ARMED NON-STATE ACTORS IN INTERNATIONAL HUMANITARIAN AND HUMAN RIGHTS LAW

Armed Non-State Actors in International Humanitarian and Human Rights Law

Foundation and Framework of Obligations, and Rules on Accountability

KONSTANTINOS MASTORODIMOS
Hellenic Coast-Guard

Routledge
Taylor & Francis Group
LONDON AND NEW YORK

First published 2016 by Ashgate Publishing

2 Park Square, Milton Park, Abingdon, Oxfordshire OX14 4RN
711 Third Avenue, New York, NY 10017

Routledge is an imprint of the Taylor & Francis Group, an informa business

First issued in paperback 2017

British Library Cataloguing in Publication Data
A catalogue record for this book is available from the British Library.

Library of Congress Cataloging-in-Publication Data
Mastorodimos, Konstantinos, author.
Armed non-state actors in international humanitarian and human rights law : foundation and framework of obligations, and rules on accountability / By Konstantinos Mastorodimos.
pages cm
Based on author's thesis (doctoral – Queen Mary, University of London, 2012) issued under title: The accountability of armed non-state actors in international humanitarian and human rights law.
Includes bibliographical references and index.
ISBN 978-1-4724-5616-8 (hardback)
1. Non-state actors (International relations) 2. Humanitarian law. 3. War (International law) 4. Human rights. 5. International criminal law. I. Title.
KZ6405.N66M37 2015
341.6'7–dc23

2015016914

ISBN 978-1-4724-5616-8 (hbk)
ISBN 978-0-8153-9341-2 (pbk)

Contents

Table of Case Law

International Court of Justice

Accordance with International Law of the Unilateral Declaration of Independence in Respect of Kosovo (Advisory Opinion) [2010] ICJ Reports 403

Dissenting Opinion of Judge Koroma, Accordance with International Law of the Unilateral Declaration of Independence in Respect of Kosovo (Advisory Opinion) [2010] ICJ Reports 467

Dissenting Opinion of Judge Bennouna, Accordance with International Law of the Unilateral Declaration of Independence in Respect of Kosovo (Advisory Opinion) [2010] ICJ Reports 500

Dissenting Opinion of Judge Skotnikov, Accordance with International Law of the Unilateral Declaration of Independence in Respect of Kosovo (Advisory Opinion) [2010] ICJ Reports 515

Separate Opinion of Judge Yusuf, Accordance with International Law of the Unilateral Declaration of Independence in Respect of Kosovo (Advisory Opinion) [2010] ICJ Reports 618

Separate Opinion of Judge Weeramantry, Application of the Convention on the Prevention and Punishment of the Crime of Genocide (Bosnia and Herzegovina v Serbia and Montenegro) (Preliminary Objections: Judgment) [1996] ICJ Reports 640

Application of the Convention on the Prevention and Punishment of the Crime of Genocide (Bosnia and Herzegovina v Serbia and Montenegro) (Merits) [2007] ICJ Reports 43

Dissenting Opinion of Vice-President Al-Khasawneh, Application of the Convention on the Prevention and Punishment of the Crime of Genocide (Bosnia and Herzegovina v Serbia and Montenegro) (Merits) [2007] ICJ Reports 241

Application of the International Convention on the Elimination of all Forms of Racial Discrimination (Georgia v Russian Federation) (Provisional Measures: Order) [2008] ICJ Reports 353

Armed Activities on the Territory of the Congo (Democratic Republic of the Congo v Uganda) (Merits) [2005] ICJ Reports 168

Armed Activities on the Territory of the Congo (New Application: 2002) (Democratic Republic of the Congo v Rwanda) (Jurisdiction and Admissibility, Judgment) [2006] ICJ Reports 6

Separate Opinion of Judge ad hoc Dugard, Armed Activities on the Territory of the Congo (New Application: 2002) (Democratic Republic of the Congo v Rwanda) (Jurisdiction and Admissibility) [2006] ICJ Reports 86

Dissenting Opinion of Judge van den Wyngaert, Arrest Warrant of 11 April 2000 (Democratic Republic of the Congo v Belgium) [2002] ICJ Reports 137

East Timor (Portugal v Australia) (Merits) [1995] ICJ Reports 90

Dissenting Opinion of Judge Skubiszewski, East Timor (Portugal v Australia) (Merits) [1995] ICJ Reports 224

Case Concerning United States Diplomatic and Consular Staff in Tehran (United States of America v Iran) (Merits) [1980] ICJ Rep 3

Frontier Dispute (Burkina Faso/Republic of Mali) (Merits) [1986] ICJ Reports 554

Legal Consequences for States of the Continued Presence of South Africa in Namibia (South West Africa) notwithstanding Security Council Resolution 276 (1970) (Advisory Opinion) [1971] ICJ Reports 16

Separate Opinion of Vice-President Ammoun, Legal Consequences for States of the Continued Presence of South Africa in Namibia (South West Africa) notwithstanding Security Council Resolution 276 (1970) (Advisory Opinion) [1971] ICJ Reports 67

Separate Opinion of Judge Petrén, Legal Consequences for States of the Continued Presence of South Africa in Namibia (South West Africa) notwithstanding Security Council Resolution 276 (1970) (Advisory Opinion) [1971] ICJ Reports 128

Separate Opinion of Judge Castro, Legal Consequences for States of the Continued Presence of South Africa in Namibia (South West Africa) notwithstanding Security Council Resolution 276 (1970) (Advisory Opinion) [1971] ICJ Reports 170

Legal Consequences of the Construction of a Wall in the Occupied Palestinian Territory (Advisory Opinion) [2004] ICJ Reports 136

Legality of the Threat or Use of Nuclear Weapons (Advisory Opinion) [1996] ICJ Reports 226

Declaration of President Bedjaoui, Legality of the Threat or Use of Nuclear Weapons (Advisory Opinion) [1996] ICJ Reports 268

Separate Opinion of Judge Guillaume, Legality of the Threat or Use of Nuclear Weapons (Advisory Opinion) [1996] ICJ Reports 287

Dissenting Opinion of Judge Shahabuddeen, Legality of the Threat or Use of Nuclear Weapons (Advisory Opinion) [1996] ICJ Reports 375

Military and Paramilitary Activities in and Against Nicaragua (Nicaragua v United States of America) (Merits) [1986] ICJ Reports 14

Nuclear Tests (Australia v France) (Merits) [1974] ICJ Reports 253

Nuclear Tests (New Zealand v France) (Merits) [1974] ICJ Reports 457

International Criminal Tribunal for the Former Yugoslavia

Prosecutor v Blaskic (Judgment on the Request of the Republic of Croatia for Review of the Decision on Trial Chamber II of 18 July 1997) ICTY-95-14 (29 October 1997)

Prosecutor v Boškoski et al. (Judgment) ICTY-04-82-T (10 July 2008)

Prosecutor v Delalic (Judgment) ICTY-96- 21-T (16 November 1998)

Prosecutor v Delalic (Appeals Judgment) ICTY-96-21 (20 February 2001)

Prosecutor v Furundzija (Judgment) ICTY-95-17/1-T (10 December 1998)

Prosecutor v Galic (Judgment) ICTY-98-29-T (5 December 2003)
Prosecutor v Galic (Appeals Judgment) ICTY-98-29-A (30 November 2006)
Prosecutor v Hadžihasanović et al. (Judgment) ICTY-01-47-T (15 March 2006)
Prosecutor v Haradinaj (Jurisdiction) ICTY-04-84-T (3 April 2008)
Prosecutor v Kunarac (Judgment) ICTY-96–23-T & IT-96–32/1-T (22 February 2001)
Prosecutor v Kupreskic (Judgment) ICTY-95-16-T (14 January 2000)
Prosecutor v Limaj et al. (Judgment) ICTY-03-66-T (30 November 2005)
Prosecutor v Milošević (Decision on Motion for Judgment of Acquittal) ICTY-02-54-T (16 June 2004)
Prosecutor v Milutinovic (Judgment) ICTY-05-87-T (26 February 2009)
Prosecutor v Tadic (Jurisdiction) ICTY-94-1 (10 August 1995)
Prosecutor v Tadic (Jurisdiction Appeals) ICTY-94-1 (2 October 1995)
Prosecutor v Tadic (Judgment) ICTY-94-1-T (7 May 1997)
Prosecutor v Tadic (Judgment) ICTY-94-1-A (15 July 1999)

International Criminal Court

Prosecutor v Jean-Pierre Bemba Gombo (Decision Pursuant to Article 61(7)(a) and (b) of the Rome Statute on the Charges) ICC-01/05-01/08 (15 June 2009)
Prosecutor v Bahar Idriss Abu Garda (Decision on the Confirmation of Charges) ICC-02/05-02/09 (8 February 2010)
Prosecutor v Katanga (Decision on the Confirmation of Charges) ICC-01/04-01/07 (30 September 2008)
Prosecutor v Thomas Lubanga Dyilo (Decision on the Confirmation of Charges) ICC- 01/04-01/06-803 (29 January 2007)
Prosecutor v Thomas Lubanga Dyilo (Judgment) ICC-01/04-01/06 (14 March 2012)
Prosecutor v Thomas Lubanga Dyilo (Decision Establishing the Principles and Procedures to Be Applied to Reparations) ICC-01/04-01/06 (7 August 2012)
Prosecutor v Callixte Mbarushimana (Decision on the Confirmation of Charges) ICC-01/04-01/10 (16 December 2011)
Prosecutor v Bosco Ntagnanda (Decision on the Confirmation of Charges) ICC-01/04-02/06 (9 June 2014)

International Criminal Tribunal for Rwanda

Prosecutor v Akayesu (Judgment) ICTR-96-4-T (2 September 1998)
Prosecutor v Musema (Judgment) ICTR-96-13-T (27 January 2000)
Prosecutor v Rutaganda (Judgment) ICTR-96-3 (6 December 1999)

Special Court for Sierra Leone

Prosecutor v Brima et al. (Judgment) SCSL-04-16-T (20 June 2007)
Prosecutor v Fofana et al. (Judgment) SCSL-04-15-T (2 August 2007)
Prosecutor v Sam Hinga Norman (Decision on Preliminary Motion Based on Lack of Jurisdiction (Child Recruitment)) SCSL-2004-14-AR72(E) (31 May 2004)
Prosecutor v Sesay et al. (Decision on Challenge to Jurisdiction: Lomé Accord Amnesty) SCSL 04-16-AR72(E) (13 March 2004)
Prosecutor v Sesay et al. (Judgment) SCSL-04-15-T (2 March 2009)

European Court of Human Rights

Aksoy v Turkey (App no 21987/93) Reports 1996-VI
Bijelic v Montenegro and Serbia (App no 11890/05) ECHR 2009
Catan and Others v Moldova and Russia (Apps nos 43370/04 et als) ECHR 2012
Cyprus v Turkey (App no 25781/94) ECHR 2001-IV
Demopoulos and others v Turkey (Apps nos 46113/99 et als) ECHR 2010
Foka v Turkey (App no 28940/95) ECHR 24 June 2008
Gustafsson v Sweden (App no 15573/89) Reports 1996-II
Ilascu and Others v Moldova and Russia (App no 48787/99) ECHR 2004-VII
Kilic v Turkey (App no 22492/93) ECHR 2000-III
Loizidou v Turkey (App no 15318/89) Reports 1996-VI
Osman v United Kingdom (App no 23452/94) ECHR 1998-VIII
Ould Dah v France (App no 13113/03) ECHR 2009
VgT Verein Gegen Tierfabriken v Switzerland (App no 24699/94) ECHR 2001-VI
Xenides-Arestis v Turkey (App no 46347/99) ECHR 22 December 2005
Zdanoka v Latvia (App no 58278/00) ECHR 17 June 2004
Zontul v Greece (App no 12294/07) ECHR 2012

Inter-American Court of Human Rights

Communities of the Jiguamiandó and the Curbaradó (Provisional Measures) Inter-American Court of Human Rights Series E (6 March 2003)
Judicial Guarantees in States of Emergency (Arts. 27(2), 25 and 8 American Convention on Human Rights), Advisory Opinion OC-9/87, Inter-American Court of Human Rights Series A No. 9 (6 October 1987)
Juridical Condition and Rights of the Undocumented Migrants, Advisory Opinion OC-18, Inter-American Court of Human Rights Series A No. 18 (17 September 2003)
Mapiripán Massacre Case (Judgment) Inter-American Court of Human Rights Series C No. 134 (15 September 2005)
Matter of the Peace Community of San José de Apartadó (Provisional Measures) Inter-American Court of Human Rights Series E (18 June 2002)

Matter of Pueblo Indígena de Kankuamo (Provisional Measures) Inter-American Court of Human Rights Series E (5 July 2004)
Matter of Pueblo Indígena Sarayaku (Provisional Measures) Inter-American Court of Human Rights Series E (6 July 2004)
Velasquez Rodriguez Case (Judgment) Inter-American Court of Human Rights Series C No. 4 (29 July 1988)

African Commission on Human and Peoples' Rights

Commission Nationale des Droits de l'Homme et des Libertés v Chad, 74/92, African Commission on Human and Peoples' Rights, 11 October 1995
Ilesanmi v Nigeria, 268/03, African Commission on Human and Peoples' Rights, 11 May 2005
Katangese Peoples' Congress v Zaire, 75/92, African Commission on Human and Peoples' Rights, 22 March 1995
Sudan Human Rights Org v Sudan; Center for Housing Rights & Evictions v Sudan, 279/03-296/05, African Commission on Human and Peoples' Rights, 25 July 2010
Zimbabwe Human Rights NGO Forum v Zimbabwe, 245/02, African Commission on Human and Peoples' Rights, 15 May 2006

Inter-American Commission on Human Rights

Juan Carlos Abella v Argentina, Case 11.137, Report No 55/97, Inter-American Commission on Human Rights, OEA/Ser.L/V/II.95 Doc. 7 rev. at 271 (1997)
William Andrews v United States, Case 11.139, Report No 57/96, Inter-American Commission on Human Rights, OEA/Ser.L/V/II.95 Doc. 7 rev. at 570 (1997)

National Courts

Reference re Secession of Quebec, 1998 CanLII 793 (SCC)
HCJ 769/02 *The Public Committee Against Torture in Israel v the Government of Israel* (14 December 2006)

Table of International Conventions

Article 29
Article 32

Convention on the Prohibition of the Development, Production and Stockpiling of Bacteriological (Biological) and Toxin Weapons and on their Destruction (adopted 10 April 1972, entered into force 26 March 1975) 1015 UNTS 163

Protocol Additional to the Geneva Conventions of 12 August 1949, and relating to the Protection of Victims of International Armed Conflicts (adopted 8 June 1977, entered into force 7 December 1978) 1125 UNTS 3

Article 1
Article 43
Article 47
Article 48
Article 51
Article 54
Article 86
Article 90
Article 91
Article 96
Article 99

Protocol Additional to the Geneva Conventions of 12 August 1949, and relating to the Protection of Victims of Non-International Armed Conflicts (adopted 8 June 1977, entered into force 7 December 1978) 1125 UNTS 609

Preamble
Article 2
Article 4
Article 5
Article 6
Article 7
Article 8
Article 9
Article 13
Article 14
Article 19
Article 25

OAU Convention for the Elimination of Mercenarism in Africa (adopted 3 July 1977, entered into force 22 April 1985) OAU Document CM/817 (XXIX) Annex II Rev.1

Article 1

Convention on the Elimination of All Forms of Discrimination Against Women (adopted 18 December 1979, entered into force 3 March 1981) 1249 UNTS 13

Article 2
Article 16

Convention on Prohibitions or Restrictions on the Use of Certain Conventional Weapons Which May Be Deemed to Be Excessively Injurious or to Have Indiscriminate Effects (adopted 10 October 1980, entered into force 2 December 1983) 1342 UNTS 137

Convention on Prohibitions or Restrictions on the Use of Certain Conventional Weapons Which May Be Deemed to Be Excessively Injurious or to Have Indiscriminate Effects, Amendment Article 1 (adopted 21 December 2001, entered into force 18 May 2004) 2260 UNTS 82

Article 1

Arab Charter on Human Rights (adopted 22 May 2004, entered into force 15 March 2008) <http://www1.umn.edu/humanrts/instree/loas2005.html>[1]

Article 1
Article 4
Article 5
Article 8
Article 9
Article 10
Article 13
Article 14
Article 15
Article 18
Article 19
Article 20
Article 22
Article 27
Article 29
Article 30

African Union Convention for the Protection and Assistance of Internally Displaced Persons in Africa (adopted 23 October 2009) (2010) 49 ILM 86

Article 1
Article 5
Article 7
Article 15

---

1 All internet sources were accessed at 6 February 2015.

Table of Other Agreements

The Uganda Peace Talks Agreement for the Restoration of Peace to the Sovereign State of the Republic of Uganda, Nairobi, Kenya, 17 December 1985 <http://nointervention.com/archive/Africa/Uganda/nairobi-peace-agreement.html>

Preamble

Article 1

Article 16

Administrative Arrangement between the Government of Malaysia and the Communist Party of Malaya Pursuant to the Agreement to Terminate Hostilities, Haadyai, Thailand, 2 December 1989 <http://theirwords.org/media/transfer/doc/my_cpm_1989_01-2aa2b0cc70df62b0ef0b5f519d5b3065.pdf>

Agreement on Human Rights, San José, *Costa Rica,* 26 July 1990 <http://www.usip.org/files/file/resources/collections/peace_agreements/pa_es_07261990_hr.pdf>

Preamble

Article 2

Article 4

Article 5

Article 6

Article 7

Article 8

Peace Accords for Angola, Bicesse, Portugal, 15 May 1991 <http://www.incore.ulst.ac.uk/services/cds/agreements/pdf/ang1.pdf>

Preamble

Agreement on Implementing the Cease-fire and on Modalities of Disarmament, Addis Ababa, Ethiopia, 15 January 1993, UN Doc S/25168

Article III

Comprehensive Agreement on Human Rights, Mexico, D.F., 29 March 1994 <http://www.usip.org/files/file/resources/collections/peace_agreements/guat_hr_940329.pdf>

Preamble

Article I

Article V

Article IX

Agreement on a Cease-Fire and Separation of Forces, Moscow, Russia, 14 May 1994 <http://reliefweb.int/report/georgia/agreement-cease-fire-and-separation-forces-signed-moscow-14-may-1994>

Lusaka Protocol, Lusaka, Zambia, 15 November 1994 <http://www.usip.org/files/file/resources/collections/peace_agreements/lusaka_11151994.pdf>

Annex 8, Art A.I

General Framework Agreement for Peace in Bosnia and Herzegovina, Paris, 21 November 1995 <http://www.ohr.int/dpa/default.asp?content_id=380>
  Annex 3
  Annex 7

SPLM/OLS (Operation Lifeline Sudan) Agreement on Ground Rules, 1995 <http://www.google.gr/url?sa=t&rct=j&q=&esrc=s&source=web&cd=1&ved=0CCIQFjAA&url=http%3A%2F%2Fwww.unicef.org%2Fpathtraining%2FDocuments%2FSession%25204%2520Humanitarian%2520Principles%2FTrainer%2520Resources%2F4.11%2520SPLM%2520Operation%2520Lifeline%2520Sudan%2520Ground%2520Rules.doc&ei=3_d6UO2gOeiG4gTT1IHgDQ&usg=AFQjCNE9zPa2idAjFDAkO_yjB9LWZ8B3VQ>
  Preamble

Peace Agreement between the Government of the Republic of Sierra Leone and the Revolutionary United Front of Sierra Leone, Abidjan, Ivory Coast, 30 November 1996 <http://www.usip.org/files/file/resources/collections/peace_agreements/sierra_leone_11301996.pdf>
  Article 19

Agreement on the Definitive Ceasefire, Oslo, Norway, 4 December 1996 <http://www.incore.ulst.ac.uk/services/cds/agreements/pdf/guat8.pdf>

Lincoln Agreement on Peace, Security and Development on Bougainville, Christchurch, New Zealand, 23 January 1998 <http://www.usip.org/sites/default/files/file/resources/collections/peace_agreements/bougain_19980123.pdf>>
  Article 1

Comprehensive Agreement on Respect for Human Rights and International Humanitarian Law between the Government of the Republic of the Philippines and the National Democratic Front of the Philippines, The Hague, The Netherlands, 16 March 1998 <http://www.incore.ulst.ac.uk/services/cds/agreements/pdf/phil8.pdf>
  Preamble
  Part II, Article 4
  Part III, Article 2
  Part III Articles 11–2
  Part IV, Article 4
  Part IV, Article 6
  Part VI, Article 2

General Framework of Agreement of Intent between the Government of the Republic of Philippines (GRP) and the Moro Islamic Liberation Front (MILF), Dawah Center, Crossing Simuay, Sultan Kudarat, Maguindanao, the Philippines, 27 August 1998 <http://www.incore.ulst.ac.uk/services/cds/agreements/pdf/phil9.pdf>
  Article II

Agreement on Ceasefire in Sierra Leone, Lomé, Togo, 18 May 1999 <http://peacemaker.un.org/sierraleone-ceasefire99>
  Article 2
  Article 4
  Article 5

Peace Agreement between the Government of Sierra Leone and the Revolutionary United Front of Sierra Leone, Lomé, Togo, 7 July 1999 <http://www.usip.org/files/file/resources/collections/peace_agreements/sierra_leone_07071999.pdf>
- Article XII
- Article XXIV
- Article XXIX
- Article XXXI

Ceasefire Agreement, Lusaka, Zambia, 10 July 1999 <http://www.un.org/Docs/s815_25.pdf>
- Article I
- Article III

Agreement on the Implementation of Principles Governing the Protection and Provision of Humanitarian Assistance to War Affected Civilian Populations, Geneva, Switzerland, 15 December 1999 <http://reliefweb.int/report/sudan/sudan-agreement-implementation-principles-governing-protection-and-provision>
- Preamble
- Part III

Accord De Cessez-Le-Feu et de Cessation des Hostilités Entre le Haut Commandement de la Force Publique et le Haut Commandement des Forces D'Autodéfense de la Résistance (FADR) en République Du Congo-Brazzaville, Brazzaville, 29 December 1999 <http://voxhumana.perso.neuf.fr/accord99.html>
- Article 5

Arusha Peace and Reconciliation Agreement for Burundi, Arusha, Tanzania, 28 August 2000 <http://www.issafrica.org/AF/profiles/Burundi/arusha.pdf>
- Article 1
- Protocol I, Article 6
- Protocol II

Acte d'Engagement, Gaborone, Botswana, 24 August 2001 <http://peacemaker.un.org/drc-engagementgaberone2001>
- Article 2
- Article 4
- Article 6
- Article 7

Agreement between the United Nations and the Government of Sierra Leone on the Establishment of a Special Court for Sierra Leone, Freetown, Sierra Leone, 16 January 2002 <https://www.icrc.org/applic/ihl/ihl.nsf/b0d5f4c1f4b810204125673900 3e6366/65cb6be7caca532cc1256c1d0027f549?OpenDocument >
- Article 3

The Nuba Mountains Cease-Fire Agreement, Bürgenstock (NW), Swiss Confederation, 19 January 2002 <http://www.sudantribune.com/spip.php?article41880>
- Article II

Agreement on a Ceasefire between the Government of the Democratic Socialist Republic of Sri Lanka and the Liberation Tigers of Tamil Eelam, 22 February 2002 <http://www.usip.org/publications/peace-agreements-sri-lanka>

Article 1
Article 2

Agreement between the Government of the Republic of Sudan and The Sudan People's Liberation Movement To Protect Non-Combatant Civilians And Civilian Facilities from Military Attack, 31 March 2002 <http://peacemaker.un.org/sites/peacemaker.un.org/files/SD_020331_Agreement%20to%20Protect%20Non-Combatant%20Civilians%20from%20Military%20Attack.pdf>
Article 1

Implementing Guidelines on the Humanitarian, Rehabilitation and Development Aspects of the GRP–MILF Tripoli Agreement on Peace of 2001, Putrajaya, Malaysia, 7 May 2002 <http://www.google.gr/url?sa=t&rct=j&q=&esrc=s&source=web&cd=1&ved=0CCEQFjAA&url=http%3A%2F%2Fwww.operationspaix.net%2FDATA%2FDOCUMENT%2F3657~v~Modalites_d_application_des_aspects_humanitaires_de_rehabilitation_et_de_developpement_de_l_accord_de_paix_de_Tripoli_entre_le_GRP_et_le_FMIL.pdf&ei=y83UVK3KJo27afGXgLAP&usg=AFQjCNEp0ypDP0yoVn4UO4ntEY4abFc2ZQ&bvm=bv.85464276,d.d2s>
Article IV

Memorandum of Understanding on Cessation of Hostilities between the Government of the Sudan and the Sudan People's Liberation Movement/Army, 15 October 2002 <http://peacemaker.un.org/sites/peacemaker.un.org/files/SD_021015_MoU%20on%20Cessation%20of%20Hostilities%20between%20the%20GoS%20and%20the%20SPLMA.pdf>
Paragraph 3
Paragraph 5

Cessation of Hostilities Framework Agreement between Government of the Republic of Indonesia and the Free Aceh Movement, 9 December 2002 <http://www.google.gr/url?sa=t&rct=j&q=&esrc=s&source=web&cd=1&ved=0CB8QFjAA&url=http%3A%2F%2Fwww.usip.org%2Fsites%2Fdefault%2Ffiles%2Ffile%2Fresources%2Fcollections%2Fpeace_agreements%2Faceh_12092002.pdf&ei=Ws7UVN__I9HvapLxgPAG&usg=AFQjCNHeO5megiDr2BnytMDO9LaZPdxOFg&bvm=bv.85464276,d.d2s>
Article 2

Global and Inclusive Agreement on Transition in the Democratic Republic of Congo, Pretoria, South Africa, 16 December 2002 <http://www.ucdp.uu.se/gpdatabase/peace/DRC%2020021216.pdf>
Article I

Linas-Marcoussis Agreement, Linas-Marcoussis, France, 23 January 2003 <http://www.usip.org/files/file/resources/collections/peace_agreements/cote_divoire_01242003en.pdf>
Annex, Article VI

Agreement on Ceasefire and Cessation of Hostilities between the Government of the Republic of Liberia and Liberians United for Reconciliation and Democracy and the Movement for Democracy in Liberia, Accra, Ghana, 17 June 2003 <http://www.usip.org/files/file/resources/collections/peace_agreements/liberia_ceasefire_06172003.pdf>

Comprehensive Peace Agreement between the Government of Liberia (GOL), The Liberians United for Reconciliation and Democracy (LURD), The Movement for Democracy in Liberia (MODEL) and the Political Parties, Accra, Ghana, 18 August 2003 <http://www.usip.org/sites/default/files/file/resources/collections/peace_agreements/liberia_08182003.pdf>

Article XII

Article XII

Article XXIV

Article XV

Humanitarian Cease Fire Agreement on the Conflict in Darfur, N' Djamena, Chad, 8 April 2004 <http://peacemaker.un.org/sudan-darfur-humanitarian2004>

Article 2

Agreement between the Government of Sudan, the Sudan Liberation Movement, and the Justice and Equality Movement, N' Djamena, Chad, 25 April 2004 <http://www.issafrica.org/AF/profiles/sudan/darfur/agmtndjamenaapr04.pdf>

Article 4

Protocol between the Government of the Sudan (GoS), the Sudan Liberation Movement/Army (SLM/A) and the Justice and Equality Movement (JEM) on the Enhancement of the Security Situation in Darfur in Accordance with the N'Djamena Agreement, Abuja, Nigeria, 9 November 2004 <http://theirwords.org/media/transfer/doc/1_sd_slm_sla_jem_2004_37-df621ac512773609ed543fbac99250bf.pdf>

Article 6

Agreement on Permanent Ceasefire and Security Arrangements Implementation Modalities between the Government of the Sudan (GOS) and the Sudan People's Liberation Movement/Sudan People's Liberation Army (SPLM/SPLA) During the Pre-interim and Interim Periods, Naivasha, Kenya, 31 December 2004 <http://www.un.org/chinese/ha/issue/sudan/docs/cpa-3.pdf>

Article 10

Declaration of Principles for the Resolution of the Sudanese Conflict in Darfur, Abuja, Nigeria, 5 July 2005 <http://peacemaker.un.org/sudan-declaration-resolution-darfur2005>

Darfur Peace Agreement, Abuja, Nigeria, 5 May 2006 <http://www.sudantribune.com/IMG/pdf/Darfur_Peac_Agreement-2.pdf>

Preamble

Article 1

Article 3

Article 17

Article 21

Article 27

Article 32

Ceasefire Code of Conduct Agreed between the Government of Nepal and CPN (Maoist), Gokarna, India, 25 May 2006 <http://www.ucdp.uu.se/gpdatabase/peace/Nep%20 20060525.pdf>

Preamble

Eastern Sudan Peace Agreement, Asmara, Eritrea, 19 June 2006 <http://peacemaker.un.org/sites/peacemaker.un.org/files/SD_061014_Eastern%20Sudan%20Peace%20Agreement.pdf>

Article 6

Article 24

Comprehensive Peace Agreement Concluded between the Government of Nepal and the Communist Party of Nepal (Maoist), Kathmandu, Nepal, 21 November 2006 <http://www.usip.org/files/file/resources/collections/peace_agreements/nepal_cpa_20061121_en.pdf>

Article 5

Article 7

Article 8

Acte d'Engagement in North Kivu, Goma, Democratic Republic of Congo, 23 January 2008 <http://peacemaker.un.org/drc-actenordkivu2008>

Article III

Agreement on a Permanent Ceasefire, Juba, Sudan, 23 February 2008 <http://peacemaker.un.org/sites/peacemaker.un.org/files/UG_080223_Agreement%20on%20a%20Permanent%20Ceasefire.pdf>

Article 2

Article 5

Agreement on Civilian Protection Component of the International Monitoring Team (IMT), Kuala Lumpur, Malaysia, 27 October 2009 <http://www.opapp.gov.ph/sites/default/files/Agreement_on_Civilian_Protection_Component.pdf>

Article 1

Agreement between the Government of the Republic of South Sudan (GRSS) and the South Sudan Democratic Movement/Army (SSDM/A), 27 February 2012 <http://peacemaker.un.org/sites/peacemaker.un.org/files/SD-SS_120227_AgreementGRSS-SSDMA.pdf>

(Central African Republic) Accord De Cessez-le-feu, Libreville, Gabon, 11 January 2013 <http://peacemaker.un.org/sites/peacemaker.un.org/files/CF._130111_AccordDeCessezLeFeu.pdf>

Article 1

Article 5

(Mali) Accord De Cessez-le-Feu, Bamako, Mali, 23 May 2014 <http://peacemaker.un.org/mali-ceasefire2014>

Table of Documents from International Organizations

1. United Nations

A. Security Council

I. Resolutions

169 (24 November 1961) The Congo Question
322 (22 November 1972) Question Concerning the Situation in Territories under Portuguese Administration
541 (18 November 1983) Cyprus
771 (13 August 1992) Former Yugoslavia
788 (19 November 1992) Liberia
794 (3 December 1992) Somalia
814 (26 March 1993) Somalia
820 (17 April 1993) Bosnia and Herzegovina
834 (1 June 1993) Angola
851 (15 July 1993) Angola
864 (15 September 1993) Angola
940 (31 July 1994) UN Mission in Haiti
950 (21 October 1994) UN Observer Mission in Liberia
955 (8 November 1994) Establishment of the International Criminal Tribunal for Rwanda (ICTR) and adoption of the Statute of the Tribunal
972 (13 January 1995) UN Observer Mission in Liberia
985 (13 April 1995) UN Observer Mission in Liberia
1001 (30 June 1995) UN Observer Mission in Liberia
1059 (31 May 1996) Liberia
1071 (30 August 1996) Liberia
1083 (27 November 1996) Liberia
1193 (28 August 1998) Afghanistan
1213 (3 December 1998) Angola
1214 (8 December 1998) Afghanistan
1216 (21 December 1998) Guinea-Bissau
1231 (11 March 1999) Sierra Leone
1244 (10 June 1999) Kosovo
1261 (30 August 1999) Children and Armed Conflict
1265 (17 September 1999) Protection of Civilians in Armed Conflict

1314 (11 August 2000) Children and Armed Conflict
1378 (14 November 2001) Afghanistan
1379 (20 November 2001) Children and Armed Conflict
1417 (14 June 2002) The Democratic Republic of the Congo
1464 (4 February 2003) Côte d'Ivoire
1479 (13 May 2003) Côte d'Ivoire
1493 (28 July 2003) Democratic Republic of the Congo
1509 (19 September 2003) Liberia
1539 (22 April 2004) Children and Armed Conflict
1556 (30 July 2004) Report of the Secretary-General on the Sudan
1559 (2 September 2004) Middle East
1565 (1 October 2004) Democratic Republic of the Congo
1574 (19 November 2004) Sudan
1592 (30 March 2005) Democratic Republic of the Congo
1612 (26 July 2005) Children and Armed Conflict
1653 (27 January 2006) The Great Lakes Region
1662 (23 March 2006) Afghanistan
1666 (31 March 2006) Georgia
1674 (28 April 2006) Protection of Civilians in Armed Conflict
1725 (6 December 2006) The Situation in Somalia
1738 (23 December 2006) Protection of Civilians in Armed Conflict
1746 (23 March 2007) Afghanistan
1756 (15 May 2007) Democratic Republic of the Congo
1765 (16 July 2007) Côte d'Ivoire
1769 (31 July 2007) Sudan
1772 (20 August 2007) Somalia
1794 (21 December 2007) Democratic Republic of the Congo
1804 (13 March 2008) The Great Lakes Region
1807 (31 March 2008) The Democratic Republic of the Congo
1814 (15 May 2008) Somalia
1828 (31 July 2008) Reports of the Secretary-General on the Sudan
1861 (14 January 2009) Chad, the Central African Republic and the Subregion
1882 (4 August 2009) Children and Armed Conflict
1894 (11 November 2009) Protection of Civilians in Armed Conflict
1960 (16 December 2010) Women and Peace and Security
1970 (26 February 2011) Peace and Security in Africa
1974 (22 March 2011) Afghanistan
1991 (28 June 2011) Democratic Republic of the Congo
1998 (12 July 2011) Children and Armed Conflict
2003 (29 July 2011) Reports of the Secretary-General on the Sudan
2011 (12 October 2011) The Situation in Afghanistan
2021 (29 November 2011) Democratic Republic of the Congo
2031 (21 December 2011) Central African Republic
2042 (14 April 2012) Middle East

2043 (21 April 2012) Middle East
2051 (12 June 2012) Middle East
2088 (24 January 2013) Central African Republic
2096 (19 March 2013) Afghanistan
2098 (28 March 2013) Democratic Republic of the Congo
2100 (25 April 2013) Mali
2109 (11 July 2013) Sudan/South Sudan
2120 (10 October 2013) Afghanistan
2121 (10 October 2013) Central African Republic
2132 (23 December 2013) Sudan and South Sudan
2136 (30 January 2014) Democratic Republic of the Congo
2143 (7 March 2014) Children and Armed Conflict
2144 (13 March 2014) Libya
2155 (27 May 2014) Reports of the Secretary-General on the Sudan and South Sudan
2158 (29 May 2014) Somalia
2173 (27 August 2014) Reports of the Secretary-General on the Sudan and South Sudan
2175 (29 August 2014) Protection of Civilians in Armed Conflict

II. Meeting Records
S/PV.2153 (22 June 1979)
S/PV.2285 (16 June 1981)
S/PV.3138 (19 November 1992)
S/PV. 3200 (18 April 1993)
S/PV. 3254 (15 July 1993)
S/PV. 3705 (16 October 1996)
S/PV.3730 (10 January 1997)
S/PV. 3765 (14 April 1997)
S/PV. 3765 (Resumption) (15 April 1997)
S/PV.3912 (30 July 1998)
S/PV.3921 (28 August 1998)
S/PV.3921 (Resumption) (28 August 1998)
S/PV.3937 (24 October 1998)
S/PV.4011 (10 June 1999)
S/PV.4046 (16 September 1999)
S/PV.4046 (Resumption 1) (17 September 1999)
S/PV.4046 (Resumption 2) (17 September 1999)
S/PV.4312 (23 April 2001)
S/PV.4312 (Resumption 1) (23 April 2001)
S/PV.4414 (13 November 2001)
S/PV.5952 (8 August 2008)
S/PV.5953 (10 August 2008)
S/PV.6061 (6 January 2009)
S/PV.6063 (8 January 2009)
S/PV.6216 (Resumption 1) (11 November 2009)

S/PV. 6494 (10 March 2011)
S/PV. 6625 (29 September 2011)
S/PV.6690 (19 December 2011)

B. General Assembly Resolutions

217A (III) (10 December 1948) Universal Declaration of Human Rights
1514 (XV) (14 December 1960) Declaration on the Granting of Independence to Colonial Countries and Peoples
2105 (XX) (20 December 1965) Implementation of the Declaration on the Granting of Independence to Colonial Countries and Peoples
2444 (XXIII) (19 December 1968) Respect for Human Rights in Armed Conflicts
2546 (XXIV) (11 December 1969) Respect for and Implementation of Human Rights in Occupied Territories
2625 (XXV) (24 October 1970) Declaration on Principles of International Law Concerning Friendly Relations and Co-operation among States in Accordance with the Charter of the United Nations
2677 (XXV) (9 December 1970) Respect for Human Rights in Armed Conflicts
2852 (XXVI) (20 December 1971) Respect for Human Rights in Armed Conflicts
3237 (XXIX) (22 November 1974) Observer Status for the Palestine Liberation Organization
3314 (XXIX) (14 December 1974) Definition of Aggression
31/152 (20 December 1976) Observer Status for the South West Africa People's Organization
36/155 (16 December 1981) Situation of Human Rights and Fundamental Freedoms in El Salvador
37/253 (13 May 1983) Question of Cyprus
38/100 (16 December 1983) Situation of Human Rights and Fundamental Freedoms in Guatemala
40/34 (29 November 1985) Declaration of Basic Principles of Justice for Victims of Crime and Abuse of Power
40/137 (13 December 1985) Question of Human Rights and Fundamental Freedoms in Afghanistan
40/140 (13 December 1985) Situation of Human Rights and Fundamental Freedoms in Guatemala
42/137 (7 December 1987) Situation of Human Rights and Fundamental Freedoms in El Salvador
43/139 (8 December 1988) Situation of Human Rights in Afghanistan
43/145 (8 December 1988) Situation of Human Rights and Fundamental Freedoms in El Salvador
44/165 (15 December 1989) Situation of Human Rights and Fundamental Freedoms in El Salvador
47/144 (18 December 1992) Situation in Myanmar
48/147 (20 December 1993) Situation of Human Rights in the Sudan

48/152 (20 December 1993)_Situation of Human Rights in Afghanistan
48/153 (20 December 1993) Situation of Human Rights in the Territory of the Former Yugoslavia
49/60 (9 December 1994)_Measures to Eliminate International Terrorism
49/196 (23 December 1994) Situation of Human Rights in the Republic of Bosnia and Herzegovina, the Republic of Croatia and the Federal Republic of Yugoslavia (Serbia and Montenegro)
49/198 (23 December 1994) Situation of Human Rights in the Sudan
51/112 (12 December 1996) Situation of Human Rights in the Sudan
51/117 (12 December 1996) Situation of Human Rights in Myanmar
52/140 (12 December 1997 Situation of Human Rights in the Sudan
52/145 (12 December 1997) Situation of Human Rights in Afghanistan
53/144 (9 December 1998) Declaration on the Right and Responsibility of Individuals, Groups and Organs of Society to Promote and Protect Universally Recognized Human Rights and Fundamental Freedoms
53/168 (10 December 1998) Fiftieth Anniversary of the Universal Declaration of Human Rights
56/83 (12 December 2001) Responsibility of States for Internationally Wrongful Acts
60/147 (16 December 2005) Basic Principles and Guidelines on the Right to a Remedy and Reparation for Victims of Gross Violations of International Human Rights Law and Serious Violations of International Humanitarian Law
61/30 (18 December 2006) Status of the Protocols Additional to the Geneva Conventions of 1949 and Relating to the Protection of Victims of Armed Conflicts
62/243 (14 March 2008) The Situation in the Occupied Territories of Azerbaijan
63/166 (18 December 2008) Torture and Other Cruel, Inhuman or Degrading Treatment or Punishment
63/245 (24 December 2008) Situation of Human Rights in Myanmar
64/11 (9 November 2009) The Situation in Afghanistan
65/8 (4 November 2010) The Situation in Afghanistan
68/152 (18 December 2013) Use of Mercenaries as a Means of Violating Human Rights and Impeding the Exercise of the Right of Peoples to Self-determination

C. Secretary General

'Annotations on the Text of the Draft International Covenants on Human Rights' (1955) UN Doc A/2929
'Respect for Human Rights in Armed Conflicts: Report' (20 November 1969) UN Doc A/7720
'Respect for Human Rights in Armed Conflicts: Report' (18 September 1970) UN Doc A/8052
'Note Transmitting the Report on the Situation of Human Rights in El Salvador Prepared by the Independent Expert of the Commission on Human Rights in Accordance with Paragraph 17 of Commission Resolution 1990/77 and Economic and Social Council Decision 1990/242' (22 October 1990) UN Doc A/45/630

'Note Transmitting the Report on the Situation of Human Rights in El Salvador Prepared by the Independent Expert of the Commission on Human Rights in Accordance with Paragraph 13 of Commission Resolution 1991/75 of 6 March 1991 and Economic and Social Council Decision 1991/257 of 31 May 1991' (11 October 1991) UN Doc A/46/529

'Note Transmitting 3rd Report of the Director of the Human Rights Division of ONUSAL' (19 February 1992) UN Doc A/46/876

'Note Transmitting Report on the Situation of Human Rights in El Salvador Prepared by the Independent Expert of the Commission on Human Rights in Accordance with Paragraph 12 of Commission Resolution 1992/62 of 3 March 1992 and Economic and Social Council decision 1992/237 of 20 July 1992' (13 November 1992) UN Doc A/47/596

'Letter Transmitting the Report of the Commission on the Truth for El Salvador' (1 April 1993) UN Doc S/25500

'Note Transmitting Report of the Secretary-General's Fact-Finding Mission to Investigate Human Rights Violations in Abkhazia, Republic of Georgia' (17 November 1993) UN Doc S/26795

'Letter Transmitting the Final Report of the Commission of Experts Established Pursuant to Security Council Resolution 780 (1992)' (27 May 1994) UN Doc S/1994/674

'Note Transmitting the Report of the Director of the United Nations Mission for the Verification of Human Rights and of Compliance with the Commitments of the Comprehensive Agreement on Human Rights in Guatemala' (1 March 1995) UN Doc A/49/856

'Note Transmitting the Report of the Director of the United Nations Mission for the Verification of Human Rights and of Compliance with the Commitments of the Comprehensive Agreement on Human Rights in Guatemala' (29 June 1995) UN Doc A/49/929

'Note Transmitting the Third Report of the Director of the United Nations Mission for the Verification of Human Rights and of Compliance with the Commitments of the Comprehensive Agreement on Human Rights in Guatemala' (12 October 1995) UN Doc A/50/482

'Human Rights and Terrorism: Report' (26 October 1995) UN Doc A/50/685

'Note Transmitting the Fourth Report of the Director of the United Nations Mission for the Verification of Human Rights and of Compliance with the Commitments of the Comprehensive Agreement on Human Rights in Guatemala' (24 February 1996) UN Doc A/50/878

'Minimum Humanitarian Standards: Report of the Secretary General' (28 January 1997) UN Doc E/CN.4/1997/77/Add.1

'Views and Comments Received from States on the Note and Revised Draft Basic Principles and Guidelines on the Right to Reparation for Victims of Gross Violations of Human Rights and International Humanitarian Law: Report of the Secretary-General' (22 December 1997) UN Doc E/CN.4/1998/34

'Minimum Humanitarian Standards: Analytical Report of the Secretary General Submitted Pursuant to Commission on Human Rights Resolution 1997/21' (15 April 1998) UN Doc E/CN.4/1998/87

'Minimum Humanitarian Standards: Analytical Report of the Secretary General Submitted Pursuant to Commission on Human Rights Resolution 1997/21: Views and Information Received from States and United Nations Bodies' (12 January 1998) UN Doc E/CN.4/1998/87/Add.1

'The Causes of Conflict and the Promotion of Durable Peace and Sustainable Development in Africa: Report' (13 April 1998) UN Doc A/52/871

'Letter Transmitting the Executive Summary, Conclusions and Recommendations of the Report of the Commission for Historical Clarification' (27 April 1999) UN Doc A/53/928

'Report of the Secretary-General to the Security Council on the Protection of Civilians in Armed Conflict' (8 September 1999) UN Doc S/1999/957

'Fundamental Standards of Humanity: Report of the Secretary-General Submitted Pursuant to Commission Resolution 2000/69' (12 January 2001) UN Doc E/CN.4/2001/91

'Report of the Secretary-General to the Security Council on the Protection of Civilians in Armed Conflict' (30 March 2001) UN Doc S/2001/331

'Note Transmitting the Interim Report of the Special Rapporteur of the Commission on Human Rights on the Situation of Human Rights in the Sudan' (7 September 2001) UN Doc A/56/336

'Children and Armed Conflict: Report of the Secretary-General' (10 November 2003) UN Doc S/2003/1053

'Report of the Secretary-General to the Security Council on the Protection of Civilians in Armed Conflict' (28 May 2004) UN Doc S/2004/431

'Extrajudicial, Summary or Arbitrary Executions, Note Transmitting the Interim Report of the Special Rapporteur' (16 August 2007) UN Doc A/62/265

'Report on Children and Armed Conflict in the Philippines' (24 April 2008) UN Doc S/2008/272

'Report of the Secretary-General on the Protection of Civilians in Armed Conflict' (29 May 2009) UN Doc S/2009/277

'Note Transmitting the Report of the Special Rapporteur on the Situation of Human Rights Defenders' (4 August 2010) UN Doc A/65/223

'Report of the Secretary-General on the Protection of Civilians in Armed Conflict' (11 November 2010) UN Doc S/2010/579

'Report of the Secretary-General on the Protection of Civilians in Armed Conflict' (22 May 2012) UN Doc S/2012/376

'Report of the Secretary-General on the Protection of Civilians in Armed Conflict' (22 November 2013) UN Doc S/2013/689

D. Commission on Human Rights

I. Resolutions

7 (1990) Use of Mercenaries as a Means of Impeding the Exercise of the Right of Peoples to Self-determination

75 (1990) Consequences of Acts of Violence Committed by Irregular Armed Groups and Drug Traffickers for the Enjoyment of Human Rights

46 (1994) Human Rights and Terrorism

59 (1994) Assistance to the Republic of Georgia in the Field of Human Rights

81 (1994) Human Rights Violations in the Papua New Guinea Island of Bougainville

74 (1995) Situation of Human Rights in Afghanistan

59 (1998) Assistance to Somalia in the Field of Human Rights

67 (1998) Situation of Human Rights in the Sudan

15 (1999) Situation of Human Rights in the Sudan

24 (2000) Situation of Human Rights in Sierra Leone

58 (2000) Situation in the Republic of Chechnya of the Russian Federation

24 (2001) Situation in the Republic of Chechnya of the Russian Federation

16 (2003) Situation of Human Rights in Burundi

37 (2003) Human Rights and Terrorism

42 (2003) The Right to Freedom of Opinion and Expression

78 (2003) Assistance to Somalia in the Field of Human Rights

44 (2004) Human Rights and Terrorism

80 (2004) Protection of Human Rights and Fundamental Freedoms While Countering Terrorism

44 (2005) Rights of the Child

56 (2005) Promotion of Peace as a Vital Requirement for the Full Enjoyment of All Human Rights by All

63 (2005) Protection of the Human Rights of Civilians in Armed Conflicts

78 (2005) Technical Cooperation and Advisory Services in Nepal

82 (2005) Situation of Human Rights in the Sudan

83 (2005) Assistance to Somalia in the Field of Human Rights

85 (2005) Technical Cooperation and Advisory Services in the Democratic Republic of the Congo

II. Reports

'Final Report on the Situation of Human Rights in El Salvador Submitted by Professor José Antonio Pastor Ridruejo in Discharge of the Mandate Conferred by Commission Resolution 32 (XXXVII)' (18 January 1982) UN Doc E/CN.4/1502

'Report of the Working Group on a Draft Declaration on the Right and Responsibility of Individuals, Groups and Organs of Society to Promote and Protect Universally Recognized Human Rights and Fundamental Freedoms' (13 March 1986) UN Doc E/CN.4/1986/40

'Report on the Human Rights Situation in the Islamic Republic of Iran by the Special Representative of the Commission, Mr. Reynaldo Galindo Pohl, Appointed Pursuant to Resolution 1986/41' (28 January 1987) UN Doc E/CN.4/1987/23

'Report of the Working Group on a Draft Declaration on the Right and Responsibility of Individuals, Groups and Organs of Society to Promote and Protect Universally Recognized Human Rights and Fundamental Freedoms' (9 March 1987) UN Doc E/CN.4/1987/38

'Report on the Situation of Human Rights in Afghanistan Prepared by the Special Rapporteur, Mr. Felix Ermacora, in Accordance with Commission on Human Rights Resolution 1988/67' (16 February 1989) UN Doc E/CN.4/1989/24

'Report on the Question of the Use of Mercenaries as a Means of Violating Human Rights and Impeding the Exercise of the Right of Peoples to Self-determination, Submitted by Mr. Enrique Bernales Ballesteros (Peru), Special Rapporteur, Pursuant to Commission Resolution 1990/7' (27 December 1990) UN Doc E/CN.4/1991/14

'Report on the Human Rights Situation in the Islamic Republic of Iran By the Special Representative of the Commission on Human Rights, Reynaldo Galindo Pohl, Pursuant to Commission Resolution 1991/82' (2 January 1992) UN Doc E/CN.4/1992/34

'Report on the Situation of Human Rights in Kuwait under Iraqi Occupation Prepared by Mr. Walter Kâlin, Special Rapporteur of the Commission on Human Rights, in Accordance with Commission Resolution 1991/67' (16 January 1992) UN Doc E/CN.4/1992/26

'Situation of Human Rights in the Sudan Report of the Special Rapporteur, Mr. Gáspár Bíró, Submitted in Accordance with Commission on Human Rights Resolution 1993/60' (1 February 1994) UN Doc E/CN.4/1994/48

'Report of the United Nations High Commissioner for Human Rights on His Mission to Rwanda of 11–12 May 1994' (19 May 1994) UN Doc E/CN.4/S-3/3

'Report by the Independent Expert, Mrs. Mónica Pinto, on the Situation of Human Rights in Guatemala, Prepared in Accordance with Commission Resolution 1994/58' (20 December 1994) UN Doc E/CN.4/1995/15

'Joint Report of the Special Rapporteur on the Question of Torture, Mr. Nigel S. Rodley, and the Special Rapporteur on Extrajudicial, Summary or Arbitrary Executions, Mr. Bacre Waly Ndiaye, Submitted Pursuant to Commission on Human Rights Resolutions 1994/37 and 1994/82: Visit by the Special Rapporteurs to the Republic of Colombia from 17 to 26 October 1994' (16 January 1995) UN Doc E/CN.4/1995/111

'Report by the Independent Expert, Mrs. Mónica Pinto, on the Situation of Human Rights in Guatemala, Prepared in Accordance with Commission Resolution 1995/51' (5 December 1995) UN Doc E/CN.4/1996/15

'Report on the Question of the Use of Mercenaries as a Means of Violating Human Rights and Impeding the Exercise of the Right of Peoples to Self-determination, Submitted by Mr. Enrique Bernales Ballesteros, Special Rapporteur, Pursuant to Commission Resolution 1995/5 and Economic and Council Resolution 1995/254' (17 January 1996) UN Doc E/CN.4/1996/27

'Situation of Human Rights in the Sudan: Report of the Special Rapporteur, Mr. Gáspár Bíró, Submitted in Accordance with Commission on Human Rights Resolution 1995/77' (20 February 1996) UN Doc E/CN.4/1996/62

'Note by the High Commissioner for Human Rights Transmitting Report of the Meeting of Special Rapporteurs/Representatives/Experts and Chairpersons of Working Groups of the Special Procedures of the Commission on Human Rights and of the Advisory Services Programme, Geneva, 28–30 May 1996' (30 September 1996) UN Doc E/CN.4/1997/3

'Situation of Human Rights in Somalia: Report of the Special Rapporteur, Ms. Mona Rishmawi, Submitted in Accordance with Commission on Human Rights Resolution 1997/47' (16 January 1998) UN Doc E/CN.4/1998/96

'Report of the Special Rapporteur on Violence against Women, its Causes and Consequences, Ms. Radhika Coomaraswamy, Submitted in Accordance with Commission Resolution 1997/44' (26 January 1998) UN Doc E/CN.4/1998/54

'Report of the Representative of the Secretary-General, Francis M. Deng, Submitted Pursuant to Commission Resolution 1997/39, Addendum: Guiding Principles on Internal Displacement' (11 February 1998) UN Doc E/CN.4/1998/53/Add.2

'Report by the United Nations High Commissioner for Human Rights' (9 March 1998) UN Doc E/CN.4/1998/16

'Report of the Workshop on Internal Displacement in Africa (Addis Ababa, 19–20 October 1998)' (15 January 1999) UN Doc E/CN.4/1999/79/Add.2

'Report of the Independent Expert on the Right to Restitution, Compensation and Rehabilitation for Victims of Grave Violations of Human Rights and Fundamental Freedoms, Mr. M. Cherif Bassiouni, Submitted Pursuant to Commission on Human Rights Resolution 1998/43' (8 February 1999) UN Doc E/CN.4/1999/65

'The Right to Restitution, Compensation and Rehabilitation for Victims of Gross Violations of Human Rights and Fundamental Freedoms: Final Report of the Special Rapporteur, M. Cherif Bassiouni, Submitted in Accordance with Commission Resolution 1999/33' (18 January 2000) UN Doc E/CN.4/2000/62

'Report of the United Nations High Commissioner for Human Rights on the Human Rights Situation in Colombia' (8 February 2001) UN Doc E/CN.4/2001/15

'Report of the High Commissioner for Human Rights on the Situation in the Republic of Chechnya of the Russian Federation' (20 February 2001) UN Doc E/CN.4/2001/36

'Report of the Human Rights Inquiry Commission Established Pursuant to Commission Resolution S-5/1 of 19 October 2000' (16 March 2001) UN Doc E/CN.4/2001/121

'Report of the Special Rapporteur, Sir Nigel Rodley, Submitted Pursuant to Commission on Human Rights Resolution 2001/62' (27 December 2001) UN Doc E/CN.4/2002/76

'The Right to a Remedy and Reparation for Victims of Violations of International Human Rights and Humanitarian Law, Note by the High Commissioner for Human Rights' (27 December 2002) UN Doc E/CN.4/2003/63

'Human Rights and Human Responsibilities, Final report of the Special Rapporteur, Miguel Alfonso Martínez, on the Study Requested by the Commission in its Resolution 2000/63, and Submitted Pursuant to Economic and Social Council Decision 2002/277' (17 March 2003) UN Doc E/CN.4/2003/105

'The Right to a Remedy and Reparation for Victims of Violations of International Human Rights and Humanitarian Law, Note by the High Commissioner for Human Rights' (10 November 2003) UN Doc E/CN.4/2004/57

'Use of Mercenaries as a Means of Violating Human Rights and Impeding the Exercise of the Right of Peoples to Self-determination; Report Submitted by Mr. Enrique Bernales Ballesteros, Special Rapporteur' (24 December 2003) UN Doc E/CN.4/2004/15

'Report of the United Nations High Commissioner for Human Rights on the Situation of Human Rights in the Darfur region of the Sudan' (7 May 2004) UN Doc E/CN.4/2005/3

'Extrajudicial, Summary or Arbitrary Executions: Report of the Special Rapporteur, Philip Alston' (22 December 2004) UN Doc E/CN.4/2005/7

'Report of the Independent Expert to Update the Set of Principles to Combat Impunity, Diane Orentlicher: Addendum' (8 February 2005) UN Doc E/CN.4/2005/102/Add.1

'Report of the Independent Expert on the Situation of Human Rights in Afghanistan, M. Cherif Bassiouni' (11 March 2005) UN Doc E/CN.4/2005/122

'Interim Report of the Special Representative of the Secretary-General on the Issue of Human Rights and Transnational Corporations and Other Business Enterprises' (22 February 2006) UN Doc E/CN.4/2006/97

'Report of the Representative of the Secretary-General on the Human Rights of Internally Displaced Persons, Walter Kälin: Addendum' (24 March 2006) UN Doc E/CN.4/2006/71/Add.7

'Extrajudicial, Summary or Arbitrary Executions: Report of the Special Rapporteur, Philip Alston, Addendum: Mission to Sri Lanka' (27 March 2006) UN Doc E/CN.4/2006/53/Add.5

'Report of the United Nations High Commissioner for Human Rights on the Situation of Human Rights in Colombia' (16 May 2006) UN Doc E/CN.4/2006/9

III. Sub-Commission Reports

'Systematic Rape, Sexual Slavery and Slavery-like Practices During Armed Conflict - Final Report Submitted by Ms. Gay J. McDougall, Special Rapporteur' (22 June 1998) UN Doc. E/CN.4/Sub.2/1998/13

'Norms on the Responsibilities of Transnational Corporations and Other Business Enterprises with Regard to Human Rights' (26 August 2003) UN Doc E/CN.4/Sub.2/2003/12/Rev.2

'Terrorism and Human Rights: Final Report of the Special Rapporteur, Kalliopi K. Koufa' (25 June 2004) UN Doc E/CN.4/Sub.2/2004/40

'Working Paper on the Relationship between Human Rights Law and International Humanitarian Law by Françoise Hampson and Ibrahim Salama' (21 June 2005) UN Doc E/CN.4/Sub.2/2005/14

'Working Paper on Human Rights and Non-State Actors Submitted by Gáspár Biró and Antoanella-Iulia Motoc' (11 July 2005) UN Doc E/CN.4/Sub.2/2005/40

E. Human Rights Council

I. Resolutions

S-3/1 (2006) Human Rights Violations Emanating from Israeli Military Incursions in the Occupied Palestinian Territory, Including the Recent One in Northern Gaza and the Assault on Beit Hanoun

6/1 (2007) Protection of Cultural Rights and Property in Situations of Armed Conflict

7/1 (2008) Human Rights Violations Emanating from Israeli Military Attacks and Incursions in the Occupied Palestinian Territory, Particularly the Recent Ones in the Occupied Gaza Strip

7/28 (2008) Missing Persons

7/35 (2008) Assistance to Somalia in the Field of Human Rights

8/9 (2008) Promotion on the Right of Peoples to Peace

S-8/1 (2008) Situation of Human Rights in the East of the Democratic Republic of the Congo

S-9/1 (2009) The Grave Violations of Human Rights in the Occupied Palestinian Territory, Particularly Due to the Recent Israeli Military Attacks against the Occupied Gaza Strip

10/19 (2009) Human Rights Violations Emanating from the Israeli Military Attacks and Operations in the Occupied Palestinian Territory

14/15 (2010) Addressing Attacks on School Children in Afghanistan

17/17 (2011) Situation of Human Rights in the Libyan Arab Jamahiriya

17/21 (2011) Assistance to Côte d'Ivoire in the Field of Human Rights

18/4 (2011) The Use of Mercenaries as a Means of Violating Human Rights and Impeding the Exercise of the Right of Peoples to Self-Determination

18/10 (2011) Human Rights and Issues Related to Terrorist Hostage-taking

18/16 (2011) Technical Assistance for the Sudan in the Field of Human Rights

20/17 (2012) Human Rights Situation in Mali

20/21 (2012) Assistance to Somalia in the Field of Human Rights

21/25 (2012) Situation of human rights in the Republic of Mali

23/1 (2013) The Deteriorating Situation of Human Rights in the Syrian Arab Republic, and the Recent Killings in Al-Qusay

23/26 (2013) The Deterioration of the Situation of Human Rights in the Syrian Arab Republic, and the Need to Grant Immediate Access to the Commission of Inquiry

24/22 (2013) The Continuing Grave Deterioration of the Human Rights and Humanitarian Situation in the Syrian Arab Republic

25/23 (2014) The Continuing Grave Deterioration of the Human Rights and Humanitarian Situation in the Syrian Arab Republic

25/26 (2014) Situation of Human Rights in Myanmar

25/36 (2014) Assistance to the Republic of Mali in the Field of Human Rights

27/10 (2014) The Use of Mercenaries as a Means of Violating Human Rights and Impeding the Exercise of the Right of Peoples to Self-Determination

27/16 (2014) The Continuing Grave Deterioration in the Human Rights and Humanitarian Situation in the Syrian Arab Republic

II. Reports

'Mission to Lebanon and Israel (7–14 September 2006): Report of the Special Rapporteur on Extrajudicial, Summary or Arbitrary Executions, Philip Alston; the Special Rapporteur on the Right of Everyone to the Enjoyment of the Highest Attainable Standard of Physical and Mental Health, Paul Hunt; the Representative of the Secretary-General on Human Rights of Internally Displaced Persons, Walter Kälin; and the Special Rapporteur on Adequate Housing as a Component of the Right to an Adequate Standard of Living, Miloon Kothari' (2 October 2006) UN Doc A/HRC/2/7

'Report of the Commission of Inquiry on Lebanon Pursuant to Human Rights Council Resolution S-2/1' (23 November 2006) UN Doc A/HRC/3/2

'Final Report on the Situation of Human Rights in Darfur Prepared by the Group of Experts Mandated by the Human Rights Council in its Resolution 4/8, Presided by the Special Rapporteur on the Situation of Human Rights in the Sudan and Composed of the Special Rapporteur on Extrajudicial, Summary or Arbitrary Executions, the Special Representative of the Secretary-General for Children and Armed Conflict, the Special Rapporteur on Violence against Women, its Causes and Consequences, the Special Representative of the Secretary-General on the Situation of Human Rights Defenders, the Representative of the Secretary-General on the Human Rights of Internally Displaced Persons and the Special Rapporteur on the Question of Torture and Other Cruel, Inhuman or Degrading Treatment or Punishment' (28 November 2007) UN Doc A/HRC/6/19

'Report of the Special Rapporteur on Extrajudicial, Summary or Arbitrary Executions, Philip Alston: Addendum, Mission to Philippines' (16 April 2008) UN Doc A/HRC/8/3/Add.2

'Protect, Respect and Remedy: A Framework for Business and Human Rights: Report of the Special Representative of the Secretary-General on the Issue of Human Rights and Transnational Corporations and Other Business Enterprises, John Ruggie' (7 April 2008) UN Doc A/HRC/8/5

'Human Rights Violations Emanating from Israeli Military Attacks and Incursions in the Occupied Palestinian Territory, Particularly the Recent Ones in the Occupied Gaza Strip: Report of the High Commissioner for Human Rights on the Implementation of Human Rights Council Resolution 7/1' (6 June 2008) UN Doc A/HRC/8/17

'Report of the High-Level Fact-Finding Mission to Beit Hanoun Established under Council Resolution S-3/1' (1 September 2008) UN Doc A/HRC/9/26

'Report of the Special Rapporteur on the Situation of Human Rights in the Palestinian Territories Occupied since 1967, Richard Falk' (11 February 2009) UN Doc A/HRC/10/20

'Human Rights Situation in Palestine and Other Occupied Arab Territories: Combined Report of the Special Rapporteur on the Right of Everyone to the Enjoyment of the Highest Attainable Standard of Physical and Mental Health, the Special Representative of the Secretary-General for Children and Armed Conflict, the Special Rapporteur on Violence against Women, its Causes and Consequences, the Representative of the Secretary-General on the Human Rights of Internally Displaced Persons, the Special Rapporteur on Adequate Housing as a Component of the Right to an Adequate

Standard of Living, and on the Right to Non-discrimination in This Context, the Special Rapporteur on the Right to Food, the Special Rapporteur on Extrajudicial, Summary or Arbitrary Executions, the Special Rapporteur on the Right to Education and the Independent Expert on the Question of Human Rights and Extreme Poverty' (20 March 2009) UN Doc A/HRC/10/22

'Outcome of the Expert Consultation on the Issue of Protecting the Human Rights of Civilians in Armed Conflict: Report of the United Nations High Commissioner for Human Rights' (4 June 2009) UN Doc A/HRC/11/31

'Report of the United Nations High Commissioner for Human Rights on the Implementation of Human Rights Council Resolution S-9/1' (19 August 2009) UN Doc A/HRC/12/37

'Report of the United Nations Fact-Finding Mission on the Gaza Conflict' (15 September 2009) UN Doc A/HRC/12/48

'Report of the Special Rapporteur on the Situation of Human Rights Defenders, Margaret Sekaggya' (30 December 2009) UN Doc A/HRC/13/22

'Report of the Special Rapporteur on Extrajudicial, Summary or Arbitrary Executions, Philip Alston: Study on Targeted Killings' (28 May 2010) UN Doc A/HRC/14/24/Add.6

'Report of the Working Group on the Use of Mercenaries as a Means of Violating Human Rights and Impeding the Exercise of the Right of Peoples to Self-determination' (2 July 2010) UN Doc A/HRC/15/25

'Report of the International Commission of Inquiry to Investigate All Alleged Violations of International Human Rights Law in the Libyan Arab Jamahiriya' (1 June 2011) UN Doc A/HRC/17/44

'Report of the Independent International Commission of Inquiry on the Syrian Arab Republic' (23 November 2011) UN Doc A/HRC/S-17/2/Add.1

'Report of the Working Group on the Use of Mercenaries as a Means of Violating Human Rights and Impeding the Exercise of the Right of Peoples to Self-determination' (4 July 2011) A/HRC/18/32

'Report of the Independent International Commission of Inquiry on the Syrian Arab Republic' (22 February 2012) UN Doc A/HRC/19/69

'Report of the Independent International Commission of Inquiry on the Syrian Arab Republic' (16 August 2012) UN Doc A/HRC/21/50

'Report of the United Nations High Commissioner for Human Rights on the Situation of Human Rights in Mali' (7 January 2013) UN Doc A/HRC/22/33

'Report of the Independent International Commission of Inquiry on the Syrian Arab Republic' (5 February 2013) UN Doc A/HRC/22/59

'Report of the Independent International Commission of Inquiry on the Syrian Arab Republic' (4 June 2013) UN Doc A/HRC/23/58

'Report of the Independent International Commission of Inquiry on the Syrian Arab Republic' (16 August 2013) UN Doc A/HRC/24/46

'Report of the Independent International Commission of Inquiry on the Syrian Arab Republic' (12 February 2014) UN Doc A/HRC/25/65

F. Human Rights Committee

'General Comment No 26' (8 December 1997) UN Doc CCPR/C/21/Rev.1/Add.8/Rev.1
'General Comment No 29' (31 August 2001) UN Doc CCPR/C/21/Rev.1/Add.11
'General Comment No 31' (26 May 2004) UN Doc CCPR/C/21/Rev.1/Add.13

G. International Law Commission Documents

International Law Commission, 'Draft Articles on the Law of Treaties with Commentaries' (1966) Yearbook of the International Law Commission Vol. II 187
Roberto Ago, 'Fourth Report on State Responsibility' (1972) Yearbook of the International Law Commission Vol. II 71
International Law Commission, 'Texts of Articles 10–15 and Commentaries Thereto as Adopted by the Commission at Its Twenty-Seventh Session' (1975) Yearbook of the International Law Commission Vol. II 59
International Law Commission, 'Draft Articles on Treaties Concluded between States and International Organizations or between International Organizations' (1978) Yearbook of the International Law Commission Vol. I 186
'Observations and Comments of Governments on Chapters I, II and III of Part 1 of the Draft Articles on State Responsibility for Internationally Wrongful Acts' (1980) Yearbook of the International Law Commission Vol. II Part One 87
Paul Reuter, 'Tenth Report on the Question of Treaties Concluded between States and International Organizations or between Two or More International Organizations' (1981) Yearbook of the International Law Commission Vol. II Part One 43
'Comments of Governments on Part One of the Draft Articles on State Responsibility for Internationally Wrongful Acts' (1981) Yearbook of the International Law Commission Vol. II Part One 71
James Crawford, 'First Report on State Responsibility' (1998) Yearbook of the International Law Commission Vol II Part One 1
'State Responsibility – Comments and Observations Received from Governments' (2001) Yearbook of the International Law Commission Vol. II Part One 33
International Law Commission, 'Draft Articles on Responsibility of States for Internationally Wrongful Acts' (2001) Yearbook of the International Law Commission Vol. II Part Two 26
International Law Commission, 'Draft Articles on Responsibility of States for Internationally Wrongful Acts, with Commentaries' (2001) Yearbook of the International Law Commission Vol. II Part Two 31
International Law Commission, 'Guiding Principles Applicable to Unilateral Declarations of States Capable of Creating Legal Obligations' (2006) UN Doc A/61/10
International Law Commission, 'Guiding Principles Applicable to Unilateral Declarations of States Capable of Creating Legal Obligations, with Commentaries Thereto' (2006) Yearbook of the International Law Commission Vol. II Part Two 369
International Law Commission, 'Text of the Draft Articles on the Responsibility of International Organizations' (2011) UN Doc A/66/10

International Law Commission, 'Text of the Draft Articles on the Effects of Armed Conflicts on Treaties' (2011) UN Doc A/66/10

H. Miscellaneous

UNGA Third Committee, 89th Meeting (1947) UN Doc A/C.3/SR.89
UNGA Third Committee, 90th Meeting (1947) UN Doc A/C.3/SR.90
UNGA Third Committee, 95th Meeting (1947) UN Doc A/C.3/SR.95
UNGA Third Committee, 153rd Meeting (1947) UN Doc A/C.3/SR.153
UNGA Third Committee, 155th Meeting (1947) UN Doc A/C.3/SR.155
UNGA Third Committee, 156th Meeting (1947) UN Doc A/C.3/SR.156
Legal Consequences for States of the Continued Presence of South Africa in Namibia (South West Africa) notwithstanding Security Council Resolution 276 (1970) (Advisory Opinion) [1971] ICJ Pleadings Vol. II
Western Sahara (Advisory Opinion) [1975] ICJ Pleadings Vol. V
'Report of the Ad Hoc Committee on the Drafting of an International Convention against the Recruitment, Use, Financing and Training of Mercenaries' (24 March 1987) UN Doc A/42/43
UN Committee on Economic, Social and Cultural Rights, 'General Comment No. 3: The Nature of States Parties' Obligations (Art. 2, Para. 1, of the Covenant)' (14 December 1990) UN Doc E/1991/23
Review Conference of the State Parties to the Convention on Prohibitions or Restrictions on the Use of Certain Conventional Weapons Which May Be Deemed to Be Excessively Injurious or to Have Indiscriminate Effects, 4th Meeting (3 October 1995) UN Doc CCW/CONF.I/SR.4
UN Committee on Economic, Social and Cultural Rights, 'General Comment No. 12' (12 May 1999) UN Doc E/C.12/1999/5
UN Committee Against Torture, *Sadiq Shek Elmi v Australia* (25 May 1999) UN Doc CAT/C/22/D/120/1998
UN Committee on Economic, Social and Cultural Rights, 'General Comment No. 14' (11 August 2000) UN Doc E/C.12/2000/4
'Victims' Compensation and Participation', Appendix to 'Letter Dated 2 November 2000 from the Secretary-General Addressed to the President of the Security Council' (3 November 2000) UN Doc S/2000/1063
'Elements of Crimes of the International Criminal Court' (2000) UN Doc PCNICC/2000/1/Add.2
'Report of the United Nations High Commissioner for Human Rights' (28 September 2001) UN Doc A/56/36
'Report of the International Commission of Inquiry on Darfur to the Secretary-General Pursuant to Security Council Resolution 1564 (2004) of 18 September 2004' (1 February 2005) UN Doc S/2005/60
UNCHR Chairperson's Statement 1 (2005) Situation of Human Rights in Colombia

UN Committee on the Rights of the Child, 'Consideration of Reports Submitted by State Parties under Article 44 of the Convention, Concluding Observations: Nepal' (21 September 2005) UN Doc CRC/C/15/Add.261

UNCHR, 57th Meeting Record (2005) UN Doc E/CN.4/2005/SR.57

UNHRC Decision 2/115 (2006) Darfur

United Nations Office of the High Commissioner for Human Rights in Nepal, 'Human Rights Abuses by the CPN-M: Summary of Concerns' (2006) <http://nepal.ohchr.org/en/resources/Documents/English/reports/IR/Year2006/2006_09_21_Human%20Rights%20Abuses%20by%20the%20CPN-M.pdf>

Working Group on Children and Armed Conflict, 'Conclusions on Children and Armed Conflict in Sri Lanka' (13 June 2007) UN Doc S/AC.51/2007/9

'Report of the Panel of Experts Established Pursuant to Resolution 1591 (2005) Concerning the Sudan Prepared in Accordance with Paragraph 2 of Resolution 1713 (2006)' (3 October 2007) UN Doc S/2007/584

Security Council Committee Established Pursuant to Resolution 1521 (2004) Concerning Liberia, 'Guidelines of the Committee for the Conduct of Its Work', 30 March 2010 <http://www.un.org/sc/committees/1521/pdf/1521_Committee_Guidelines.pdf>

Security Council Committee Established Pursuant to Resolution 1533 (2004) Concerning the Democratic Republic of the Congo, 'Guidelines of the Committee for the Conduct of Its Work', 6 August 2010 <http://www.un.org/sc/committees/1533/pdf/S%20AC.43%202010%20Guidelines%20FINAL%20%286%20August%202010%29.pdf>

ICC, *Rules of Procedure and Evidence* (2nd edn 2013)

Security Council Committee Established Pursuant to Resolution 1591 (2005) Concerning the Sudan, 'Guidelines of the Committee for the Conduct of Its Work', 23 December 2013 <http://www.un.org/sc/committees/1591/pdf/Sudan_guide_E.pdf>

2. Organization of American States

American Declaration of the Rights and Duties of Man, Res. XXX, Final Act of the Ninth International Conference of American States (Pan American Union), Bogota, Colombia, Mar. 3–May 2, 1948

Annual Report 1990–1, Inter-American Commission on Human Rights, OEA/Ser.L/V/II.79 Doc. 12 rev. 1 (1991)

Annual Report 1992–3, Inter-American Commission on Human Rights, OEA/Ser./L/V/II.83 Doc. 14 corr. 1(1993)

Fourth Report on the Situation of Human Rights in Guatemala, Inter-American Commission of Human Rights, OEA/Ser. L/V/ II.83 Doc. 16 rev. 1 (1993)

Third Report on the Human Rights Situation in Colombia, Inter-American Commission on Human Rights, OEA/Ser.L/V/II.102 Doc. 9 rev. 1 (1999)

Report on Terrorism and Human Rights, Inter-American Commission on Human Rights, OEA/Ser.L/V/II.116 Doc. 5 rev. 1 corr. (2002)

3. African Union

African Commission on Human and Peoples' Rights, *Resolution on the Situation in Rwanda*, ACHPR /Res.8 (XV) 1994

African Commission on Human and Peoples' Rights, *Resolution on South Africa*, ACHPR / Res.9 (XV) 1994

Lomé Declaration of July 2000 on the Framework for an OAU Response to Unconstitutional Changes of Government (AHG/Decl.5 (XXXVI)

African Commission on Human and Peoples' Rights, *Resolution on the Human Rights Situation in the Republic of Somalia*, ACHPR/Res.129 (Ext.OS/IV) 2008

African Commission on Human and Peoples' Rights, *Resolution on the Human Rights Situation in the Democratic Republic of the Congo (DRC)*, ACHPR/Res.139 (XXXXIV) 2008

4. European Union

Conference on Yugoslavia, Arbitration Commission, 'Opinion No 8' (1992) 31 International Legal Materials 1521

Parliament Resolution (EC) on Measures to Promote a Commitment by Non-State Actors to a Total Ban on Anti-Personnel Landmines [2002] OJ C72/352

Council Directive (EC) 2004/83 on Minimum Standards for the Qualification and Status of Third Country Nationals or Stateless Persons as Refugees or as Persons Who Otherwise Need International Protection and the Content of the Protection Granted [2004] OJ L304/12

Parliament Resolution (EC) on the Situation in Sri Lanka [2006] OJ C305/258

Independent International Fact-Finding Mission on the Conflict in Georgia, 'Report' (2009) Vol. II

5. Council of Europe

X and Y v Netherlands (App 8978/80) European Commission of Human Rights (1983)

Parliamentary Assembly Recommendation 1444 on the Conflict in Chechnya (2000)

Table of Travaux Préparatoires

Final Record of the Diplomatic Conference of Geneva of 1949 Vols I and II-B (Federal Political Department 1951)

Actes de la Conférence Convoquée par l'Organisation des Nations Unies pour l'Education, la Science et la Culture (Staatsdrukkerij- en Uitgeverijbedrijf 1961)

Official Records of the Diplomatic Conference on the Reaffirmation and Development of International Humanitarian Law Applicable in Armed Conflicts, Geneva (1974–1977) Vols 1, 4–5, 7–11 and 14 (Federal Political Department 1978)

United Nations Conference on the Law of Treaties, Official Records, First Session (United Nations 1969)

United Nations Conference on the Law of Treaties, Official Records, Second Session (United Nations 1970)

United Nations Conference on the Law of Treaties, Official Records, Documents of the Conference (United Nations 1971)

United Nations Conference on the Law of Treaties between States and International Organizations or between International Organizations Vol. 1 (United Nations 1995)

Table of National Documents

1. Documents from States

A. Documents Submitted to the International Court of Justice in the Context of the Advisory Opinion, Accordance with International Law of the Unilateral Declaration of Independence in Respect of Kosovo *(2010)*

Written Statement of the Republic of Azerbaijan <http://www.icj-cij.org/docket/files/141/15668.pdf>

Written Comments of France <http://www.icj-cij.org/docket/files/141/15680.pdf>

Written Statement of the Government of Japan <http://www.icj-cij.org/docket/files/141/15658.pdf>

Written Statement of The Islamic Republic of Iran <http://www.icj-cij.org/docket/files/141/15646.pdf>

Written Comments of the Kingdom of Netherlands <http://www.icj-cij.org/docket/files/141/15692.pdf>

Written Comments of the Kingdom of Norway <http://www.icj-cij.org/docket/files/141/15682.pdf>

Written Comments of the Kingdom of Spain <http://www.icj-cij.org/docket/files/141/15706.pdf>

Written Comments by the Swiss Confederation <http://www.icj-cij.org/docket/files/141/15698.pdf>

B. Statements in the Context of Human Rights Council Sessions

2nd Emergency Session (11 August 2006)

Intervention by the Permanent Representative of Brazil in Geneva, Ambassador Clodoaldo Hugueney <http://extranet2.ohchr.org/Extranets/HRCExtranet/portal/page/portal/HRCExtranet/2SpecialSession/Tab1/6.Brazil.pdf>

Statement by Ambassador Paul Meyer of Canada <http://extranet2.ohchr.org/Extranets/HRCExtranet/portal/page/portal/HRCExtranet/2SpecialSession/Tab1/13.Canada.pdf>

Statement by Mrs Astrid Helle Ajamay, Minister Counsellor, Norway <http://extranet2.ohchr.org/Extranets/HRCExtranet/portal/page/portal/HRCExtranet/2SpecialSession/Tab3/21.Norway.pdf>

General Statement, Philippines <http://extranet2.ohchr.org/Extranets/HRCExtranet/portal/page/portal/HRCExtranet/2SpecialSession/Tab1/14.Philippines.pdf>

Déclaration de S.E. M. Blaise Godet Représentant Permanent de la Suisse auprès de l'Office des Nations Unies et autres Organisations Internationales à Genève <http://extranet2.ohchr.org/Extranets/HRCExtranet/portal/page/portal/HRCExtranet/2SpecialSession/Tab1/12.Switzerland.pdf>

9th Emergency Session (9 January 2009)

(Angola) Statement by H.E. Ambassador Arcanjo Nascimento before the Human Rights Council Special Session on the Situation in Gaza <http://extranet2.ohchr.org/Extranets/HRCExtranet/portal/page/portal/HRCExtranet/9thSpecialSession/Oralstatements/090109/Tab15/Tab/Angola.pdf>

Austria Statement by Ambassador Christian Strohal <http://extranet2.ohchr.org/Extranets/HRCExtranet/portal/page/portal/HRCExtranet/9thSpecialSession/Oralstatements/090109/Tab/StatementsofObserverStatesandotherobservers/Austria.pdf>

Statement by Brazilian Delegation <http://extranet2.ohchr.org/Extranets/HRCExtranet/portal/page/portal/HRCExtranet/9thSpecialSession/Oralstatements/090109/Tab/Memberstates/Brazil.pdf>

Statement by H.E. Giovanni Caracciolo Di Vietri Permanent Representative of Italy <http://extranet2.ohchr.org/Extranets/HRCExtranet/portal/page/portal/HRCExtranet/9thSpecialSession/Oralstatements/090109/Tab/Memberstates/Italy.pdf>

Statement by the Republic of Korea <http://extranet2.ohchr.org/Extranets/HRCExtranet/portal/page/portal/HRCExtranet/9thSpecialSession/Oralstatements/090109/Tab15/Tab/Republic%20of%20Korea0001.pdf>

Statement by Nigeria <.http://extranet2.ohchr.org/Extranets/HRCExtranet/portal/page/portal/HRCExtranet/9thSpecialSession/Oralstatements/090109/Tab15/Tab/Nigeria0001.pdf>

Statement by Portugal <http://extranet2.ohchr.org/Extranets/HRCExtranet/portal/page/portal/HRCExtranet/9thSpecialSession/Oralstatements/090109/Tab/StatementsofObserverStatesandotherobservers/Portugal0001.pdf>

Intervention de la Délégation Sénégalaise lors de la Session Extraordinaire du Conseil des Droits de l'Homme sur le Situation à Gaza <http://extranet2.ohchr.org/Extranets/HRCExtranet/portal/page/portal/HRCExtranet/9thSpecialSession/Oralstatements/090109/Tab/Memberstates/Senegal.pdf>

(Slovenia) Statement by H.E. Andrej Logar <http://extranet2.ohchr.org/Extranets/HRCExtranet/portal/page/portal/HRCExtranet/9thSpecialSession/Oralstatements/090109/Tab/Memberstates/Slovenia0001.pdf>

Statement by H.E. Ambassador Sihasak Phuangketkeow, Permanent Representative of Thailand to the United Nations Office in Geneva <http://extranet2.ohchr.org/Extranets/HRCExtranet/portal/page/portal/HRCExtranet/9thSpecialSession/Oralstatements/090109/Tab/StatementsofObserverStatesandotherobservers/Tha%C3%AFland.pdf>

(Statement by the) Delegation of Vietnam <http://extranet2.ohchr.org/Extranets/HRCExtranet/portal/page/portal/HRCExtranet/9thSpecialSession/Oralstatements/090109/Tab/StatementsofObserverStatesandotherobservers/Vietnam.pdf>

23rd Session (29 May 2013)

Statement by Australia <https://extranet.ohchr.org/sites/hrc/HRCSessions/RegularSessions/23rdSession/OralStatements/Australia_07.pdf>

Intervention de la Belgique <https://extranet.ohchr.org/sites/hrc/HRCSessions/RegularSessions/23rdSession/OralStatements/Belgium_07.pdf>

Statement by H.E Mr. Mothusi B.R. Palai, Permanent Representative of Botswana to the UN Office in Geneva <https://extranet.ohchr.org/sites/hrc/HRCSessions/RegularSessions/23rdSession/OralStatements/ Botswana _07.pdf>

Intervention of Brazil <https://extranet.ohchr.org/sites/hrc/HRCSessions/RegularSessions/23rdSession/OralStatements/Brazil_07.pdf>

Canadian Intervention <https://extranet.ohchr.org/sites/hrc/HRCSessions/RegularSessions/23rdSession/OralStatements/Canada_07.pdf>

(Statement of) Estonia <https://extranet.ohchr.org/sites/hrc/HRCSessions/RegularSessions/23rdSession/OralStatements/Estonia_07.pdf>

Statement by H.E. Ms Iruthisam Adam, Permanent Representative of the Republic of Maldives <https://extranet.ohchr.org/sites/hrc/HRCSessions/RegularSessions/23rdSession/OralStatements/Maldives_07.pdf>

Statement by New Zealand <https://extranet.ohchr.org/sites/hrc/HRCSessions/RegularSessions/23rdSession/OralStatements/NZ_07.pdf>

C. Miscellaneous

US Department of the Army Field Manual 27–10, *The Law of Land Warfare* (1956)

Public Statement of Prime Minister of the Democratic Republic of Congo, October 21, 1964 (1965) 59 The American Journal of International Law 616

Department of State, Office of the Legal Adviser, 'The Legality of United States Participation in the Defense of Viet Nam' (1966) 75 Yale Law Journal 1085

'Mise en Œuvre des Conventions de Genève' (1967) 49 Revue International de la Croix Rouge 334

Joint Services Regulation (Z/Dv) 15/2 in Dieter Fleck (ed.), *The Handbook of Humanitarian Law in Armed Conflicts* (OUP 1995)

Declaration of Israel to the Convention on Prohibitions or Restrictions on the Use of Certain Conventional Weapons Which May Be Deemed to Be Excessively Injurious or to Have Indiscriminate Effects, 22 March 1995

Australia's Government Statement for the Meeting of Contracting Parties to the Fourth Geneva Convention, Geneva, 27–29 October 1998 (1999) 2 Yearbook of International Humanitarian Law 450

Statement of Government of Colombia Regarding the Status of FARC, 16 June 1999 (1999) 2 Yearbook of International Humanitarian Law 440

Office of the Judge Advocate General of Canada, *Law of Armed Conflict at the Operational and Tactical Levels* (2001) <http://www.fichl.org/uploads/media/Canadian_LOAC_Manual_2001_English.pdf>

Memorandum from John C. Yoo, Deputy Assistant General Counsel & Robert Delahunty, Special Counsel, Office of Legal Counsel, Department of Justice, to William J. Haynes II, General Counsel, Department of Defense, Re: Application of Treaties and Laws to al Qaeda and Taliban Detainees (January 9, 2002) <http://lawofwar.org/Yoo_Memo_html.htm>

Reservation of France to the Convention on Prohibitions or Restrictions on the Use of Certain Conventional Weapons Which May Be Deemed to Be Excessively Injurious or to Have Indiscriminate Effects, 18 July 2002

Written Statement Submitted by the Government of the Republic of South Africa, *Legal Consequences on the Construction of a Wall in the Occupied Palestinian Territory* (Advisory Opinion) [2004] <http://www.icj-cij.org/docket/files/131/1597.pdf>

(UK) Ministry of Defence, Joint Doctrine and Concepts Centre, *The Joint Service Manual of the Law of Armed Conflict* (2004)

Witness to Truth: Report of the Sierra Leone Truth & Reconciliation Commission Vol. 2 (2004)

Bellinger III, John B. & Haynes II, William J., 'A US Government Response to the International Committee of the Red Cross Study Customary International Humanitarian Law' (2007) 89 International Review of the Red Cross 443

(US) Department of the Navy, *The Commander's Handbook on the Law of Naval Operations*, NWP 1–14 M (2007)

Republic of Liberia, Truth and Reconciliation Commission, *Consolidated Final Report* Vol. 2 (2009)

Turkish National Commission of Inquiry, Report on the Israeli Attack on the Humanitarian Aid Convoy to Gaza on 31 May 2010 (2011)

Declaration of the Philippines to the Protocol Additional to the Geneva Conventions of 12 August 1949, and relating to the Protection of Victims of International Armed Conflicts, 30 March 2012

2. Documents from Armed Non-State Actors

Programme Politique du Front National de Libération du Sud Viet Nam (1967) <http://theirwords.org/media/transfer/doc/1_vn_fnl_1967_03-e7a4d62b214d4faf8a33567f467fe7b3.pdf>

'Declaration by UNITA' (1980) 20 International Review of the Red Cross 320

'Declaration of Intent by the African National Congress' (1981) 21 International Review of the Red Cross 20

'NDFP Declaration of Adherence to International Humanitarian Law', 15 August 1991 <http://theirwords.org/media/transfer/doc/ph_ndfp_1991_19-f33015876ed5c0c837380aa1fff083b7.pdf>

ELN, 'Declaración Pública del Comandante Manuel Pérez', 15 July 1995 <http://theirwords.org/media/transfer/doc/co_eln_1995_11-f5e6b47ebf049f6af76bc20fe929d588.pdf>

NDFP, 'Declaration of Undertaking to Apply the Geneva Conventions of 1949 and Protocol I of 1977', 9 August 1996 <http://www.hartford-hwp.com/archives/54a/036.html>

Constitution of the Republic of Somaliland (1997) <http://www.somalilandlaw.com/Somaliland_Constitution/body_somaliland_constitution.htm>

SPLM Political Secretariat, 'Fifteen-Point Programme of the SPLM' (1998) <http://www.splmtoday.com/index.php/programme-splm-35>

UCK (KLA), 'Undertaking of Demilitarisation and Transformation', 20 June 1999 <http://www.nato.int/kosovo/docu/a990620a.htm>

SPLM/A, 'Deed of Commitment under Geneva Call for Adherence to a Total Ban on Anti-Personnel Mines and for Cooperation in Mine Action', Geneva, 4 October 2001 <http://www.genevacall.org/wp-content/uploads/dlm_uploads/2013/12/splma.pdf>

The SPLA Act (2003) <http://theirwords.org/media/transfer/doc/1_sd_splm_a_2003_03-5fd4e4fabf407e670f236c8d3ecaf381.pdf>

North East Secretariat on Human Rights, 'Charter' (2005) <http://www.padippakam.com/document/ltte/HR_Report01/Charter-English.pdf>

NDFP Human Rights Monitoring Committee, *NDFP Adherence to International Humanitarian Law on Prisoners of War (POWs)* (2009) <http://theirwords.org/media/transfer/doc/1_ph_ndfp_2009_38-7bad5cfad8e2b3a0e2029e4fcf62d803.pdf>

Decree, No. 71 (2010): Establishment of a JEM Committee for Human Rights (JCHRs) <http://theirwords.org/media/transfer/doc/sd_jem_2010_49-03a60fff4d0b8044d99e8b15eae55d2e.pdf>

Chin National Front's Perspective on Child Protection in Armed Conflict (2010) <http://theirwords.org/media/transfer/doc/mm_cnf_cna_2010_29-4b3e18cae2b0ed244acb2cc0c50cf460.pdf>

NTC, 'The Treatment of Detainees and Prisoners', Benghazi, 25 March 2011 <http://theirwords.org/media/transfer/doc/ly_ntc_2011_05-615c0dc0f1c0ffe8dfcba03007bcead3.pdf>

NTC, 'Frontline Manual' (2011) <http://theirwords.org/media/transfer/doc/1_ly_ntc_2011_03-ef921ee4a9e2826b1ad8c267b8254c97.pdf>

Defence Commission (PKK), 'Rules for the Conduct of Warfare' (2011) <http://theirwords.org/media/transfer/doc/ut_tr_pkk_hpg_2011_04_eng-c4389828932861eb8ccc1dd849ae7603.pdf>

NDFP, 'Declaration and Program of Action for the Rights, Protection and Welfare of Children', 24 April 2012 <http://www.philippinerevolution.net/publications/ang_bayan/archives/2012/original/20120629en.pdf?1340952943>

JEM, Command Order on Recruitment and Use of Child Soldiers, 15 September 2012 <http://theirwords.org/media/transfer/doc/sd_jem_2012_48-6fc3e6e13af6a631f2afcd86e7fb22bd.pdf>

Constitution of the Republic of Abkhazia <http://apsnypress.info/en/constitution>

NDFP, 'Constitution: Organizational Principles and Policies' <http://www.ndfp.net/web2014/index.php/about/constitution/organizational-principles-and-policies>

NRA's (Uganda) Code of Conduct <http://theirwords.org/media/transfer/doc/sc_ug_nra_02-56e734a47e81ad2ebace8f1ab67b1a73.pdf>

Lasting Peace in Sierra Leone: The Revolutionary United Front Sierra Leone (Ruf/SL) Perspective and Vision <http://theirwords.org/media/transfer/doc/sl_ruf_08-8b0383b426906a2602263d3afda2c66d.pdf>

Statement by the Opposition Movements (JEM and SLM-Unity) <http://theirwords.org/media/transfer/doc/1_sd_jem_slm_a_unity_2008_18-9786ecfeda2b4605ff60bcdc4aab48b2.pdf>

Table of Documents from Non-Governmental Organizations

Institut de Droit International, 'Responsabilité Internationale des Etats à Raison des Dommages Causés sur Leur Territoire à la Personne et aux Biens des Etrangers' Resolution (1927) <http://www.idi-iil.org/idiF/resolutionsF/1927_lau_05_fr.pdf>

International Committee of the Red Cross, 'The International Committee and the Vietnam Conflict' (1966) 6 International Review of the Red Cross 399

Institut de Droit International, 'The Principle of Non-Intervention in Civil Wars' Resolution (1975) <http://www.idi-iil.org/idiE/resolutionsE/1975_wies_03_en.pdf>

International Institute of Humanitarian Law, 'Rules of International Humanitarian Law Governing the Conduct of Hostilities in Non-International Armed Conflicts' (1990) 30 International Review of the Red Cross 383

Human Rights Watch, 'World Report 1992: El Salvador' <http://www.hrw.org/reports/1992/WR92/AMW-08.htm#TopOfPage>

Committee on the Enforcement of Human Rights Law, 'Final Report on the Status of the Universal Declaration of Human Rights in National and International Law' in International Law Association Report of the Sixty-Sixth Conference (Buenos Aires, 1994) (International Law Association, London 1994) 525

Institut de Droit International, 'The Application of International Humanitarian Law and Fundamental Human Rights, in Armed Conflicts in which Non-State Entities are Parties' Resolution (1999) <http://www.idi-iil.org/idiE/resolutionsE/1999_ber_03_en.PDF>

International Council on Human Rights Policy, *Taking Duties Seriously: Individual Duties in International Human Rights Law* (1999) <http://www.ichrp.org/files/reports/10/103_report_en.pdf>

International Council on Human Rights Policy, *Ends & Means: Human Rights Approaches to Armed Groups* (2000) <http://www.ichrp.org/files/reports/6/105_report_en.pdf>

International Committee of the Red Cross, 'International Humanitarian Law and the Challenges of Contemporary Armed Conflicts: Report' (2003) <http://www.icrc.org/eng/assets/files/other/ihlcontemp_armedconflicts_final_ang.pdf>

International Committee of the Red Cross, 'Improving Compliance with International Humanitarian Law: Report' (2003) <https://www.icrc.org/eng/assets/files/other/improving_compliance_with_international_report_eng_2003.pdf >

International Institute of Humanitarian Law, *The Manual on the Law of Non-International Armed Conflict With Commentary* (Sanremo, 2006) <http://www.iihl.org/iihl/Documents/The%20Manual%20on%20the%20Law%20of%20NIAC.pdf>

The Chicago Principles on Post-Conflict Justice (2007) <http://www.concernedhistorians.org/content_files/file/to/213.pdf>

Geneva Call, *Engaging Armed Non-State Actors in a Landmine Ban: The Geneva Call Progress Report (2000–7)* (2007) <http://www.genevacall.org/wp-content/uploads/dlm_uploads/2013/12/raport.pdf>

The Montreux Document on Pertinent International Legal Obligations and Good Practices for States Related to Operations of Private Military and Security Companies during Armed Conflict (2008) <http://www.icrc.org/eng/assets/files/other/icrc_002_0996.pdf>

International Committee of the Red Cross, 'Increasing Respect for International Humanitarian Law in Non-International Armed Conflicts' (2008) <http://www.icrc.org/eng/assets/files/other/icrc_002_0923.pdf>

Committee on Aspects of the Law of State Succession, 'Final Report' in International Law Association Report of the Seventy-Third Conference (Rio de Janeiro 2008) (International Law Association, London 2008) 250

Committee on Compensation for Victims of War, 'Report' in International Law Association Report of the Seventy-Third Conference (Rio de Janeiro 2008) (International Law Association, London 2008) 459

Assembly of the International Committee of the Red Cross, 'Interpretive Guidance on the Notion of Direct Participation in Hostilities under International Humanitarian Law' (2008) 90 International Review of the Red Cross 991

'Expert Meeting on Procedural Safeguards for Security Detention in Non-international Armed Conflict' (2009) 91 International Review of the Red Cross 859

Committee on Reparation for Victims of Armed Conflict, 'Draft Declaration of International Law Principles on Reparation for Victims of Armed Conflict (Substantive Issues)' in International Law Association Report of the Seventy-Fourth Conference (The Hague, 2010) (International Law Association, London 2010) 295

Committee on Non-State Actors, 'Non-State Actors in International Law: Aims, Approach and Scope of Project and Legal Issues – First Report' in International Law Association Report of the Seventy-Fourth Conference (The Hague 2010) (International Law Association, London 2010) 630

Committee on the Use of Force, 'Final Report on the Meaning of Armed Conflict in International Law' in International Law Association Report of the Seventy-Fourth Conference (The Hague, 2010) (International Law Association, London 2010) 676

Committee on Non-State Actors, 'Non-State Actors in International Law: Lawmaking and Participation Rights' in International Law Association Report of the Seventy-Fifth Conference (Sofia 2012) (International Law Association 2012) 658

Committee on Reparation for Victims of Armed Conflict, 'Reparation for Victims of Armed Conflict (Procedural Issues)' in International Law Association Report of the Seventy-Fifth Conference (Sofia 2012) (International Law Association 2012) 580

Committee on Non-State Actors, 'Third Report' in International Law Association Report of the Seventy-Sixth Conference (Washington 2014) (International Law Association 2014) 686

Committee on Reparation for Victims of Armed Conflict, 'Draft Procedural Principles for Reparation Mechanisms' in International Law Association Report of the Seventy-Sixth Conference (Washington 2014) (International Law Association 2014) 780

'Deed of Commitment under Geneva Call for Adherence to a Total Ban on Anti-Personnel Mines and for Cooperation in Mine Action' <http://www.genevacall.org/resources/deed-of-commitment/f-deed-of-commitment/doc.pdf>

List of Abbreviations

ACHR	American Convention on Human Rights
ANC	African National Congress
ANSA	Armed Non-State Actor
CCW	Convention on Prohibitions or Restrictions on the Use of Certain Conventional Weapons Which May be Deemed to Be Excessively Injurious or to Have Indiscriminate Effects
CIS	Commonwealth of Independent States
CPN (Maoist)	Communist Party of Nepal (Maoist)
DRC	Democratic Republic of Congo
ELN	National Liberation Army (Colombia)
FARC	Revolutionary Armed Forces of Colombia
FDLR	Forces Démocratiques de Libération du Rwanda
FMLN	Farabundo Martí National Liberation Front
GA	General Assembly
ICC	International Criminal Court
ICCPR	International Covenant on Civil and Political Rights
ICESCR	International Covenant on Economic, Social and Cultural Rights
ICRC	International Committee of the Red Cross
ICTY	International Criminal Tribunal for the former Yugoslavia
ICTR	International Criminal Tribunal for Rwanda
IHL	International Humanitarian Law
ILA	International Law Association
ILC	International Law Commission
JEM	Justice and Equality Movement
LTTE	Liberation Tigers of Tamil Eelam
NDFP	National Democratic Front of the Philippines
NTC	(Libyan) National Transitional Council
OAS	Organization of American States
OAU	Organization of African Unity
PKK	Kurdistan Workers' Party (Turkey)
PLO	Palestinian Liberation Organization
POW	Prisoner of war
SC	Security Council
SCSL	Special Court for Sierra Leone
SG	Secretary General
SPLM	Sudan People's Liberation Movement
SWAPO	South West African People's Organization

TRNC	Turkish Republic of Northern Cyprus
UDHR	Universal Declaration of Human Rights
UNCHR	United Nations Commission on Human Rights
UNHRC	United Nations Human Rights Council
UCK (KLA)	Kosovo Liberation Army
VCLT	Vienna Convention on the Law of Treaties

Preface

This book started its slow journey as soon as I became involved with issues pertaining to non-international armed conflicts. The original idea for starting it bears only a little resemblance to the present outcome. In essence, the obligations and accountability of armed non-state actors are still evolving, as states, the international community and doctrine are still unsure about how to deal with them. The hope is that this book will contribute towards setting a road map.

My interest in humanitarian law and armed non-state actors owes a lot to Professor Sassòli of the University of Geneva and his practical approach thereto. Moreover, Professor Okowa of Queen Mary College, University of London has challenged my ideas and given me additional food for thought. The publishing team at Ashgate has been patient in answering my endless questions on numerous aspects of this book, while the anonymous reviewers have offered substantial mental stimulation.

A special thanks goes to Eleni, Dimitra and Stelios for their affection, support, help and overall encouragement during the preparation of this project. My parents have also provided me with everything they had and my gratitude cannot be expressed adequately. This book is dedicated to two little children who are fighting for their life, with the wholehearted wish that they make it safely.

This book represents solely the personal views of the author and does not relate in any way to his current or previous affiliations.

Introduction

It is commonplace that the vast majority of conflicts around the globe involve at least one armed non-state actor (hereinafter ANSA). This reality emerged mainly in the aftermath of the Second World War and persists until now, despite the 'upgrade' of certain non-inter-state armed conflicts (wars of national liberation) by Additional Protocol I.[1] The erosion of the state's monopoly on violence and the grave implications of conflict for human rights and peace have increasingly made ANSAs a matter of international concern. However, this concern has not resulted in the development of a uniform (or even principled) approach concerning ANSAs treatment or status.[2] Instead a variety of parallel, but essentially different, approaches have been adopted: a re-affirmation/elucidation of the rules of state responsibility for wrongful acts, including the attribution of certain ANSAs' conduct towards existing or future-to-be states; a significant strengthening of individual responsibility in the event of an international crime committed; the attitudes and perceptions of the international community towards ANSAs as mere outlaws/ international terrorists which should be eliminated by a variety of international and national measures;[3] an increased role of the Security Council in situations where non-state actors are involved; the approbation of the international community to certain cases of entities entitled to self-determination; and the regulation of their conduct in the event of an armed conflict. At times these approaches intermingle, as several actors on the international plane take different views, sometimes following policy aims rather than legal standards. The outcome of these approaches is incoherency and partiality, revealing a profound difficulty on the part of international law to adjust to the challenges posed by ANSAs.[4] The only substantial exception is the law applicable during armed conflicts, where, after significant initial reluctance, the international community of states has

1 Protocol Additional to the Geneva Conventions of 12 August 1949, and relating to the Protection of Victims of International Armed Conflicts (adopted 8 June 1977, entered into force 7 December 1978) 1125 UNTS 3 (Protocol I).

2 Noemi Gal-Or, 'Observations on the Desirability of an Enhanced International Legal Status of the Non-State Actor' in Marth Noortmann and Cedric Ryngaert (eds), *Non-State Actor Dynamics in International Law: From Law-Takers to Law-Makers* (Ashgate 2010) 125.

3 On the danger that this approach could pose towards radicalization of armed groups see UNSG, 'Report of the Secretary-General on the Protection of Civilians in Armed Conflict' (22 May 2012) S/2012/376, 11–12.

4 See the comments of Jan Klabbers, 'Rebel with a Cause? Terrorists and Humanitarian Law' (2003) 14 EJIL 299, 300, Fergus Green, 'Fragmentation in Two Dimensions: The ICJ's Flawed Approach to Non-State Actors and International Legal Personality' (2008) 9 Melb.J. Int'l L. 47, 49 and a broader debate in Rafael Domingo, 'The Crisis of International Law' (2009) 42 Vand.J.Transnat'l L. 1543–93.

conceded to the application of certain rules to all fighting parties. Yet this framework has been formulated, almost exclusively, by states and its content was mostly determined with states in mind; the opposing armed group only played a residual role, if any at all.[5]

The need for an examination of the obligations and accountability of ANSAs in certain branches of international law relates firstly to their impact on international relations,[6] as evidenced by their transboundary (armed) activities or the effect of their internal armed activities outside the borders of a state. Secondly, ANSAs have been a concern (and that only recently and partially) for international humanitarian law (hereinafter IHL), notwithstanding the fact that other human rights are endangered and that ANSAs might be operating outside the strict confines of an armed conflict.[7] Even the framework of obligations was not coupled in a coherent manner with accountability tools for ANSAs.[8] The reason for this lack is explained, partly, by the perception of legitimacy that a collective entity could gain.[9] The collective character of a group might put the representativeness and legitimacy of a government into question, especially when it appears to attract the support of a significant segment of the population of a state. Therefore it makes sense to 'downgrade' ANSAs and leave the matter of their accountability aside.

Thirdly, the individualization of responsibility for violations of humanitarian law and the extended focus on it leads to decreased attention being paid to the accountability of the entity as such. Individuality was itself '... a reaction to the monolithic and sometimes powerless principles of state responsibility'[10] and the lack of serious implementation

5 Similarly Zakaria Daboné, 'International Law: Armed Groups in a State-Centric System' (2011) 93 IRRC 395, 396.

6 Gérard Cahin, 'The Responsibility of other Entities: Armed Bands and Criminal Groups' in James Crawford, Alain Pellet and Simon Olleson (eds), *The Law of International Responsibility* (CUP 2010) 332.

7 Emmanuel Decaux, 'The Definition of Traditional Sanctions: Their Scope and Characteristics' (2008) 90 IRRC 249, 251, notices that except for humanitarian law, non-state entities '... exist in a legal vacuum'.

8 Marco Sassòli, 'Taking Armed Groups Seriously: Ways to improve their Compliance with International Humanitarian Law' (2010) 1 Journal of International Humanitarian Legal Studies 5, 7, 'the international responsibility of non-State actors remains largely uncharted waters' and Jann K. Kleffner, 'The Collective Accountability of Organized Armed Groups for System Crimes' in Harmen van der Wilt and André Nollkaemper (eds), *System Criminality in International Law* (CUP 2009) 257.

9 States '... prefer to pass over the group and address the individuals that make up the group', Liesbeth Zegveld, *Accountability of Armed Opposition Groups in International Law* (CUP 2002) 223. This approach is particularly evident in the African Union Convention for the Protection and Assistance of Internally Displaced Persons in Africa (adopted 23 October 2009) (2010) 49 ILM 86 (hereinafter *Kampala Convention*), arts 7.4 and 5, especially when compared with the initial draft, see Flavia Zorzi Giustiniani, 'New Hopes and Challenges for the Protection of IDPs in Africa: the Kampala Convention for the Protection and Assistance of Internally Displaced Persons in Africa'(2010–2011) 39 Denv.J. Int'l L. & Pol'y 347, 360.

10 André Nollkaemper, 'Concurrence between Individual Responsibility and State Responsibility in International Law' (2003) 52 ICLQ 615, 631.

mechanisms.[11] In fact, 'collective entities such as states, international organizations, non-state actors, groups, and corporations may benefit from the crimped narratives that international criminal law produces'.[12] In terms of accountability, though, the individualist approach is not adequate. It is confined to certain acts that are criminalized[13] and it is associated with a degree of gravity, while it demands a high level of evidence as well. Furthermore, the accountability of the individual might be more difficult to ascertain within the activities of a group, if it is not 'lost' altogether. The possibility of obtaining reparations increases if the respondent is a collectivity rather than an individual. More importantly, individual responsibility does not take account of the fact that without the collectivity (and even the ensuing climate that this collectivity, be it a state or non-state actor, has created) the individual would be fairly unable to commit a wrongful act, while it fails to include system criminality.[14] Group accountability could also create a culture of deterrence and compliance, since only '… groups may take preventive steps, which cannot be and are not requested from every individual involved in a conflict …'[15] – steps that can 'address the systemic causes of individual criminality'.[16] Consequently it appears that intense focus on the individual carries significant problems with it as well.

Fourthly, ANSAs '… are less frequently acting as proxies of other states (as used to be the case almost invariably with the former Soviet Union and the United States during the Cold War)'.[17] Consequently any recourse to the rules on state responsibility appears less relevant than ever. And generally, when there is no control, the responsibility of the state will arise when it has not shown due diligence, because 'it is in practice impossible for a state to prevent all injurious acts which a private person might commit against a foreign state'.[18] Such a concept is 'difficult to quantify'[19] and 'various parameters operate when assessing whether a State has duly discharged the obligation concerned'.[20] Such

---

11 For André Nollkaemper, 'Systemic Effects of International Responsibility for International Crimes' (2010) 8 Santa Clara J. Int'l L. 313, 331, 'in respect to international crimes committed by armed groups, rebel movements etc., the law of individual responsibility remains, at least within the paradigm of responsibility, the only option'.

12 Mark A. Drumbl, 'Accountability for System Criminality' (2010) 8 Santa Clara J. Int'l L. 373, 377.

13 UNSG, 'Report of the Secretary-General on the Protection of Civilians in Armed Conflict' (29 May 2009) S/2009/277, 15.

14 *Drumbl* 2010, 373 and *Nollkaemper* 2010, 314.

15 Marco Sassòli, 'Possible Legal Mechanisms to Improve Compliance by Armed Groups with International Humanitarian and International Human Rights Law' (2003) 3.

16 *Nollkaemper* 2003, 639.

17 Aristotle Constantinides, 'Human Rights Obligations and Accountability of Armed Opposition Groups: The Practice of the UN Security Council' (2010) 4 HR&ILD 89, 90–91.

18 Robert Jennings and Arthur Watts (eds), *Oppenheim's International Law* Vol. 1 (9th edn, Longman 1992) 549.

19 Malcolm N. Shaw, *International Law* (5th edn, CUP 2003) 706.

20 *Application of the Convention on the Prevention and Punishment of the Crime of Genocide (Bosnia and Herzegovina v Serbia and Montenegro)* (Merits) [2007] ICJ Rep 154. See also Ian Brownlie, *Principles of Public International Law* (7th edn, OUP 2008) 454–6.

parameters have hardly been demystified, although it is certain that 'the circumstances of an insurrection or civil war will significantly affect the way that [due diligence] is applied'.[21] Furthermore state responsibility rules are rarely invoked,[22] probably because 'international responsibility [is] an area of law often intentionally laced with the ambiguity of political expediency'.[23] It is this lack of effectiveness (and occasionally observance[24]) that appears to justify a move towards the accountability of ANSAs.[25] All these factors as well as the diverse approaches towards accountability of ANSAs call for a reconsideration in order to formulate a principled approach towards this phenomenon.

It seems striking that the debate on ANSA accountability did not expand considerably in the previous decade in comparison to similar debates over the accountability of other non-state entities. The 9/11 attacks have largely moved focus towards the legality of counteraction against terrorist groups.[26] This shift of interest is certainly expectable from a political point of view, but rather incomprehensible if one takes into account the fact that armed conflicts are far more destructive than terrorist attacks. Possibly it has its own significance that the effects of terrorism are (or have been) felt by powerful states that are in principle unaffected by an internal conflict. It is also possible that the individualization of accountability through international criminal law has also played a role along with the persistent fear of legitimacy.

To a certain extent, the present book forms part of the greater debate on the role of non-state actors in international law,[27] albeit confined to certain types of non-state actors (ANSAs) and certain legal regimes (international humanitarian law and human rights law). IHL serves as the starting point of analysis, as it acknowledges the existence of ANSAs. However, the present work does not focus on the exact content of obligations *via*

---

21 *Jennings* and *Watts*, 553.

22 Jutta Brunnée, 'International Legal Accountability through the Lens of the Law of State Responsibility' (2005) 36 NYIL 21, 55.

23 Jonathan Somer, 'Jungle Justice: Passing Sentence on the Equality of Belligerents in Non-International Armed Conflict' (2007) 89 IRRC 655, 674.

24 See Karl Zemanek, 'Does the Prospect of Incurring Responsibility Improve the Observance of International Law?' in Maurizio Ragazzi (ed.) *International Responsibility Today: Essays in Memory of Oscar Schachter* (Martinus Nijhoff 2005) 132.

25 *Cahin*, 335–6.

26 Even that debate was entangled in the state-centred approach of international law. This is evident from the conscious effort to lower the degree of interaction between states and ANSAs, so that the conduct of the latter would be attributed to a state or that a state should be subject to some use of force for its failure to inhibit ANSAs' activities from its territory. Additionally, this debate focused almost exclusively on the legal/legitimate responses of states to the use of force by ANSAs.

27 Philip Alston (ed.), *Non-State Actors and Human Rights* (OUP 2005), Andrew Clapham, *Human Rights Obligations of Non-State Actors* (OUP 2006) and Marth Noortmann and Cedric Ryngaert (eds), *Non-State Actor Dynamics in International Law: From Law-Takers to Law-Makers* (Ashgate 2010). The International Law Association (hereinafter ILA) has set up a Committee to research on the topic of Non-State Actors in International Law.

humanitarian law, as they have been debated in a variety of humanitarian law books.[28] It is rather the triggering mechanism and the framework of obligations that will be discussed, especially with regard to the actual capacity of ANSAs.

This book focuses on accountability of the entity as such, and therefore issues of state responsibility[29] as well as individual accountability are only treated incidentally. In addition, the author does not focus exclusively on periods of armed violence, while the issue of obligations under human rights law is treated more extensively and in light of recent developments.[30] The scope of obligations under human rights law is also treated in some detail, given that international legal discourse has generally refrained from touching upon this topic to date.

There is also a conscious attempt to support many of the findings, as far as possible, with practice, not only by states and international organizations but by (a variety of) ANSAs as well;[31] otherwise this book would only constitute a further instance of the state-centred international legal discourse. It will actually be argued that ANSAs should not be ignored, at least with regard to certain issues. Practical realities should indicate that in order to gain compliance with international law, a role could (or should) be given to them.[32] The present book tries, additionally, to link certain ANSA characteristics with their obligations and accountability in order to explain the variable approaches according to IHL and to build a principled approach in respect of their obligations and accountability under human rights law.

In terms of structure, the notion of ANSAs will be examined, chiefly as it has appeared in IHL. Thereafter a number of factors which could have significance for their obligations and accountability will be suggested. These attributes will also be pertinent for a basic classification of armed non-state actors into three different types, already familiar to international lawyers: *de facto* entities, ANSAs in control of territory; and armed actors without territorial control (common article 3 ANSAs). National liberation movements as such will only be mentioned as historical paradigms, since it does not appear possible to

28 See, particularly, Lindsay Moir, *The Law of Internal Armed Conflict* (CUP 2002) and Sandesh Sivakumaran, *The Law of Non-International Armed Conflict* (OUP 2012). The scope of humanitarian law rules is also debated in depth in the commentaries to the Geneva Conventions and the Additional Protocols as well as in Jean-Marie Henckaerts and Louise Doswald-Beck, *Customary International Humanitarian Law* Vol. 1–2 (CUP 2005) (hereinafter CIHL Study).

29 We do not suggest that state responsibility rules (to the extent that an ANSA is somehow involved) are pellucid. On the contrary there is much ambiguity on their content and relevance to factual situations, see Chapter 3, sub-chapter on *Non-State Actors within State-Centred International Law*, at 117–21.

30 Mohamed Abdelsalam Babiker, *Application of International Humanitarian and Human Rights Law to the Armed Conflicts of the Sudan: Complementary or Mutually Exclusive Regimes?* (Intersentia 2007) 116, notes the lack of concern in legal literature and further contains, probably, the more extensive discourse, so far, on practice relating to human rights and armed groups.

31 Agreements signed between states or international organizations and ANSAs have been listed in a separate table after international conventions so as to indicate their significance and role.

32 See also Sophie Rondeau, 'Participation of Armed Groups in the Development of the Law Applicable to Armed Conflicts' (2010) 93 IRRC 649, 654.

resurrect their significance in international law. Then, the study will turn to the obligations and accountability of ANSAs in humanitarian law. This includes an examination of the mechanisms which trigger the applicability of humanitarian law to ANSAs and the extent of obligations, as well as the potential for accountability in the event of violations. The same pattern will be followed with regard to accountability under human rights law, although the examination will be more tentative; in the current state of affairs there is hardly any agreement on whether ANSAs are or should be held accountable for human rights violations. The author will assess the several arguments in favour of extending their accountability to human rights law violations and the possible legal bases, as well as the tendencies of various international actors in this regard. In sequence the range of actors subject to human rights law and the scope of obligations will be examined according to a qualified approach based on the particularities of each type of ANSA. The potential for putting accountability into operation is also a thorny issue which calls for innovative solutions, if we are not to create imperfect obligations.

The inquiry of accountability under these legal regimes will finally reveal that there is a need to move away from the state-centred approach and to adapt international law to the particularities of armed non-state actors, especially as the potential bases for ANSA obligations appear to be expanding. But firstly, it is necessary that the framework of the book regarding the terms 'non-state actor' and 'ANSA' be inscribed.

Chapter 1
Notion of Armed Non-State Actors

Non-State Actors: the Genus of Armed Non-State Actors

Non-state actor is an umbrella term for all entities which are not assimilated to a state.[1] The term is used in the negative, compared to the phrase 'state actor' (or agent), and for Alston[2] the term was ' … intentionally adopted in order to reinforce the assumption that the state is not only the central actor, but also the indispensable and pivotal one around which all other entities revolve'. The Articles on the Responsibility of States for Internationally Wrongful Acts[3] (hereinafter State Responsibility Articles), art 4,[4] define the state organ as

> any person or entity which has that status in accordance with the internal law of the State and exercises legislative, executive, judicial or any other functions, whatever position it holds in the organization of the State, and whatever its character as an organ of the central Government or of a territorial unit of the State.

Therefore any organ or entity which is not officially part of the state (although at times it might be under the control of one) is a non-state actor.

A variety of actors have been classified under this heading. With reference only to collective entities whose actions (could) have some international repercussions, international organizations, terrorist groupings, non-governmental organizations, (multi) national corporations, national liberation movements and rebel groups are included.[5] All

1 See also UNCHR (Sub-Commission), 'Working Paper on Human Rights and Non-State Actors Submitted by Gáspár Biró and Antoanella-Iulia Motoc' (11 July 2005) E/CN.4/Sub.2/2005/40, 8–9, defining (political) non-state actors by the fact that they are missing an attribute of the state and the *Zimbabwe Human Rights NGO Forum v Zimbabwe*, 245/02, African Commission on Human and Peoples' Rights, 15 May 2006 [136].

2 Philip Alston, 'The "Not-a-Cat" Syndrome: Can the International Human Rights Regime Accommodate Non-State Actors?' in Philip Alston (ed.), *Non-State Actors and Human Rights* (OUP 2005) 3. See also Peter Willets, 'Transnational Actors and International Organizations in Global Politics' in John Baylis and Steve Smith (eds), *The Globalization of World Politics. An Introduction to International Relations* (OUP 2001) 357.

3 International Law Commission, 'Draft Articles on Responsibility of States for Internationally Wrongful Acts' (2001) YILC Vol. II Part Two, 26–30.

4 This rule is considered as customary, *Armed Activities on the Territory of the Congo (Democratic Republic of the Congo v Uganda)* (Merits) [2005] ICJ Rep 242 and *Genocide Case*, ICJ Rep 202.

5 The definition used by the Committee on Non-State Actors, 'Non-State Actors in International Law: Aims, Approach and Scope of Project and Legal Issues – First Report' in International Law Association Report of the Seventy-Fourth Conference (The Hague 2010) (International Law Association 2010) 637 (hereinafter ILA Committee on Non-State Actors 2010) excludes international organizations and territorial entities such as Kosovo and Palestine.

these entities pursue different aims and carry out their activities in variable environments. In light of this, it is questionable whether a doctrinal general category of non-state actors is viable or even desirable, especially since the status of certain non-state actors differs substantially from that of others.

International organizations stand out at large because they have a full legal personality within their area of competence.[6] They have been created, mostly, by states, although membership might not be confined to states alone. Their international regulation is moving towards the direction of a state, with the necessary adaptations to their particularities. For example, after the adoption of the Vienna Convention on the Law of Treaties (hereinafter VCLT),[7] a comparable agreement was adopted on the law of treaties between states and international organizations or between international organizations.[8] After the adoption of the State Responsibility Articles, a comparable work was recently concluded by the International Law Commission (hereinafter ILC) on international organizations.[9]

Non-governmental organizations and corporations are entities which operate under the umbrella of a state's national law.[10] Their importance has grown considerably[11] and they both might even undertake to operate a certain governmental activity, mostly with the consent of the respective state or in the absence or default of one. The debate on corporations, particularly, has sparked a considerable wave of interest from international legal scholarship,[12] since the impact of their activities might be more significant than that of states.

---

6 *Brownlie*, 61 and Anthony Aust, *Handbook of International Law* (2nd edn, CUP 2010) 15.

7 Vienna Convention on the Law of Treaties (adopted 23 May 1969, entered into force 27 January 1980) 1115 UNTS 331.

8 Vienna Convention on the Law of Treaties between States and International Organizations or between International Organizations (adopted 21 March 1986) (1986) 25 ILM 543 (hereinafter 1986 Vienna Convention).

9 'Text of the Draft Articles on the Responsibility of International Organizations' (2011) A/66/10.

10 See the European Convention on the Recognition of the Legal Personality of International Non-Governmental Organisations (adopted 24 April 1986, entered into force 1 January 1991) ETS No. 124, which recognizes the legal personality of NGOs within member states other than the one where it was formed. Although the Convention refers to personality in the context of internal law, it is not immaterial that international NGOs might be seen in the future as possessing a measure of international personality. See also, indicatively, Steve Charnovitz, 'Nongovernmental Organizations and International Law' (2006) 100 AJIL 348, 355–7.

11 See, for example, the Separate Opinion of Judge Guillaume, *Legality of the Threat or Use of Nuclear Weapons* (Advisory Opinion) [1996] ICJ Rep 287–8, regarding the influence of NGOs to states and inter-governmental organizations to submit to the ICJ the request for an opinion.

12 See, for example, Barbara Frey, 'The Legal and Ethical Responsibilities of Transnational Corporations in the Protection of International Human Rights' (1997) 6 Minn.J.Global Trade 153–88, UNCHR (Sub-Commission), 'Norms on the Responsibilities of Transnational Corporations and Other Business Enterprises with Regard to Human Rights' (26 August 2003) E/CN.4/Sub.2/2003/12/Rev.2, *Clapham* 2006, 195–270, UNHRC, 'Protect, Respect and Remedy: A Framework for Business and Human Rights: Report of the Special Representative of the Secretary-General on the Issue of Human Rights and Transnational Corporations and

Rebel groups (including national liberation movements) and 'terrorist' organizations are associated with the use of violence in order to achieve their aims. Both of them typically operate within the borders of one state, although there is an increasing tendency for rebel groups (and a particular terrorist group, Al-Qaeda) to defy this reality. These entities are considered as illegal organizations under national laws, unlike non-governmental organizations and corporations. They are also distinct from other non-state actors, because of their temporary and provisional character;[13] yet some of them carry the potential to become a government of a pre-existing or new state. In that sense they differ from other non-state actors, because their aspirations usually include a significant change in their legal status, close to the archetypical example of the international law subject that is the state. As for the differentiation between rebel groups and terrorist organizations, this is sometimes totally blurred and September 11 has substantially contributed to this outcome: certain rebel groups have been designated as terrorist organizations in an effort, usually by their opponents, to de-legitimize their goals. Certainly the use of illegal tactics from the rebel groups contributed significantly to them acquiring a 'terrorist' status. This characterization, which sparks the applicability of a separate legal regime (the law of international terrorism), will not form part of the present book and our understanding of ANSAs will not be influenced by any designation as a terrorist organization. The next sub-chapter will be devoted to the notion of ANSAs, in order to clarify their unique characteristics.

Armed Non-State Actors

Terminology

A variety of terms have been used in order to describe armed non-state actors:[14] rebel groups, armed opposition groups, insurrectional movements,[15] non-state armed groups[16]

Other Business Enterprises, John Ruggie' (7 April 2008) A/HRC/8/5, Larissa Van den Herik and Jernej Letnar Cernic, 'Regulating Corporations under International Law, From Human Rights to International Criminal Law and Back Again' (2010) 8 JICJ 725–43 and Peter Muchlinski, 'Multinational Enterprises as Actors in International Law: Creating "Soft Law" Obligations and "Hard Law" Rights' in Marth Noortmann and Cedric Ryngaert (eds), *Non-State Actor Dynamics in International Law: From Law-Takers to Law-Makers* (Ashgate 2010) 9–39.

13 See Roberto Ago, 'Fourth Report on State Responsibility' (1972) YILC Vol. II, 71, 129 and Gérard Cahin, 'Attribution of Conduct to the State: Insurrectional Movements' in James Crawford et al. (eds), *The Law of International Responsibility* (CUP 2010) 248 (hereinafter Cahin2).

14 The term has been used by Andrés Franco, 'Armed Nonstate Actors' in David M. Malone (ed.), *The UN Security Council: From the Cold War to the 21st Century* (Rienner 2004) 117, Churchill Ewumbue-Monono, 'Respect for International Humanitarian Law by Armed Non-State Actors in Africa' (2006) 88 IRRC 905–24 and Annyssa Bellal, Gilles Giacca and Stuart Casey-Maslen, 'International Law and Armed Non-State Actors in Afghanistan' (2011) 93 IRRC 1–33.

15 State Responsibility art 10.

16 UNGA Res 63/245 (24 December 2008) [2(d)].

or simply armed groups,[17] armed dissident groups,[18] non-state entities[19] and non-governmental entities.[20] All of these terms have in essence almost the same meaning,[21] pointing at a collective entity which possesses certain characteristics as a minimum. They also 'have in common … an attempt to find a neutral terminology that captures the idea that the group uses force and operates beyond state control or authorisation'.[22]

The term ANSA is also preferred for the following reason: in contrast to armed groups, which was (and to a certain extent still is) the predominant term used, it could capture in a more neutral way the idea that a political branch might be also included or even be in charge of the armed elements of the group. Certainly the method used to achieve the aim is not differentiated; but the means to achieve it might also be additional to an armed conflict.

Besides neutral terminology, though, ANSAs have certain features. Depending on the existence of these features, certain consequences derive with regard to both their obligations and accountability.

The Characteristics of Armed Non-State Actors

ANSAs are principally the non-state parties in a non-international armed conflict. Nonetheless, this does not imply that ANSAs are necessarily defined only in that context, since other features might become important and lead to a different status and obligations. The evolution of the notion of ANSAs in international humanitarian law will be examined, before turning the discourse to other characteristics.

The Evolution of the Notion

ANSAs were not unknown in international law, before the appearance of modern international humanitarian law. Civil wars were a reality for centuries and belligerency recognition sought to capture this phenomenon, whenever the existence of the ANSA had repercussions outside the parent state.

---

17 Art 1.1 of the Protocol Additional to the Geneva Conventions of 12 August 1949, and relating to the Protection of Victims of Non-International Armed Conflicts (adopted 8 June 1977, entered into force 7 December 1978) 1125 UNTS 609 (Protocol II) and art 1e of the Kampala Convention.

18 *Third Report on the Human Rights Situation in Colombia*, Inter-American Commission on Human Rights, OEA/Ser.L/V/II.102 Doc. 9 rev. 1 (1999), chapter IV.

19 Institut de Droit International, 'The Application of International Humanitarian Law and Fundamental Human Rights, in Armed Conflicts in which Non-State Entities are Parties' Resolution (1999) (hereinafter IDI 1999 Resolution).

20 UNSC Res 1807 (31 March 2008) [1].

21 At least the term insurrectional movement has been used in a more restrictive manner. *Constantinides*, 89, uses the term 'armed opposition groups' restrictively as well.

22 International Council on Human Rights Policy, *Ends & Means: Human Rights Approaches to Armed Groups* (2000) 5 (hereinafter ICHRP 2000).

The Doctrine of Belligerency Recognition[23]

The provisional entrance of ANSAs into international relations was possible through recognition of belligerency: subject to fulfilment of certain objective criteria and governmental recognition of belligerent status, an ANSA was vested with a limited international personality[24] and certain international legal norms were applicable.

These objective criteria corresponded to the ANSA's characteristics and the quantity of violence: large-scale hostilities, occupation of a substantial part of a state's territory, a measure of orderly administration,[25] observance of the laws of war and whether the entity acts under a responsible authority.[26] A further criterion for recognition by a third state is the need for definition of its relations with the warring parties.[27]

These criteria require that the ANSA consists of a large number of combatants, owns heavy material and has a trained hierarchy.[28] Simultaneously, its own capacity to exercise a governmental function should not be neglected.[29]

Besides these objective characteristics, the subjective feature of recognition was indispensable. For Lauterpacht[30] the lawful government was bound to grant recognition when the large scale of hostilities demanded the operation/applicability of the relevant rules of warfare. However, recognition is usually a voluntary act and belligerency recognition does not escape this rule.[31] Consequently, only policy reasons[32] could justify recognition.

The act of recognition entails both the state and the ANSA coming under an obligation to respect the laws of war in force in their mutual relations. When recognition comes from a third state '... it brings about the operation of the laws of war just in relation between the rebels and the recognising government',[33] namely the application of the laws of neutrality.

---

23 Parts of this sub-chapter have been previously published in Konstantinos Mastorodimos, 'Belligerency Recognition: Past, Present and Future' (2014) 29 Conn.J.Int'l L. 301–26.

24 Ti-Chiang Chen, *The International Law of Recognition* (Preager 1951) 305 and Erik Castren, *Civil War* (Suomalainen Tiedeakatemia 1966) 137.

25 See Sam Foster Halabi, 'Traditions of Belligerent Recognition: The Libyan Intervention in Historical and Theoretical Context' (2012) 27 Am.U.Int'l L.Rev. 321, 362–3.

26 Hersch Lauterpacht, *Recognition in International Law* (CUP 1947) 176, G.I.A.D. Draper, 'Humanitarian Law and Internal Armed Conflicts' (1983) 13 GaJICL 253, 257 and Yair M. Lootsteen, 'The Concept of Belligerency in International Law' (2000) 166 Mil.L.Rev. 109.

27 *Lauterpacht* 1947, 176. See also William Edward Hall, *A Treatise on International Law* (8th edn, Clarendon Press 1924) 39. But see *Halabi*, 326.

28 Maurice Flory, 'Algérie et Droit International' (1959) 5 AFDI 817, 826.

29 *Chen*, 307.

30 *Lauterpacht* 1947, 175 and 243 ff. See also Denmark, *Final Record of the Diplomatic Conference of Geneva of 1949* Vol. II-B (Federal Political Department 1951) 332 (hereinafter 1949 Records).

31 For this majority opinion see, indicatively, *Hall*, 39 and Yoram Dinstein, 'The International Law of Civil Wars and Human Rights' (1976) 6 Israel Yrbk Hum Rts 62, 77.

32 *Castren*, 145–6.

33 Richard Baxter, 'Jus in Bello Interno: The Present and Future Law' in John N. Moore (ed.), *Law and Civil War in the Modern World* (Johns Hopkins University Press 1974) 518 and Dietrich Schindler, 'The Different Types of Armed Conflicts According to the Geneva Conventions and Protocols' (1979-II) 163 Recueil des Cours de l'Académie de Droit International 145.

Recognition by the parent state triggers the applicability of the customary law of war.[34] Additionally, the recognized belligerent incurs human rights obligations.[35] The rules of international responsibility become applicable (including attribution) and the insurgent entity becomes liable to pay compensation for its wrongdoings.[36] In parallel the territorial state is deemed to be free from international responsibility for the acts of rebels.[37]

Academic sources[38] cite the Nigeria/Biafra conflict as the last recorded recognition of belligerency by the incumbent government. But the current existence of the doctrine is controversial. Several international institutions[39] have rather recently mentioned the customary international law doctrine of recognition of belligerency, along with members of the academia.[40] The practice of some states also appears to endorse its existence. The proclamation by the Philippines of a state of rebellion in 2003[41] is relative proof,[42] although the government denies that any of its actions has ever implied recognition.[43]

---

34 But see *Castren*, 153–4.

35 José Maria Ruda, 'Recognition of States and Governments' in Mohammed Bedjaoui (ed.), *International Law: Achievements and Prospects* (UNESCO 1991) 461.

36 *Castren*, 155.

37 Institut de Droit International, 'Responsabilité Internationale des Etats à Raison des Dommages Causés sur Leur Territoire à la Personne et aux Biens des Etrangers' Resolution (1927), art 7 and Gerhard Von Glahn, *Law among Nations: An Introduction to Public International Law* (5th edn, Collier Macmillan 1986) 87.

38 Ingrid Detter, *The Law of War* (2nd edn, CUP 2000) 40 and François Bugnion, '*Jus Ad Bellum, Jus in Bello* and Non-International Armed Conflicts' (2003) 6 YIHL 167, 181. But see, indicatively, Louise Doswald-Beck, 'The Legal Validity of Military Intervention by Invitation of the Government' (1985) 56 British YIL 189, 197 and James Crawford, *The Creation of States in International Law* (2nd edn, Clarendon Press 2006) 406.

39 *Prosecutor v Tadic* (Jurisdiction) ICTY-94-1 (10 August 1995) [69], *IDI 1999 Resolution*, art II and *Annual Report 1990–1*, Inter-American Commission on Human Rights, OEA/Ser.L/V/II.79 Doc. 12 rev. 1 (1991) chapter V.

40 Michael Bothe, 'Article 3 and Protocol II: Case Studies of Nigeria and El Salvador' (1981–2) 31 Am.U.L.Rev. 899, 901; Julio A. Barberis, 'Nouvelles Questions Concernant la Personnalité Juridique Internationale' (1983) 179 Recueil Des Cours 240; L.C. Green, *The Contemporary Law of Armed Conflict* (2nd edn, Manchester University Press 2000) 59; A.P.V. Rogers, *Law on the Battlefield* (2nd edn, Manchester University Press 2004) 224; Gary D. Solis, *The Law of Armed Conflict* (CUP 2010) 152–3; and *Halabi*, 327–8.

41 See Soliman M. Santos, Jr., 'Correspondent's Report: The Philippines' (2003) 6 YIHL 561–2.

42 Rebellion is a sub-classification of internal strife according to traditional international law. For this taxonomy see *Lootsteen*, 113–14.

43 Atty. Soliman Santos, Jr., 'The Recent MILF Agreements, Belligerency Status, International Law and the Philippine Constitution'. In fact, in the Declaration of the Philippines to the Protocol Additional to the Geneva Conventions of 12 August 1949, and relating to the Protection of Victims of International Armed Conflicts, 30 March 2012, the state clarified that 'no claim of status of belligerency may be invoked … ' from the application of Protocol I, thus recognizing that recognition of belligerency still holds a certain contemporary relevance. See also National Democratic Front of the Philippines (hereinafter NDFP) Human Rights Monitoring Committee, *NDFP Adherence to International Humanitarian Law on Prisoners of War (POWs)* (2009) 4.

The Venezuelan's National Assembly vote ' ... to support ... Chavez's call for Colombia to recognize the "belligerent status" of the Revolutionary Armed Forces of Colombia (FARC) and the National Liberation Army (ELN)'[44] suggests also the continuing existence of belligerency recognition. Yet the actual prospects of revival are rather faint, since the occurrence of the objective features continues to be infrequent.[45] Moreover this legal concept was designed for a completely different world order. The source of power in the international system lay exclusively with states, as evidenced by the effects of recognition solely towards the recognizing state, whereas nowadays the role of international organizations has increased up to the point that they are capable of intervening during intrastate conflicts.[46]

Recognition of belligerency did not have a great impact in the practice of internal wars, although it was the only institution which sought to cover the interrelations of the parties and third states during civil wars and it would clarify both the primary rules of conduct and the secondary rules of responsibility. Yet with regard to the first set of rules, the international community has not entirely left the gap open, since common article 3 to the Geneva Conventions[47] is meant to apply in non-international armed conflicts.

Common Article 3 to the Geneva Conventions of 1949

The first explicit reference to ANSAs in a global IHL treaty[48] was this (common) Article of the Geneva Conventions, (presumably) applying to each 'Party to the conflict'. The Article and more generally the Conventions do not give any hint of the characteristics of ANSAs; consequently the preparatory works to the Conventions could give a measure of states' understanding.

44 Venezuelan Legislature Supports Belligerent Status for Colombian Rebels, 19 Jan 2008, by Kiraz Janicke – Venezuelanalysis.com, <http://venezuelanalysis.com/print/3080>. See also ELN, 'Declaración Pública del Comandante Manuel Pérez', 15 July 1995 (hereinafter: ELN Declaration) and Arturo Carrillo-Suarez, 'Hors de Logique: Contemporary Issues in International Humanitarian Law as Applied to Internal Armed Conflict' (1999) 15 Am.U.Int'l L.Rev. 1, 58, on the FARC position.

45 This was the main reason offered by *Lauterpacht* 1947, 182–3 and remains the principal justification today.

46 *Halabi*, 331.

47 Geneva Convention for the Amelioration of the Condition of the Wounded and Sick in Armed Forces in the Field (adopted 12 August 1949, entered into force 21 October 1950) 75 UNTS 31 (First Geneva Convention); Geneva Convention for the Amelioration of the Condition of Wounded, Sick and Shipwrecked Members of Armed Forces at Sea (adopted 12 August 1949, entered into force 21 October 1950) 75 UNTS 85 (Second Geneva Convention); Geneva Convention Relative to the Treatment of Prisoners of War (adopted 12 August 1949, entered into force 21 October 1950) 75 UNTS 135 (Third Geneva Convention); and Geneva Convention Relative to the Protection of Civilian Persons in Time of War (adopted 12 August 1949, entered into force 21 October 1950) 75 UNTS 287 (Fourth Geneva Convention).

48 See also art 1 of the regional Convention on Duties and Rights of States in the Event of Civil Strife (adopted 20 February 1928, entered into force 21 May 1929) 134 LNTS 45, referring to 'rebel forces'.

As Frédéric Siordet[49] wrote in the influential Commentary of the International Committee of the Red Cross (hereinafter ICRC), which is typically (and wrongly) attributed to Pictet in its entirety, 'different conditions [exist], although in no way obligatory, that constitute convenient criteria'. These criteria were drawn from the negotiating table and their common characteristic is that they exhibit a significant threshold of organization and power. The French proposition[50] referred to ' … organized military forces belonging to a responsible authority capable of respecting, or enforcing respect for the Convention, in a given territory'. The US view[51] resembles the objective criteria for recognition of belligerency. Recognition of belligerency as such, or for the purpose of the Conventions' applicability, was also discussed, after an Australian proposal.[52] However, none of them became part of written (treaty) law, showing that there was no uniform view on the characteristics of the ANSA and, primarily, that, in light of the object and purpose of the treaty (humanization of internal wars), even ANSAs who did not meet all these demanding criteria *could* be parties to the conflict.[53] In fact these criteria were discussed at the proposition of the ICRC that all Conventions should be applicable during a non-international armed conflict.[54] In the final version, territorial control and a measure of orderly administration do not appear to form a necessary part of the attributes of ANSAs (at least for purposes of the article's applicability). Recognition of any kind (from the incumbent government or a third party) is equally unnecessary.

As a minimum, the ANSA should fulfil the following criteria:

1. It should constitute a group. A group is made up of two people at least, but with such a low level of participation it would not be able to initiate and sustain a conflict. Therefore an ANSA should (and usually does) consist of, at least several hundreds or thousands of individuals, although much would depend on the context within which the group is operating. The resources of the state and the coverage of national territory could indicate what sort of manpower is necessary for the ANSA to become a party to the conflict.
2. Naturally, as well, the group should be armed. This indicates the existence of weapons and war materials in the hands of the members of the group.[55] Without this feature the group will not be able to create the violent conditions amounting to an armed conflict.

---

49 'Common Article 3' in Jean Pictet (ed.), *Commentary to the Geneva Convention for the Amelioration of the Condition of the Wounded and Sick in Armed Forces in the Field* (International Committee of the Red Cross 1952) 49–50.

50 *1949 Records* Vol. II-B, 10. It was supported by Spain, 11, Italy, 40 and Norway, 44.

51 *1949 Records* Vol. II-B, 12. It received support from China, 12.

52 *1949 Records* Vol. II-B, 15. But see Norway, 11.

53 The International Criminal Tribunal for Rwanda (hereinafter ICTR) in *Prosecutor v Akayesu* (Judgment) ICTR-96-4-T (2 September 1998) [619] mentioned them but did not use them in practice. The International Criminal Tribunal for the former Yugoslavia (hereinafter ICTY), on the other hand, rejected them for the interpretation of common article 3, *Prosecutor v Boškoski et al.* (Judgment) ICTY-04-82-T (10 July 2008) [196].

54 *1949 Records* Vol. I, 47.

55 *Prosecutor v Limaj et al.* (Judgment) ICTY-03-66-T (30 November 2005) [121] and *Boškoski* [281].

3. The group should be organized.[56] This indicates that the group is not randomly formed and some structure exists, which usually follows a system of hierarchy,[57] like that of a state army, at least on a micro-level. Of course it can follow the model of a state (for example having an executive and other branches),[58] although this presupposes several resources that most armed groups do not normally have. Usually there will be some allocation of responsibilities between the group's members – although there is no need for formally defined roles – and an authority (civilian or military, individual or collective[59]) responsible for the group's acts. However, a strict hierarchy/command structure might be absent, as for example in the case of a group where there is tacit or express agreement on the role of each member and all members act as a collective authority.[60] Regardless of whether such a scheme is possible, viable or effective, the organized character of the group should not be contested at first sight. In the vast majority of cases, though, there will be some rudimentary form of hierarchy/command structure.[61] It is not necessary that it should also be effective, in the sense that the commands of superiors are respected *at all times* by subordinates.[62] If they are respected, the ANSA could be able to implement its obligations (if there is awareness of them) and the organized character of the entity would be sufficiently proved. The ability to implement its obligations is only an indication and it is not constitutive of the ANSA organization.[63] In that case

56 Switzerland, *1949 Records* Vol. II-B, 335.

57 See for example the UCK (KLA) Regulations which created a chain of military hierarchy between the various levels of commanders and further affirmed the existence of organization, *Limaj* [111]. See also *Prosecutor v. Callixte Mbarushimana* (Decision on the Confirmation of Charges) ICC-01/04-01/10 (16 December 2011) [104] on the Forces Démocratiques de Libération du Rwanda (hereinafter FDLR).

58 See for example the model of FLN's (Algeria) organization in Mohammed Bedjaoui, *Law and the Algerian Revolution* (International Association of Democratic Lawyers 1961) 81 ff. and Arnold Fraleigh, 'The Algerian Revolution as a Case Study in International Law' in Richard Falk (ed.), *The International Law of Civil War* (Johns Hopkins University Press 1971) 188–9

59 *ICHRP 2000*, 18:

> [a]rmed groups are under military or political (civilian) control. In either case they can be authoritarian. Many armed groups are led by a single individual or a small cadre of leaders. In others, by contrast, the leadership is accountable to its members to a significant extent and could be considered democratic.

60 Similarly for armed resistance forces see Waldemar A. Solf, 'Article 43, Protocol I' in Michael Bothe, Karl Josef Partsch and Waldemar A. Solf (eds), *New Rules for Victims of Armed Conflicts: Commentary on the Two 1977 Protocols Additional to the Geneva Conventions of 1949* (Martinus Nijhoff Publishers 1982) 237.

61 *Limaj* [89], 'This degree [of organisation] need not be the same as that required for establishing the responsibility of superiors for the acts of their subordinates within the organisation … ' and, in agreement, Anthony Cullen, *The Concept of Non-International Armed Conflict in International Humanitarian Law* (CUP 2010), 155.

62 *Boškoski* [196] and [205]. Opposite *Cullen*, 155.

63 *Limaj* [88–9]. See also the Committee on the Use of Force, 'Final Report on the Meaning of Armed Conflict in International Law' in International Law Association Report of the Seventy-

many ANSAs that were not able to apply, for example, the (burdensome) provision on regularly constituted courts, would be considered as unorganized and no armed conflict present. Certainly the ANSA cannot function in a totally unorganized way, meaning that some plan should be followed, at least voluntarily, by its members. It is the collective planned action as an outcome of an organized entity, generating an armed conflict, which matters most rather than the (form of) structure of the ANSA or its ability to implement the laws of armed conflict.

Reliance on the above-mentioned three criteria, and especially organization, was not so obvious before the conclusion of Protocol II and the creation of the ICTY. In fact, before 1977 common article 3 seemed to be interpreted in accordance with the 'convenient' criteria suggested at the negotiating table of the Geneva Conventions.[64] The applicability of common article 3 was accepted, usually, in conflicts of large proportions, where the respective ANSA was fairly organized and even had control over territory, such as in Algeria (1954–62);[65] otherwise there was a frequent denial, usually by the governmental party to the conflict.[66] The negotiating records of Protocol II reveal also that (some) states wanted to link their understanding of common article 3 applicability with the high threshold of what would then become the Protocol.[67] The inclusion of the territorial control element in Protocol II marked, in the end, the express differentiation between an ANSA subject to common article 3 (which does not necessarily have to occupy territory)[68] and ANSAs subject to this Protocol.

Fourth Conference (The Hague, 2010) (International Law Association 2010) 692 (hereinafter ILA Committee on the Use of Force), that this element is not necessary for the existence of an armed conflict. There is strong support, though, that this ability is constitutive of an armed group: see, among others, *Schindler*, 147, *Moir*, 36 and Jelena Pejic, 'Status of Armed Conflicts' in Elizabeth Wilmshurst and Susan Breau (eds), *Perspectives on the ICRC Study on Customary International Humanitarian Law* (CUP 2007) 86. A good reason to disassociate such capacity is that many IHL rules were not formulated with ANSAs in mind.

64 See Venezuela, *1949 Records* Vol. II-B, 333 and the Memorandum from John C. Yoo, Deputy Assistant General Counsel and Robert Delahunty, Special Counsel, Office of Legal Counsel, Department of Justice, to William J. Haynes II, General Counsel, Department of Defense, Re: Application of Treaties and Laws to al Qaeda and Taliban Detainees (January 9, 2002) 8–9, on the understanding at the negotiating table. See also *Cullen*, 49–51 and 146 and *Draper* 1983, 270, arguing that the nature of substantive obligations incurred in the article demand a level and degree of organization similar to that of a recognized belligerent.

65 See *Bedjaoui*, 38–42 and 46–55 and *Castren*, 74. The acceptance of humanitarian laws' applicability only took place in 1956, Jean Siotis, *Le Droit de la Guerre et les Conflits Armés d'un Caractère Non-International* (Librairie Générale de Droit et de Jurisprudence 1958) 211.

66 James E. Bond, 'Internal Conflict and Article Three of the Geneva Conventions' (1971–2) 48 DenLJ 263, 271–2.

67 See for example the propositions of Pakistan, *Official Records of the Diplomatic Conference on the Reaffirmation and Development of International Humanitarian Law Applicable in Armed Conflicts, Geneva (1974 –1977)* Vol. 4 Part II (Federal Political Department 1978) 6 (hereinafter 1977 Records) and the German Democratic Republic, *1977 Records* Vol. 4, Part II, 8.

68 That was firstly supported by *Siordet* 1952, 50. See also some recent corroborations in *Juan Carlos Abella v Argentina*, Case 11.137, Report No 55/97, Inter-American Commission on Human Rights, OEA/Ser.L/V/II.95 Doc. 7 rev. at 271 (1997) [152] and Republic of Liberia, Truth and

The reference of the *Tadic* decision[69] to an organized armed group gave a further impetus to discuss its elements more thoroughly. Rather recently a Trial Chamber of the ICTY[70] has made a useful (but non-exhaustive) enumeration of indicative criteria in the Tribunal's previous jurisprudence, which confirm the existence of a sufficient and effective organization: 'factors signalling the presence of a command structure';[71] 'indicating that the group could carry out operations in an organised manner';[72] 'indicating a level of logistics';[73] 'relevant to determining whether an armed group possessed a level of discipline and the ability to implement the basic obligations of Common Article 3';[74] 'and indicating that the armed group was able to speak with one voice'.[75] References to the entity from international organs could also be an indication.[76]

The quantitative and qualitative decrease of ANSA characteristics, from the objective criteria of belligerency recognition to the requirement that the armed group is organized, has appeared to expand in more recent practice. The UN Security Council[77] and the (extinct) Commission on Human Rights applied common article 3[78] to a wide range of groups apparently lacking any real effectiveness or organization, such as those present in the Somali conflict.[79] This practice could either be a positive step towards the applicability

---

Reconciliation Commission, *Consolidated Final Report* Vol. 2 (2009) 52–3 (hereinafter Liberia Truth and Reconciliation Report). But see Zeray Yihdego, 'Darfur and Humanitarian Law: The Protection of Civilians and Civilian Objects' (2009) 14 J.C. & S.L. 37, 50.

69 ICTY, *Prosecutor v Tadic* (Jurisdiction Appeals) ICTY-94-1 (2 October 1995) [70].

70 *Boškoski* [199–203]. See also *Prosecutor v Haradinaj et al.* (Jurisdiction) ICTY-04-84-T (3 April 2008) [51]–[60].

71 *Boškoski* [199] and *Haradinaj* [60]. These could include the existence of headquarters, *Prosecutor v Milošević* (Decision on Motion for Judgment of Acquittal) ICTY-02-54-T (16 June 2004) [23–24] or the implementation of strategic policies to further their aims, *Prosecutor v Milutinovic et al.* (Judgment) ICTY-05-87-T (26 February 2009) [840].

72 *Boškoski* [200]. These could include the coordination between the different units, *Limaj* [108].

73 *Boškoski* [201]. These could include the ability to recruit and train new members, *Limaj* [118 ff.], the establishment of a financial operation, *Milutinovic* [840] and the wearing of uniforms, *Prosecutor v Brima* (Judgment) SCSL-04-16-T (20 June 2007) [545].

74 *Boškoski* [202]. These could include the existence of an internal disciplinary system, *Limaj* [116] and *Haradinaj* [60]. Obviously, compliance with those rules could also affirm that the group is sufficiently organized. *Sivakumaran* 2012, 175, notices that the indicia of organization in the ICTY are predominantly related to intensity of violence rather than the ability to implement its obligations.

75 *Boškoski* [203] and *Haradinaj* [60]. See also *Limaj* [129]:

> by July 1998 the KLA had become accepted by international representatives, and within Kosovo, as a key party involved in political negotiations to resolve the Kosovo crisis. This discloses and confirms that by that time the KLA had achieved a level of organisational stability and effectiveness. In particular this gave it the recognised ability to speak with one voice and with a level of persuasive authority on behalf of its members.

76 In *Prosecutor v Tadic* (Judgment) ICTY-94-1-A (7 May 1997) [567], the Chambers used it as an element relevant to the intensity of violence.

77 Res 794 (3 December 1992) [4], 814 (26 March 1993) [13] and 1772 (20 August 2007) [19].

78 Res 59 (1998) [3].

79 In a case concerning Somalia a Belgian Military Court did not apply common article 3, because the groups involved were not organized, see Marc Cogen, 'Correspondents' Report:

of common article 3 to situations of non-international armed conflicts where the totality of ANSAs (or certain ones) are not even organized; or a humanitarian 'concession' of the Council in situations where a central government does not exist.[80] For Moir[81] the opinion of Siordet[82] on the application of common article 3 'as widely as possible'[83] relates to unorganized armed groups as parties to an internal armed conflict; however, Siordet made this call in comparison to the highly demanding convenient criteria proposed by states. Moreover, his contradistinction with these criteria is on low-level and unorganized armed violence, not unorganized armed groups.[84] Consequently it is not proper to associate his call with the practice of the Security Council.

The possibility that an unorganized ANSA would participate in a non-international armed conflict should be dismissed because the entity's accountability goes hand in hand with its capability to uphold the relevant standards.[85] Consequently the failed-state exception appears more plausible: the relevant UN organs could call for voluntary compliance with relevant international law standards or, in the case of the Security Council, they could even create them.[86]

Belgium' (1998) 1 YIHL 412, 415.

80 See also Robin Geiss, 'Armed Violence in Fragile States: Low-Intensity Conflicts, Spillover Conflicts, and Sporadic Law Enforcement Operations by Third Parties' (2009) 91 IRRC 127, 136:

> first, concerns that have traditionally supported a heightened threshold for non-international armed conflicts in contradistinction to internal disturbances and tensions, namely states' concerns about outside interference in their internal affairs, are attenuated in the absence of effective government control. Second, the application of IHL might simply seem politically desirable. In an environment in which the domestic legal order is dysfunctional, where the communitarian value system is indeed profoundly disturbed and the central addressee of human rights obligations no longer exists, IHL could provide an internationally accepted (lowest) common denominator on which the warring factions could potentially agree and which could serve as a starting point for attempts to regulate their behaviour.

81 37–8.

82 1952, 50. Similarly Anton Schlögel, 'Civil War' (1970) 10 IRRC 123, 131.

83 His argument is that such norms 'were already recognized as essential in all civilized countries, and enacted in the municipal law of the States in question, long before the Convention was signed'. *Moir*, 37, notices that international human rights law (subject to derogations) would be adequate in this regard. However, at that point, international human rights law did not exist, so Siordet's position appears legitimate.

84 Unorganized armed violence could be generated by (organized) armed groups; it is more difficult to envisage unorganized armed groups (practically armed individuals) generating organized armed incidents.

85 See also the similar comments of *Moir*, 38 and *Babiker*, 129–30 and 132. The *ILA Committee on Non-State Actors* 2010, 637, did not include unorganized groups in the scope of its work.

86 Security Council resolutions could create obligations for ANSAs, so that this organ performs its duties of maintaining international peace and security. On the understanding that ANSAs should comply with the resolutions of the Security Council see, indicatively, the statements from Kenya and Japan, UN Doc S/PV.3937 (24 October 1998) 8 and 9 respectively, Russia, USA and United Kingdom, UN Doc S/PV.4011 (10 June 1999) 7, 14–15 and 18 respectively and Costa

Nonetheless such practices might not have any tangible results, as the individual criminal responsibility would remain the only available path for accountability. An ICTY Chamber[87] went as far as commenting that Security Council resolutions ' ... are made on a political, not legal, basis, and cannot be directly interpreted as evidence of, or a legal interpretation of, a factual state of affairs, despite the fact that such resolutions may have legal consequences'. However, and in light of the repercussions of the Council's resolutions, it is not easy to discount its views.

Article 3 was almost the only[88] applicable treaty law[89] for ANSAs that were not recognized as belligerents, for a time period of almost 30 years. The next codification of IHL, the Additional Protocols of 1977, had two major consequences: a particular group of ANSAs, national liberation movements fighting against colonial domination, foreign occupation and racist regimes, would be qualified as parties to an international armed conflict, while Protocol II would enumerate certain criteria, pertinent to ANSAs, for the purpose of its applicability.

The Additional Protocol II of 1977

This treaty, currently ratified by the vast majority of the international community of states (168 parties at 11 February 2015), has offered new evidence on ANSAs' features.

In the Draft Additional Protocol to Article 3 Common to the Four Geneva Conventions of August 12, 1949[90] from the ICRC, there is a reference to organized armed forces and responsible command. Similarly, the 'collective nature of hostilities' also implied the existence of an organized armed force. In the end, Protocol II has re-affirmed that the

Rica, UN Doc S/PV.6063 (8 January 2009) 6. See also the Dissenting Opinions of Judge Bennouna and Skotnikov in the *Accordance with International Law of the Unilateral Declaration of Independence in Respect of Kosovo* (Advisory Opinion) [2010] ICJ Rep 513 and 519–20 respectively as well as Rüdiger Wolfrum and Christiane E. Philipp, 'The Status of the Taliban: Their Obligations and Rights under International Law' (2002) 6 Max Planck Yrbk UN L 559, 583 and Kirsti Samuels, *Political Violence and the International Community: Developments in International Law and Policy* (Nijhoff 2007) 47–9. But see also *Kosovo* Opinion, ICJ Rep 452 and the Written Comments of the Kingdom of Norway in the *Kosovo* Opinion, 5. On several resolutions with language suggesting that ANSAs are expected to comply with, see, indicatively, UNSC Res 864 (15 September 1993) [10], 1193 (28 August 1998) [16], 1265 (17 September 1999) [4], 1674 (28 April 2006) [6], 1769 (31 July 2007) [22] and 1828 (31 July 2008) [16]. See also several agreements referring to respect for Security Council resolutions, such as the Lusaka Protocol, Lusaka, Zambia, 15 November 1994, Annex 8, art A.I.1, the Declaration of Principles for the Resolution of the Sudanese Conflict in Darfur, Abuja, Nigeria, 5 July 2005, preamble (hereinafter Darfur Declaration of Principles) and the Darfur Peace Agreement, Abuja, Nigeria, 5 May 2006, preamble.

87 *Boškoski* [192].

88 See also the Convention for the Protection of Cultural Property in the Event of Armed Conflict (adopted 14 May 1954, entered into force 7 August 1956) 249 UNTS 240 (1954 Hague Convention) art 19.

89 In the *Military and Paramilitary Activities in and Against Nicaragua (Nicaragua v United States of America)* (Merits) [1986] ICJ Rep 114, the ICJ confirmed the customary nature of the article.

90 Text in James Bond, *The Rules of Riot: Internal Conflict and the Law of War* (Princeton University Press 1974) 209 ff.

group should be organized, while referring also to a responsible command. For Sylvie-Stoyanka Junod[91]

> the existence of a responsible command implies some degree of organization of the insurgent armed group or dissident armed forces .... It means an organization capable, on the one hand, of planning and carrying out sustained and concerted military operations, and on the other, of imposing discipline in the name of a *de facto* authority.[92]

Both the ICTR and the Special Court for Sierra Leone (hereinafter SCSL)[93] refer to responsible command as a separate element, though the explanation given by the ICTR[94] does not appear to add anything to the element of organization; the ability to follow a planned action and to carry it out collectively is implicit in the organization of the ANSA, while this ability cannot be realized without discipline. Therefore it is not self-evident that the reference to responsible command is significant.[95]

The imposition of discipline appears to be an additional element of the organizational features of ANSAs in the context of Protocol II. It is also suggested that 'the degree of organisation required to engage in "protracted violence" is lower than the degree of organisation required to carry out "sustained and concerted military operations"'.[96] This is generally right, but it might not apply at all times, as the ability to mount an armed conflict of significant proportions could equally depend on the level of manpower and other war material resources, as well as the ability of the territorial state to fight back. It is the requirement of control over territory that suggests a more advanced stage of organization in comparison to common article 3 ANSAs.

The territorial element is part of the definition of ANSAs according to Protocol II.[97] But not every occupation of territory is sufficient for the Protocol to apply: control should

91 'Article 1, Protocol II' in Yves Sandoz, Christophe Swinarski and Bruno Zimmermann (eds), *Commentary on the Additional Protocols of 8 June 1977 to the Geneva Conventions of 12 August 1949* (International Committee of the Red Cross 1987) 1352.

92 This part of the commentary was adopted *verbatim* in *Prosecutor v Musema* (Judgment) ICTR-96-13-T (27 January 2000) [257] and by the International Criminal Court (hereinafter ICC), *Prosecutor v Thomas Lubanga Dyilo* (Decision on the Confirmation of Charges) ICC-01/04-01/06 (29 January 2007) [232].

93 *Akayesu* [623], *Musema* [255], *Prosecutor v Fofana et al.* (Judgment) SCSL-04-15-T (2 August 2007) [126] and *Prosecutor v Sesay et al.* (Judgment) SCSL-04-15-T (2 March 2009) [97].

94 *Akayesu* [626].

95 *Moir*, 105, describes it as superfluous. See also the disagreement of Jean Siotis, 'La Protection de la Personne Humaine dans les Conflits Armés ne Présentant pas un Caractère International' (1973) 12 Mil.L. & L. War Rev. 281, 283, based on its subjective character. But see *Yihdego*, 44 and the opposition of *Sivakumaran* 2012, 175 as well as the sources cited therein.

96 *Boškoski* [197].

97 Several states at the negotiating table for Protocol II have expressed their disappointment for the territorial element, such as Germany, *1977 Records* Vol. 8, 220, Egypt, 235 and Norway, 293. This could indicate readiness to ditch the criterion in their practice; see for example the USA's position in Michael. J. Matheson, 'Session One: The United States Position on the Relation of

be such as to enable 'them to carry out sustained and concerted military operations'[98] and to implement the Protocol. Consequently there has to exist some stability in the area controlled by the insurgents,[99] although this is not a *conditio sine qua non*. Otherwise it would bring about the criterion of 'continuous control over territory', as proposed by Indonesia.[100] 'Even a small part of the national territory (e.g. 1 per cent of the whole) could be enough (depending on circumstances) for the ability to carry out military operations and implement the Protocol.'[101]

Control over territory, even if not substantial, should create a presumption of the organized character of the ANSA, as it evinces its effectiveness, along with the generation of an armed conflict. Of course this presumption is refutable, when, for example, control is gained randomly and without any fight, in the environment of a semi-failed state. However in the vast majority of cases the existence and the extent of territorial control would indicate an organized entity with substantial resources and power in its hands.

While the differentiation of recognized belligerents and ANSAs subject to Protocol II is fairly obvious,[102] there seems to be a significant confusion around the meaning of the phrase ' … exercise such control over a part of its territory as to enable them to carry out sustained and concerted military operations and to implement this Protocol', despite repeated assertions at the negotiating table of the 'reasonably objective [conditions that] … could be applied without great difficulty'.[103] The proper focus lies on the degree of control over territory which gives the *ability* to carry out military operations and the *ability* to implement the law.[104] Certainly the prior implementation of the law is not a condition,

---

Customary International Law to the 1977 Protocols Additional to the 1949 Geneva Conventions: Remarks' (1987) 2 Am.U.J.Int'l L. & Pol'y 419, 430 and Canada, René Provost and Joseph Rikhof 'Correspondent's Report: Canada' (2000) 3 YIHL 440–441.

98 Theoretically even the occupation of an uninhabited strategic point could give rise to the applicability of the Protocol. For Robert Kolb and Richard Hyde, *An Introduction to the International Law of Armed Conflicts* (Hart 2008) 79, 'the ICRC has held that a minimum control suffices'.

99 *Junod* 1987, 1353. See also *L.C. Green*, 321.

100 *1977 Records* Vol. 7, 71. See also Brazil, *1977 Records* Vol. 4, 8.

101 *Mastorodimos* 2014, 313.

102 See, in this regard, ibid., 312–3.

103 USA, *1977 Records* Vol. 8, 292. See also Italy and Belgium, *1977 Records* Vol. 8, 290 and 291 respectively, as well as the 'Note of the Directorate for Public International Law of the (Swiss) Federal Department of Foreign Affairs' (1986) in Marco Sassòli and Antoine A. Bouvier, *How Does Law Protect in War* (2nd edn, International Committee of the Red Cross 2006) 1384. See also *Junod* 1987, 1351, Peter H. Kooijmans, 'In the Shadowland between Civil War and Civil Strife: some Reflections on the Standard-Setting Process' in Astrid J.M. Delissen and Gerard J. Tanja (eds), *Humanitarian Law of Armed Conflict Challenges ahead: Essays in Honour of Frits Kalshoven* (Nijhoff Publishers 1991) 231 and *Cullen*, 102, referring also to objective criteria. On the other hand, 'those new criteria offered every opportunity for subjective interpretation', as Netherlands, rightly commented, *1977 Records* Vol. 8, 288. See also similar statements from Argentina, *1977 Records* Vol. 8, 291 as well as Colombia, Kenya and Yemen, *1977 Records* Vol. 7, 78, 82 and 235 respectively and the similar thoughts of *Detter*, 205–6.

104 This appears to be the position of Norway, *1977 Records* Vol. 8, 293.

as suggested,[105] because it would free even the signatory party to the conflict from its humanitarian (treaty) obligations, contrary to both the object and purpose of the relevant treaty as well as the ordinary meaning of the article; such interpretation would return us to the doctrine on recognition of belligerency. In addition, neither the ability to implement the law, nor the execution of operations (or the corresponding ability), are necessary qualifying factors for the ANSA to become a party to the conflict, although the degree of violence will be relevant for the existence of an armed conflict.

The ICRC Commentary to the Additional Protocols examines territorial control (of the above-mentioned quality), the sustained and concerted nature of military operations and the capability to implement the Protocol as three different features relevant to the Protocol's applicability.[106] The ICTR[107] and the SCSL[108] link territorial control with the ability to execute military operations, while the ability to implement the Protocol is the second criterion.[109] The preparatory works of the Protocol do not enlighten us much: Canada seems to profess that, apart from territorial control, the ability to implement the Protocol is linked with the scale of operations[110] (thus offering another variation), while Belgium[111] appears to follow the Commentary's approach.

There are two reasons why the capability to implement the Protocol[112] should not be a stand-alone condition for its applicability: while this capability is important for the quality, compliance and accountability of the ANSA, it must be presumed to exist once the ANSA

---

105 See Pakistan, *1977 Records* Vol. 4, Amendments to Draft Additional Protocol II, 6. For Antonio Cassese, 'The Status of Rebels under the 1977 Geneva Protocol on Non-International Armed Conflict' (1981) 30 ICLQ 416, 424–5 and A.P.V. Rogers, 'Armed Forces and the Development of the Law of War' (1982) 21 Rev Dr Milit 201, 203, the insurgents should implement the Protocol beforehand. See the disagreement of Switzerland in *Sassòli and Bouvier*, 1384 and Helen Duffy, *The 'War on Terror' and the Framework of International Law* (CUP 2005) 222.

106 *Junod* 1987, 1351–3, although, overall, her position is confusing because in the beginning of her discourse she seems to imply that the other elements are only defining the extent of territorial control. See also Sylvie Junod, 'Additional Protocol II: History and Scope' (1983) 33 Am.U.L.Rev. 29, 37–8. Karl Josef Partsch, 'Article 1, Protocol II', in Bothe et al. (eds), *New Rules for Victims of Armed Conflicts: Commentary on the Two 1977 Protocols Additional to the Geneva Conventions of 1949* (Martinus Nijhoff Publishers 1982) 627, refers to effective control of a certain quality, the capacity for operations and the capacity to implement the Protocol.

107 *Akayesu* [623], *Musema* [254] and *Prosecutor v Rutaganda* (Judgment) ICTR-96–3-T (6 December 1999) [95]. Yet in *Akayesu* [627] some value was given to the fact that the ANSA 'carried out continuous and sustained military operations'.

108 *Sesay* Judgment [97] and *Fofana* [126].

109 This appears to be the majority opinion. See also *Schindler*, 148, *Babiker*, 42–3 and Noelle Higgins, *Regulating the Use of Force in Wars of National Liberation, the Need for a New Regime: A Study of the South Moluccas and Aceh* (Nijhoff 2010) 133.

110 *1977 Records* Vol. 7, 77. Similarly, Djamchid Momtaz, 'Le Droit International Humanitaire Applicable aux Conflits Armés Non Internationaux' (2001) 292 Recueil Des Cours 49–51.

111 *1977 Records* Vol. 8, 291. See also *Carrillo-Suarez*, 91 ff. and the *ILA Committee on the Use of Force* 690.

112 This capability is described as objective by *Partsch* 627, *Junod* 1987, 1353, *Akayesu* [624], *Musema* [254] and *Sesay* Judgment [97].

is organized. Otherwise it would amount to a condition of reciprocity:[113] the governmental forces would be freed of obligations because the ANSA is not judged as being able to live up to humanitarian standards. Such interpretation would defeat the object and purpose of the Protocol, which is to humanize internal conflicts. It can be argued[114] that this is not significant because human rights law would apply – the exception being those states that are not party to any major human rights treaty, such as China, Comoros, Cuba, Israel, the Solomon Islands and Toga. Yet human rights can be crippled by derogations, although this is more of a theoretical danger than a practical reality.

In addition it is a different issue, as an evidentiary matter, whether the ANSA is capable of implementing the Protocol and whether ANSAs hold territory which enables them to implement the Protocol. The first assessment requires information about the organization of the ANSA, which will usually come from the manner in which it executes military operations, as well as other elements (for example knowledge of the rules) which might not be available to the state party to the conflict or external actors.[115] The second assessment can also be done in the abstract, even *before* any outbreak of hostilities, because it would take into account the provisions of the Protocol, the characteristics of the state's territory (mountainous and so on) *and* what sort of ANSA (for example in terms of manpower and organization) can implement the treaty. The crucial element would be control of territory by the ANSA rather than positive knowledge of its characteristics and organization.

More significantly, the ability to implement the Protocol could be denied without prior knowledge of the rules; but to deny applicability of the rules because there was no proper dissemination, according to art 19 of Protocol II, appears, equally, not to serve the treaty's purpose, especially since it is mainly[116] an obligation of the state even in times of peace.

---

113 Charles Lysaght, 'The Scope of Protocol II and its Relation to Common Article 3' (1983) 33 Am.U.L.Rev. 9, 22 and, similarly, *Moir*, 108. The *CIHL Study* Vol. 1, 498–9, rules out reciprocity in all types of conflicts, although practice, Vol. II, 3187–96, does not seem particularly convincing with regard to non-international armed conflicts. See also the mixed proposals of states, *1977 Records* Vol. 10, 109–10, leaving room for reprisals and reciprocity in the event of persisting violations by the ANSA.

114 *Sivakumaran* 2012, 68.

115 The treatment of the relevant criterion from ICTR, *Akayesu* [627], was extremely liberal; the Court was satisfied by the fact that there was structure and discipline in the ANSA and by the ANSA's statement to the ICRC that it was bound by the rules of international humanitarian law. However, this last element suggests the willingness to apply humanitarian law or, in the least, a self-assessment that they have the objective capacity. It does not demonstrate the actual capacity of the ANSA. At least it would not be possible to claim lack of knowledge, which would definitely impair the (objective) ability to implement.

116 See also Rules 142–3 of the *CIHL Study* Vol. 1, 501–8. David Turns, 'Implementation and Compliance' in Elizabeth Wilmshurst and Susan Breau (eds), *Perspectives on the ICRC Study on Customary International Humanitarian Law* (CUP 2007) 362, finds Rule 142, to the extent that it extends IHL instructions to the ANSA's forces as 'unrealistic', 'aspirational … and … unlikely to reflect an actual rule of customary international law'. But see the *IDI 1999 Resolution*, art XII, that 'all States and non-State entities must disseminate the principles and rules of humanitarian law … which are applicable in internal armed conflicts' as well as Gauthier de Beco, 'Compliance with International Humanitarian Law by Non-State Actors' (2005) 18 HuV 190, 197 and Anne-Marie La

Consider for example a pre-conflict situation where the state has refrained from making the rules known to the public (including the future individual members of the ANSA). Consequently when the conflict breaks out, the protection of the public, from the state and the non-state actor would be delayed until such time that the ANSA has proper knowledge of the rules. Such interpretation appears to be self-defeating.

The appearance of ANSAs with the features of Protocol II was not infrequent (before and after its adoption); nevertheless the Protocol's applicability has been relatively scarce because states that have been involved with internal armed conflicts refrained from acceding to the Protocol or insisted on a high threshold of applicability[117] or denied applicability.[118] Such attitudes have had a double effect. Firstly they lead to calls for a '… progressive and flexible interpretation of the application clauses of Protocol II'.[119] The customization of certain rules of the Protocol does not carry the same threshold of application, but that of common article 3 and, therefore, to a large extent, this criterion has been invalidated in practice. Secondly it paved, up to a point, the road for the conclusion of a new treaty (the Rome Statute for the International Criminal Court[120]) which would supplement common article 3 (in terms of its substantive provisions), while getting rid of the territorial control feature.

The Rome Statute

The latest development in treaty law relevant to ANSAs came from the area of international criminal law. Partly reproducing the *Tadic* formula,[121] the Statute has departed from the criteria of Protocol II. More specifically, there is no express reference, in art 8.2, to responsible command, territorial control, ability to implement the laws of war or to carry out sustained and concerted military operations (either on its own or linked to territorial control). The only reference with regard to ANSAs is a requirement for organization. An ICC Chamber[122] explains the organizational element '… insofar as such groups acted under a responsible command and had an operative internal disciplinary system'. The 'responsible command' element does not seem to differentiate from the organizational requirement.[123]

Rosa and Carolin Wuerzner, 'Armed Groups, Sanctions and the Implementation of International Humanitarian Law' (2008) 90 IRRC 327, 333.

117 See also the interpretation of *L.C. Green*, 66–7.

118 See the example of Colombia, *Carillo-Suarez*, 41–2 and El Salvador, *Tadic* Appeals Decision [117] and Michel Veuthey, 'Implementation and Enforcement of Humanitarian Law and Human Rights Law in Non-International Armed Conflicts: The Role of the International Committee of the Red Cross' (1983) 33 Am.U.L.Rev. 83, 87.

119 *Zegveld*, 53. In UNHRC, 'Report of the International Commission of Inquiry to Investigate All Alleged Violations of International Human Rights Law in the Libyan Arab Jamahiriya' (1 June 2011) A/HRC/17/44, 30, not much attention was given to territorial control.

120 (adopted 17 July 1998, entered into force 1 July 2002) 2187 UNTS 90 (Rome Statute).

121 *Tadic* Appeals Decision [70].

122 *Prosecutor v Katanga et al.* (Decision on the Confirmation of Charges) ICC-01/04-01/07 (30 September 2008) [239].

123 *Prosecutor v Jean-Pierre Bemba Gombo* (Decision Pursuant to Article 61(7) (a) and (b) of the Rome Statute on the Charges) ICC-01/05-01/08 (15 June 2009) [234], 'responsible command entails some degree of organization of those armed groups, including the possibility to impose

Several Chambers[124] so far have also given significant probative value to the 'the ability to plan and carry out military operations for a prolonged period of time' or the ability to sustain the conflict, considering that in such cases the organization element is confirmed. Overall there is no significant difference from common article 3. The crimes which are the subject matter of the ICC imply also a certain planned action, which can only be the effect of an organized entity: genocide requires 'conduct [which] took place in the context of a manifest *pattern* of similar conduct'[125] (emphasis added); the notion of crimes against humanity includes 'acts … committed as part of a *widespread or systematic* attack' (art 7.1 of the Statute) (emphasis added); and the jurisdiction of the ICC with regard to war crimes concerns particularly their perpetration '*as part of a plan or policy or as part of a large-scale commission*' (article 8.1 of the Statute) (emphasis added). The internal disciplinary system would also constitute significant evidence of the organized character of the ANSA[126] as well as the elements that were deemed relevant in the context of common article 3.[127]

There is, however, an omission in the Statute, which could have repercussions for its applicability, and which relates to the features of an armed group. There are two different sub-paragraphs dealing with the criminalization of violations of non-international armed conflict law. Art 8.2(c) duplicates common article 3 and the subsequent paragraph does not make any reference to the quality of the group. Art 8.2(e) criminalizes other violations of laws and customs of war and the subsequent paragraph makes an express reference to the (organized) quality of the ANSA. Therefore it can be argued that in terms of the application of common article 3 (and art 8.2(c) of the Rome Statute) even a non-organized group can generate an internal armed conflict. Such interpretation would come in sharp contrast to the dominant position regarding the quality of the non-state party in common article 3; on the other hand it would appear to be consonant with the applicability of common article 3 in situations of chaotic armed conflicts that have been addressed by UN organs.[128] It is expected that the jurisprudence of the ICC will shed more light on

---

discipline and the ability to plan and carry out military operations'. The pedigree from the ICRC's Commentary is evident. In *Prosecutor v Thomas Lubanga Dyilo* (Judgment) ICC-01/04-01/06 (14 March 2012) [535–6], Trial Chamber I notes the reliance on Protocol II language, but rejects the significance of 'responsible command' for the applicability of the Rome Statute.

124 *Lubanga* Decision 2007 [234] and [237], *Bemba* [233], *Mbarushimana* [103] and, similarly, *Lubanga* Judgment [536]. See also *Prosecutor v. Bosco Ntagnanda* (Decision on the Confirmation of Charges) ICC-01/04-02/06 (9 June 2014) [17].

125 Elements of Crimes of the International Criminal Court' (2000) UN Doc PCNICC/2000/1/Add.2.

126 *Lubanga* Judgment [544] and *Mbarushimana* [104].

127 See *Lubanga* Judgment [537] and its reference to the judgments of the ICTY in *Limaj, Haradinaj and Boškoski*. In *Mbarushimana* [106], 'the armed group's capacity to oppose state and peace-enforcement forces' was mentioned as an element of the organized character of the ANSA, while in *Bosco Ntagnanda* [16], some value was given to the 'effective system of communication', both being elements which come under the broad jurisprudence of the ICTY.

128 See sub-chapter *Common Article 3 to the Geneva Conventions of 1949*, at 17–18.

the various features of ANSAs' organization, although so far the difference between arts 8.2(d) and (f) has been rejected in terms of any legal significance[129] – or went unnoticed.[130]

Synthesis

The common element of the above-mentioned treaties with regard to the quality of the ANSA is organization. Although there is hardly any agreement on what this entails exactly, the collective and planned military activities would be the most significant element of proof, while they would also satisfy the violence requirement, as a necessary trigger for the applicability of humanitarian law and accountability for its violations. The existence of a command structure or hierarchy would affirm that feature as well. It is possible that for common article 3 and the corresponding article of the Rome Statute, the element of organization does not include a responsible command,[131] although the need and the ability for the ANSA to act as a collective entity is necessary. The temporary or permanent occupation of a territory would be another element which relates to the organization of the ANSA. If that control has the quality elements that are required by Protocol II,[132] this treaty would be applicable. In any case it would appear that without the organizational element, it would be difficult to establish the accountability of the ANSA. Yet in light of the vast differences between ANSAs, in terms of size, power and degrees of success, among others, it might be questioned whether other elements besides organization and effectiveness would be important for the existence of the ANSA and/or its accountability. In the forthcoming part we will examine three elements which have been linked at various times with actors in the international arena: recognition, representativeness and legitimacy. These features have the potential to change both the obligations of ANSAs and the accountability for their actions.

Additional Features

Recognition

Shaw defines recognition as ' ... a statement [or act] by an international legal person as to the status in international law of another real or alleged international legal person or of the validity of a particular factual situation'.[133] This statement/act has certain legal

129 *Bemba* [232]. Similarly Herman von Hebel and Darryl Robinson, 'Crimes within the Jurisdiction of the Court' in Roy S. Lee (ed.), *The International Criminal Court: The Making of the Rome Statute – Issues, Negotiations, Results* (Kluwer Law International 1999) 120 and *Cullen*, 175 ff.

130 In *Prosecutor v Bahar Idriss Abu Garda* (Decision on the Confirmation of Charges) ICC-02/05–02/09 (8 February 2010), *Mbarushimana* and *Bosco Ntagnanda* the Chambers did not differentiate between the crimes under the relevant sub-paragraphs. In any case, if the 'higher' threshold of 8.2(f) is satisfied, the lower 8.2(c) will also be satisfied. Therefore the potential legal significance will only be evident if the alleged crimes fall exclusively under art 8.2(c).

131 For Yves Sandoz, 'International Humanitarian Law in the Twenty-First Century' (2003) 6 YIHL 3, 14, it is part of the organizational element. Contra *Cullen*, 157.

132 Significantly, these elements are not considered to be customary, see *Lootsteen*, 128–9 and *Cullen*, 114. The different way that they are interpreted supports this view, as well as the fact of (purported) customization of the substantive rules, even in other situations of lower levels of violence.

133 At 368. See also *Von Glahn* 1986, 82.

consequences, regardless of its constitutive or declaratory character,[134] although it '... may be [a] pure act ... of policy not purporting to be legal characterization ... '.[135]

Under traditional international law, recognition of belligerency has the effect of vesting a limited legal personality in the ANSA and subjecting it to certain international rules. Recognition as a state has the effect that the recognizing entity acknowledges the recognized as a full subject of international law[136] and the rules and principles of international law become applicable in their relations. Recognition as a government[137] implies its stability,[138] willingness to honour its (international) obligations[139] and, possibly, legitimacy (in the sense of having the consent of the constituency),[140] ultimately being able to lead to the creation and/or continuance of (e.g. diplomatic or treaty) relations with the recognizing state.

In limited cases ANSAs were recognized as states (for example in the case of Algeria[141] or Biafra) or governments (as with the Taliban regime[142] or the (Libyan) National Transitional Council (hereinafter NTC)[143]). While these acts did not transform the relevant actors into states/governments, as the need for collective recognition is prevalent in borderline cases[144] and the consent/recognition by the parent state still constitutes one of the most significant factors in state recognition matters, they carry with them certain political and legal significance. The newly recognized entity can enter into diplomatic, treaty and other relations with the recognizing state. The factual importance of even one recognition (as a state or government) might be paramount, especially when there is a duty

134 See this dichotomy in James Crawford, *The Creation of States in International Law* (2nd edn Clarendon Press 2006) 19–26 and John Dugard and David Raič, 'The Role of Recognition in the Law and Practice of Secession' in Marcelo G. Kohen (ed.), *Secession: International Law Perspectives* (CUP 2006) 97–9.

135 *Brownlie*, 86.

136 See art 10 of the Charter of the Organization of American States (adopted 30 April 1948, entered into force 13 December 1951) 119 UNTS 3 (hereinafter OAS Charter). For a brief description of the repercussions of recognition, see Brad Roth, *Governmental Illegitimacy in International Law* (OUP 2000) 122–3.

137 This is considered as outdated in general, see *Shaw*, 380, if it not in desuetude, *Crawford*, 155. But see Stefan Talmon, 'Recognition of Opposition Groups as the Legitimate Representative of a People' (2013) 12 Chinese JIL 219, 226 ff.

138 Usually recognition of governments has also included the element of effectiveness, even if it is partial, see Sean D. Murphy, 'Democratic Legitimacy and the Recognition of States and Governments' (1999) 48 ICLQ 545, 579 and *Shaw*, 377.

139 *Von Glahn* 1986, 94.

140 See *Flory*, 839. For *Aust* 2010, 25, '[t]he question of recognition of a government arises only when it has come to power unconstitutionally ... recognition may be withheld as an indication of political displeasure.'

141 *Fraleigh*, 210–13.

142 *Bellal* et al., 3.

143 See the reference in Christian Tomuschat, 'The Arabellion: Legal Features' (2012) 72 ZaöRV 447, 464, although it is not crystal clear that it constituted recognition as a government. For acts in the Syrian context that could be deemed as governmental recognition see *Talmon* 2013, 244.

144 With regard to governmental recognition, there might be a need for legal de-recognition of the standing government, see *Talmon* 2013, 239.

of non-recognition;[145] the recognized entity has the potential to normalize its international relations and gain some limited access within other states.

The meaning of recognition, however, is not static, as it is not confined only to belligerency, states or governments. An act that recognizes an ANSA as representative of peoples[146] can have a certain impact on its status, as it might imply a limited legal standing in international law or certain privileges attached to this characterization.[147] This was obvious in the cases of national liberation movements.

While the UN constituted the international organization with the general competence for decolonization processes, it implicitly left the matter of recognition to regional organizations, notably the Organization of African Unity (hereinafter OAU) and the League of Arab States. The latter examined the '... level of effectiveness[148] with regard to the organisation concerned ... and ... exclude[d] in practice secessionist movements',[149] while ascertaining their representativeness.[150] Such recognition differed substantially from traditional forms of recognition in international law, although it resembled recognition of government in line with its representativeness and legitimacy[151] or a government-in-exile,[152] in the event of total lack of internal territorial control.

---

145 Non-recognition will be a duty, if the breached rule is of an *erga omnes* character (State Responsibility art 41.2) or if the Security Council has made a relevant pronouncement on the illegality of a situation, such as in Res 402 (22 December 1976). Otherwise any act of recognition appears to be a purely voluntary act of the state, see the Dissenting Opinion of Judge Skubiszewski, *East Timor (Portugal v Australia)* (Merits) [1995] ICJ Rep 264.

146 See the example of recognition by France of the Libyan National Council in *Halabi*, 376 and of the Syrian opposition from other states in *Talmon* 2013, 220–21.

147 See also Jonte van Essen, 'De Facto Regimes in International Law' (2012) 28 Merkourios 31, 43. *Talmon* 2013, 243, while noting its '... symbolic value, indicating political support for the opposition group recognized and implying that the recognizing State is ready to engage with the group, its institutions and representatives', acknowledges also the 'increased practical, i.e. material and financial support', excluding military assistance.

148 Effectiveness is important with regard to control over territory and the ability to mount an armed conflict. See this interpretation of effectiveness in the context of the Organization of African Unity in Heather A. Wilson, *International Law and the Use of Force by National Liberation Movements* (Clarendon 1988) 144. See also Georges Abi-Saab, 'Wars of National Liberation in the Geneva Conventions and Protocols' (1979) 165 Recueil des Cours 413. If opposed to a legal right/title, 'effectiveness is likely to be more strictly applied', *Crawford*, 59. That could explain why effectiveness in the context of national liberation movements was not a particularly rigid condition.

149 *Shaw*, 220–221. Only those movements which were claiming representation of the whole peoples in the colonial territory would be recognized, *Wilson*, 145.

150 Claude Lazarus, 'Le Statut des Mouvements de Libération Nationale à l'Organisation des Nations Unies' 20 (1974) AFDI 173, 180 and Fatsah Ouguergouz, 'La Palestine et les Conventions de Genève du 12 Août 1949 ou l'Histoire d'une Adhésion Avortée' in Laurence Boisson de Chazournes and Vera Gowlland-Debbas (eds), *The International Legal System in Quest of Equity and Universality: Liber Amicorum Georges Abi-Saab* (Nijhoff 2001) 521.

151 Liberation movements were 'perceived as future authoritative governments ... responsible for the ... well-being of their people', Eric Suy, 'The Status of Observers in International Organizations' (1978) 160 Recueil des Cours 100.

152 *G. Abi-Saab*, 412.

Subsequent to national liberation movements' recognition by regional organizations, the General Assembly has taken the initiative to grant them observer status several times.[153] Their 'privileges' included participation in the Security Council discussions.[154] A number of international conferences included liberation movements as participants.[155] Recognition also led to the creation of relations between states and national liberation movements. The PLO signed various multilateral agreements[156] in the context of the Organization of Islamic States and the then European Economic Community accorded the movement preferential treatment in trade relations.[157] At times, national liberation movements were admitted as states in regional organizations. As well as the example of Western Sahara, which was accepted as a member in the OAU in 1984, the PLO had already been admitted (as Palestine) to the Organization of Islamic States in 1969. The possibility that inter-state humanitarian law[158] could apply in the relation between the movement and states, was another effect of recognition. In light of the above, the limited international legal personality of national liberation movements has been acknowledged widely.[159]

Besides the unique (and probably extant) case of national liberation movements, the recent situations in Libya and Syria incited a discussion on criteria of recognition as a legitimate representative of a people. Talmon[160] identifies among these criteria that the 'government of the State must have lost legitimacy and the opposition group must be representative, broad, and enjoy a reasonable prospect of permanence'. In essence such criteria are not substantially different from national liberation movements' recognition; only that the consequences appear to be more limited in the case of ANSAs.

Even 'recognition' that the insurgent entity should be considered as a significant interlocutor in the resolution of internal turmoil could have repercussions, not so much in legal terms but at least in the political/legitimacy sphere; when France and Mexico '... issued a joint statement in which they recognised the Alliance of the Frente de Liberacion Nacional Farabundo Marti and the Frente Democratico Revolucionario as being a representative

153 See UNGA Res 3237 (XXIX) (22 November 1974) and 31/152 (20 December 1976).

154 See the participation of Polisario, UN Doc S/PV. 2153 (22 June 1979) 5 ff. and the Palestinian Liberation Organization (hereinafter PLO), UN Doc S/PV. 2285 (16 June 1981) 4, in Security Council deliberations.

155 In the context of the UN see *Lazarus*, 195. The conference that led to the adoption of Protocol I also took place with their participation.

156 On the character of these texts as treaties see Shabtai Rosenne, 'The Perplexities of Modern International Law: General Course on Public International Law' (2001) 291 Recueil des Cours 289 and *Ouguergouz*, 522. Canada, *1977 Records* Vol. 6, 365, rejected their corresponding competence.

157 Elizabeth Chadwick, *Self-determination, Terrorism and the International Humanitarian Law of Armed Conflict* (Martinus Nijhoff 1996) 56. For other examples see *Ouguergouz*, 522.

158 See arts 1.4 and 96.3 of Protocol I. Note, though, that the procedure for the applicability of Protocol I to conflict with national liberation movements did not materialize even once.

159 See Senegal, *1977 Records* Vol. 8, 45, the German Democratic Republic in UNCHR, 'Report of the Working Group on a Draft Declaration on the Right and Responsibility of Individuals, Groups and Organs of Society to Promote and Protect Universally Recognized Human Rights and Fundamental Freedoms' (13 March 1986) E/CN.4/1986/40, 5, *Kooijmans*, 230 and *Momtaz*, 57.

160 2013, 237–8.

political force ... ',[161] it was implied that a final solution to the conflict without the participation of the insurgent entity was deemed unacceptable. But, generally, it is recognition by the parent state which is bound to have more significance, as revealed mainly by recognition as belligerent or state,[162] and this is denied in the overwhelming majority of cases.

While, however, recognition is significant for the extent of relations (and responsibility) between the state and the recognized ANSA and might allow ANSAs to claim an international legal status more persuasively, it is not a necessary precondition for the rise of ANSA accountability,[163] with the exception of national liberation movements. This is obvious not only in the regime of IHL and the lack of recognition as a precondition for the applicability of Common Article 3,[164] which was an implicit aim of the drafters, but also in general international law: a revolutionary group which establishes a general *de facto* government may be held responsible by governments which refused to recognize it. Moreover the responsibility of insurrectional movements (State Responsibility art 10) is not conditioned on the prior recognition of the former ANSA as a state/government. However, the lack of recognition (or of any other interactions) could create difficulties for an injured State to 'present ... a claim and bring ... home the responsibility'.[165] Furthermore, and using an IHL paradigm again, the collective recognition of an ANSA as a state (or even a single recognition, if it comes from the 'parent' or the opposing state) could transform the nature of a previously internal armed conflict[166] and the extent of obligations of the (former) ANSA as well as, possibly, the applicable accountability norms.[167] It is also possible that an act of recognition would constitute a direct or indirect

---

161 UNCHR, 'Final Report on the Situation of Human Rights in El Salvador Submitted by Professor José Antonio Pastor Ridruejo in Discharge of the Mandate Conferred by Commission Resolution 32 (XXXVII)' (18 January 1982) E/CN.4/1502, 16.

162 The importance of recognition by the parent state was evident in a number of cases, including Bangladesh and the Baltic states. Even in the case of Yugoslavia, 'none of the constituent republics was admitted to the United Nations prior to the adoption by Serbia-Montenegro of its new Constitution, which clearly implied renunciation of any territorial claim to the territory of the other republics', *Crawford*, 399.

163 *Shaw*, 386, ' ... it should not be assumed that non-recognition ... will deprive that entity of rights and duties before international law'.

164 Similarly two states in conflict which are parties to the Geneva Conventions are bound to apply it, even if they are not mutually recognized. See arts 43.1 of Protocol I, 13.3 of the First and Second Geneva Convention and 4.3 of the Third Geneva Convention. The example of the conflict between Israel and the Arab States, mutually unrecognized, is illustrative. The character of the conflict between Algeria and Guinea-Bissau with France and Portugal, respectively, changed after their accession to the Geneva Conventions, even though their state character was debatable up to a point.

165 ILC, 'Texts of Articles 10–15 and Commentaries Thereto as Adopted by the Commission at Its Twenty-Seventh Session' (1975) YILC Vol. II, 61, 93.

166 *Dinstein* 1976, 80.

167 But it should not be assumed that the scheme works vice-versa, because an acknowledgement (recognition) that an international armed conflict exists in a situation where a state is fighting an armed non-state actor could have an impact mainly on the obligations rather than accountability mechanisms.

acknowledgement of the ANSA's effectiveness,[168] representativeness or legitimacy, while it could also constitute significant proof that the non-state entity is organized and capable of being a party to an armed conflict.

The element of recognition revealed that representativeness might be a constitutive part of it; therefore it is necessary to examine whether it could have a significance of its own, with regard to the character of ANSAs.

Representativeness

One of the defining characteristics of the state is its population. Due to the principle of self-determination, the state and its government are presumed to be representative of this population.[169] in accordance with art 21.3 of the Universal Declaration of Human Rights (hereinafter UDHR).[170] Self-determination was recognized in the Charter of the United Nations[171] as a principle (arts 1.2 and 55)[172] and in subsequent General Assembly resolutions as a right (such as 1514 (XV)[173] and 2625 (XXV)[174]). The 1966 Covenants recognized also a (human) right of peoples, under common art 1.[175] The International Court of Justice (hereinafter ICJ) confirmed, rather recently, its *erga omnes* character,[176] while it is considered occasionally as *jus cogens.*[177]

---

168 This is not necessary though, since 'massive recognition by states in combination with membership to the United Nations can have a significant impact in overcoming the lack of effectiveness in the internal or external sphere', Konstantinos Mastorodimos, 'The Character of the Conflict in Gaza: Another Argument towards Abolishing the Distinction between International and Non-International Armed Conflicts' (2010) 12 Int'l. C.L.Rev. 437, 442. See the examples of state recognition before attaining effective governance (Bangladesh and the ex-Yugoslav Republics) in *Dugard and Raič*, 135.

169 *Roth*, 2. In fact 'representation … is a necessary condition for law creation and legislative power', *Gal-Or*, 138. But until recently, ' … international law [was] not greatly concerned with whether a given government is or is not the representative of the "true" national will', *ILC* 1975, 100, while the effectiveness of the government was given a much more prominent role.

170 UNGA Res 217A (III) (10 December 1948).

171 (adopted 26 June 1945, entered into force 24 October 1945) 1 UNTS XVI (hereinafter UN Charter).

172 Yet these references were mostly implying the moral and political character of the principle.

173 (14 December 1960).

174 (24 October 1970).

175 International Covenant on Economic, Social and Cultural Rights (adopted 16 December 1966, entered into force 3 January 1976) 993 UNTS 3 (ICESCR) and International Covenant on Civil and Political Rights (adopted 16 December 1966, entered into force 23 March 1976) 999 UNTS 171 (ICCPR). See also art 20.1 of the African Charter on Human and Peoples' Rights (adopted 27 June 1981, entered into force 21 October 1986) 1520 UNTS 217, 245 (African Charter).

176 *East Timor*, ICJ Rep 102.

177 Sierra Leone, *United Nations Conference on the Law of Treaties, Official Records*, First Session (United Nations 1969) 300 (hereinafter 1969 Records First Session), Algeria, *Western Sahara* (Advisory Opinion) [1975] ICJ Pleadings Vol. V, 319–20 and the written statement of South Africa in *Legal Consequences on the Construction of a Wall in the Occupied Palestinian Territory* (Advisory Opinion) 2004, 11.

Representativeness 'refers to the qualitative diversity of the represented sections or segments of the society'.[178] Increasingly, 'the representative and democratic nature of the government has … been put forward as a requirement' for statehood[179] as well as a prerequisite of good governance in post-conflict societies.[180] Yet the presence of ANSAs appears to refute the presumption on the representativeness of governments. These entities do not appear from a vacuum: they usually constitute the vehicle of a local community[181] that cannot find an alternative way to express its voice and exercise its rights (including self-determination, if they constitute a people[182]) in its state of residence. This is not, of course, an absolute rule, but it constitutes the majority of cases where armed conflicts break out and ANSAs appear. In such cases, 'the presumption in favour of the established government is arbitrary from the standpoint of popular sovereignty'.[183]

At many times, ANSAs represent ethnic communities, at least partially. This is more evident in the cases of national liberation movements which represent peoples. Since a population is an indispensable element of states, the representative character of an ANSA could give a better claim for state creation. In other cases the ANSA might be affiliated with or represent religious or political groups. Non-representativeness of any kind is

178 *Talmon* 2013, 240.

179 *Shaw*, 183, *Murphy*, 558–9 and 565–6 and Anne Peters, 'Statehood after 1989: "*Effectivités*" between Legality and Virtuality' (2010) 10.

180 See, among others, the Uganda Peace Talks Agreement for the Restoration of Peace to the Sovereign State of the Republic of Uganda, Nairobi, Kenya, 17 December 1985 (hereinafter Uganda Peace Talks Agreement), art 16, the Protocol II to the Arusha Peace and Reconciliation Agreement for Burundi, Arusha, Tanzania, 28 August 2000 and Annex 3 of the General Framework Agreement for Peace in Bosnia and Herzegovina, Paris, 21 November 1995. See also Rüdiger Wolfrum, 'Legitimacy in International Law from a Legal Perspective: Some Introductory Considerations' in Rüdiger Wolfrum and Volker Rφben (eds) *Legitimacy in International Law* (Springer 2008) 8, on '… an increasing tendency in international law to induce States to establish a democratic national structure … '.

181 See also Ron Dudai, 'Closing the Gap: Symbolic Reparations and Armed Groups' 93 (2011) IRRC 783, 794.

182 Most definitions of a 'peoples' contain a combination of objective and subjective elements, see M.G. Kaladharan Nayar, 'Self Determination beyond the Colonial Context: Biafra in Retrospect' (1975) 10 Texas Int'l.L.J. 321, 340 and the *Sudan Human Rights Org v Sudan; Center for Housing Rights & Evictions v Sudan*, 279/03–296/05, African Commission on Human and Peoples' Rights, 25 July 2010 [220]. Increasingly, though, it is acknowledged that the peoples are not necessarily limited to that of a state as a whole, *Sudan Human Rights Org Case* [222] and the Written Comments of the Kingdom of Netherlands, 3 ff. in the *Kosovo* Opinion.

183 *Roth*, 196.

rare.[184] But, at the same time, a clear standard of representation, especially when there are competing claims, is lacking in international law.[185]

In general, representativeness will not have an effect on the accountability of ANSAs,[186] save for the case of national liberation movements. But this is not an absolute rule because 'the state, as member of the international community, can be represented in the international plane by an entity other than the government in place'.[187] This representation, though, is destined to take place only when the government is considered as illegitimate and there has been a process of de-recognition and/or recognition of the ANSA as the government (whether in exile or not). In such situations (evidenced partly by the recent situation in Libya) the ANSA accountability could be treated as part of the state responsibility architecture. At the very least, the illegitimacy of the government (especially if coupled with suppression of the population) might generate some positive attitude of the international community or individual states towards the representative ANSA.

Besides these limited and, to a certain extent, infrequent cases, representativeness might have an impact on the legitimate expectations of the international community towards the ANSA;[188] on the role that the ANSA will play during peace negotiations; and

184 As an indication only, in almost 42 non-international armed conflicts after 1945, and in particular in Afghanistan (Taliban), Algeria (war of independence), Angola (UNITA), Bosnia-Herzegovina (Republica Srpska), Burundi (FNL), Colombia (FARC), Cyprus, Eritrea (war of independence), Georgia (Abkhazia), Greece, Israel (Hamas), Lebanon (Hezbollah), Liberia (NPFL), Burma/Myanmar (Karen National Union), Namibia, Nepal (Communist Party of Nepal (Maoist), hereinafter CPN (Maoist)), Nigeria (Biafra), the Philippines (MNLF and MILF), Russia (Chechnya), Rwanda (Rwandan Patriotic Front), Senegal (Casamance), Serbia (UCK (KLA)), Sierra Leone (RUF and AFRC), Somalia (Somali National Movement), Sri Lanka (LTTE), the Sudan People's Liberation Movement (hereinafter SPLM), FYROM (NLA), Turkey (PKK), Uganda (LRA), Yemen (Royalists), Yemen (Al Houthi), Angola (war of independence), the Philippines (NPA), Mozambique (RENAMO), the Sudan (SLA and Justice and Equality Movement (hereinafter JEM)), South Africa (African National Congress (hereinafter ANC)), Zimbabwe (Rhodesia), Rwanda (FDLR), Croatia (Republic of Serbia Krajina), only the ANSAs of Sierra Leone were considered as lacking any representativeness. RENAMO was also considered as a vehicle of South Africa's intervention against Mozambique, but in the first post-peace elections it gained a significant percentage of the popular vote. The cases of NPFL, FARC and LRA are on the borderline, as they were or are lacking any external (and possibly internal) legitimacy, mainly because of their terror-like tactics. But on FARC see Elena M. Valencia, 'Theories of Compliance in International Conflict: The Place of the Third Geneva Convention in the Colombian Armed Conflict' (2007) 21 Temple Int'l & Comp.L.J. 445, 449–50, while the NPFL (Liberia) won the 1997 elections, which were considered as free and fair, *Samuels*, 170. The other ANSAs were either representing peoples or ethnic, political or religious groups or a combination thereof.

185 *Talmon* 2013, 240.

186 See the rejection of such possibility in the context of State Responsibility art 10 in Patrick Dumberry, 'New State Responsibility for Internationally Wrongful Acts by an Insurrectional Movement' (2006) 17 EJIL 605, 610–611.

187 *Momtaz*, 58.

188 Armed groups lacking representativeness or a substantial measure thereof are usually liable for significant violations of humanitarian law, as the examples of Liberia and Sierra Leone evince. It is also quite possible – although it needs corroboration – that armed groups representing an ethnic group tend to show more respect for IHL when compared with those representing ideologies (for

mainly on the place of the ANSA in the final peace agreement. If there is some provision for the post-conflict role of the ANSA, obviously as an entity embedded in the political system (usually a political party), it is probable that the ANSA was/is representing part of the local population. At times post-conflict elections had the effect of former ANSAs becoming the new government, as the examples of Burundi in 2005 and Nepal in 2009 attest. In such cases, the ANSA should, thereafter, form part of the state and follow the corresponding obligations and responsibility rules. In other cases ANSAs which were considered as not representing any substantial group within a state gained a commendable place in the elections (such as RENAMO in Mozambique, with 30 per cent of votes). Of course there might be various non-legal reasons that lead to these outcomes such as fatigue of the public from previous governments or state conduct during the conflict. Nonetheless, this example shows that there is a degree of subjectivity on assertions relevant to the representative character of ANSAs and therefore some objective way would be needed to ascertain the relations of ANSAs with other non-state groups. Only in limited cases (such as a coup d'état in previously functioning democracies) will it be possible to speak with absolute certainty on whether an ANSA actually represents an ethnic, religious or political group. Obviously the possibility of referendums, ballots and similar procedures is unlikely to happen. Strikes, sit-ins or demonstrations that have been realized under the aegis of the ANSA could ascertain, up to a point, popular support.[189] Recognition also tends to be decisive in this context, especially if it has a collective character and/or it comes from UN organs.

Possibly, though, it is effectiveness (in the sense of sustaining a conflict) that could also provide a relative indication,[190] because the asymmetrical type of warfare in which, usually, an ANSA exists could not be sustained without some voluntary help from the local population. Of course there is a possibility that this help is involuntary and, therefore, effectiveness is not necessarily a safe indication. But if representativeness is proved, there is an increased possibility for the legitimation of the ANSA.

Legitimacy

This term has been used in a variety of contexts, referring to norms,[191] factual situations[192] and actors.[193] With regard to norms, legitimacy refers to their capacity to extract voluntary compliance. Therefore, legitimacy in the international system might be significant, since this legal system does not possess enforceability mechanisms similar to those of national systems. In the case of lack of (positive) norms, legitimacy has been used in order to imply the morality/justness of certain action and/or to generate agreement when there

example communism and so on) – the reason could be that in the first paradigms people matter where in the second people are simply means to a cause.

189 See such measures in Algeria, *Bedjaoui*, 63 and 67–70.

190 *G. Abi-Saab*, 413.

191 Thomas M. Franck, 'Legitimacy in the International System' (1988) 82 AJIL 705–59.

192 Enrico Milano, *Unlawful Territorial Situations in International Law Reconciling Effectiveness, Legality and Legitimacy* (Martinus Nijhoff 2004).

193 *Roth* and Jean d'Aspremont, 'La Légitimité des Rebelles en Droit International' (2008).

are different opinions on legality or illegality.[194] With regard to such situations, the usual connotation is that of implying a just cause and it 'can work *beyond the positive norms* to allow a recognition of an originally unlawful situation by a legal system'.[195] In the same sense, legitimacy might imply 'soft legality'.[196]

As regards actors, 'the term mostly refers to the justification of authority – this notion is understood as the equivalent of having the power to take binding decisions'.[197] Consequently it is a reference to entities in power, such as governments, or other entities which exercise authority, such as ANSAs (possibly would-be governments or would-be states).

The legitimacy of governments did not play, until recently, any significant role in international relations, since it mostly concerned the internal-constitutional legal system,[198] a matter which lies within the domestic affairs of a state (art 2.7 of the UN Charter). However, the emergence of human rights (including self-determination and the existence of an individual right to vote and be elected[199]) and/or the conduct of certain governments towards their citizens (in disregard of these and other rights) made art 2.7 less relevant. Therefore the legitimacy of the government will be measured not only in accordance with the constitutional system or else its establishment in accordance with these rules but also with regard to compliance to certain international rules.[200] The conduct of governments *per se* or their specific disregard of democracy rules would be the vehicles of (de)legitimization and might have other effects, since recognition was occasionally related to internal legitimacy.[201]

The legitimacy of ANSAs tends to interrelate with the legitimacy of the government.[202] Depending on how the latter is viewed by the international community, there are prospects (although not automatic) that the ANSA will be viewed as something more than an armed organization. National liberation movements are probably the exemplary

194 See, for example, UNGA Res 2105 (XX) (20 December 1965) [10] and UNSC Res 322 (22 November 1972) [3].

195 *Milano*, 17. See also *Peters*, 8.

196 Hanspeter Neuhold, 'Legitimacy: A Problem in International Law and for International Lawyers?' in Rüdiger Wolfrum and Volker Rφben (eds), *Legitimacy in International Law* (Springer 2008) 351.

197 *Wolfrum*, 6 and Mark A. Drumbl, 'Collective Violence and Individual Punishment: The Criminality of Mass Atrocity' (2004–5) 99 Nw.U.L.Rev. 539, 548.

198 *Chen*, 105 and *Dinstein* 1976, 62.

199 See, in the universal level, UDHR, art 21 and ICCPR, art 25 and, in the regional level, the Protocol to the Convention for the Protection of Human Rights and Fundamental Freedoms (adopted 20 March 1952, entered into force 18 May 1954) CETS No.: 009, art 3, American Convention on Human Rights (adopted 21 November 1969, entered into force 18 July 1978) 1144 UNTS 143 (ACHR), art 23 and African Charter, art 13.1.

200 Even beyond the human rights regime in a broad sense, non-compliance with the basic norms of international relations (non-use of force) or, generally, Security Council resolutions could have the same effect.

201 *Shaw*, 379. Many such examples existed in the pre Second World War era, see *Chen*, 113–4.

202 *D'Aspremont* 2008, 2. See *Ends & Means*, 34: '[t]he existence of an active armed group in a country suggests that either the state or the government in power is considered illegitimate by at least that segment of the population which supports armed struggle.'

paradigm. Their existence was deemed as legitimate not only because of the emergence of the decolonization process (which matched their cause of future independence) but also because the government was actively opposing this process in many cases. Apartheid regimes, similarly, lent legitimacy to ANSAs, since they were widely perceived as violating basic international human rights norms (for example racial discrimination). Even the illegality of certain conduct by ANSAs did not reduce their overall legitimacy in the international plane.

National liberation movements, though, were a special case, since their legitimacy was also combined with their representativeness and recognition. It is actually the latter elements that mattered with regard to their obligations (and accountability). The treatment (and accountability) of ANSAs will depend mostly on the legitimacy of the government (mainly regarding its conduct[203] and/or representativeness) and less on the activities,[204] cause[205] and representativeness of the ANSA. For example, in its initial stages the UCK (KLA) was regarded as a terrorist organization; but after Serbia was deemed a human rights violator, the UCK (KLA) became an ally and a significant party for the resolution of the dispute.[206] Similarly the Gaddafi and Taliban regimes were discredited internationally due to their respective activities, while their oppositions were regarded more favourably

203 See the example of 'remedial secession', according to which a repressive and non-representative government towards a certain group cannot expect this group to remain loyal to it and therefore the gates of secession could open up, as a last viable and realistic resort to self-determination. It has received support from states, see Written Comments by the Swiss Confederation and Finland in the *Kosovo* Opinion, 2–3 and 3 respectively, judicial formations, see Separate Opinion of Judge Yusuf in the *Kosovo* Opinion [2010] ICJ Rep 622–3, Reference re Secession of Quebec, 1998 CanLII 793 (SCC) [134–8] and *Katangese Peoples' Congress v Zaire*, 75/92, African Commission on Human and Peoples' Rights, 22 March 1995 [6], ANSAs, see Bereket Habte Selassie, 'Self-determination in Principle and Practice: The Ethiopian-Eritrean Experience' (1997) 29 Colum.Hum.Rts.L.Rev. 91, 107 and *N. Higgins* 2010, 181 and writers, indicatively, *Nayar*, 338, Robert McCorquodale, 'Self-Determination: A Human Rights Approach' (1994) 43 ICLQ 857, 879–80, René Provost, *International Human Rights and Humanitarian Law* (CUP 2002) 255 and Christian Tomuschat, 'Secession and Self-determination' in Marcelo G. Kohen (ed.), *Secession: International Law Perspectives* (CUP 2006) 38–42. Another example is the possibility that a prominent member of the government (e.g. prime minister, president) is to stand trial in front of an international criminal court. See also *Talmon* 2013, 238.

204 Certainly an acceptance of international rules and a corresponding respect for them could, potentially, play some role. This scheme works *vice versa*, as the illegal and shocking conduct of an ANSA might generate a more positive view of a government, M. Cherif Bassiouni, 'The New Wars and the Crisis of Compliance with the Law of Armed Conflict by Non-State Actors' (2007–8) 98 J.Crim.L. & Criminology 711, 786.

205 For *Franco*, 120, 'on many occasions the [Security] Council determines the legitimacy of [ANSAs'] aspirations based on judgements of ANSA's behaviour rather than on its stated objectives'.

206 But its (increasing) effectiveness also played a significant role, see Klejda Mulaj, 'Resisting an Oppressive Regime: The Case of Kosovo Liberation Army' (2008) 31 Studies in Conflict & Terrorism 1103, 1109. *D'Aspremont* 2008, 21 and Christine Bell, *On the Law of Peace: Peace Agreements and the Lex Pacificatoria* (OUP 2008) 34, also believe that it is effectiveness (of ANSAs) that drives states to accept a certain legitimacy of the ANSAs.

by the international community. The cause behind an ANSA also plays a part,[207] although relatively small: it could lend legitimacy in the case where the aim is to democratize the state or stop human rights violations by the government,[208] while it could go the other way if the aim is highly criminal (the genocide of a certain part of the population), contrary to democratic principles[209] or secessionist.[210]

On the other hand, a government in confrontation with ANSAs will not lose its presumption (of legitimacy) if there are no legal (and political[211]) reasons for it to do so. ANSAs would then be deemed as illegal[212] and more focus might be given to individual members rather than the ANSA as a collective entity.[213] In certain situations ANSAs could also be regarded as terrorist organizations, thus losing any legitimacy in the eyes of the international community.

However, it is to be questioned whether legitimacy should not play a more active role in the (international) position of ANSAs. Certainly, they are illegal entities under national law and, therefore, they cannot be established lawfully. On the other hand, they might be the continuation of a perfectly legal entity in a national system which has been discontinued for whatever reasons, legitimate or not; or it could be the collective vehicle of a right to resist in unconstitutional changes which exists in several legal systems. Besides the legitimacy of establishment, the decision making, the conduct and the outcomes that the

---

207 *ICHRP 2000*, 32, 'legitimacy is partly rooted in the armed group's *aims*'.

208 See *Willets*, 368, 'legitimacy in using violence is increased in four ways: (1) when a group appears to have widespread support within their constituency; (2) when political channels have been closed to them; (3) when the target government is exceptionally oppressive, and (4) when the violence is aimed at "military targets" without civilian victims'.

209 Lomé Declaration of July 2000 on the Framework for an OAU Response to Unconstitutional Changes of Government (AHG/Decl.5 (XXXVI). For *Samuels*, 194, there is 'a new norm of international policy and international law prohibiting recourse to force to overthrow a democratically elected government'.

210 While there is an opinion that secession is a matter of fact, chiefly unregulated by international law, see *Aust* 2010, 24, the Written Statement of the Government of Japan, 3 and the Written Comments of France, 5 in the *Kosovo* Opinion, there is a strong disinclination towards unilateral secession. See, for example, Res 169 (24 November 1961) [1] and an OAU resolution on Nigeria in Anthony Hamilton Millard Kirk-Greene (comp.), *Crisis and Conflict in Nigeria: A Documentary Sourcebook 1966–1970*, Vol. II, June 1967–January 1970 (OUP 1971) 172–3. Furthermore see, indicatively, a general denial of a right to secede in Hurst Hannum, 'The Right of Self-Determination in the Twenty-First Century' (1998) 55 Wash. & Lee L. Rev. 773, 776, Photini Pazartzis, 'Secession and International Law: The European Dimension' in Marcelo G. Kohen (ed.), *Secession: International Law Perspectives* (CUP 2006) 371 and *Crawford*, 388. See also the Written Statement of the Republic of Azerbaijan, 5, the Written Statement of The Islamic Republic of Iran, 8 and the Written Comments of the Kingdom of Spain, 4 in the *Kosovo* Opinion.

211 One consideration being the government as a stabilizing entity in a turbulent region and so on. In that case, even recognition might come after, *van Essen*, 48.

212 Occasionally the Security Council refers to ANSAs as 'illegal', see Res 940 (31 July 1994) [3], 1794 (21 December 2007) [6] and 2096 (19 March 2013) preamble, [23] and [27]. See also the UNCHR Chairperson's Statement 1 (2005) [5].

213 UNCHR Res 78 (2005) [4–7].

ANSA produces should lend certain legitimacy to the entity; in an era when the rule of law is championed, there is more than one reason not to discourage responsible non-state entities and to maintain a certain line of communication with them. Of course there is a need for caution and clear distinguishing criteria, as '... legitimacy has too often been used as a pretext for political bargaining'[214] in the past.

But overall, it appears that the effects of an ANSA's legitimacy will be residual (and similar to those relating to its representativeness): it could imply that the international community would expect the ANSA to act as a responsible entity. Legitimacy might increase the role of ANSAs in peace negotiations and the post-conflict society. It could also generate a sort of political recognition of representativeness with the outcome of gaining, at least, moral/political support from other states.[215] Overall, legitimacy is not constitutive of ANSAs and would not generally matter in terms of the existence of their accountability,[216] although it could matter as to whether (and how) accountability is actively pursued.

Concluding Remarks

Overall it follows that the existence of ANSAs is mostly linked to their organized character and the effectiveness of their action, as evidenced by their ability to mount an armed conflict and/or to control territory. Recognition could play a significant role in the status of the ANSA, the extent of obligations and the corresponding accountability for its actions, even when its effectiveness is almost non-existent, as the government-in-exile paradigm could demonstrate. Representativeness, on the other hand, could induce recognition of the ANSA, but on its own it would lend, at best, only certain legitimacy to the ANSA. This last element might have some significance – although not in the context of accountability – when the incumbent government is disfavoured by the international community. The differences, however, between ANSAs create a need to classify them and treat their obligations and accountability accordingly, especially since international law and practice have drawn different consequences for different types of ANSAs.

214 *Chen*, 115.

215 See *Talmon* 2013, 231, on Syria.

216 *ILC* 1975, 105 and 'Draft Articles on Responsibility of States for Internationally Wrongful Acts, with Commentaries' (2001) YILC Vol. II Part Two 31, 51 (hereinafter Responsibility Commentary). Also Jean D'Aspremont, 'Rebellion and State Responsibility: Wrongdoing by Democratically Elected Insurgents' (2009) 58 ICLQ 427, 434–5. It could matter, though, indirectly, if it leads to recognition and the subsequent change of the primary obligations of the ANSA.

Chapter 2
Classification of Armed Non-State Actors

Despite some common characteristics, ANSAs do not form a single category. *De facto* entities exercise effective governance over people and territory, yet they only move in the periphery of the international community, despite claims of self-determination and resemblance to states. The importance of other ANSAs depends largely on effectiveness in the sense of control over territory and the generation of an armed conflict. If both these criteria apply, international practice ascribes certain consequences, at times extending beyond the armed conflict period.[1] If they do not occupy territory, then there is a tendency to simply regard them as terrorist or even common criminal organizations which, nevertheless, have certain (limited) duties originating from international law.

De Facto Entities

This term[2] is inspired by '*de facto* regimes' which comes from German international law scholarship. One could designate as *de facto* regimes all entities which possess the attributes of a state (territory, population, government and external relations capacity), in variable degrees, although they were most of the time created through a violation of a principle of international law (usually the prohibition on use of force, [non-intervention in the internal affairs of a state,] territorial integrity and/or self-determination of peoples).[3]

The common understanding is that the term '*de facto* regimes' includes illegitimate and unrecognized governments (such as the Taliban regime in Afghanistan[4]), entities which have been partially recognized as states (such as the former German Democratic Republic and Taiwan)[5] and non-recognized secessionist movements (such as Biafra and Somaliland).[6]

---

1 See, for example, *infra* sub-chapter *The Role of Effectiveness*, at 44 ff., on the implied mandate doctrine, as well as art 2.2 of Protocol II, regarding obligations towards detained persons.

2 Jonathan I. Charney and John Robert Victor Prescott, 'Resolving Cross-Strait Relations between China and Taiwan' (2000) 94 AJIL 453, 475, use it as synonymous to *de facto* regimes. Anne Hsiu-An Hsiao, 'Is China's Policy to Use Force Against Taiwan a Violation of the Principle of Non-Use of Force Under International Law?' (1998) 32 New Eng.L.Rev. 715, 716, uses the same term for Taiwan.

3 *Mastorodimos* 2010, 448.

4 See also the use of the term in S/RES/940, preamble and [3], referring to the *de facto* government in Haiti.

5 Jochen Frowein, 'De Facto Regimes' in Rudolf Bernhardt (ed.), *Encyclopaedia of Public International Law* Instalment 10 (North-Holland 1987) 73. See also *Crawford*, 469.

6 Michael Schoiswohl, *Status and (Human Rights) Obligations of Non-Recognized De Facto Regimes in International Law: the Case of 'Somaliland': the Resurrection of Somaliland against all International 'Odds':*

The differences between these categories are quite substantial. Unrecognized/*de facto* governments' conduct would trigger the international responsibility of the state it governs,[7] so that their inclusion among *de facto* regimes is partially misleading. Partially recognized entities would function as states for the part of the international community that has accorded state recognition. As regards states that have been refused recognition, implicitly or explicitly, they (together with secessionist entities) would be largely ignored (as if not existing). These *de facto* entities will be the focus of the present sub-chapter, as there is uncertainty as to whether they enjoy any status under international law.

De facto entities have usually arisen as a direct or by- product of an armed conflict (sometimes with the direct involvement of third states). The existence itself of these entities reveals that the temporary outcome of these conflicts was the defeat of the incumbent government or, in the least, a serious blow to its effectiveness as well as a permanent danger to the territorial integrity of the respective state. As a distinct category of ANSAs they aspire to become or be considered/recognized as states. They usually claim to (and probably do) represent a certain segment of the country's inhabitants which differs ethnically (or otherwise) from the rest of the population. They seem to possess the features of a state (territory with a relatively stabilized 'boundary', population, an effective administrative structure[8] and possibly even the capacity to enter into relations with states[9]) and exercise exclusive authority over people and land, to the detriment of the parent state. Their military power is significant and they have reached a major degree of organization. Provided that these entities are not *de facto* organs of these neighbouring states (which is a usual claim by the incumbent government coupled with a designation of the territory as occupied[10]), the ANSA is, most of the time, in a 'state of war' with the parent state. But as a matter of fact the relations between states and *de facto* entities are pacified in the majority of cases for a number of years (or there are clashes of limited duration and, possibly, intensity).[11] In fact the high level of organization, the existence and stability of the governmental function and the usual preservation of the regime in a relatively pacified situation are the attributes which distinguish *de facto* entities from ANSAs in control of territory (subject to Protocol II). And although their structure resembles a state much more than an armed group, their international marginalization seems to place their accountability outside the state responsibility context.

State Collapse, Secession, Non-Recognition and Human Rights (Nijhoff 2004) and *van Essen*, 33.

7 *Responsibility Commentary*, 49.

8 The most important criterion of statehood, *Crawford*, 56.

9 The essence of such capacity is independence, *Shaw*, 181 and *Brownlie*, 71–2.

10 The European Court of Human Rights has at times vested responsibility for acts of unrecognized *de facto* entities in supportive neighbouring states (Turkey, Russia). See also UNGA Res 37/253 (13 May 1983) [8], '*demand[ing]* the immediate withdrawal of all occupation forces from the Republic of Cyprus' and UNGA Res 62/243 (14 March 2008) on 'The Situation in the Occupied Territories of Azerbaijan', with regard to Nagorno Karabakh. See also *Aust* 2010, 19–20, considering these entities more or less as under the control of other states. In such case their obligations and accountability falls under the inter-state paradigm.

11 The Serb Republic of Bosnia and Biafra were the main exceptions.

While non-recognition appears to be a defining characteristic of these entities, if one followed exclusively the declaratory theory of state recognition,[12] then some of the *de facto* entities resemble states much more than other fictitious, disintegrating entities such as Somalia. However, this non-recognition, or even the existence of *de facto* entities, is actually some evidence that an act of recognition itself has some probative[13] and/or constitutive value and that the declaratory theory of recognition is not followed exclusively. In borderline cases the act of recognition has a 'semi-constitutive' character,[14] acknowledging that a state exists (and it possesses the attributes of one) and that the recognizing state wishes to regulate its relations with the entity. The lack of recognition denotes that other states refuse to acknowledge its existence as a state, and the entity cannot act within the realm of the international community. However, this refusal (usually implicit) does not itself mean that *de facto* entities are ignored completely by international law.

Application of Public International Law Norms to De Facto Entities

It is maintained, mainly by German writers, that *de facto* regimes are [to be] treated as partial subjects of international law.[15] Such acceptance would entail that certain rules of international law will function for and against the *de facto* entity. But, as Schoiswohl explains persuasively,

> it is not their international legal personality which enables them to enter into international relations, but the other way round: it is the *abstract* acceptance by the international legal community – necessitated by the practical needs to acknowledge its existence – to treat it as an entity with some sort of personality, which correspondingly endows it with its international legal status to the extent necessary to meet the needs of international society.[16]

---

12 This appears to be the prevailing opinion, see *Von Glahn* 1986, 84, *Ruda*, 454, the Conference on Yugoslavia, Arbitration Commission, 'Opinion No 8' (1992) 31 ILM 1523 and the Independent International Fact-Finding Mission on the Conflict in Georgia, 'Report' (2009) Vol. II 127 (hereinafter Mission to Caucasus Report).

13 John Quigley, 'The Israel-PLO Interim Agreements: Are They Treaties?' (1997) 30 Cornell Int'l L.J. 717, 729. See also the Arbitration Commission, ibid. and art 10 of the OAS Charter.

14 *Schoiswohl* 2004, 181. Similarly *Shaw*, 378.

15 *Bothe* 1981–2, 900–901, who claims that this treatment has acquired the status of customary law; Hans-Joachim Heintze, 'Are De Facto Regimes Bound by Human Rights?' (2009) 15 OSCE Yearbook 267, 269; Beate Rudolf, 'Non-State Actors in Areas of Limited Statehood as Addressees of Public International Law Norms on Governance' (2010) 4 HR&ILD 127, 136; and *van Essen*, 34. *Ago*, 129, refers to 'insurrectional movements' as 'a separate subject of international law', with ' … its limited international capacity, [… being] perfectly capable of committing internationally wrongful acts … '. Although the meaning of an insurrectional movement is not crystal clear, it appears to include actors similar to *de facto* entities, with regard to control over territory and their performance of certain governmental functions. See also *Jennings and Watts*, 553, accepting the existence of rights and/or obligations, without necessarily having an international personality.

16 Michael Schoiswohl, '*De facto* Regimes and Human Rights Obligations – the Twilight Zone of Public International Law?' (2001) 6 ARIEL 45, 53–4.

There is equally support that the norms on inter-state use of force are applicable to these entities;[17] this is easily discernible for partially recognized entities which, undoubtedly, constitute states. According to the OAS Charter (art 9), 'even before being recognized, the State has the right to defend its integrity and independence … ', thus implying the illegality of force. In addition, in the United Nations Special Committee on Principles of International Law concerning Friendly Relations and Cooperation among States 'non-recognition of the statehood of a political entity was held not to affect the international application of this cardinal rule of general international law'.[18] UNGA Res 3314 (XXIX) also contains an explanatory note according to which the term 'state' is used without prejudice to questions of recognition or whether a state is a member of the UN. While such clauses were made with divided states in mind, such as Germany and Korea, it is to be questioned whether they should not also apply in matters of *de facto* entities, especially since any use of force, following a pacified period, might create a threat to international peace and security. Additionally, art 2.4 of the UN Charter is considered to apply wherever there is an international line of demarcation, including armistice lines,[19] 'established by or pursuant to an international agreement to which it is a party or which it is otherwise bound to respect'.[20] There is also support that even a *de facto* boundary brings the prohibition of art 2.4 of the Charter into place.[21]

It is interesting that two states during Security Council deliberations have condemned the first use of force by Georgia towards South Ossetia. The first one was Russia,[22] as expected, which has claimed that 'the aggression has been carried out in violation of the

17 Albrecht Randelzhofer, 'Article 2(4)' in Bruno Simma (ed.), *The Charter of the United Nations: A Commentary* (2nd edn, OUP 2002) 121 and Jochen Frowein and Phillip Kirsch, 'Introduction to Chapter VII' in Bruno Simma (ed.), *The Charter of the United Nations: A Commentary* (2nd edn, OUP 2002) 721. Christian Henderson and James A. Green, 'The *Jus ad Bellum* and Entities Short of Statehood in the Report on the Conflict in Georgia' (2010) 59 ICLQ 129, 135 and 138, seem to give support to such interpretation with regard to the Caucasus entities, although overall 'the application of the *jus ad bellum* to non-State entities is aspirational, or, at best, an emerging principle of *lex ferenda*'. Similarly *Peters*, 5. See also *Charney and Prescott*, 471 and 476 and *van Essen*, 37, although they do not seem to accept the generality of the rule. Opposite Yoram Dinstein, *War, Aggression and Self-Defence* (4th edn, CUP 2005) 85; Olivier Corten, 'Are there Gaps in the International Law of Secession?' in Marcelo G. Kohen (ed.), *Secession: International Law Perspectives* (CUP 2006) 251–2 and Phil C.W. Chan, 'The Legal Status of Taiwan and the Legality of the Use of Force in a Cross-Taiwan Strait Conflict' (2009) 8 Chinese JIL 455, 482 ff.

18 Marjorie Whiteman, *Digest of International Law* Vol. 12 (Department of State Publications 1963) 281.

19 See also Department of State, Office of the Legal Adviser, 'The Legality of United States Participation in the Defense of Viet Nam' (1966) 75 Yale L.J. 1085, 1090, Natalino Ronzitti, 'Resort to Force in Wars of National Liberation' in Antonio Cassese (ed.), *Current Problems of International Law: Essays on U.N. Law and on the Law of Armed Conflict* (Dott. A. Giuffrè 1975) 327 and the Joint Services Regulation (Z/Dv) 15/2 in Dieter Fleck (ed.), *The Handbook of Humanitarian Law in Armed Conflicts* (OUP 1995) (hereinafter German Manual) 59.

20 A/RES/2625.

21 *Ronzitti* 1975, 327 and *Hsiao*, 728.

22 UN Doc S/PV.5952 (8 August 2008) 3.

fundamental principle of the Charter of the United Nations concerning the non-use of force'. The second was Panama[23] which condemned 'the decision taken by the Georgian Government to seek to impose its authority over South Ossetia through the use of force', thus implying its inadmissibility. The rest of the states, although staying silent on this issue, also refrained from endorsing at any time the permissibility of using force in order to bring the *de facto* entities under the jurisdiction of Georgia. Since international law is supposed to leave the use of intra-state force unregulated, this lack of support can signify a change of attitude in certain cases, although definite conclusions are not safe: it can equally be implied that the initial act of Georgia was politically imprudent.

Besides *jus ad bellum*, the accountability of these entities could also be said to include inter-state IHL rules[24] and human rights law.[25] The capacity to conclude agreements (even multilateral) with other states is not generally contested.[26] Their responsibility for injuries to states is accepted in doctrine[27] and, in practice, it was invoked by injured states and compensation was granted.[28] Depending, however, on the time of invocation, the accountability of *de facto* entities could form part of a new state responsibility, in accordance with State Responsibility art 10.

While there is serious support for the application of certain norms of international law to *de facto* entities, this is far from evident or settled. On the other hand, it was relatively easy for the community of states to accept the validity of certain acts of administration on the part of *de facto* entities and the principle of effectiveness played exactly this role.

The Role of Effectiveness

Despite non-recognition, territory, people and effective governance do not disappear just because states choose to ignore their existence. A certain *modus vivendi* would have to emerge in the relations between *de facto* entities and states as well as in the internal relations of the *de facto* entity, and the principle of effectiveness took up this role, at least with regard to the latter. The international community could not wholly disregard the phenomenon of *de facto*

---

23 UN Doc S/PV.5953 (10 August 2008) 15.

24 See Chapter 3, sub-chapter on *De* Facto *Entities and International Humanitarian Law,* at 59–61.

25 The applicability of human rights to ANSAs will be treated extensively in Chapter 4 on *Obligations and Accountability of Armed Non-State Actors in International Human Rights Law.*

26 For an impressive number of agreements to which Taiwan participates, see *Hsiao*, 734. For Sandesh Sivakumaran, 'Binding Armed Opposition Groups' (2006) 55 ICLQ 369, 390–91, 'as de facto entities in control of a portion of territory have the competence to enter into treaties relating to the territory under their control'. See also *Von Glahn* 1986, 106 and *Rudolf*, 135. Nonetheless such treaties are usually 'on administrative and technical issues', *van Essen*, 46. Opposite Anthony Aust, *Modern Treaty Law and Practice* (CUP 2007) 61–2, although accepting the treaty-making capacity of the Turkish Republic of Northern Cyprus (hereinafter TRNC).

27 *Jennings and Watts*, 553, *Schoiswohl* 2001, 64–5 and *Brownlie*, 87.

28 See *Ago*, 139 ff., *ILC* 1975, 98–9, Stephan Talmon, *Recognition of Governments in International Law: With Particular Reference to Governments in Exile* (Clarendon Press 1998) 32 and *Schoiswohl* 2004, 257.

entities and consequently gave, sometimes, precedence to the principle of effectiveness, as long as other rules or principles (especially of a *jus cogens* quality) are accommodated.

As a principle of international law effectiveness denotes the adaptation of law to realities and status quo.[29] In light of the under-development of international law (and society), effectiveness was a useful tool of law's adaptation to international realities (*ex factis jus oritur*). But the steadily increasing reach of law in a variety of international relations as well as its relatively current inclination towards value- and justice-orientated goals (evidenced by the emergence of peremptory norms) appears to cause the retraction of effectiveness, although it has retained a (significant) place in international legal discourse.[30]

According to the implied mandate/state of necessity doctrine certain acts of the *de facto* regime might be valid *ab initio*, provided that they are of an apolitical nature or relevant to the everyday life in the territory (acts of normal administration).[31] The ICJ has endorsed this doctrine in the *Legal Consequences for States of the Continued Presence of South Africa in Namibia (South West Africa) notwithstanding Security Council Resolution 276 (1970)*[32], holding that

> ... non-recognition of South Africa's administration of the Territory should not result in depriving the people of Namibia of any advantages derived from international co-operation. In particular, while official acts performed by the Government of South Africa on behalf of or concerning Namibia ... are illegal and invalid, this invalidity cannot be extended to those acts, such as, for instance, the registration of births, deaths and marriages, the effects of which can be ignored only to the detriment of the inhabitants of the Territory.[33]

Consequently, this doctrine appears to apply in civil (and private international) law issues and acts of organs of *de facto* entities relative to such relationships. It might, however, be difficult at times to draw definite lines on the (il)legality of certain acts of the entity.[34] Therefore, the doctrine itself creates insecurity and might be applied ad hoc and according

29 *Milano* 2004, 3 and Theodore Christakis, 'The State as a "Primary Fact": Some Thoughts on the Principle of Effectiveness' in Marcelo Cohen (ed.), *Secession-International Law Perspectives* (CUP, 2006) 139 ff.

30 See *Milano* 2004, 44–5.

31 *Ruda*, 460, *Roth*, 155–9 and *Schoiswohl* 2004, 270 ff. Thomas M. Franck and Nigel S. Rodley, 'Legitimacy and Legal Rights of Revolutionary Movements with Special Reference to the Peoples Revolutionary Government of South Vietnam' (1970) 45 N.Y.U.L.Rev. 679, 693, do not differentiate on the nature of acts, as long as 'they vest within the area of the regime's effective control'.

32 (Advisory Opinion) [1971] ICJ Rep 56. See also the Separate Opinion of Judge Castro, ICJ Rep 218–9, the (more expanding) Separate Opinion of Judge Petrén, ICJ Rep 134 and 137 and the representatives of the Netherlands and USA, ICJ Pleadings Vol. II, 130 and 503 respectively. It was also accepted by the European Court in *Loizidou v Turkey* (App no 15318/89) Reports 1996-VI [45] and acknowledged by the ILC, *Responsibility Commentary*, 115.

33 *Aust* 2010, 21, refers also to commercial matters.

34 See several examples in *Lauterpacht* 1947, 146 ff. and Jonathan L. Alder, 'The Unrecognized Government in the Courts of the United States' (1964–5) 5 Va. J. Int'l L. 36, 47 ff. See also the English courts' denial of validity of divorce decrees issued by Rhodesian courts in *Brownlie*, 100.

to circumstances. Obviously its practical application should not lead to violations of individual human rights of the inhabitants in addition to those who have been expelled,[35] because it would run counter to its initial existence.

There is also support in doctrine and practice that ANSAs' actions can generate further effects:

> Rebels who have received no recognition of any kind may be regarded to some extent as having such powers (of government and administration of the area) … the rebel regime may be regarded as competent to perform local acts of administration, such as levying taxes and imposing custom duties, and may be regarded as entitled to exercise the powers of the *de iure* government in relation to contracts requiring performance in the territory under the control of the rebels.[36]

To the extent that such actions could require even a piece of legislation,[37] this could have a valid effect even after the disappearance of ANSAs. But the legitimacy and continuing validity of these (official) acts in the post-conflict environment by the national authorities would appear to depend on whether they are used for or constitute 'normal governmental functions'[38] with due respect for human (and constitutional) rights. If, on the other hand, the rebel aim is furthered, there are dimmer prospects for their validity and binding character.[39]

When the European Court of Human Rights was faced with the applicant's argument that 'no deprivation of liberty imposed by its agents might be regarded as "lawful" within the meaning of the Convention' as '"TRNC" was not a valid and recognised State under international law', it responded that

> it would not be consistent with … responsibility under the Convention if the adoption by the authorities of the 'TRNC' of civil, administrative or criminal law measures, or their

35 Yet some balancing might be necessary, as the Dissenting Opinion of Judge Baka in *Loizidou* reveals: ' … the principle has some application in the field of real property in a situation such as that pertaining in the "TRNC" where it can be said that the interests of the community required, if not necessitated, some form of regularisation'. Ultimately it was accepted by the Court in *Demopoulos and others v Turkey* (Apps nos 46113/99 et al) ECHR 2010 [116].

36 *Jennings and Watts*, 167–8 and Chris N. Okeke, *Controversial Subjects of Contemporary International Law* (Rotterdam University Press 1974) 171.

37 See *Chen*, 319–20, on several administrative acts and the corresponding pieces of legislation which were held valid, without the existence of recognition, during the period of the civil war in Spain. See also Zaim M. Nedjati, 'Acts of Unrecognized Governments' (1981) 30 ICLQ 388, 413.

38 Daniel Patrick O' Connell, *International Law* (2nd edn, Stevens 1970) 971. See also *Chen*, 316 and Robert D. Powers Jr., 'Insurgency and the Law of Nations' (1962) 16 JAG J. 55, 58.

39 *Alder*, 42.

> application or enforcement within that territory, were to be denied any validity or regarded as having no 'lawful' basis in terms of the Convention.[40]

Even more, the existence of laws/structures that would give the ability to the *de facto* entity to protect human rights could not be viewed as illegal.[41] Consequently it appears that effectiveness could permit a rather large variety of acts by *de facto* entities to be considered as valid and legal (with the serving character behind it as maintaining law and order and/or aiding the ANSA's cause pending) or, conversely, it could lead to accountability of such entities in cases where their actions infringed certain rights.[42]

Effectiveness would probably cause some sort of interactions with subjects of international law, but their consequences are less than crystal clear. It is possible though that at certain times these entities will only be treated as ANSAs in control of territory, without, necessarily, possessing the state-like function. In essence these entities are the predecessors of *de facto* entities and will be examined subsequently.

Armed Non-State Actors in Control of (a Certain) Territory

This category represents the 'classic' rebel group with a rather permanent control over certain territory (and possibly, but not necessarily, some form of basic administration), although the 'boundary' could change at times. These ANSAs trigger the applicability of Protocol II, on the conditions that control over territory is of a certain quality, that the 'parent' state has signed and ratified this treaty and that there is armed violence. The Protocol has been applicable, at times with the acknowledgement of the state-party as

40 *Foka v Turkey* (App no 28940/95) ECHR 24 June 2008 [81–3]. A similar argument was raised by the Cypriot government in *Demopoulos* [65], regarding the validity of a law (and institution) providing remedies for violations of the right to property. The Court, however, could not accept this argument [95 ff.], because the existence of such acts was the outcome of its previous judgments, see below, and, in a sense, it was required to be taken. Of course, we should not lose track of the fact that Turkey is still considered responsible for everything that goes on in Northern Cyprus, but it would be wrong to assume that different considerations would apply in the event of TRNC's accountability.

41 See *Cyprus v Turkey* (App no 25781/94) ECHR 2001-IV [98], concerning the need to have appropriate organs in order to ensure respect for human rights and, similarly, *Xenides-Arestis v Turkey* (App no 46347/99) ECHR 22 December 2005 [40], with regard to remedies on the violations of the rights to home and property.

42 Note though that express ratification and approval of such acts by the government, particularly after the end of the armed conflict, could shift responsibility to the state, see Michael Akehurst, 'State Responsibility for the Wrongful Acts of Rebels – an Aspect of the South Rhodesian Problem' (1968–9) 43 British YBIL 49, 61.

well, to the conflicts in El Salvador,[43] Colombia,[44] Philippines,[45] Rwanda,[46] Sierra Leone[47] and Libya[48] and, possibly, Georgia (with regard to its breakaway territories[49]) and Russia (Chechnya[50]), while it could also fit, at times, in other conflicts such as those in Sudan,[51] Ethiopia (versus the Eritrean People's Liberation Front),[52] Darfur in Sudan,[53] Sri Lanka[54] and Nepal.[55]

---

43 See the preamble of UNGA Res 42/137 (7 December 1987); the opinion of Switzerland in *Sassòli and Bouvier*, 1383–5; the 'Letter Transmitting the Report of the Commission on the Truth for El Salvador' (1 April 1993) S/25500, 21; Theodor Meron, *Human Rights and Humanitarian Norms as Customary Law* (Clarendon Press 1989) 76; and *N. Higgins* 2010, 134. Opposite, Waldemar A. Solf, 'Comment' (1981–2) 31 Am.U.L.Rev. 927, 932.

44 See the position of the Constitutional Court of Colombia, Ruling No. C-225/95, Re: File No. L.A.T.-040 in *Sassòli and Bouvier*, 2266, the *Third Report on the Human Rights Situation in Colombia*, chapter IV, *Valencia*, 457–61 and *Solis*, 131. See also the self-assessment in the *ELN Declaration*. However, the government tends to deny that an armed conflict exists, *Carillo-Suarez*, 41–2 and Constantin von der Groeben, 'The Conflict in Colombia and the Relationship between Humanitarian Law and Human Rights Law in Practice: Analysis of the New Operational Law of the Colombian Armed Forces' (2011) 16 J.C.& S.L.141, 145 and 147 ff., although it appears that in the end it applies IHL.

45 Christopher Greenwood, 'A Critique of the Additional Protocols to the Geneva Conventions of 1949', in Christopher Greenwood, *Essays on War in International Law* (Cameron May 2006) 203 and *N. Higgins* 2010, 134. See also the relevant self-assessment in NDFP, 'Declaration of Undertaking to Apply the Geneva Conventions of 1949 and Protocol I of 1977', 9 August 1996 (hereinafter 1996 NDFP Declaration).

46 See art 4 of the Statute of the International Tribunal for Rwanda, Annex to UNSC 955 (8 November 1994) and *N. Higgins* 2010, 134.

47 Art 3 of the Statute of the Special Court for Sierra Leone, Annex to the Agreement between the United Nations and the Government of Sierra Leone on the Establishment of a Special Court for Sierra Leone, Freetown, 16 January 2002.

48 UN Doc A/HRC/17/44, 3 and 30.

49 *Mission to Caucasus Report*, 300. Georgia, however, seems to favour the international armed conflict option.

50 See the relevant assessment by the Constitutional Court of the Russian Federation, Judgment of July 31, 1995, Presidential Decrees and Federal Government's Resolution on the Situation in Chechnya in *Sassòli and Bouvier*, 2429–33, the Reply by the Federal Government to the Written Question Submitted by the Parliamentary Social Democratic Party, Document 13/437 (hereinafter Federal Government Reply) in *Sassòli and Bouvier*, 2415–6 as well as UNCHR Res 58 (2000), referring to the Protocol in the preamble. *N. Higgins* 2010, 135 is reluctant.

51 UNGA Res 48/147 (20 December 1993) [6], Res 49/198 (23 December 1994) [9] and Res 51/112 (12 December 1996) [9]. Significantly, Sudan was not a party to the Protocols at that time.

52 *Schindler*, 149 and John Baloro, 'International Humanitarian Law and Situations of Internal Armed Conflicts in Africa' (1992) 4 AFJICL 449, 460. However, there was a claim that the conflict should have been treated as international, due to the alien domination of Eritrea by Ethiopia.

53 See *Yihdego*, 52 and, similarly, *Sivakumaran* 2012, 191.

54 Implicitly opposite, Michael H. Hoffman, 'The Application of International Humanitarian Law in Sri Lanka: A Compliance Based Case Study on the Rules of War' (2001) 30 Israel Yrbk Hum Rts 209, 226.

55 But see *Somer*, 681, being more reluctant.

Unlike national liberation movements (and sometimes *de facto* entities), these actors do not necessarily represent a group with an identity distinct from the rest of the country's population. However, in many cases, the end of the conflict signalled their transformation into political parties and even their triumph in elections (in Nepal and El Salvador). In other cases (Sierra Leone) the ANSA lacked almost any legitimacy among the local population, especially since their brutal practices alienated a part of it. Not surprisingly external legitimacy was also lacking.

Depending on the duration of the conflict, whether actual or frozen, and the existence of administration of the territory they control, these ANSAs might resemble *de facto* entities. The LTTE in Sri Lanka has fought a long war which was frozen with the Agreement on a Ceasefire between the Government of the Democratic Socialist Republic of Sri Lanka and the Liberation Tigers of Tamil Eelam.[56] For a number of years the Tigers have administered a significant part of the territory. The recurrence of violence has altered the situation, since LTTE's control over territory was lost, until its final defeat. However, it appears that at no time was it considered a *de facto* entity and only political and/or legitimacy reasons could justify this outcome as well as the lack of interaction with third states. In essence *de facto* entities, which do not enjoy the support and/or recognition of a (usually neighbouring) state, might be treated as ANSAs falling under this heading.

Overall the key ingredient of these ANSAs is effectiveness (although more limited than that of *de facto* entities), while recognition, representativeness and legitimacy will only play a marginal role, if any at all. As such these actors are regulated mainly by the body of humanitarian law. However, it would be wrong to assume that their relevance to international law is necessarily confined to this legal regime. Their acts pertaining to the administration of the controlled territory could be subject to human rights standards. Furthermore, they might be held accountable for breaches of the law of nations. For the ILC, the definition of ANSAs in Protocol II could be taken as a guide for the notion of 'insurrectional movements' in the State Responsibility art 10,[57] showing therefore that the previous conduct of the ANSA in control of territory can be the basis of liability of the future state-to-be or the new government of the state. Roberto Ago endorsed not only the international responsibility of insurrectional movements but also their character as a subject of international law.[58] While it can be contested whether these ANSAs have any status in international law, it is, nevertheless, certain that they can be disassociated

---

56 22 February 2002 (hereinafter Sri Lanka Ceasefire).

57 *Responsibility Commentary*, 51. See also the similar proposition of Czechoslovakia in 'Comments of Governments on Part One of the Draft Articles on State Responsibility for Internationally Wrongful Acts' (1981) YILC Vol. II Part One 71, 73. Yet this should not be taken to exclude the conduct of ANSAs without control of territory, see Chile in 'Observations and Comments of Governments on Chapters I, II and III of Part 1 of the Draft Articles on State Responsibility for Internationally Wrongful Acts' (1980) YILC Vol. II Part One 87, 98 and Marco Sassòli, 'State Responsibility for Violations of International Humanitarian Law' (2002) 84 IRRC 401, 410.

58 *Ago*, 129 ff. and Hazem Atlam, 'National Liberation Movements and International Responsibility' in Marina Spinedi and Bruno Simma (eds), *United Nations Codification of State Responsibility* (Oceana Publications 1987) 35. But see *Responsibility Commentary*, 50, referring to the state as ' … the only subject of international law to which responsibility can be attributed'.

from other ANSAs which do not even have the resources nor the capacity to control any territory in a permanent manner.

Common Article 3 Armed Non-State Actors

This category represents the majority of ANSAs (and internal conflicts) around the globe. Such conflicts are regulated as a matter of treaty law mainly by common article 3 and the Rome Statute. These entities create many significant problems and they are, on many occasions, equated with terrorist organizations, carrying, thus, all the problems and consequences that such a designation implies. Examples of this kind of ANSA were or are operating in Chile,[59] Burma/Myanmar,[60] Turkey (the Kurds),[61] Mexico (the Zapatistas movement), Guatemala,[62] Thailand, China, Iraq,[63] Syria[64] and other corners worldwide. In these relatively low-intensity conflicts, there are substantial differences in power between the state army and the ANSA and a factual inequality between the belligerents, creating at times an asymmetric conflict.

Armed resistance movements in occupied territories could also be classified in this sub-category provided of course that they have the minimum characteristics required for an ANSA.[65] However this is probably the exception: if the movement belongs to a party to the (international) conflict, in accordance with the four criteria of art 4.2(b) of the Third Geneva Convention or otherwise art 43 of Protocol I, then it forms part of the machinery of a state and accountability for its actions falls under the State Responsibility articles.

It is equally possible that a group of mercenaries could form (or be included in) an ANSA. According to art 47.1 of Protocol I, which applies only to international conflicts, mercenaries are not entitled to combatant and/or prisoner-of-war (hereinafter POW) status, but mercenarism as such is not prohibited: such a role was accorded to other treaties. The

---

59 German Democratic Republic, *1977 Records* Vol. 5, 136. See also the assessment of the criminal Appeal Court of Santiago in *Sassòli and Bouvier*, 1360.

60 UNGA Res 47/144 (18 December 1992) [10] and 51/117 (12 December 1996) [15].

61 Sadi Cayci, 'Countering Terrorism and the Law of Armed Conflict: the Turkish Experience' (2002) 8 I.P. 333, 340 and William Abresch, 'A Human Rights Law of Internal Armed Conflict: The European Court of Human Rights in Chechnya' (2005) 16 EJIL 741, 755.

62 UNGA Res 40/140 (13 December 1985) preamble and UNSG, 'Note Transmitting the Report of the Director of the United Nations Mission for the Verification of Human Rights and of Compliance with the Commitments of the Comprehensive Agreement on Human Rights in Guatemala' (1 March 1995) A/49/856, 31.

63 *Solis*, 153–4.

64 UNHRC, 'Report of the Independent International Commission of Inquiry on the Syrian Arab Republic' (16 August 2013) A/HRC/24/46, 7 and 18, indirectly, and Carla Del Ponte, 'The case of Syria' in Michel Veuthey and Gian Luca Beruto (eds), *Respecting International Humanitarian Law: Challenges and Responses* (Franco Angeli 2014) 53.

65 See this possibility in *Mastorodimos* 2010, 459, with further references.

OAU Convention for the Elimination of Mercenarism in Africa,[66] in addition to a direct prohibition of mercenarism, follows the definition of Protocol I, and potentially it could be interpreted as applying only to international conflicts.[67] The International Convention against the Recruitment, Use, Financing, and Training of Mercenaries[68] is more expansive and can cover civil conflicts.[69] However, the low participation of states in the UN treaty might suggest that there is no established international *customary* rule (on prohibition of mercenary activity) for internal conflicts,[70] although the international community is probably moving in this direction, to the extent that mercenaries are considered as potential violators of legal standards. Mercenaries have fought alongside ANSAs during the secessionist movement of Katanga in the 1960s, in Biafra, Angola, Mozambique and Liberia/Sierra Leone.[71] They could even become a party to a (non-international) armed conflict, although this is more of a theoretical possibility, as mercenaries (or a group thereof) are usually integrated in the command structure of the ANSA. There is actually no compelling reason, apart from legitimacy, to differentiate between ANSAs and a mercenary army: the only substantial difference is that mercenarism is partially prohibited in international law while participation in ANSAs is not.[72]

Private military companies differ from 'typical' ANSAs, because they are a business enterprise that was created under the law of a state. So, in essence, they are organized entities, recognized as a legal person and, therefore, being legitimate to perform the duties that their country of origin allows them to. As such they are not bound by humanitarian law, unless they are integrated into a state's army (in an international armed conflict) either

---

66 (adopted 3 July 1977, entered into force 22 April 1985) OAU Document CM/817 (XXIX) Annex II Rev.1, art 1.

67 *Contra* Luisa Vierucci, 'Private Military and Security Companies in Non-International Armed Conflicts: "Ius ad Bellum" and "Ius in Bello" Issues' in Francesco Francioni and Natalino Ronzitti (eds) *War by Contract: Human Rights, Humanitarian Law and Private Contractors* (OUP 2011) 253. See also UN Doc A/HRC/17/44, 65–8, who takes for granted that this treaty applied to the non-international armed conflict in Libya.

68 (adopted 4 December 1989, entered into force 20 October 2001) 2163 UNTS 75, art 1.

69 'Report of the Ad Hoc Committee on the Drafting of an International Convention against the Recruitment, Use, Financing and Training of Mercenaries' (24 March 1987) A/42/43, 3 and Edward Kwakwa, 'The Current Status of Mercenaries in the Law of Armed Conflict' (1990) 14 Hastings Int'l & Comp.L.Rev. 67, 85.

70 But see UNCHR, 'Report on the Question of the Use of Mercenaries as a Means of Violating Human Rights and Impeding the Exercise of the Right of Peoples to Self-determination, Submitted by Mr. Enrique Bernales Ballesteros, Special Rapporteur, Pursuant to Commission Resolution 1995/5 and Economic and Council Resolution 1995/254' (17 January 1996) E/CN.4/1996/27, 26 '[t]he condemnation of mercenarism is a universally accepted fact, even in those States which have not yet specifically categorized it as a crime.'

71 See S/RES/169 [1], UNCHR, 'Report on the Question of the Use of Mercenaries as a Means of Violating Human Rights and Impeding the Exercise of the Right of Peoples to Self-determination, Submitted by Mr. Enrique Bernales Ballesteros (Peru), Special Rapporteur, Pursuant to Commission Resolution 1990/7' (27 December 1990) E/CN.4/1991/14, 5–6 and *Liberia Truth and Reconciliation Report*, 327 ff.

72 In essence, mercenarism is more a *jus ad bellum* issue rather than a *jus in bello* consideration.

affiliated to the armed forces of a party to the conflict (in the sense of a paramilitary/militia group or as civilians accompanying the armed forces) or as part of them (armed forces).[73] They could also form part of the state army or an ANSA in a non-international armed conflict. The (still) theoretical possibility of becoming an autonomous party to a non-international conflict cannot be excluded[74] and would not play any significant role in their accountability: its individual members do not have a right to participate in hostilities (as any individual would), unless they are integrated in a state army. Whether they, additionally, are classified as mercenaries under international law is a matter of assessment in accordance with existing definitions. Initially there was a tendency to regard such companies as only a different face of mercenarism.[75] Nevertheless, this appears to be changing[76] and their legitimacy is increasing, not only because the privatization of the use of force is becoming acceptable but also because it corresponds to present-day needs (for example protection of vessels in the high seas against pirates, use of relevant companies' services by the United Nations).

Territorial control is not a decisive factor for the factual importance of the ANSA and for their impact on people and material things. Hezbollah (and Hamas in Palestine before the 2006 elections) offer examples of political parties in the respective territories, having a significant military wing and exercising segments of state power in parallel with the official administration. In any case, even without significant territorial control, ANSAs are able to generate a non-international armed conflict. If, however, any of the above-mentioned groups (armed resistance movements, mercenaries or private military companies) occupy territory, then Protocol II might be applicable, with all the entailed consequences.

The question of status of ANSAs without control of territory appears to be a difficult puzzle. Quite apart from the classical approach where the state is the only subject of international law,

---

73 See also The Montreux Document on Pertinent International Legal Obligations and Good Practices for States Related to Operations of Private Military and Security Companies during Armed Conflict (2008) 12. In this case, this is a matter of state responsibility. However, as Lindsey Cameron, 'Private Military Companies: their Status under International Humanitarian Law and its Impact on their Regulation' (2006) 88 IRRC 573, 583, rightly writes, 'the whole point of privatization is precisely ... to devolve on the private sector what was previously the preserve of government authorities. It would seem to be at variance with the philosophy of outsourcing to contend that private military companies are nonetheless members of a state's armed forces.'

74 *Vierucci*, 252.

75 *Witness to Truth: Report of the Sierra Leone Truth and Reconciliation Commission* Vol. 2 (2004) 89 (hereinafter Sierra Leone Truth and Reconciliation Report) and UNCHR, 'Use of Mercenaries as a Means of Violating Human Rights and Impeding the Exercise of the Right of Peoples to Self-determination' (24 December 2003) E/CN.4/2004/15, 14.

76 See UNHRC, 'Report of the Working Group on the Use of Mercenaries as a Means of Violating Human Rights and Impeding the Exercise of the Right of Peoples to Self-determination' (2 July 2010) A/HRC/15/25, 11 and 'Report of the Working Group on the Use of Mercenaries as a Means of Violating Human Rights and Impeding the Exercise of the Right of Peoples to Self-determination' (4 July 2011) A/HRC/18/32, 15.

> the needs of the community determine the nature of an entity as a participant of international law … As the needs change, so do the international legal participants … Given that there are a large number of internal armed conflicts; that armed opposition groups play an important role in these conflicts and hence in the international community; that internal armed conflicts result in human rights abuses, refugees and internally displaced persons; and that the international community rates the protection of human rights as significant, the needs of the community require that the actions of armed opposition groups be effectively regulated.[77]

If the meaning of community involves only the archetypical subjects of international law, Fergus Green[78] is right to contend that 'the expansion of non-state actors would therefore appear to depend on the interests and needs of *states* to interact with non-state actors (but not vice versa)'. Otherwise, it is also the interests of individuals and peoples, among others, that could accord a sort of personality to an entity. Giving the prevalent role of humanitarian law in relation to the interests of individuals, the need to objectify ANSAs in international law appears significant.

Regardless of community needs, it is not certain whether it suffices that 'the subjects must be the direct and intended addressee of the rights and duties'[79] or whether some form of (community) acceptance is also needed.[80] Shaw[81] refers also to participation which denotes 'some degree of influence upon the international plane'. As we will examine later, there is an almost unanimous opinion *nowadays* that ANSAs have become the intended addressees of duties, at least for IHL purposes, a move dictated not so much by states' interests but by the needs of individuals. This community acceptance, though, is denied with regard to personality.[82] However, the initial concern of the negotiating states was the

---

77 *Sivakumaran* 2006, 373.

78 At 54.

79 Bin Cheng, 'Introduction to Subjects of International Law' in Mohammed Bedjaoui (ed.), *International Law: Achievements and Prospects* (UNESCO 1991) 29.

80 *Shaw*, 177. See also *F. Green*, 71 ff. referring, similarly, to factual capacity to possess certain international rights/duties as well as recognition and conferral of rights and responsibilities and Alfred P. Rubin, 'The Status of Rebels under the Geneva Conventions of 1949' (1972) 21 ICLQ 472, 475.

81 Ibid. See also *van Essen*, 39 and 49 as well as the more extensive taxonomy of *Gal-Or*, 136, including, among others, the capacity of law-making, law adjudication and law enforcement.

82 Common art 3 to the Geneva Conventions; arts 19 and 22.6, respectively, of the 1954 Hague Convention and its Second Protocol (adopted 26 March 1999, entered into force 9 March 2004) 2253 UNTS 172; art 1.6 of the Protocol on Prohibitions or Restrictions on the Use of Mines, Booby-Traps and Other Devices as Amended on 3 May 1996 (Protocol II as Amended on 3 May 1996) Annexed to the Convention on Prohibitions or Restrictions on the Use of Certain Conventional Weapons Which May be Deemed to Be Excessively Injurious or to Have Indiscriminate Effects (adopted 3 May 1996, entered into force 3 December 1998) 2048 UNTS 93; and art 1.6 of the Convention on Prohibitions or Restrictions on the Use of Certain Conventional Weapons Which May be Deemed to Be Excessively Injurious or to Have Indiscriminate Effects, Amendment Article 1 (adopted 21 December 2001, entered into force 18 May 2004) 2260 UNTS 82 (Amended Article 1 to the CCW). See also art 4.3 of the Optional Protocol to the Convention on the Rights of the

possibility that the automatic applicability of certain laws of war would accord belligerency status to an insurgent entity. Such status could have indirect ramifications outside humanitarian law, such as the possibility of neutrality towards the incumbent government and the impossibility of trying rebels for treason, at least during the war. Later on, though, as belligerency recognition tended to be confined to textbooks, the concern of states was equally tied to international legitimacy. Protocol II even dropped any reference to 'parties to the conflict' in order not to suggest that rebels had equal status with governmental forces. All those fears, though, do not preclude the possibility that ANSAs might have an international legal personality for *IHL purposes*.[83] The majority of the academic community also seems to accept[84] that some form of status is accorded to ANSAs in general, as parties to a conflict, including those without any control over territory. But even so, while their character as passive subjects of international law is rather uncontested, their capacity as active subjects/participants to international law is debatable and exceptional; not only are there not any appropriate procedures but the possibility that ANSAs can create law (or at least contribute to law's development) is constantly denied.[85]

In conclusion it appears that the international status of ANSAs in general, and common article 3 ANSAs in particular, depends on how we define the term 'personality', although it appears possible to argue that they possess such personality for certain and limited purposes. Due to their enormous factual importance, as exercising power over individuals, and in combination with the needs of the community to regulate their conduct, certain primary rules (should) apply to them, thus creating accountability in the event of their breach. Yet it is not possible in general to deny the instrumentality of states (and international organizations), as their consent, recognition or acquiescence is a significant factor in conferring the status of ANSA as well as the extent of their obligations and accountability in international law. We will now turn to an examination of certain branches of international law which are particularly important for the needs of the community, namely humanitarian and human rights law.

Child on the Involvement of Children in Armed Conflict (adopted 25 May 2000, entered into force 12 February 2002) 2173 UNTS 222 (hereinafter Optional Protocol) as well arts 7.1 and 15.2 of the Kampala Convention. Yet see the acceptance of Burma, *1949 Records* Vol. II-B, 329, that '[the ANSA] is thus being, rightly or wrongly, given a place in international law' and 330, 'the mere inclusion of this Article in an international Convention will automatically give the insurgents a status as high as the legal status which is denied to them'.

83 Similarly *Siotis* 1958, 218; *Castren*, 87; Denise Plattner, 'La Portée Juridique des Déclarations de Respect du Droit International Humanitaire qui Emanent de Mouvements en Lutte dans un Conflit Armé', (1984–5) 18 RBDI 298, 320; and *Sassòli and Bouvier*, 266.

84 See, indicatively, G.I.A.D. Draper, *The Red Cross Conventions* (Stevens 1958) 17; *Solf* 1981–2, 931; *Schoiswohl* 2001, 52; and *Provost*, 283.

85 See this discussion in sub-chapter *Customary International Law*, at 90–91, and the possibility in sub-chapter *Common Article 3 Agreements*, at 66, that a common article 3 agreement is a form of (international) law-making.

Chapter 3
Obligations and Accountability of Armed Non-State Actors in International Humanitarian Law

Introduction

International humanitarian law is directly concerned with situations of armed conflict, including non-international ones. The latter type of conflict is by definition a situation which includes, at least, one ANSA as a warring party. The insertion of common article 3 into the Geneva Conventions was intended to limit the government's leeway in its use of means and methods during such conflicts. The reference to 'each Party to the conflict [which] shall be bound to apply' suggests that the ANSA would also have the same obligations as the government,[1] although the comments of several states during negotiations reveal a different intention or serious ambiguity, to such extent that the final text might not match their views. The US/UK,[2] 'proposed to replace the words "each Party to the conflict" by the word "these" referring to the High Contracting Parties',[3] while for Burma[4] the Convention ' … proposed an impossible condition: to bind down a non-contracting party … '. Other

---

1 The provision on the conclusion of agreements also suggests the binding character of the article to ANSAs, otherwise it would not be possible to ' … bring into force … all or part of the *other* provisions … '.

2 Some years later the UK has tried to exclude art 19, which has almost identical content with common article 3, from the ambit of the 1954 Hague Convention, because it would be rendered inapplicable, *Actes de la Conférence Convoquée par l'Organisation des Nations Unies pour l'Education, la Science et la Culture* (Staatsdrukkerij- en Uitgeverijbedrijf 1961) 188 (hereinafter Actes de la Conférence). During these negotiations, there was little discussion on the matters that culminated around common article 3, although India, *Actes de la Conférence*, 123, expressed some caution on how a non-contracting party would have to apply the treaty's content.

3 *1949 Records* Vol. II-B, 90. See also the Australian consideration, *1949 Records* Vol. II-B, 94. For Monaco, *1949 Records* Vol. II-B, 79 'the rebels *might* be regarded as already bound by the Convention … because the humanitarian provisions of the Geneva Conventions are of a super-contractual character … ' (emphasis added). On the opposing side see Greece, *1949 Records* Vol. II-B, 94, 'insurgents and even bandits were obviously nationals of some State, and were thereby bound by the obligations undertaken by the latter'. Significantly its position in the context of the 1954 Hague Convention, *Actes de la Conférence*, 188–9, seemed to envisage a declaration from the part of the insurgent entity.

4 *1949 Records* Vol. II-B, 328.

states were contradicting themselves, such as Switzerland,[5] for which 'the formula "each Party to the conflict" was not acceptable as only the *de jure* governments were bound by the Convention. This term should be replaced by "High Contracting Parties"'; later on, though, it supported that 'where the term "Parties to the conflict" … refer […] to Parties to a non-international conflict, Article 2A enumerates the only obligations by which they are bound'.[6] In the end, the provision was voted by 34 votes to 12 with 1 abstention.[7]

In the initial negotiations phase, where the discussions centred on the possibility of applying all Conventions, several states indicated that the volition or actual conduct of the ANSA would be necessary for their (reciprocal) application.[8] Furthermore, any mention of belligerency recognition[9] would imply that the ANSA has not only accepted but applied in fact the standards of the laws of war. These comments do not exclude the possibility that humanitarian law *could* be binding on ANSAs. In all probability, though, the intention of (at least some of) the parties was not to pronounce on the potential applicability of the Conventions to ANSA conduct but rather to exempt their own activities from (automatic) international scrutiny. Obviously such interpretation could defeat the object and purpose of the treaty, let alone that reciprocity would confer a measure of legitimacy to ANSAs. In addition, once states accepted that there was an armed conflict, usually after some form of leverage by outside parties (such as the ICRC), they had a distinct incentive to place obligations on ANSAs regardless of the latter's volition. Consequently it appears absurd to free ANSAs from accountability. But overall, it is far from evident that ANSAs would *automatically* be bound to apply these rules and this could explain why it was suggested that only the final text should be taken into account.[10]

The immediate practice after the conclusion of the conventions shows that states were reluctant to apply common article 3.[11] The most plausible explanation is that they did not want to limit their freedom of action, but a reason might be that the article was thought to

---

5 *1949 Records* Vol. II-B, 99.

6 *1949 Records* Vol. II-B, 335. Similarly see the confusing comments of Denmark in *1949 Records* Vol. II-B, 99 and 332.

7 *1949 Records* Vol. II-B, 339. The similar provision of the 1954 Hague Convention was voted in with a 62 per cent (instead of 72 per cent in common article 3), but with fewer opposing votes and a 30 per cent abstention, see *Actes de la Conférence*, 219.

8 See Romania, *1949 Records* Vol. II-B, 11 (subjection of its applicability subject to its observance), US, 12 (the insurgent civil authority agrees to be bound by the provisions of the Convention), Italy, 46 (the party must apply it in fact) and Australia, 50 (both Parties to the conflict must declare themselves bound by the Convention). In fact the initial Stockholm text, provided for reciprocity with regard to the Third and Fourth Convention, unlike the others, *1949 Records* Vol. I, 47, 61, 73 and 113, respectively.

9 See Australia, *1949 Records* Vol. II-B, 15 as well as Spain in *Actes de la Conférence*, 117.

10 Frédéric Siordet, 'Les Conventions de Genève et la Guerre Civile' (1950) 32 RIRC 104, 105. Additionally, the lack of clarity in the preparatory works tends to diminish their importance and to obscure, rather than clarify, the meaning of the article.

11 See David P. Forsythe, 'Legal Management of Internal War: The 1977 Protocol on Non-International Armed Conflicts' (1978) 72 AJIL 272, 275–6.

be non-binding for ANSAs.[12] Scholar comments, on the other hand, were acknowledging that ANSAs would be bound.[13]

Protocol II does not make a reference similar to that of common article 3 to 'parties to the conflict'. Yet the understanding of the majority, at the negotiation table, was that the insurgent entity would be bound automatically.[14] There were states, though, which did not accept that ANSAs would be equally obliged by the treaty.[15] The great difference from 1949 appears that the Western bloc has changed attitudes and the objectors came from 'third world' states that were specially affected or prone to revolutionary changes. Some states have also argued in favour of a declaration of intention by the ANSA to observe humanitarian rules,[16] thus implying that it could be bound, but not automatically. Overall it was certainly not ' ... abundantly clear to states that provisions of international humanitarian law applied equally to all parties ... '[17] but neither was it clear that 'the view opposed to any extension of legal rights or duties to rebels was far more widespread'.[18] Instead we could refer to a growing community acceptance from the core subjects of international law, although yet not unanimous.

In more recent years it became well settled that 'mandatory provisions of common art. 3 expressly bind and apply equally to both parties to internal conflicts, that is government and dissident forces'.[19] The language of Protocol II as Amended on 3 May 1996 is also instructive as to the volition of the drafters, since it refers to 'the application of the provisions of this Protocol to parties to a conflict ... ' (art 1.6) as well as to the responsibility of each party to the conflict (art 3.2), and also revisits the formulation of

---

12 See the example of France in *Provost*, 157. However see the opposite position of Congo, 'Public Statement of Prime Minister of the Democratic Republic of Congo, October 21, 1964' (1965) 59 AJIL 616.

13 Indicatively, *Siotis* 1958; *Draper* 1958, 17; and *Castren*, 86. On the other hand see Raymund T. Yingling and Robert W. Ginnane, 'The Geneva Conventions of 1949' (1952) 46 AJIL 393, 396; Richard Baxter, 'Forces for Compliance with the Law of War' (1964) 58 Am. Soc'y Int'l L. Proc. 82, 87; and Gerhard Von Glahn, 'The Protection of Human Rights in Time of Armed Conflicts' (1971) 1 Israel Yrbk Hum Rts 208, 217.

14 Belgium, *1977 Records* Vol. 7, 76, Canada, Vol. 8, 205, Zaire (currently known as the Democratic Republic of Congo (hereinafter DRC)), Vol. 7, 219; UK, Vol. 8, 236; Ukraine, Vol. 9, 239; and Australia, Vol. 4, 17.

15 Colombia, *1977 Records* Vol. 7, 79 and Pakistan, Vol. 8, 225. Iraq's comments, Vol. 9, 235, show that it also did not adhere to the applicability of IHL to ANSAs, while the Bangladeshi view, Vol. 5, 186, implied the same.

16 Pakistan, *1977 Records* Vol. 8, 226. See also Brazil accepting, on the one hand, the binding force of the Protocol, Vol. 5, 98, but expecting recognition by the adverse Party in order to apply, Vol. 8, 286.

17 Sandesh Sivakumaran, 'Courts of Armed Opposition Groups: Fair Trials or Summary Justice?' (2009) 7 JICJ 489, 497.

18 *Cassese* 1981, 423.

19 *Abella v Argentina* [174]. See also *Prosecutor v Sam Hinga Norman* (Decision on Preliminary Motion Based on Lack of Jurisdiction (Child Recruitment)) SCSL-2004-14-AR72(E) (31 May 2004) [22], the Constitutional Court of Colombia in *Sassòli and Bouvier*, 2267 and the *IDI 1999 Resolution*, art II.

common article 3 in art 1.3.[20] The follow-up from the Second Protocol to the 1954 Hague Convention and the Amended Article 1 to the CCW only corroborate the firm belief of the international community towards this path.

However, the mechanism under which ANSAs are bound by IHL is somewhat obscure, since the ANSAs cannot become parties to the relevant conventions (with the sole and limited exception of national liberation movements). This is an important part of our discourse on the accountability of ANSAs,[21] because it will define not only their international status, if any, but also the basis and extent of their obligations and accountability. The following part will shed some light on this discussion, by distinguishing the obligations of ANSAs based on their status or active volition (direct) or through their passive volition or regardless of it (indirect). The rest of the chapter will be dedicated to the primary and secondary rules, by examining on the one hand the richness of primary rules, at times going beyond the objective capabilities of the ANSA and, in other instances, being under-comprehensive. The scope of secondary rules on accountability will also be examined as they are a necessary part of the enforcement of primary rules.

The Legal Basis of Obligations of Armed Non-State Actors

ANSAs cannot become parties to international treaties although they are considered to be bound by international humanitarian law. There are two possible ways to explain this outcome. The first one relates to their own status, which gives them a role as a subject of international law. We have seen that while this is dubious for common article 3 ANSAs as well as ANSAs in control of territory, *de facto* entities have a better prospect in this regard. If they lack any status, their obligations could be explained on the basis that they elect to be bound through alternative law-making means to which they have access. These two possibilities appear to give a certain role to ANSAs, since their status or active volition would appear to be the vehicle of their obligations. The alternative is that the ANSA becomes bound through the medium of a state, probably with the latter's consent. This does not necessarily mean that the ANSA lacks any autonomy in this regard. But it is probable that its freedom of action would be more restrained and within a pre-existing corpus. These two alternatives will be examined successively.

---

20 See also arts 5.3, 5.4, 9.2, 10.2 and 10.4. The negotiating records reveal a similar understanding, see, indicatively, the positions of China and Cuba in the Review Conference of the State Parties to the Convention on Prohibitions or Restrictions on the Use of Certain Conventional Weapons Which May Be Deemed to Be Excessively Injurious or to Have Indiscriminate Effects, 4th Meeting (3 October 1995) CCW/CONF.I/SR.4, 8 and 14.

21 Similarly Jann K. Kleffner, 'The Applicability of International Humanitarian law to Organized Armed Groups' (2011) 93 IRRC 443, 444, noting also that the strategies for ensuring compliance will depend on how the ANSA is bound.

Direct Obligations

Since the idea of binding non-contracting parties was considered a juridical heresy,[22] it is natural to examine whether ANSAs can become bound through their own status or by their active volition. This has been denied, on the one hand, during the negotiations for several international conventions, as it was rejected that any ANSA act (for example declaration of intention) could bring the convention into operation for the ANSA. On the other hand, though, states and other actors on the international plane have signed agreements with ANSAs or attached a certain normative significance to unilateral acts of ANSAs. Similarly *de facto* entities were occasionally considered to carry a status that increases the extent of their humanitarian law obligations to the level of a participant in an international armed conflict. This last option is examined in the following part.

De Facto *Entities and International Humanitarian Law*

We have noted previously the existing, mainly doctrinal, support that *de facto* regimes constitute subjects of international law. The question then is whether we should distinguish *de facto* regimes (especially *de facto* entities) from other ANSAs and consider whether they are (or have become) parties to an international armed conflict.

The first draft of what would then become common article 3[23] suggests that the negotiating states to the Geneva Conventions foresaw the possibility that *de facto* regimes could become parties to international conflicts, subject to a declaration and compliance on the part of ANSAs: the description of the non-state parties to a non-international conflict coincides significantly with that of a *de facto* regime. However, this proposition was dropped in favour of a more modest (and all-inclusive as regards ANSAs) provision, where ANSAs did not have a role regarding the applicability of IHL.

The cases of partially recognized entities (as states) have been solved in the past pragmatically. The various divided states, such as Korea, Vietnam, Yemen and Germany, were admitted as parties to the Geneva Conventions 'because of the eagerness of the Swiss Federal Council … to have as many parties to the Convention as possible'.[24] Therefore, their treatment as states for IHL purposes is not contestable. The problematic cases are those entities which exhibit, to a certain extent, the characteristics of a state but are not recognized as such; or those cases of entities that have been recognized by some states but for which the issue of relations with other states is unresolved. Obviously enough then, even for states that were admitted as parties to the Geneva Conventions, the status of conflicts before that moment is not self-evident. The case of Korea represents, exactly, the first appearance of this problem.

Before the outbreak of the conflict, Korea was already *de facto* divided. The conflict was generally considered to be international,[25] although it is unlikely that the status of the

22 *Siordet* 1950, 120.

23 *1949 Records* Vol. II-B, 124.

24 *Baxter* 1974, 521.

25 *Castren*, 70–1, Vaughn A. Ary, 'Concluding Hostilities: Humanitarian Provisions in Cease-fire Agreements' (1995) 148 Mil.L.Rev. 186, 225 and *Detter*, 46. For Julian G. Verplaetse, 'The *Ius in*

basic fighting parties (North and South Korea) mattered; instead it was the involvement of individual states (China) and international organizations (United Nations) that internationalized the conflict. On the other hand, the different segments of Vietnam, despite being parties to the Geneva Conventions,[26] treated the conflict differently for reasons relating to the status of South Vietnam as well.[27] Since North Vietnam denied its involvement in South Vietnam, there was technically no armed conflict.[28] But as soon as there were clashes between North and South Vietnam/US, there was an international conflict,[29] despite non-recognition between the parties to the conflict or lack of acknowledgement by one of the parties. POW status was granted to North Vietnamese,[30] unlike South Vietnamese and US soldiers.[31] Consequently there was no real consensus, although the conflict between North and South Vietnam was to all appearances a clear case of *de facto* regimes being obliged to apply the Geneva Conventions in their mutual relations.

These two examples show that the purported international subjectivity of *de facto* entities is hardly an argument for the existence of an international conflict. Beyond these limited cases, in older and recent cases of conflicts between unrecognized secessionist entities and the parent state, there has been an overwhelming uniformity of opinion and practice towards the (initial) non-international character of the conflict.[32] Biafra and Katanga, in the past, were almost never[33] considered to be powers subject to the customary law of international armed conflict. The fact that there was not any pacified period did not really matter, because even the recent conflicts in South Ossetia, Abkhazia and, a little earlier,

---

Bello and Military Operations in Korea 1950–1953' (1963) 23 ZaöRV 679, 723, there was a '*de facto* agreement that the relevant provisions [of the Geneva Conventions] were *de facto* applicable to the operations'. But see *Schindler*, 129, for whom North Korea considered itself bound by common article 3 only and *Detter*, 48 on the similar position of the then USSR.

26 See International Committee of the Red Cross, 'The International Committee and the Vietnam Conflict' (1966) 6 IRRC 399.

27 See the positions of the USA and North Vietnam in Quincy Wright, 'Legal Aspects of the Viet-Nam Situation' (1966) 60 AJIL 750–2.

28 North Vietnam denied that a conflict existed even when it was bombarded by American forces, *Schindler*, 129.

29 Roger Pinto, 'Les Règles du Droit International Concernant la Guerre Civile' (1965) 114 Recueil des Cours 456. But see *Wright*, 756.

30 *Rubin*, 479. See also Rosalyn Higgins, 'Internal War and International Law' in Richard A. Falk and Cyril E. Black (eds), *The Future of the International Legal Order* Vol. III (Princeton University Press 1971) 92, on the position of the USA more generally.

31 Anonymous, 'The Geneva Convention and the Treatment of Prisoners of War in Vietnam' (1966–7) 80 Harv. L.Rev. 851, 858 ff.

32 Whether involvement by third parties could change the qualification of the conflict is a different issue, see *Mastorodimos* 2010, 461–2. Also the *de facto* applicability of the Geneva Conventions or a unilateral declaration in this regard by one (or all) of the fighting forces does not transform the nature of the conflict; only the extent of obligations.

33 Michel Veuthey, 'Les Conflits Armés de Character Non-internationals' in Antonio Cassese (ed.), *Current Problems of International Law: Essays on U.N. Law and on the Law of Armed Conflict* (Dott. A. Giuffrè 1975) 239 ff.; *Solf* 1981–2, 927; and *Moir*, 74 ff. See the exception of *Bothe* 1981–2, 901.

Chechnya were also termed as non-internationals.[34] The LTTE controlled territory and exercised governance in Sri Lanka to such an extent that it resembled a *de facto* entity, but it was never considered as such. Consequently, its purported international subjectivity and the possible applicability of certain international law norms to it do not appear to generate effects in IHL. There are actually only (policy) arguments to support a claim to extend the applicability of humanitarian law to *de facto* entities besides the rules applicable to non-international armed conflict, at least in those cases that they consider themselves bound. In many of the above-mentioned cases the armed forces of the *de facto* entity resembled a state army and, therefore, the potential for destructive effects is increased and the need for a more comprehensive corpus of rules might be compelling. Yet in the absence of positive practice, we cannot but consider them as subject to the same rules as other ANSAs.

It is to be noted that the Institut de Droit International,[35] in a different context, excluded from the ambit of civil wars 'armed conflicts between political entities which are separated by an international demarcation line or which have existed de facto as States over a prolonged period of time, or conflicts between any such entity and a State'. But this should not be taken to imply the status of an international armed conflict in the case of clashes between two such entities. From the existing partially recognized *de facto* entities, only the (unlikely possibility of) an armed conflict between Kosovo and Serbia could be a test of status as regards the participants and the character of the conflict.

There is also a logical argument to consider a *de facto* (secessionist) entity's clash with a third state as an international armed conflict, provided that the third state does not intervene at the genuine request of the government: a conflict beyond the borders of a state cannot be described as internal, while the opposing parties do not share the same 'nationality'.[36] Nonetheless, in such cases (that to the author's knowledge have not materialized so far) it is not the status of the *de facto* entity which changes the character to the conflict; it is rather the act of the third state beyond its borders that tends to call for a qualification of the conflict as international. Beyond this paradigm, any obligations of ANSAs could be predicated either on agreements with the opposing forces or unilateral declarations.

Agreements Between the Parties to the Conflict

The basic body of humanitarian law, the Geneva Conventions, provides for a whole series of agreements in the event that the opposing forces decide to proceed accordingly. The Third Geneva Convention only provides for 17 different special agreements as well as an article (6) regarding the general competence of the fighting parties to move beyond the ambit of the substantive obligations of the Convention. Such types of agreements would be open to national liberation movements and any other type of ANSAs in the event that they are classified as actors in an international armed conflict. There is also a paragraph in

34 Chapter 1, sub-chapter on *The Additional Protocol II of 1977*, at 47.

35 'The Principle of Non-Intervention in Civil Wars'- Resolution (1975) art 1.2b.

36 See the relevant argumentation in *Mastorodimos* 2010, 444–5. But 'when a State enters into conflict with a nongovernmental armed group located in the territory of a neighbouring State … not acting on behalf of a government, in the absence of two States opposing each other, there is no international armed conflict', *Lubanga* Judgment [541].

common article 3 that provides the competence for agreements in the context of a non-international armed conflict, while other types of agreements (on ceasefire and peace) are concluded with ANSAs as signatories. These conventional obligations, characterized as hybrid treaties,[37] will comprise the focus of the following sub-chapters.

Common Article 3 Agreements

Common article 3 of the Geneva Conventions[38] foresees the applicability of parts (or all the Geneva Conventions) 'by means of special agreements'. Such agreements could prove a useful tool for humanitarian protection, especially when there is controversy on the qualification of the conflict,[39] the applicability of certain rules and/or protective gaps of the law. In cases of concluding such agreements, the ANSA is bound directly, according to the well-known general principle of law '*pacta sunt servanda*'.

From the formulation of the article, it appears that its content would include only those agreements that increase (and/or even supersede[40]) the applicable rules, not those that narrow them. Consequently the contractual freedom of the parties is limited. This stands equally true for international armed conflicts, as evidenced by common art 6 of the First, Second and Third Geneva Convention and arts 7 and 47 of the Fourth Geneva Convention – the difference is that the relevant provisions for international armed conflicts specifically prohibit the curtailment of protection. It is less evident whether an agreement whose content falls outside the existing provisions of humanitarian law treaties should also be considered a common article 3 agreement. The object and purpose of the article would probably militate in favour of such interpretation. After all, the Geneva Conventions might not be 'compatible' to apply as they are,[41] since they are largely predicated on the difference in nationality, and, therefore, some form of adaptation might be needed to the exigencies of a non-international conflict setting.

Declaratory agreements that only re-affirm existing obligations might not be considered as common article 3 agreements,[42] although they could be important for two reasons. Firstly, they would be firm evidences of the ANSA's will to uphold humanitarian law standards. Secondly, they could induce compliance to the extent that the ANSA perceives that it has

---

37 Committee on Non-State Actors, 'Non-State Actors in International Law: Lawmaking and Participation Rights' in International Law Association Report of the Seventy-Fifth Conference (Sofia 2012) (International Law Association 2012) 663 (hereinafter ILA Committee on Non-State Actors 2012)

38 See also art 19.2 of the 1954 Hague Convention. Arts 9.2 and 10.4 of Protocol II as Amended on 3 May 1996 provide for agreements of a more limited content.

39 Nonetheless an explicit common article 3 agreement would imply that the signatories regard the conflict as non-international.

40 *Siordet* 1952, 48 and Jelena Pejic, 'Procedural Principles and Safeguards for Internment/administrative Detention in Armed Conflict and Other Situations of Violence' (2005) 87 IRRC 375, 378.

41 See *Baxter* 1974, 529 ff. on some problems that could arise.

42 But see International Committee of the Red Cross, 'Increasing Respect for International Humanitarian Law in Non-International Armed Conflicts' (2008) 16 (hereinafter ICRC 2008).

contributed to law creation. Both points are particularly important since certain ANSAs have denied applicability of IHL, because they did not participate in the relative processes.[43] Similarly, agreements that 'execute' or interpret the provisions of the applicable law might also not be considered as coming under the scope of common article 3 agreements, as they only concretize pre-existing obligations. If, however, we include them in common article 3 agreements, they would be considered to have an international pedigree and this could enhance compliance and, maybe, an increased scrutiny from international actors.

Writers[44] have occasionally referred to tacit or *ad hoc* agreements by parties[45] to the conflict. This is not the same as common article 3 agreements; they are either unilateral declarations of the same (or similar) content or compliance in practice with certain rules/ principles by both parties to the conflict. Such 'agreements' probably denote the level of animosity between the parties and the fact that they could not even sit at the same table. In terms of substance they might have the same consequences to written and formal agreements, but they do not (necessarily) carry the same legal significance,[46] especially since tacit compliance might denote policy, not law. The rejected article 38 of Protocol II, referring to 'mutual declarations'[47] as a substitute to agreements, could probably be considered as tacit agreement,[48] although it is not entirely certain that they should not be treated as binding unilateral declarations.[49] Much would depend on the initial opinion of the parties to the conflict (whether considering it as agreements or unilateral declarations) as well as their reactions in the event of violations by the opposing party. Such 'agreements' tend to be a past practice, as there has been a formalization of their conclusion.

Predictably, there is no obligation to conclude an agreement and this is acknowledged by the ICRC[50] as well. The language of diplomacy would use the verb 'shall' instead of 'should', in the case that it implied a legal obligation of the parties.

Parties to these agreements would necessarily be an ANSA and a state or ANSAs exclusively, although we are still lacking examples of the latter. Accords with the ICRC or

---

43 See the National Liberation Front in International Committee of the Red Cross, 'The International Committee and the Vietnam Conflict' (1966) 6 IRRC 400 and FARC in Daniel Garcia-Pena Jaramillo, 'Humanitarian Protection in Non-International Conflicts: A Case Study of Colombia' (2001) 30 Israel Yrbk Hum Rts 179, 189.

44 Henri Meyrowitz, 'Le Droit de la Guerre dans le Conflit Vietnamien' (1967) 13 AFDI 153, 157; *Forsythe* 1978, 275; *Solf* 1981–2, 931; and Robert Kogod Goldman, 'International Humanitarian Law and the Armed Conflicts in El Salvador and Nicaragua' (1987) 2 Am.U.J.Int'l L.& Pol'y 539, 545. See also the (UK) Ministry of Defence, Joint Doctrine and Concepts Centre, *The Joint Service Manual of the Law of Armed Conflict* (2004) [15.56] (hereinafter UK Manual).

45 The examples offered refer to Yemen and Nigeria in the 1960s.

46 Similarly *Sivakumaran* 2012, 445. Opposite *Schindler*, 148 and Neil Boister, 'The Legal Regulation of the South African "Armed Conflict" by Common Article 3 of the 1949 Geneva Conventions' (1988–9) 14 SAYIL 129, 136.

47 *1977 Records* Vol. 10, 157.

48 See ICRC, *1977 Records* Vol. 9, 245. But see the Federal Republic of Germany, 246.

49 See sub-chapter *Unilateral Declarations*, at 71–8.

50 *1977 Records* Vol. 9, 245. See also UNSG, 'Respect for Human Rights in Armed Conflicts: Report' (20 November 1969) A/7720, 37.

international organizations are also considered as falling under the scope of the article.[51] However, the language of the article, clearly referring to parties to the conflict, does not warrant such conclusion. In addition, a commitment to the adversary cannot be equated with a commitment to third parties: to the extent that the latter includes rights for the benefit of the state, its assent might be needed. Reciprocity might also prove a crucial factor in the implementation of these agreements and its lack (as one of the parties to the conflict is not bound) might lead the ANSA to skip its obligations in practice. Nonetheless, the common article provides measures for individuals, rather than the adversary party and accountability for its breach might also be owed to the international community as a whole,[52] to the extent that the agreements contain such rules. These two factors could induce us to consider agreements with third parties as being common article 3 agreements. After all, the humanitarian initiative of the ICRC forms part of common article 3.

An interesting case in point of an agreement with a third party is the 1995 SPLM/OLS (Operation Lifeline Sudan) Agreement on Ground Rules. This agreement is written in a legalized form, while it provides for responsibilities of the signing parties. Furthermore it was signed by the leader of the SPLM/A[53] and it was invoked by the Operation Lifeline Sudan, when some of its provisions were breached.[54] There is also a preambular reference of support to (the provisions and principles of) humanitarian law instruments, including the Geneva Conventions and the Protocols. As regards its content, it is an enhancement of IHL protection, to the extent that facilitation of humanitarian assistance becomes a binding obligation for the ANSA. Consequently this agreement lies inside the spirit of common article 3, but outside its language. At least it should be considered as a binding humanitarian agreement[55] and not only a written unilateral declaration and it would imply the competence of ANSAs to conclude agreements beyond the guise of common article 3 (and without, necessarily, any state consent). Much, however, could depend on the content of each agreement and generalized conclusions might not be possible.

The most famous example of a common article 3 agreement is the one concluded under the auspices of the ICRC, between the warring parties in Bosnia-Herzegovina.[56] That agreement provided for the application of parts of the Geneva Conventions to this conflict, and it was used in the ICTY's jurisprudence, initially as evidence for the intent

---

51 *Zegveld*, 29, *Ewumbue-Monono*, 911 ff. and Dieter Fleck, 'Non-International Armed Conflicts' in Dieter Fleck (ed.), *Handbook of International Humanitarian Law* (2nd edn, OUP 2008) 621. This is, however, not evident from the comments of the ICRC, *1977 Records* Vol. 9, 245.

52 See the *Responsibility Commentary*, 33: '[e]very State, by virtue of its membership in the international community, has a legal interest in the protection of certain basic rights and the fulfilment of certain essential obligations'.

53 UNCHR, 'Situation of Human Rights in the Sudan: Report of the Special Rapporteur, Mr. Gáspár Bíró, Submitted in Accordance with Commission on Human Rights Resolution 1995/77' (20 February 1996) E/CN.4/1996/62, 15.

54 Ibid., 20–21.

55 The intention of the parties becomes evident also from its quotation in the Memorandum of Understanding on Cessation of Hostilities between the Government of the Sudan and the Sudan People's Liberation Movement/Army, 15 October 2002, [5].

56 Agreement No. 1, Geneva, 22 May 1992 in *Sassòli and Bouvier*, 1765 ff.

of the parties to punish individuals[57] and, lately, with regard to obligations of conduct undertaken by the same parties. In *Prosecutor v Furundzija*[58] the Chambers found that torture was prohibited due to this agreement, among other reasons. In *Prosecutor v Galic*[59] the Chambers found that by virtue of the agreement the parties to the conflict clearly agreed to abide by the provisions of Protocol I protecting civilians from hostilities.

Another example is the Comprehensive Agreement on Respect for Human Rights and International Humanitarian Law between the Government of the Republic of the Philippines and the National Democratic Front of the Philippines (hereinafter Philippines Comprehensive Agreement),[60] although it appears to be mostly a re-affirmation of existing obligations[61] rather than a forward-looking agreement. The Agreement between the Government of the Republic of Sudan and The Sudan People's Liberation Movement To Protect Non-Combatant Civilians And Civilian Facilities from Military Attack[62] can be considered a re-affirmation of customary law obligations, only if the rules on the conduct of hostilities were customary at the time of its conclusion; otherwise it is an expansion of international armed conflict rules to a non-international armed conflict setting. Significantly this agreement was applicable for one year only, a provision that is not prohibited by common article 3 – in fact it is expectable that such agreements will be temporary. Obviously if the rules were customary, this temporal clause might be insignificant as to the extent of obligations of the parties[63]. Note also that the General Assembly has been treating the Additional Protocols as applicable to the Sudan conflict since 1995,[64] despite the fact that Sudan was not a party to the relevant conventions at that time. A possible reading is that the relevant conventions were considered as customary, but there are serious doubts whether states intended or envisaged such an outcome.

The Comprehensive Agreement on Human Rights in Guatemala,[65] although technically not a humanitarian law agreement, went to great pains to exclude that (art IX.2) 'these *statements* by the Parties do not constitute a special agreement, in the terms of article 3 (Common) … ' (emphasis added). This eagerness could serve as evidence that common

57 *Tadic* Appeals Decision [136].

58 (Judgment) ICTY-95-17/1-T (10 December 1998) [135].

59 (Judgment) ICTY-98-29-T (5 December 2003) [25]. Note though that the Appeals Chambers in *Prosecutor v Galic* (Appeals Judgment) ICTY-98-29-A (30 November 2006) [86] avoided addressing the argument of the defendant on the non-binding character of the agreement, on the ground that the offence was firmly established in customary law.

60 The Hague, 16 March 1998. See also the Agreement on Civilian Protection Component of the International Monitoring Team (IMT), Kuala Lumpur, Malaysia, 27 October 2009, which concretizes pre-existing obligations, which are also to be found in customary law.

61 See also Roselle C. Tenefrancia, 'A Breed of its Own: Characterizing the CARHRIHL as a Legal Document' (2009) 59 Ateneo L.J.149, 158.

62 31 March 2002. *Babiker*, 180–81, does not seem to consider it a common article 3 agreement.

63 That would depend on the effect of customary IHL to ANSAs, see sub-chapter *Customary International Law*, at 89–92.

64 See A/RES/49/198 [10], A/RES/51/112 [9] and Res 52/140 (12 December 1997) [9].

65 Mexico, D.F., 29 March 1994.

article 3 agreements are international in nature[66] – article 3 of the VCLT recognizes the existence of other international agreements. More importantly, the possibility that they can supersede or amend the applicable international law,[67] even to a certain extent, could not but evince a corresponding status.[68] It would not make sense to consider it as a piece of internal law because that could lead a state to terminate it or amend it[69] and therefore it would be opposite to the object and purpose of common article 3. Furthermore, it would cripple its enforcement, especially if the agreement does not provide for something, instead of the (admittedly weak) international treaty enforcement rules. Even the remote possibility that such an agreement is turned into an internal piece of legislation, in order to make it binding on the state party (and even the ANSA), would evince its international pedigree.[70]

In such case the ANSA is accorded a law-making role in international (humanitarian) law, with the simultaneous state consent, which is significant evidence of (at least a limited) international subjectivity. Moreover it could have a substantial effect on its continuing validity, despite violations by the other side, in accordance with art 60.5 of the VCLT. This presupposes that the article is a reflection of customary law[71] and applicable in relations that are not purely inter-state.

Its exclusion from the initial draft of the ILC[72] would suggest that this provision was not customary – yet this exclusion seemed to relate to the understanding of the ILC that another provision covered the substantive content.[73] The clause was proposed orally by Switzerland[74] and was finally voted by 87 states to none with nine abstentions. The difference in formulation between the initial proposal (referring to multilateral treaties) and the final text would suggest that bilateral agreements are also covered. It would therefore appear that its analogous application to common article 3 agreements is not out of

66 See also Ezequiel Heffes and Marcos D. Kotlik, 'Special Agreements Concluded by Armed Opposition Groups: Where is the Law?'. But see *Prosecutor v Sesay et al.* (Decision on Challenge to Jurisdiction: Lomé Accord Amnesty) SCSL 04-16-AR72(E) (13 March 2004) [48] as well as the Constitutional Court of Colombia, *Sassòli and Bouvier*, 2271.

67 This includes not only treaty law but also customary law, since the latter is prone to changes through treaty law, see *Shaw*, 116.

68 See also, indirectly, *de Beco*, 194. But see the disagreement of *Tenefrancia*, 153, regarding the specific document.

69 *Heffes and Kotlik*.

70 But a similar argument was rejected in the *Sesay Decision* [43–4].

71 See some relevant indications in *Provost*, 171. For Bruno Simma and Christian J Tams, 'Article 60 (1969)' in Olivier Corten and Pierre Klein, *The Vienna Conventions on the Law of Treaties: A Commentary* (OUP 2011) 1367, the Court in *Namibia* considered this clause as customary.

72 'Draft Articles on the Law of Treaties with Commentaries' (1966) YILC Vol. II 187–274 (hereinafter ILC 1966).

73 *Simma and Tams*, 1367. See also Greece, *United Nations Conference on the Law of Treaties, Official Records*, Second Session (United Nations 1970) 113–14 (hereinafter 1969 Records Second Session).

74 *1969 Records* First Session, 354. See also the written form in *United Nations Conference on the Law of Treaties, Official Records*, Documents of the Conference (United Nations 1969) 269. The oral amendment received the approbation of Ukraine, *1969 Records* First Session 355, Denmark, 358 and Austria, 359. The written amendment was supported by Costa Rica, *1969 Records* Second Session, 112, Brazil, Ecuador, Israel, Finland and Greece 113, India, Iceland, Italy and El Salvador, 114.

question, if it has not become in the meantime a customary rule with application outside the inter-state context. The 1986 Vienna Convention includes the same provision and it was adopted in the conference with no discussion at all. The ICTY's position, considering the agreement in Bosnia as valid despite repeated violations, could be evidence, although it could alternatively signify the lack of any procedure for its termination or suspension by the contracting parties or their reluctance to do so, probably for political reasons.

Overall, though, these agreements can only supplement applicable IHL standards, especially since they are not frequent. A valid explanation turns on the fact that they require large-scale civil wars[75] – the paradigms referred to above correspond almost entirely to armed conflicts where Protocol II is or could have been applicable – a measure of symmetry between the parties[76] as well as channels of communication between the belligerents which are usually lacking.[77] In addition, the organization of the contracting parties and good faith are, obviously, indispensable for the actual implementation of the agreement.[78] On the other hand, they are not to be lightly dismissed as ineffective or useless, not only because they can increase the level of protection but also because they can induce the compliance of non-contracting parties to humanitarian law treaties. Even the claims of ineffectiveness are not self-evident, because there is a possibility that without their existence, humanitarian law violations might have been increased in scope and content.

Overall, these agreements do not alter the fact that certain inter-state treaties are addressing non-contracting parties that did not have any evident role in the treaties' formation. In fact, since the basis for such agreements is common article 3, the applicability of this article to non-contracting parties is pre-supposed. Consequently there is a need to search for alternative justifications in order to conclude how ANSAs are bound by humanitarian law.

Humanitarian Law in Ceasefire and Peace Agreements

As the international society has grown stronger after the Cold War, so have its efforts to bring a temporary or permanent stoppage of violence in armed conflicts. The number of ceasefire and peace agreements, has, therefore, increased when compared with the past.[79] The binding nature of such agreements at the intra-state level is not contested, regardless of the character of the ANSA, on the condition that the parties intended to be bound. The *pacta sunt servanda* rule is a general principle of law applicable to the national and international level.

---

75 See UK, *1949 Records* Vol. II-B, 98 and similarly *Pejic* 2005, 378.

76 ICRC, *1977 Records* Vol. 9, 245 and *ICRC* 2008, 17.

77 For *La Rosa and Wuerzner*, 332–3, the reasons are 'states' concerns … about … armed groups' legitimacy, or because the parties do not want to commit themselves to more than the minimum for fear of their own members being prosecuted, or because the intention of one or both parties to respect international humanitarian law is not sincere'.

78 Colin Smith, 'Special Agreements to Apply the Geneva Conventions in Internal Armed Conflicts: The Lessons of Darfur' (2007) 2 Irish YBIL 91, 99.

79 *Bell* 2008, 27.

The intention of the parties can be ascertained from its text[80] and ' … surrounding evidence …, such as the subject matter of the obligations and the choice of language',[81] the context and structure of the agreement as well as 'the rank and standing of those who made it … and who authenticated it'.[82] Security Council involvement, usually after their conclusion, is also an indication – if not an affirmation – of their binding nature.[83] The Council '*call[ed] on* the two sides … to comply fully with previous agreements … ' (Res 1666 (31 March 2006) [3]), urged parties ' … to adhere to agreements reached in their dialogue' (Res 1725 (6 December 2006) [2]) or '*demand[ed]* that the parties to the conflict in Darfur fulfil their … commitments under relevant agreements … '(S/RES/1828 [16]). Consequently, parties are expected to honour their bilateral commitments, but generalized conclusions are not possible to reach and everything would depend on the context of each case and agreement.

A characteristic of these agreements is that they occasionally reserve a certain role for international humanitarian law in their text and the purpose of this part is to explain whether these agreements *create* the basis of corresponding obligations of ANSAs.

The terms 'truce', 'cessation of hostilities' and 'armistice' have been equally used as synonymous to ceasefire agreements in inter-state conflicts.[84] Although the content of relevant agreements is hardly uniform, armistice agreements, as entrenched in arts 36–41 of the Annex to the 1907 Hague Convention (IV),[85] could include, *inter alia*, provisions on the relation of the armies with the local inhabitants, acts to be prohibited during the armistice and disposition of prisoners of war.[86] Consequently the existence of humanitarian law stipulations, either new in content or as a re-affirmation of previously applicable rules, was already a fact. Armistice agreements (or local arrangements/ agreements) are also provided for in the Geneva Conventions (arts 15 of the First Geneva Convention, 18 of

80 It is not uncommon the parties state the binding character of these agreements. See for example art 1 of the Arusha Peace and Reconciliation Agreement for Burundi, the preamble of the Peace Accords for Angola, Bicesse, Portugal, 15 May 1991 and art 24.89 of the Eastern Sudan Peace Agreement, Asmara, Eritrea, 19 June 2006.

81 *Bell* 2008, 128.

82 *Rosenne* 2001, 356.

83 For Karel Wellens, 'The Practice of the (UN) Security Council with regard to Treaties and (Other) Agreements Governed by International Law' (2003) 2 Revista Colombiana de Derecho Internacional 11, 70–71, 'the overall objective to maintain or restore international peace and security may have considerably reduced … any inclination on the part of the Council to ascertain the precise legal status of instruments relevant to the matter before it … '.

84 See Sydney D. Bailey, 'Cease-fires, Truces, and Armistices in the Practice of the UN Security Council' (1977) 71 AJIL 461, 462; Office of the Judge Advocate General of Canada, *Law of Armed Conflict at the Operational and Tactical Levels* (2001) [1403.2] (hereinafter Canadian Manual) and the *UK Manual* [10.13.1].

85 Convention (IV) Respecting the Laws and Customs of War on Land and its Annex: Regulations Concerning the Laws and Customs of War on Land (adopted 18 October 1907, entered into force 26 January 1910) 3 Martens Nouveau Recueil (ser. 3) 461 (hereinafter Hague Convention).

86 See in more detail the US Department of the Army Field Manual 27–10, *The Law of Land Warfare* (1956) 173–4 and the *UK Manual* [10.24].

the Second Geneva Convention and 17 of the Fourth Geneva Convention), for the benefit of sick or wounded combatants and/or civilians.

Inter-state peace agreements[87] are much less concerned with humanitarian law, since their aim is to end the conflict and to solve the dispute that initially brought the states into conflict. The fate of prisoners of war, criminal prosecutions for previous violations of the laws of war and reparations could feature in these treaties and, therefore, present some interest with regard to humanitarian law.

Ceasefire agreements in intra-state conflicts resemble armistice as regards their content and they usually include, *inter alia*, the specific acts to be prohibited, in addition to political and military stipulations. References to the relations with the local inhabitants and the disposition of prisoners or detainees are less usual,[88] although there is a clear (and rather recent) tendency to define the ceasefire with regard to the human rights of the local population, at least to a certain extent.[89] One such example is the Agreement on Ceasefire and Cessation of Hostilities between the Government of the Republic of Liberia and Liberians United for Reconciliation and Democracy and the Movement for Democracy in Liberia (hereinafter Liberia Ceasefire),[90] providing for security guarantees on safe and unhindered access by humanitarian agencies to vulnerable groups, free movement of persons and goods, as well as for the return and resettlement of refugees and internally displaced persons and several prohibitions (as violations of the ceasefire) such as 'harassment, attacks, hostage taking or unlawful arrest of civilians and personnel of humanitarian agencies as well as seizure of properties of individuals and corporations'.[91]

Peace agreements are, of course, more comprehensive, since their subject matter includes many aspects of the post-conflict life in their respective countries. Since they are designed to regulate a situation which no longer constitutes an armed conflict, it would make sense if there were no (or minimum) mention of humanitarian law and this is indeed what happens most of the time. References to the peacetime equivalent law (that is, human rights) are more usual, as well as to international criminal law as the means to punish past violations of IHL. Examples of references to humanitarian law can be found in the Darfur Declaration of Principles where the parties stress their ' ... commitment to respect international humanitarian law ... ' (preambular [5]). The Philippine government

87 Wilhelm G. Grewe, 'Peace Treaties' in Rudolf Bernhardt (ed.) *Encyclopaedia of Public International Law* Instalment 4 (North-Holland 1982) 104–5.

88 This could depend on whether the ceasefire agreement is a preliminary for peace, in which case it could have a scope similar to definitive peace agreements.

89 See also *Ary*, 192.

90 Accra, Ghana, 17 June 2003, [5] and [9].

91 See also the Agreement on Ceasefire in Sierra Leone, Lomé, Togo, 18 May 1999, arts 2, 4–5, the Nuba Mountains Cease Fire Agreement, Bürgenstock (NW), Swiss Confederation, 19 January 2002, arts II.2 and II.3d and the *Memorandum of Understanding on Cessation of Hostilities between the Government of the Sudan and the Sudan People's Liberation Movement/Army*, [3] and [5]. Note though that many ceasefire agreements did not contain any relevant clauses, for example Agreement on a Cease-Fire and Separation of Forces, Moscow, 14 May 1994 and the (Guatemala) Agreement on the Definitive Ceasefire, Oslo, 4 December 1996, but they are overwhelmingly dated from the previous century.

and the MILF have agreed[92] to observe more than what is provided for by humanitarian treaty rules,[93] while violations of the agreement would be investigated and prosecuted. In the Comprehensive Peace Agreement between the Government of Liberia (GOL), The Liberians United for Reconciliation and Democracy (LURD), The Movement for Democracy in Liberia (MODEL) and the Political Parties (hereinafter Liberia Peace Agreement)[94] (art XV) 'the Parties undertake to respect … the principles and rules of International Humanitarian law in post conflict Liberia'.

The existence of such stipulations in ceasefire and peace agreements should not be overstated. References to international humanitarian law *per se* in ceasefire agreements are rare.[95] If there are any, they might serve either as a reminder of the existence and value of this legal regime or as a basis of obligations, especially if one of the parties was not prepared to accept humanitarian law as applicable beforehand. It is more usual to agree on provisions which are equivalent with those of humanitarian treaty law. This makes sense because a ceasefire agreement could signal the end of applicability of humanitarian law.[96] In any case the breadth of obligations under ceasefire agreements is usually limited in scope and purpose, if they exist at all. Consequently the chances of binding ANSAs to humanitarian law obligations through ceasefire agreements are not particularly promising, while they might also be of limited duration, even if renewable upon agreement.[97]

Reliance on them once fighting is renewed seems equally difficult, because it is not at all certain that the agreement, or parts of it, survives its breach.[98] Since the object and purpose of the ceasefire agreement is defeated, it should be considered as becoming a dead letter. Even if art 60.5 of the VCLT applied, it is not certain that it could cover an agreement whose object is not purely humanitarian.[99] Moreover, separability of provisions seems equally difficult, especially if humanitarian law-style provisions are part and parcel of the definition of ceasefire. Consequently the role of humanitarian law in ceasefire agreements is mostly symbolic and it could offer proof of the positive inclination of an ANSA (or generally the parties to the conflict) towards IHL and serve as a reminder of existing obligations,[100] particularly if the agreement breaks down or expires and hostilities resume.

---

92 Implementing Guidelines on the Humanitarian, Rehabilitation and Development Aspects of the GRP–MILF Tripoli Agreement on Peace of 2001, Putrajaya, Malaysia, 7 May 2002.

93 See art IV.3–4, providing access of the ICRC to detainees and the function of the ICRC tracing mechanism.

94 Accra, Ghana, 18 August 2003.

95 See the (Mali) Accord De Cessez-le-feu, Bamako, Mali, 23 May 2014, point 2.

96 See *Akayesu* [627] and Andrew Clapham, 'Human Rights Obligations of Non-State Actors in Conflict Situations' (2006) 88 IRRC 491, 507. That would equally depend, though, on the fact that after the agreement hostilities ceased. But see the *Uganda Peace Talks Agreement*, art 1i, which explicitly provides for the application of common article 3 during the ceasefire period.

97 The majority of agreements quoted within this sub-chapter are of an unlimited duration.

98 But see the International Committee of the Red Cross, 'International Humanitarian Law and the Challenges of Contemporary Armed Conflicts: Report' (2003) 66.

99 Positive *Simma and Tams*, 1368.

100 *ICRC 2008*, 24.

The references to IHL in peace agreements appear even more symbolic. These agreements are destined to put an end to the conflict and to introduce or restore amicable relations between the parties. Consequently humanitarian law appears inappropriate, apart from provisions relevant to post-conflict obligations of the parties. It would make sense to resort to a peace agreement 'if [it] was concluded at an early stage of the peace process and fighting remains ongoing',[101] in order to improve compliance, but it is difficult to accept their relevance 'if the peace process subsequently breaks down':[102] in such case, the peace agreement is probably nothing more than a piece of paper and its relevance for IHL purposes should be considered as non-existent for the same reasons as for ceasefire agreements. The fact that, at times, the stipulations relevant to humanitarian law are of a general nature and difficult to implement[103] contributes to the relevant unimportance of IHL references within peace agreements. Furthermore, both ceasefire and peace agreements might come at a late stage of the conflict and, consequently, the time gap on the applicability of humanitarian law might prove detrimental for its purpose of existence. Therefore other forms of commitment to humanitarian obligations might be needed and unilateral declarations appear to have a certain prospect in this regard.

Unilateral Declarations

Unilateral declarations of states may create legal obligations, if 'publicly made and manifesting the will to be bound … '.[104] The determination of their legal effects depends on content,[105] factual circumstances in which they were made (publicity and formality) and reactions to which they gave rise.[106] The author of the declaration is, of course, important, and there are certain presumptions regarding its functions within a state.[107] Concerned states may then rely on them and they ' … are entitled to require that such obligations be respected'.[108]

---

101 *Sivakumaran* 2006, 389.

102 Ibid. See, also, a similar assessment in the Lasting Peace in Sierra Leone: The Revolutionary United Front Sierra Leone (Ruf/SL) Perspective and Vision, 6 and 9.

103 See *infra*, the references to the Nepali and Liberian Peace Agreements.

104 ILC, 'Guiding Principles Applicable to Unilateral Declarations of States Capable of Creating Legal Obligations' (2006) A/61/10, Principle 1 (hereinafter ILC Guiding Principles). See also *Nuclear Tests (Australia v France)* (Merits) [1974] ICJ Rep 267–8 and *Nuclear Tests (New Zealand v France)* (Merits) [1974] ICJ Rep 472–3.

105 It should not be 'an offer or otherwise dependent on reciprocal undertakings … ', *Brownlie*, 641.

106 See the 'Guiding Principles Applicable to Unilateral Declarations of States Capable of Creating Legal Obligations, with Commentaries Thereto' (2006) YILC Vol. II Part Two, 369, 372: 'the importance of the reactions of other States concerned in evaluating the legal scope of the unilateral acts in question, whether those States take cognizance of commitments undertaken (or, in some cases, rights asserted), or, on the contrary, object to or challenge the binding nature of the "commitments" at issue' (footnotes omitted). Significantly, compliance does not appear to be an element of its legal validity.

107 *ILC Guiding Principle* 4.

108 *ILC Guiding Principle* 1.

The legal validity of unilateral declarations by ANSAs is less evident.[109] In 1946 the ICRC suggested a formula whereby parties to a civil conflict would declare their intention to apply the principles of the Geneva Conventions, subject to reciprocity,[110] while several states regarded such declaration as a precondition for the applicability of humanitarian law in non-international armed conflicts.[111] However, such declarations would not have a unilateral effect; they were rather the extra step that was needed in order to bring about the applicability of humanitarian treaty law. Similar voices were raised (and rejected) during negotiations for Protocol II. The ICRC Draft Protocol II[112] contained an article (38) that would permit declarations addressed to the depositary of the Geneva Conventions or to the ICRC to function as substitutes for the lack of common article 3 agreements. Although reciprocity would imply that only declarations by both parties would in practice be made, the language of the article could leave[113] a window of opportunity for unilateral declarations as well. In any case the role of declarations was perceived as a substitute for common article 3 agreements, which were manifestly absent until that time, rather than a formal means to make humanitarian law exclusively applicable to ANSAs.

According to art 96.3 of Protocol I, the representing authority of a national liberation movement would be able to enter into treaty relations with state parties to the Protocol by a unilateral declaration addressed to the depositary. But this constituted rather a semi-formal instrument of accession, modified to the realities of liberation movements and intended to produce mutual rather than unilateral obligations.[114]

Despite the lack of formal status, the validity of unilateral declarations and the responding capacity of ANSAs should not be doubted: if they can become parties to an international agreement, lesser forms of law-making should be considered possible and acceptable. Furthermore, while international law is generally reluctant to accept the legal validity of unilateral declarations, as evidenced by the principle that in case of doubt it should not be considered as such,[115] such principle might not be applicable to ANSAs. States (and to a certain extent national liberation movements) have other law-making means, while for ANSAs this is more doubtful and more difficult, to the extent that it requires channels of communication with the outside world. In addition, a conflict situation would hinder the enemies, in principle, from concluding an agreement that could

109 See the reluctant position of the *ILA Committee on Non-State Actors* 2012, 663.

110 *Siordet* 1950, 115.

111 See the relevant references in *supra* sub-chapter *Introduction*, at 56.

112 *1977 Records* Vol. 1, 44.

113 See *1977 Records* Vol. 9, 245. But see the opinion of (the then West) Germany, 246, referring only to declarations by both sides and Indonesia, 291, referring to reciprocal obligations.

114 However, if Konstantinos D. Magliveras, 'Devising New Rules for Regulating International Terrorism Warfare and Engaging Non-State Actors in the Negotiations' in Noëlle Quenivet and Shilan Shah-Davis (eds), *International Law and Armed Conflict* (TMC Asser Press 2010) 349, is right that it was non-revocable, there is a substantial difference with accession. For *Daboné*, 411–12, it is hard to classify such declarations among unilateral acts, but it is also not appropriate to refer to accession. He also confines the effect of this declaration to the liberation movement and the concerned state, coming to the conclusion that it appears to be a new type of special agreement.

115 *ILC Guiding Principle* 7.

make humanitarian law applicable or extend the scope of obligations.[116] In fact states might not want to sign an agreement with an ANSA for legitimacy reasons or they might not want to extend their obligation. These varying circumstances would therefore militate in favour of the legal validity of a unilateral declaration by an ANSA. It could be different, though, if the circumstances for the conclusion of an agreement existed, for example the state was ready to proceed accordingly, and the ANSA rejected such offer. In that case a subsequent unilateral declaration (to apply IHL or to extend obligations) might not be intended to have legal consequences. On the contrary, if the ANSA has appealed to the government or other entity to conclude a relevant agreement and there was an outright rejection, a subsequent unilateral declaration should be serious evidence of the intention of the ANSA to incur legal obligations. The intention is more easily discernible whenever the ANSA declares that it will abide by quantitative obligations which exceed common article 3 and Protocol II (on the condition that it is applicable in the respective conflict). Similarly, the intention is more apparent when the ANSA was previously not accepting humanitarian law as applicable.

Roberts and Sivakumaran argue that 'when declarations on humanitarian norms are issued in the midst of a non-international armed conflict or cast in legal language, there should be a presumption that they are binding'.[117] This would, rightly, suggest that the content of the declaration could be a condition for its validity. But it is not adequate that the circumstance (the midst of the conflict) evinces the seriousness of the declaration, because the ANSAs' intentions might rest on internal and/or international legitimacy.[118] The publicity of the declaration should be considered indispensable,[119] as otherwise it would be impossible to communicate the scope of obligations and the declaration could not lead to any form of accountability. The formality of the declaration should also be serious proof of the intention of the author. The seriousness of the declaration itself could also be judged depending on the organ that makes it: it would be different if it came from a regional commander or the central organ of the ANSA. Finally I would suggest that the representativeness of the group could give a better argument as to the validity of the declaration, if not as a legal prerequisite but at least as a political criterion. The constituency of the ANSA might matter both for the intention behind the declaration and its perception by third parties.

Practice is quite extensive.[120] Algeria declared its intention to apply the Third Geneva Convention to French soldiers.[121] The fighting parties in Yemen stated that they would

116 In the *Frontier Dispute (Burkina Faso/Republic of Mali)* (Merits) [1986] ICJ Rep 574, the Court judged that since there was nothing to hinder the parties from concluding a formal agreement, there were no circumstances that prove that the (unilateral) declaration could have legal consequences.

117 Anthea Roberts and Sandesh Sivakumaran, 'Lawmaking by Nonstate Actors: Engaging Armed Groups in the Creation of International Humanitarian Law' (2012) 37 Yale J.Int'l L. 107, 142.

118 *Bugnion*, 194 and *Valencia*, 72–3.

119 *Sassòli* 2010, 25, also subscribes to the public announcement.

120 There is an entire database devoted to unilateral declarations/statements, <http://theirwords.org/pages/home>, listing 230 such entries at 04/02/2015.

121 *Wilson*, 51.

respect the principles of the Geneva Conventions,[122] while a similar statement of accepting 'humanitarian principles' was made by Katanga.[123] In more recent years the NDFP had made a 'Declaration of Adherence to International Humanitarian Law'.[124] Since the ANSA 'formally declares its adherence to international humanitarian law', it appears that humanitarian law was considered (formally) inapplicable before that date[125] and that this declaration is the vehicle for the creation of obligations for the ANSA. It is to be noted that the state had the same obligations by virtue of its accession to the Geneva Conventions and Protocol II. Therefore, if there was not an indirect way to bind the ANSA, the ANSA would be bound by this unilateral declaration – at least its *intention* is quite evident in this regard.

The SPLM in its Fifteen-Point Programme made a reference that 'whenever an enemy soldier is disarmed or unarmed, his/her life must be spared, protected, respected, and considered as a Prisoner of War (POW)'.[126] However, a careful reading of the Programme, which is online and therefore public, would reveal that in the same paragraph there is a reference to *policy* on human rights, denoting that the movement might not have intended to create legal obligations. In addition the rest of this policy is formulated in legal terms (The Movement shall …), unlike the relevant stipulation for the benefit of enemy combatants.

National liberation movements have also made declarations of intention to apply humanitarian law rules.[127] Such pledges were made in public and originated from the president of the movements. However, it is not evident whether these movements intended to bypass the mechanism of art 96.3 Protocol I without addressing the declaration to the depository or to produce unilateral effects, especially since there was an alternative. SWAPO's Declaration referred to the future prospect of accession to the Protocol, thus differentiating its legal consequences from an art 96.3 declaration. ANC's declaration seems to exclude application of the Protocol *in toto* and it resembles an attempt to apply art 96.2, regarding ad hoc acceptance and application of the Protocol (or parts of it) by a

122 Kathryn Boals, 'The Relevance of International Law to the Internal War in Yemen' in Richard E. Falk (ed.), *The International Law of Civil War* (Hopkins 1971) 315 and *Veuthey* 1975, 240–1. This implied more than common article 3.

123 Donald W. McNemar, 'The Post Independence War in Congo' in Richard E. Falk (ed.), *The International Law of Civil War* (Johns Hopkins University Press 1971) 260. Other declarations were made in Hungary, *Veuthey* 1975, 236–7; by Biafra, *Veuthey* 1975, 242; LTTE, *M. Hoffman*, 213; and PKK, Susan Breau, 'The International Law Implications of the Turkish/Kurdish Conflict' (2008) 41 RBDI 426, 437. For a list of unilateral declarations in the African context see *Ewumbue-Monono*, 907–10.

124 15 August 1991 (hereinafter 1991 NDFP Declaration).

125 See also another reference in the declaration on 'voluntary adherence to Protocol II of the Geneva Conventions and to international humanitarian law in general'. Furthermore in the *1996 NDFP Declaration* it proclaims that '[i]t has declared accession [sic] to Protocol II since 15 August 1991'.

126 SPLM Political Secretariat, 'Fifteen-Point Programme of the SPLM' (1998) [2.13].

127 See the 'Declaration of Intent by the African National Congress' (1981) 21 IRRC 20 and the South West African People's Organization (SWAPO) declaration in *Ewumbue-Monono*, 909.

party to the conflict.[128] Consequently, if their intention can be discerned from the content of the declarations, these would have a unilateral effect. However, the declaration by the ANC refers to 'principles of international humanitarian law' and that ' … it will endeavour to respect the rules … ' whenever practically possible, a language that is quite vague and equivocal. SWAPO's Declaration, on the other hand, did not carry the same restrictions and, thus, seemed to be a better prospect as a tool for the creation of obligations.[129]

In the same vein, declarations of intention by self-proclaimed (and therefore unrecognized) liberation movements (to apply the Geneva Conventions) might also be considered as unilateral declarations extending the applicability of IHL norms in the conduct of the ANSA – this was how the 1996 NDFP Declaration was treated.[130] However, the NDFP expects that 'by virtue of this unilateral declaration … the GRP is bound as before by the Geneva Conventions and henceforth by Protocol I in accordance with Article 96, paragraph 3(c) of Protocol I'. Since the Philippines had not acceded to Protocol I at that time, it is not evident that the ANSA's intention was to self-impose obligations without reciprocity from the other party to conflict. The highly politicized language used in the declaration as well as the fact that it seems to exceed the applicable rules of IHL (with regard to legitimate targets) are also counter-arguments on the legal validity of the declaration. On the other hand, subsequent statements by the NDFP[131] show that it stood up to the content of the declaration and, therefore, its intention might be construed more broadly. Subsequent practice, though, does not form part of the validity of a unilateral declaration and, therefore, it is not certain how to judge this case overall.

An interesting case is offered by the already mentioned 1995 SPLM/OLS (Operation Lifeline Sudan) Agreement on Ground Rules, to the extent that it makes a reference in the preamble on support to (the provisions and principles of) humanitarian law instruments, including the Geneva Conventions and the Protocols. A Special Rapporteur urged 'the two signatories to the document to treat in practice the relevant provisions of the cited international instruments as not only worthy of support, but as unequivocal and unilaterally assumed obligations and to direct their future actions in this spirit'.[132] The General Assembly[133] has been '[c]all[ing] upon parties to the hostilities to respect fully the applicable provisions of international humanitarian law, including article 3 common to the

128 See also *Provost*, 156.

129 *Barberis*, 258, suggests that all of these acts had the effect of a unilateral declaration wherever the opposing state has not acceded to the Protocol.

130 *ICRC 2008*, 20.

131 See its statement in *Santos Jr.* 2003, 564, that it treats police and army personnel as prisoners of war in accordance with the Geneva Conventions and the respective agreement with the government. In fact the NDFP has published three pamphlets in order to show its implementation and adherence to humanitarian law rules regarding POWs. See also the 'NDFP Declaration and Program of Action for the Rights, Protection and Welfare of Children', 24 April 2012, preamble (hereinafter NDFP's Children Declaration), where it is claimed that by proclaiming the 1996 NDFP Declaration, 'the NDFP has assumed rights and duties under Protocol I'.

132 UN Doc E/CN.4/1996/62, 24.

133 A/RES/49/198 [10], A/RES/51/112 [9] and A/RES/52/140 [9]. But in subsequent resolutions this reference is lacking.

Geneva Conventions of 12 August 1949, and the Additional Protocols thereto, of 1977 … '. Similarly the Commission of Human Rights, in Res 67 (1998) [6], has called upon 'all parties to the hostilities to respect fully the applicable provisions of … the Additional Protocols … of 1977'. At that time Sudan was not a party to either Protocol. Therefore it can be suggested that both the Assembly and the Commission relied on relevant unilateral pledges from the SPLM and another (unknown) declaration from the state. There is, however, an alternative explanation: that the Protocols were considered customary back then. In a similar vein, in the 'Report of the International Commission of Inquiry on Darfur to the Secretary-General Pursuant to Security Council Resolution 1564 (2004) of 18 September 2004'[134] evidence was found for the intention of the parties to apply humanitarian law treaties based on ceasefire agreements. I would suggest though that both these inferences are at best hyper-ambitious and one reason is that, although the parties could make an agreement (or even issue a clear unilateral declaration) in this regard, they did not do that expressly. Obviously they might be a good basis for advocacy, but hardly an extension of already accepted obligations.

The above-mentioned examples show, up to a point, the limits of ANSA practice. For a start, it is not always evident whether they are intending to create new obligations or simply re-affirming pre-existing obligations. Moreover, the generality of references,[135] for example on principles of the Geneva Conventions, might be a good base for advocacy, but it does not clarify the extent of obligations. Expectations of reciprocity also cripple the validity of declarations. There are good reasons, then, to measure intention with subsequent compliance,[136] as it would, in addition, evince more clearly the good faith of the author (of the declaration). This could suggest the way in which the 1996 NDFP's Declaration becomes binding, while it could also give an answer as to how to treat general references to IHL within ANSAs' declarations.

Compliance should also be important when the ANSA declares adherence to rules that exceed its factual capacity.[137] No accountability could be pursued over obligations that cannot be followed in practice. It is no coincidence that certain opinions later in this sub-chapter interrelate the strength of the group with the validity and/or value of the unilateral declaration. But its factual capacity should be disassociated from its juridical competence, as suggested by Plattner:[138] in essence a common article 3 ANSA might be incapable of applying the whole of Protocol II, but it is not incompetent to unilaterally declare its (partial) applicability. If, subsequently, the ANSA manages to comply, the unilateral declaration should be considered as having full effect. As an example, if there is a pledge to apply the Third Geneva Convention by an ANSA without territorial control,

134 (1 February 2005) S/2005/60, 50–51 (hereinafter Darfur Inquiry).

135 See, for example, the 'Declaration by UNITA' (1980) 20 IRRC 320, that the ANSA ' … subscribes to the fundamental rules of international law applicable in armed conflicts', as well as the declarations from Katanga and the Yemeni ANSA in the 1960s.

136 See *Plattner* 1985, 315. This would suggest, though, that before exhibition of compliance, the unilateral undertaking would have no legal effect.

137 *Plattner* 1985, 317, made the link between capability to adhere and the validity of the unilateral declaration.

138 Ibid, at 315.

its legal validity is compromised, to the extent that POW camps require such control. If, however, the ANSA succeeds in setting up such camps, the unilateral declaration would acquire legal significance. The state could legitimately expect similar conduct in the future as a legal obligation and the ANSA could be held accountable for breaches of the law, at least for the period that it is materially competent to act towards this end.

Increasingly, unilateral pledges come to be considered as an important tool for the implementation of humanitarian law in specific sectors,[139] especially since an NGO (Geneva Call) and the UN Secretary-General's Special Representative for Children and Armed Conflict are actively pursuing ANSAs in order to extract their commitments not to use anti-personnel mines[140] and not to recruit or use children in armed conflict respectively. The LTTE agreed in June 1998 ' … not to use children under 18 in combat and not to recruit those under 17',[141] while in March 2003 it signed an action plan for children affected by war. The Security Council has called parties to the conflict to 'abide by the concrete commitments they have made to the Special Representative of the Secretary-General for Children and Armed Conflict, as well as relevant United Nations bodies … ',[142] while in Res 1998 (12 July 2011) it called upon ANSAs ' … to address all other violations and abuses committed against children and undertake specific commitments and measures in this regard',[143] including action plans.[144]

Participants in a seminar organized by the ICRC[145] noted the usefulness of unilateral declarations

> … especially where the State is unwilling to enter into a special agreement [and] as an additional tool of leverage available to encourage compliance with international humanitarian law. For greater enforceability, a number of participants suggested that the unilateral declaration be combined with a verification mechanism that might supervise compliance with international humanitarian law in the conflict … .'

139 *ICRC* 2008, 19. See also Parliament Resolution (EC) on Measures to Promote a Commitment by Non-State Actors to a Total Ban on Anti-Personnel Landmines [2002] OJ C72/352.

140 The character of the 'Deed of Commitment under Geneva Call for Adherence to a Total Ban on Anti-Personnel Mines and for Cooperation in Mine Action' (hereinafter Geneva Call's Deed of Commitment) as a unilateral declaration is obvious in arts 9–10 of the text. Its written character and the fact that a sub-state entity receives it as custodian attach to it an increased level of significance.

141 UNSG, 'Children and Armed Conflict: Report of the Secretary-General' (10 November 2003) S/2003/1053, 14.

142 Res 1379 (20 November 2001) [8d]. See also Res 1261 (30 August 1999) [9], 1314 (11 August 2000) [10], 1539 (22 April 2004) [4] and 1612 (26 July 2005) [15].

143 [6d]. See also 1882 (4 August 2009) [5c].

144 S/RES/1539 [5a] and S/RES/1612 [5].

145 International Committee of the Red Cross, 'Improving Compliance with International Humanitarian Law: Report' (2003) 21 (hereinafter ICRC 2003).

Philip Alston also proposed that 'in cases in which such groups are willing to affirm their adherence to human rights principles ... it may be appropriate to encourage the adoption of formal statements to that effect'.[146]

Unilateral declarations of ANSAs appear to have induced states to accede to international humanitarian law treaties.[147] The UN Secretary General has also noted[148] that the signatories to the Geneva Call's Deed of Commitment ' ... have, for the most part, refrained from using anti-personnel mines, cooperated in mine action in areas under their control and destroyed stockpiles'.[149] There is also a preambular paragraph in Res 2068 (19 September 2012) on the ' ... generated progress, in particular the demobilization of thousands of children, the signing of action plans between parties to armed conflict and the United Nations and the delisting of parties to conflict from the Annexes to the Secretary-General's annual report'.[150] Consequently it appears to be a promising tool in the applicability of humanitarian norms to ANSAs and it has the potential to be all-encompassing, in the case that the unilateral declaration refers to the full body of IHL. However, their not-so-frequent occurrence would suggest the evaluation of unilateral declarations as being a *complementary* tool for the creation of obligations. It is therefore necessary to examine if there is an indirect way to oblige ANSAs to respect humanitarian law.

Indirect Obligations

Although ANSAs constitute the half-part of an armed conflict, it appears that neither their status nor their volition is judged by international practice as necessary or adequate for the applicability of humanitarian law to them. Certainly the number of agreements and

146 UNCHR, 'Extrajudicial, Summary or Arbitrary Executions: Report of the Special Rapporteur, Philip Alston' (22 December 2004) E/CN.4/2005/7, 21. The Rapporteur meant a group that ' ... exercises significant control over territory and population and has an identifiable political structure'. The inference is that the validity of unilateral declarations would depend on the organization and effectiveness of the ANSA to abide by the declaration. See also *Detter*, 189, submitting that unilateral declarations are 'valid undertaking[s], binding on the groups making [them], provided that the group fulfils the condition of being a belligerent'.

147 Sudan accessed the Convention on the Prohibition of the Use, Stockpiling, Production and Transfer of Anti-Personnel Mines and on Their Destruction (adopted 18 September 1997, entered into force 1 March 1999) 2056 UNTS 211 (hereinafter Ottawa Convention) in 2003 after the main ANSA, SPLM/A, made a declaration not to use landmines, see the 'Deed of Commitment under Geneva Call for Adherence to a Total Ban on Anti-Personnel Mines and for Cooperation in Mine Action', Geneva, 4 October 2001. It appears that the decision of Sudan was motivated by this factor as well, *Roberts and Sivakumaran*, 129. The accession of Iraq might also have been induced by relevant declarations of the Kurdish ANSAs in the north of Iraq.

148 UN Doc S/2009/277, 9.

149 See Geneva Call, *Engaging Armed Non-State Actors in a Landmine Ban: The Geneva Call Progress Report (2000–7)* (2007) 34, which reports an overall compliance of ANSAs to their unilateral undertakings.

150 But see the website of the Office of the Special Representative of the Secretary General, <https://childrenandarmedconflict.un.org/our-work/action-plans/>, showing that ANSAs have mostly failed to implement the signed action plans.

unilateral declarations has increased and some normative significance is attached to them. Nonetheless, they are not adequate either in quantity or quality for bringing the regime of humanitarian law in force. Consequently other mechanisms have been suggested in order to achieve this result.

Legislative Jurisdiction

The most common explanation for the applicability of humanitarian law rules to insurgent entities comes from the principle of legislative jurisdiction. This can be described as the power to make rules.[151] International rules will either be implemented through national legislation or they might apply directly in the national legislative order if they are self-executing. The assumption is that when an international rule becomes voluntarily binding on the state, this includes also individuals and collectivities which reside within the territory/jurisdiction of the state, provided that the international and the local law or the local law exclusively addresses such third parties as well.

The legislative jurisdiction principle is generally a satisfactory legal explanation in theory and enjoys some support from states, including Greece[152] and the former USSR.[153] However, apart from states that did not accept the applicability of Protocol II to insurgent movements, other states considered it necessary for the ANSA to accept IHL treaties in some way (tacitly, recognition and so on).[154] Obviously such proposals are direct acceptances that this justification is hardly a satisfactory basis. In addition, not many states made an express reference to the legislative jurisdiction, while Turkey took a negative view in a similar context.[155]

The ICRC[156] has also 'acceded' to this justification, while it found substantive support from legal scholarship.[157] The purported applicability of the Ottawa Convention and the Convention on the Prohibition of the Development, Production, Stockpiling and Use

151 *Brownlie*, 299.

152 *1949 Records* Vol. II-B, 94.

153 *1977 Records* Vol. 14, 314 and, implicitly, Zaire (DRC), *1977 Records* Vol. 7, 219 and Mongolia, *1977 Records* Vol. 9, 238. See also the *German Manual* in *Fleck* 1995, 33 and the (US) Department of the Navy, *The Commander's Handbook on the Law of Naval Operations*, NWP 1–14 M (2007) [5.2].

154 See *supra* sub-chapter *Introduction*, at 56.

155 See UNSG, 'Minimum Humanitarian Standards: Analytical Report of the Secretary General Submitted Pursuant to Commission on Human Rights Resolution 1997/21: Views and Information Received from States and United Nations Bodies' (12 January 1998) E/CN.4/1998/87/Add.1, 27–8.

156 *1977 Records* Vol. 9, 241. Similarly for the General Director of UNESCO with regard to art 19 of the 1954 Hague Convention, *Actes de la Conférence*, 323.

157 See, indicatively, G.I.A.D. Draper, 'Human Rights and the Law of War' (1971–2) 12 Va.J.Int'l L. 326, 342; *L.C. Green*, 331; and Hans-Joachim Heintze, 'Do Non-State Actors Challenge International Humanitarian Law?' in Wolff Heintschel von Heinegg and Volker Epping (eds), *International Humanitarian Law Facing New Challenges: Symposium in Honour of Knut Ipsen* (Springer 2007) 164. See also *Sivakumaran* 2006, 381 ff. See though, the disagreement of *Baxter* 1964, 87 and *Boister*, 135.

of Chemical Weapons and on Their Destruction[158] in all circumstances, including armed opposition groups and non-international armed conflicts, is also an indirect argument in favour of this thesis. The Ottawa Convention, specifically, is not addressed to ANSAs as humanitarian treaties are; instead, 'each State Party shall take all appropriate legal, administrative and other measures, including the imposition of penal sanctions, to prevent and suppress any activity prohibited ... under this Convention undertaken by persons or on territory under its jurisdiction or control' (art 9). It, therefore, imposes an obligation on states to prohibit mine-related activities from individuals and, possibly, collectivities as well. There is substantial support for the thesis that this suffices with regard to ANSAs. The understanding of Colombia that ' ... the Convention applied to all warring parties ... '[159] was not contested. The Security Council has called upon ' ... all parties to armed conflict to: (a) Respect fully the relevant provisions of applicable international law relating to the ... protection of children in armed conflict, in particular the ... Ottawa Convention ... ',[160] along with the UN Human Rights Commission and the UN High Commissioner for Human Rights.[161] However, the CIHL Study[162] seems to reject its applicability to ANSAs. Truly, such interpretation would disregard the object and purpose of Amended Article 1 to the CCW, which is to apply to ANSAs and non-international armed conflicts, as well as the work of Geneva Call, mentioned above. In addition it disregards, partly, the equality of belligerents before IHL, since the treaty leaves some leniency to states to keep anti-personnel mines in their arsenal.[163]

There are a number of reservations relating to the validity of legislative jurisdiction. It is possible that an international treaty is not incorporated automatically in countries with a dualist system;[164] therefore neither sub-state entities nor individuals will be bound, if the state does not transpose its international obligations into a piece of national legislation.

158 (adopted 3 September 1992, entered into force 29 April 1997) 1974 UNTS 45, art I, see *CIHL Study* Vol. 1, 261, *Moir*, 146 and William H. Boothby, *Weapons and the Law of Armed Conflict* (OUP 2009) 138. A similar understanding pertains to the Convention on the Prohibition of the Development, Production and Stockpiling of Bacteriological (Biological) and Toxin Weapons and on their Destruction (adopted 10 April 1972, entered into force 26 March 1975) 1015 UNTS 163.

159 Stuart Maslen and Peter Herby, 'An International Ban on Anti-personnel Mines: History and Negotiation of the "Ottawa Treaty"' (1998) 38 IRRC 693, 699. But the *Parliament Resolution (EC) on Measures to Promote a Commitment by Non-State Actors to a Total Ban on Anti-Personnel Landmines* suggests that this is not a universally accepted position.

160 S/RES/1379 [8a]. Note, though, that it was not duplicated in other Council resolutions with a similar subject matter.

161 UNCHR Chairperson's Statement 1 (2005) [25] and UNCHR, 'Report of the United Nations High Commissioner for Human Rights on the Situation of Human Rights in Colombia' (16 May 2006) E/CN.4/2006/9, 2. See also the International Institute of Humanitarian Law, *The Manual on the Law of Non-International Armed Conflict With Commentary* (2006) 3, 32 and 38 (hereinafter IIHL Manual), *Fleck* 2008, 622 and the *ILA Committee on the Use of Force*, 686.

162 Vol. 1, 282. See also *Zegveld*, 177 and Marco Sassòli, 'The Implementation of International Humanitarian Law: Current and Inherent Challenges' (2007) 10 YIHL 45, 63–4

163 See, also, *Boothby* 2009, 135, on riot control agents.

164 See for example how the Geneva Conventions do not form part of Israeli law in Yoram Dinstein, *The International Law of Belligerent Occupation* (CUP 2009) 28–9.

Past experiences have shown that states were less than diligent in this regard,[165] although the situation is probably rectified with the passage of time. In fact even the quality of the internal law will be relevant for its applicability, particularly for the Chemical and Biological Weapons Conventions. Problems could appear if the incorporated treaty does not enjoy a status higher than other sources of municipal law[166] – in such cases it could even be superseded by subsequent laws. In addition, if the local law is repealed, the ANSA would not continue to be bound, although the international responsibility of the state is incontestable to the extent that it has not denounced the treaty. According to the relevant provisions of the four Geneva Conventions (arts 62, 63, 142 and 158 respectively), Protocol I (art 99.1) and Protocol II (art 25.1), if denunciation takes place during an armed conflict, only its end would terminate the applicability of the relevant provisions. In that case, the state would continue to be bound through international law, despite the lack of a relevant municipal law; the ANSA will not be bound, in accordance with the effects of the legislative jurisdiction. However, the fact that part of the treaties contains self-executing provisions[167] could balance this potential problem,[168] provided that the internal state law allows for such applicability.[169] It is certain, though, that the Ottawa Convention and other similarly drafted ones are not self-executing with regard to sub-state entities or individuals.[170]

Zegveld,[171] rightly, differentiates between individual and group obligations, claiming that the latter are not covered by the legislative jurisdiction. Her argument is that the treaty obligations of IHL cannot be adhered to by individuals only, as they are not simply termed as prohibitions. This is partly true for several of the obligations contained in common article 3 and Protocol II.

---

165 For example the Republic of Vietnam has transposed the Conventions with a governmental Decree only in 1967, despite being a party to the Conventions since 1953, see 'Mise en Œuvre des Conventions de Genève' (1967) 49 RICR 334, 336–7. Under the legislative jurisdiction the National Liberation Front was not bound until then. Fiji was a party to the Conventions from 1959, but it implemented legislation only in 2007, Aziz Mohammed, 'Correspondent's Report: Fiji' (2007) 10 YIHL 326.

166 Similar problems could exist in the way that international customary law is incorporated in the national legal system of a state.

167 That concerns the majority of common article 3 and Protocol II.

168 See *Sivakumaran* 2006, 383. Russia's Constitutional Court, in *Sassòli and Bouvier*, 2431, seems to accept the application of Protocol II to the parties of the conflict despite the lack of amendments to the relevant internal legislation. See also the Constitutional Court of Hungary on the direct applicability of the Geneva Conventions in Péter Kovács, 'Correspondent's Report: Hungary' (1998) 1 YIHL 451 ff. But see *Carrillo-Suarez*, 38–9.

169 See Carlos M. Vasquez, 'Direct vs. Indirect Obligations of Corporations under International Law' (2004–5) 43 Colum. J. Transnat'l L. 927, 935–6.

170 See *Aust* 2010, 79: '... a treaty will not be self-executing if it clearly envisages implementing legislation'.

171 *Zegveld*, 16. The *German Manual* in *Fleck* 1995, 33, gives support to such thesis. But see the approach of *Sivakumaran* 2012, 242. See also the comments of G.I.A.D. Draper, 'The Geneva Conventions of 1949' (1965-I) 114 Recueil des Cours 96 and *Kleffner* 2011, 450–451.

The legislative jurisdiction also poses a question of legitimacy. An ANSA would be rather reluctant to adhere to national legislation from a government whose legitimacy it doubts. Consequently the practicability of this justification might be at stake. Finally, legislative jurisdiction could not justify by itself the direct accountability of ANSAs for violations of international law,[172] since it is treated as an entity subordinate to a state and, therefore, a third state could barely ask for reparations due to ANSA conduct.[173]

In sum it would appear that legislative jurisdiction might not be a satisfactory justification for the obligations and accountability of ANSAs, for both legal and pragmatic reasons. Nonetheless it is probably the pedigree of the way that ANSAs or, at least, individuals came to be bound by certain international law rules. In many respects it is a product of the statist approach to international law, as the ANSA is clearly treated as subordinate and any faults of the state's implementation of treaties will have an impact on the ANSA, both regarding its obligations and accountability.

Effect of Treaties on Third Parties

This theory found its more committed (and probably sole) advocate in the early writings of the late Judge Antonio Cassese. Its foundation is that arts 34–5 of the VCLT are customary and that third parties are all (possible) subjects of international law.[174] Under the Convention's articles, two conditions should be met: 1) the contracting parties must have intended the treaty to impose obligations on third parties and 2) the third party must accept the obligations.

Intention of the parties can be derived from the language of common article 3 and reference to 'each party to the conflict'. On the other hand, there is no such reference in Protocol II, although this language resumed in subsequent treaties. Cassese argued that the intention of the contracting parties (with regard to Protocol II) is evidenced by the following:

i) the Protocol supplements common article 3 and the latter is clearly believed to confer rights and duties upon ANSAs.
ii) Based on the wording of the Protocol and the certain features that the rebel armies should have,

> the Protocol only begins to apply when rebels prove to be able to, and do in fact, implement it … [T]his of necessity must entail that once they prove to be able to implement the Protocol, its provisions become legally binding on them. A contrary interpretation would render the whole Protocol nugatory … .[175]

---

172 *Anonymous*, 857 and *Bellal* et al., 10. Similarly, it could not justify the limited legal personality, even for IHL purposes.

173 The possibility to bring a civil claim in a national court would also depend on the internal personality of the ANSA, the stage of the conflict and so on.

174 *Cassese* 1981, 423 and *Moir*, 53.

175 *Cassese* 1981, 424–5.

iii) According to art 6.5 of Protocol II 'at the end of hostilities, the authorities in power shall endeavour to grant the broadest possible amnesty … '. This is (a kind of) duty imposed (possibly) upon armed groups as well, should they succeed in defeating the government. As Cassese continues his reasoning,

> if this duty is made incumbent on the rebels once they seize power in the territory, it is logical … that the other rules of the Protocol also bind the rebels before that … moment. Otherwise one could reach the strange conclusion that the Protocol, while it does not grant any legal status to rebels, nevertheless takes them into account once they have attained power … .[176]

It is also equally possible to claim that the object and purpose of the treaty was to humanize non-international armed conflicts and this goal cannot be fulfilled without the imposition of certain duties on rebels. Consequently the intention of the parties would be realized only if the ANSAs have duties alongside the contracting state.

The second criterion of art 35 is that the third party should accept[177] the duties imposed. It is expected that: a) rebel groups would be willing to undertake IHL duties, in order to gain some kind of enhanced group legitimacy as political actors; and b) fear of reciprocity could also lead them towards the same outcome.

This theory rests on several debatable foundations. Firstly, it starts from the pre-supposition that ANSAs are subjects of international law. This is not, however, entirely certain, especially since common art 3.4 and other humanitarian treaties do not affect the legal status of the parties to the conflict. Even if a certain status is accepted, one should verify the customary status of these particular provisions with regard to other subjects of international law.[178]

The general rule of art 34 is not particularly problematic. Morocco claimed that it ' … reflected existing international law'[179] and the provision was adopted without any dissent.[180] There was also complete agreement in the ILC:[181] agreements do not impose obligations upon third parties. Art 35 was accepted by 99 votes to none, with one abstention[182] and, today, the majority of the international community has adhered to the VCLT. A comparable clause was also inserted in the 1986 Vienna Convention (art 35). Consequently one could

176 Ibid., 427.

177 See ibid., 428, listing several possible ways to show this acceptance: a unilateral declaration, tacit compliance or a request to the ICRC to intervene and guarantee respect. However, tacit compliance would point to the objective criteria of belligerency, because the ANSA would have to apply the Protocol first, before it becomes legally binding to the actor. Moreover, a request to the ICRC could also be addressed in the event of internal disturbances which do not constitute an armed conflict and therefore where the Protocol cannot be applicable.

178 See the similar reservations of *Sivakumaran* 2006, 377.

179 *1969 Records* First Session, 192. Similarly, Eric David, 'Article 34 (1969)' in Olivier Corten and Pierre Klein, *The Vienna Conventions on the Law of Treaties: A Commentary* (OUP 2011) 888–9.

180 *1969 Records* Second Session 59.

181 *ILC* 1966, 226 ff.

182 *1969 Records* Second Session, 60.

argue in favour of the customary status of art 35,[183] while academic commentaries support this thesis.[184]

As regard the formality of written acceptance by the third party, as required by the VCLT, there is a two-way argument. The original article by the Commission only required express acceptance[185] and the relevant amendment of Vietnam[186] was considered by the UK as running 'counter to the fundamental principle of international customary law ..., namely that States were free to bind themselves otherwise than by written treaties'.[187] In the end, Vietnam's amendment was adopted by 44 votes to 19, with 31 abstentions,[188] but the customary status of written acceptance is less than evident. The 1986 Vienna Convention followed the same path with regard to written form and arts 34–5 were adopted without a vote.[189] For the ICTY Appeals Chamber in *Blaskic*[190] it was sufficient that acceptance was inferred by the passing of an internal law. Therefore even an indirect written acceptance could create legal obligations for the ANSA. On the other hand an oral assurance might not suffice, unless we consider the written form as too formal for the settings and the actor[191] and in light of the object and purpose of the relevant treaties.

Subsequently we would also have to ascertain the customary law status of art 35 with regard to obligations of third parties other than states. Although states could take this path in order to accommodate their interests and there was no dissent in the adoption of the comparable clauses, the low participation of states in the 1986 Vienna Convention (only 30 as of 10 February 2015, while the treaty is not yet in force) does not fortify the argument.

Even after taking for granted the customary status of the relevant articles, the intention of the contracting parties cannot necessarily be evidenced according to Cassese's arguments: a) the language of common article 3 serves as an argument – in fact his interpretation,

---

183 On the tendency of the ICJ to consider the provisions of the VCLT as customary see *Aust* 2007, 12–13.

184 Mark E. Villiger, *Commentary on the 1969 Vienna Convention on the Law of Treaties* (Nijhoff 2009) 472 and 479 and Caroline Laly-Chevalier, 'Article 35 (1969)' in Olivier Corten and Pierre Klein, *The Vienna Conventions on the Law of Treaties: A Commentary* (OUP 2011) 905.

185 *ILC* 1966, 227.

186 *1969 Records* Second Session, 59.

187 Ibid., 60.

188 Ibid.

189 *United Nations Conference on the Law of Treaties between States and International Organizations or between International Organizations* Vol. 1 (United Nations 1995) 16 and 22. See also Paul Reuter, 'Tenth Report on the Question of Treaties Concluded between States and International Organizations or between Two or More International Organizations' (1981) YILC Vol. II Part One 43, 67, where the Rapporteur shows a tendency to informalize the requirement of written assent, whenever there are ties between a state and an international organization. However, in a situation of a non-international armed conflict such ties will not exist and the formality seems more important.

190 *Prosecutor v Blaskic* (Judgment on the Request of the Republic of Croatia for Review of the Decision on Trial Chamber II of 18 July 1997) ICTY-95-14 (29 October 1997) [26].

191 See also Stephen Schwebel in 'Draft Articles on Treaties Concluded between States and International Organizations or between International Organizations' (1978) YILC Vol. I, 189 claiming that the requirement of the ' ... formal expression of consent ... [arose] from the need to protect the independence of States ... ' something that cannot be applicable as such to ANSAs.

giving more weight to the ordinary meaning of the convention rather than the *travaux préparatoires*, is acceptable, if not required, under the VCLT. However, the contemporary (1949) understanding departed from such interpretation and to a lesser extent the same applies for 1977. Today, however, where this acceptance is hardly disputable, it would not necessarily imply that the intention of the contracting parties has changed with regard to ANSAs' status. b) Prior implementation by ANSAs is not *sine qua non* for the applicability of Protocol II.[192]

The value of acceptance of obligations by the third party (the ANSA) can also be disputed. In 1949 it appeared to be a significant factor only when the full application of the Conventions was discussed. In the negotiations for the conclusion of Protocol II, states have argued in favour of a declaration of intention by the insurgent entity to observe humanitarian rules or recognition of the Protocol's applicability by the ANSA.[193] Neither proposition made it into the final text, probably for fear of conferring legitimacy on the ANSA; conditioning the applicability of *international* law according to the wishes of a non-international entity could have this effect at the very least.[194] Apart from legitimacy, the evaluation of humanitarian law as the lowest common denominator of conduct during armed conflict might have an impact on the exclusion of an ANSA's consent in this regard.[195] Overall it is probable that humanitarian law drafters did not intend to give any relevant freedom of action to ANSAs, although such requirement would enhance the legitimacy of the relevant rules and, possibly, compliance in certain cases.[196] Moreover, it is not certain that ANSAs would accept their responsibilities in any case,[197] as there are mainly policy and not legal arguments in this regard.

In light of the above, the effect of treaties for third parties could bring selectivity in the application of IHL and it would not sit comfortably with the principle of equality (that is, the equal application of the laws to both parties to the conflict). Consequently, the uncertain status of arts 34–5 (whether customary with regard to non-state actors) and the weakness of this justification to bind all belligerents from the beginning of a conflict, which appears unacceptable from a humanitarian angle, would militate towards looking for another possible foundational basis.

---

192 See this discussion, Chapter 1, at sub-chapter *The Additional Protocol II of 1977*, at 22–3.

193 See *supra* sub-chapter *Introduction*, at 57.

194 But see the *Philippines Comprehensive Agreement* which, in art 4 of Part II, could be deemed to limit the application of humanitarian law instruments signed by the state only to those that are acceptable by the ANSA as well.

195 See *Zegveld*, 17 and Cedric Ryngaert, 'Imposing International Duties on Non-State Actors and the Legitimacy of International Law' in Marth Noortmann and Cedric Ryngaert (eds), *Non-State Actor Dynamics in International Law: From Law-Takers to Law-Makers* (Ashgate 2010) 70.

196 *Ryngaert* 2010, 76 and 84.

197 See the cases of National Liberation Front and FARC, *supra* sub-chapter *Common Article 3 Agreements*, at 63. The *1991 NDFP Declaration* reveals that humanitarian law was considered inapplicable before that date.

Claims of Representation of the State

One alternative justification, as explained by Moir,[198] is that

> insurgents are bound by reason of the fact and to the extent that they purport to represent the state or part of it. This would appear to follow logically from the fact that treaties are binding for a government that assumes power through revolution, since the legal personality of the state remains unchanged. It would be anomalous for insurgents to find themselves bound by the obligations of article 3 on attaining overall control of the state, whereas up to that point the article has been unconcerned with their actions … despite controlling a sizeable portion of the state's territory.

Siordet subscribes to this position,[199] but there are lots of reservations surrounding its validity.

First of all, it is not obvious why a claim of being the (future and representative) government of a state would only bring about obligations under the laws of war. On the contrary it would make more sense that all treaties ratified by the state or, at least, those unaffected by an armed conflict,[200] would bind rebel armies, even before they become (if they are to become) the government of the state. However, in this case, it might be too onerous for ANSAs and unrealistic to abide by all rules. *De facto* entities would probably find fewer difficulties in this regard, whereas it would be almost impossible for common article 3 ANSAs to act accordingly. Consequently we would have to limit the scope of ANSAs' obligations only to the extent of their capabilities.

Secondly, if the rebels do not claim to represent the state, but instead they aim at creating a new state, it would be absurd to bind them on this basis.[201] In fact such a claim could change the way such an ANSA views the conflict and it could 'transform' the ANSA, in theory, into a nascent state (with all the responding obligations). But regardless of self-perceptions, the character of the conflict would not change. In essence, the aim of a new state creation could be equal to a claim of representing *a* future state and, therefore, would not be so different from the reviewed justification; yet such a claim might, again, burden the ANSA with more obligations[202] than its objective capacity suggests.

---

198 At 55, although he does not endorse it.

199 1952, 51. See also Jean Pictet (ed.), *Commentary to the Geneva Convention IV Relative to the Protection of Civilian Persons in Time of War* (International Committee of the Red Cross 1958) 37, while Joseph B. Kelly, 'Legal Aspects of Military Operations in Counterinsurgency' (1963) 21 Mil.L.Rev. 95, 102, could be seen to endorse this justification. See, on the other hand, the negative opinion of David Elder, 'The Historical Background of Common Article 3 of the Geneva Convention of 1949' (1979) 11 Case W.Res.J.Int'l L. 37, 55 and the doubts of *Sivakumaran* 2006, 380. For *Kleffner* 2011, 451, this approach implies effectiveness, rather than representation.

200 According to the International Law Commission, 'Text of the Draft Articles on the Effects of Armed Conflicts on Treaties' (2011) A/66/10, humanitarian and human rights law treaties stand among those treaties which remain unaffected, while the articles are destined to apply during non-international armed conflicts as well.

201 *Moir*, 55–6.

202 This could entail not only customary law obligations but also treaty obligations that could devolve with control over territory. There is a strong case, internationally, for automaticity in the

Another valid objection would be in cases where rebels do not claim (or want) to represent a state,[203] but they rather represent one ethnic, national, linguistic or other group. This partial representation claim is covered, supposedly, by this justification, but it appears to constitute an even more problematic case: a claim of state representation (as a whole) implies a certain status (along with rights and obligations) in international law, much like that of a government-in-exile or a national liberation movement. A claim of partial state representation could, at best, imply the status of those represented, but it is not at all obvious that this is sufficient to make the ANSA a subject of IHL.

Even if we disregard the fact that in the vast majority of cases the ANSA is not considered as representing the state internationally, thus reminding us of the effect of recognition, a claim which is not supported factually would barely serve as a tool for imposing obligations on ANSAs. Although it is rare for ANSAs not to represent a segment of the population of a state, it is also seldom that the ANSA represents a majority within the state, unless a minority ruled the country effectively before the appearance of the ANSA. The examples of South Africa and Namibia were included in the national liberation movements' paradigm. Other cases such as Nepal and Burundi, where the ANSA became the elected government after the end of armed conflict, are not only the exceptions, but they were also difficult to substantiate during the armed conflict period.

Finally, even if we assume that the claim is valid and that ANSAs become subject to IHL obligations, this would only be a deferral of the problem. What would then be the status of the non-representative government? Depending on its characteristics (effectiveness, recognition and so on), it could constitute a *de facto* government, a *de facto* regime/entity or simply an ANSA with or without control of territory. With the exception of the first option, which denotes that it would incur the responsibilities of the state as a whole, including humanitarian law obligations, in all other cases we would have to search for a basis to bind the non-representative government. Therefore the claim of representation would not be particularly useful without being combined with another justification in order to bind *both* parties to the conflict.

Presumably, the present justification is also attached to the condition of territorial control and this could be linked with a theory of devolution to humanitarian law obligations. It is a matter of common sense that states evade (direct) international responsibility in principle, when a part of their territory is outside its jurisdiction.[204] The *de facto* replacement of the

---

succession of international humanitarian law treaties, see *Prosecutor v Delalic* (Appeals Judgment) ICTY-96-21 (20 February 2001) [111] and Menno T. Kamminga, 'State Succession in Respect of Human Rights Treaties' (1996) 7 EJIL 469–84. Opposite Akbar Rasulov, 'Revisiting State Succession to Humanitarian Treaties: Is There a Case for Automaticity?' (2003) 14 EJIL 141, 167 ff. and *Aust* 2010, 366. But probably the right approach is that of *Brownlie*, 661 and 663 that 'non-transmissibility forms part of general international law', although there is an indication of *opinio juris* towards succession.

203 Cedric Ryngaert, 'Human Rights Obligations of Armed Groups' (2008) 41 RBDI 355, 358 and *Kleffner* 2011, 453.

204 *Ago*, 132, 'the acts committed by the organs of an insurrectional movement – apart from situations where the latter is transformed into something else following the favourable outcome of its struggle – cannot be attributed to the State against which the movement is, or has been, directed.

territorial state's jurisdiction with the ANSA's authority/control entails that it is actually the ANSA who is accountable for whatever happens in the territory and has external repercussions, at least with regard to interactions with third parties (non-nationals of the territorial state and third states as well). Consequently, the ANSA inherits at least *partly* the obligations of the state in the territory it controls.[205] Effectiveness suffices to create a basis for international accountability. But it would be wrong to assume that accountability is limited towards third states, because the sovereign and its citizens under the control of the ANSA should also be protected. Therefore humanitarian reasons imply that the ANSA should also be held accountable for its conduct towards anyone under its sphere of influence.

In a sense, the justification of devolution of responsibilities explains what happens before article 10 on State Responsibility comes into play and how a *de facto* government inherits its predecessor's obligations. The provisional status of an ANSA is not problematic as such, because devolution would cover only the time period until there is some certainty on the fate of the ANSA or else the preceding state obligations would fully resume.

Although effectiveness (as succession to the governmental position)[206] would not necessarily exclude devolution of responsibility for the whole body of IHL treaties,[207] there are a number of reasons why its effects are limited: to start with, the character of the conflict as non-international does not change in principle and states would disfavour anything that could amount to automatic recognition of belligerency, even for IHL purposes; secondly, the factual capability of ANSAs, which is usually subordinate to those of the state, point, also, to the need to limit the obligations of ANSAs only to a certain extent.

This claim could additionally have a legal significance, if viewed as a unilateral declaration entailing the willingness and capacity of the ANSA to incur at least certain state obligations. Claims of representation would probably be made as an assurance to the community of states that the ANSA is capable of undertaking and respecting the international obligations of the state. Moreover, it is likely that the credibility of such claim would depend on the representativeness of a group within the borders of the state and its capacity to uphold the effects of the unilateral declaration, in combination with its actual strength (including control over territory). In such a scenario it is possible that other actors (states or international organizations) would interact with the ANSA, on a limited scale. Of course any act of recognition (as a state, government, representative of peoples or belligerent) could entail certain rights and responsibilities for the ANSA.

In addition, the significance of this claim could appear in the context of violence between a third state and the ANSA. In the event that the non-representative government

---

Responsibility can be attached to that State only because of some possible failure by its own organs to discharge the habitual obligations of vigilance, prevention and, in particular, punishment.'

205 *Pinto*, 528. This is even more important and appropriate in failed or semi-failed states where in reality the territorial state could not logically bear any responsibility for any violation of treaty rules.

206 See Shigeki Miyazaki, 'The Application of the New Humanitarian Law' (1980) 20 IRRC 184, 187, noting this theory and linking it with the claim of representation. *Wilson*, 51, rejects, though, its validity, considering it as 'artificial … to assume obligations based on succession'.

207 It is probably for this reason that *Meyrowitz*, 172, does not support such thesis. Possibly respect for outside borders and objective regimes could also be justified under this rationale.

invites a third state which, then, clashes with the ANSA, the claim of the ANSA that it represents the national will might also suggest the character of the conflict as being international. In addition it could suggest its inclination and/or willingness to apply the corresponding rules. This would be more evident if this claim is coupled with a declaration on the applicable rules of international armed conflict. The legitimacy of the non-representative government will have a role to play; in such scenario, the third state could be regarded as a military occupier and the (representative) ANSA as the resistance force – Afghanistan in the 1980s could fit such a paradigm.[208] It might not even be necessary to resort to such justification, provided that the ANSA is deemed to be the legitimate government or a legitimate representative of the people. Similarly, in a situation of military occupation where there is no government-in-exile, the ANSA could be the only vehicle of the state representation and the conflict could be considered international.[209]

Overall, though, a claim of representation, which is certainly difficult to substantiate during an armed conflict period, would not be an adequate basis, apart from, arguably, very specific cases of ANSAs representing a majority in the state. Even in these cases, which would probably have to be combined with a large measure of effectiveness, it would be difficult to explain the position of the non-representative government with regard to its international humanitarian law obligations. At best it could provide a basis of obligations as a unilateral declaration and/or during a conflict with a third state. The need for alternatives, in consequence, becomes obvious.

Customary International Law

In the doctrine of belligerency recognition, the (voluntary) act of the state vests a limited personality in the non-state belligerent and the latter incurs, as a consequence, the corresponding rights and obligations which flow from the customary laws of international armed conflict (in relation to the recognizing state). The question that will occupy us is whether customary law can bind ANSAs who have not attracted this privilege.

Customary international law is based on the general (representative, widespread and consistent) practice of nations occurring out of a sense of obligation[210] and would apply in the relations between subjects of international law. Although it is rather uncontroversial that liberation movements have some limited personality and, arguably *de facto* entities, the case for common article 3 ANSAs seems much grimmer. States seem resistant to this idea, as evidenced by the continuing existence in treaties of the clause excluding any legal status

---

208 See also the Programme Politique du Front National de Libération du Sud Viet Nam (1967) 2, where the Front affirms that it is the only authentic representative of the South Vietnamese population. Significantly, its self-assessment included a claim that it has liberated four-fifths of the country. But in this programme, it does not make any reference to IHL proper, only to rules with a similar content, and it is not obvious how the conflict is judged. See also *1977 Records* Vol. 6, 154, where Mozambique indirectly considered the conflict in Vietnam as a national liberation war.

209 See *Solf* 1982, 235.

210 See however Antonio Cassese, 'The Martens Clause: Half a Loaf or Simply Pie in the Sky?' (2000) 11 EJIL 187, 213 ff., advocating that the Martens clause might have an impact on the formation of customary law.

of the parties to the conflict that are not High Contracting Parties. Yet it is uncontested that entities with no status have duties under customary IHL.[211]

The possibility that ANSAs in conflict have a limited international status for humanitarian purposes only has already been mentioned and it would explain how they have duties under this justification.[212] But in such a possibility, their practice should also be considered as able (although not essential) to contribute to the formation of custom, at least for matters that are left unregulated by the existing law and concern the scope of their duties and rights. After all, they are 'specially affected' actors and, to an extent, much more so than states that have never experienced (in the years of law formation for non-international armed conflicts) any internal armed conflict. Furthermore their representativeness of or affiliation with ethnic or other groups could also suggest that their views carry a certain importance beyond the ANSA itself and could be considered an element of interpretation from a civil society. Even the fact that they occasionally become governments of a state, either a new one or a pre-existing, should indicate an increased significance of at least certain ANSAs. Yet the legal significance of practice by ANSAs is rather unclear and that was accepted, also, by the CIHL Study,[213] although there is occasional mention thereof.[214] It has been suggested, by the ICTY[215] and academia, that states should 'not deny the reality that armed opposition groups are important actors ... and can contribute to the formation of customary law'[216] and possibly even to the

211 See, for example, Costa Rica, UN Doc S/PV. 3765 (14 April 1997) 20; Sweden on behalf of EU, UN Doc S/PV.4312 (Resumption 1) (23 April 2001) 6; UNCHR, 'Situation of Human Rights in Somalia: Report of the Special Rapporteur, Ms. Mona Rishmawi, Submitted in Accordance with Commission on Human Rights Resolution 1997/47' (16 January 1998) E/CN.4/1998/96, 5; UN Doc A/HRC/17/44, 33; William Walker, 'The International Law Applicable to Guerrilla Movements in Internal Armed Conflicts: A Case Study of Contra Attacks on Nicaraguan Farming Cooperatives' (1988–9) 21 N.Y.U.J.Int'l L. & Pol'y 147, 154; and Jean-Marie Henckaerts, 'Binding Armed Opposition Groups through Humanitarian Treaty Law and Customary Law' (2003) 27 Collegium 123, 128. See also the *1996 NDFP Declaration*.

212 The reference of the *Darfur Inquiry*, 51, that ' ... insurgents that have reached a certain threshold of organization, stability and effective control of territory, possess international legal personality and are therefore bound by the relevant rules of customary international law on internal armed conflicts ... ', would, on the one hand, substantiate the relevance of personality with customary obligations while it would also suggest that certain ANSAs, though nonetheless parties to a conflict, would not be bound by such rules.

213 Vol. 1, xlii. Such practice is listed along with NGOs' statements.

214 In Vol. 2, containing practice, there are 163 examples of ANSAs' conduct.

215 In the *Tadic* Appeals Decision [102–3] and [107], the Court used the practice of an ANSA as evidence for the creation of customary IHL, although in subsequent cases it did not do so, *Roberts and Sivakumaran*, 150. See also a passing general reference in the *Darfur Inquiry*, 44. Significantly even the UNSG, 'Respect for Human Rights in Armed Conflicts: Report' (18 September 1970) A/8052, 47, has envisaged that the 'present-day practices of Governments and insurgents' should play a role in the definition of active hostilities.

216 *Henckaerts* 2003, 128–9. See also *Anonymous*, 856–7; *M. Hoffman*, 209; *Sassòli* 2003, 6; Claude C. Emanuelli, 'Comments on the ICRC Study on Customary International Humanitarian Law' (2006) 44 Canadian YBIL 437, 444; *Bellal* et al., 15; and *Rondeau*, 668. The lowest level of participation

creation of rules that apply to such conflicts.[217] The signatories of the Geneva Call's Deed of Commitment state, in the preamble, that they are '*resolved* to play [their] role … as participants in the practice and development of legal and normative standards for such conflicts … ', even though this practice does not affect their legal status ([6] of the Deed). The only legal argument,[218] though, is that art 38 of the Statute of the International Court of Justice,[219] which is considered as the definitive statement on sources of international law, does not refer explicitly to state practice and therefore appears permissive with regard to the legal significance of practice by entities other than states.[220]

The results of such inclusion could be that sense of ownership (on the part of ANSAs) and, possibly, compliance could grow. This form of law-making is easier for states to accept in comparison to any form of direct law-making by ANSAs.[221] There is also a danger that states might agree to unachievable standards[222] and, therefore, ANSA practice could have positive results in the architecture and viability of the rules. Yet this exclusion reveals persisting fears of legitimacy,[223] which are, in a sense, more substantiated with regard to other non-state actors, because many ANSAs seek to replace the government that they are fighting. Additionally, such exclusion might also demonstrate the concern that their practice could tone down the minimum applicable rules of conduct.[224] Any relevant corroboration, though, does not exist: the verbal departure of ANSAs from existing rules is not extensive[225] or, at least, not more extensive than state usage, which has, at many times, exhibited disregard for humanitarian rules. If ANSAs have a different understanding, it is

---

could be envisaged in the case that there is controversy regarding the existence of a purported rule of customary law and the practice of ANSAs affirms or denies its customary character.

217 See the reluctant position of *ILA Committee on Non-State Actors* 2012, 665.

218 Robert McCorquodale, 'An Inclusive International Legal System' (2004) 17 LJIL 477, 498 and Jan Arno Hessbruege, 'Human Rights Violations Arising from Conduct of Non State Actors' (2005) 11 Buff. Hum. Rts. L.Rev. 21, 38.

219 Annex to the UN Charter.

220 See also the Dissenting Opinion of Judge van den Wyngaert in the *Arrest Warrant of 11 April 2000 (Democratic Republic of the Congo v Belgium)* [2002] ICJ Rep 156: 'the opinion of *civil* society … cannot be completely discounted in the formation of customary international law today' as well as Anthea Roberts, 'Righting Wrongs or Wronging Rights? The United States and Human Rights Post-September 11' (2004) 15 EJIL 721, 738–9.

221 Certainly, it is even more unimaginable that states would invite ANSAs to participate in the creation of IHL treaties, as suggested by *de Beco*, 192.

222 See this discussion *infra*, sub-chapter *Between Over- and Under- Regulation: Does One Size Fit All Armed Non-State Actors?*, at 105–6.

223 But see *Kleffner* 2011, 455: '[t]he fact that a given entity enjoys certain rights under international law and is subject to certain obligations does not necessarily confer legitimacy on that entity. Indeed, even states as the undisputed and only primary subjects of international law are not necessarily legitimate'.

224 *Somer*, 662, notes that ' … neither the ICTY Appeals Chamber nor the Darfur Commission pointed to any rebel practice that contradicted IHL norms created by states'.

225 See such practices in *CIHL Study* Vol. II, 574, 870, 929 and 972, but they constitute the minority of cited examples.

virtually impossible to change the law, unless states consent in this regard.[226] In fact there are examples where ANSAs appear to have moved beyond the existing rules of IHL.[227]

This justification would present an overall disadvantage: not all rules on non-international armed conflicts are of customary nature and, therefore, it could not be all-encompassing, although if the CIHL Study is a correct restatement of customary rules, then there will be very little difference between treaty law and customary rules.[228] In this case there could be a difference between the obligations of a state (based on treaty and customary law) and the ANSA (based only on customary law).[229] Consequently, it appears necessary that the customary law justification applies in parallel with any kind of treaty obligations applicable to ANSAs in order to avoid an inequality between the actors within the conflict.

An alternative justification is to focus rather on the status of the ANSA as a customary *recipient* of humanitarian law obligations, rather than the international persona of the ANSA, even if the latter is confined only to the needs of the community to bind this collective entity. This justification is attractive in the sense that it conforms to the literal meaning of common article 3.4, while it would be adequate for creating a foundation of obligations for customary law and (self-executing) treaty rules alike. It has not attracted, so far, any significant support. Only an Appeals Chamber of the SCSL[230] opined (without any reference to other sources or even the pedigree of the idea) that '... a convincing theory is that they are bound as a matter of international customary law to observe the obligations declared by Common Article 3 which is aimed at the protection of humanity'. Obviously such theoretical construction cannot explain how common article 3 was initially applicable to ANSAs and therefore we would need to resort to other justifications to find the root of ANSAs' obligations. Moreover we would need to ascertain *when* this customary rule arose and whether the *opinio juris* of states or the practice of ANSAs is the decisive factor for the emergence of a relevant rule, as, obviously, actual state *practice* cannot exist in this regard. Consequently, while this possibility seems attractive, it will not be easy to support.

In line with a basic hierarchy of international norms, certain of them have achieved a higher legal status. These norms have a potential as a basis for obligations for ANSAs.

Jus Cogens *Rules*

The notion of *jus cogens* appeared in written form through the VCLT (art 53), in the equivalent term of peremptory norms of international law. It designates norms (whether in treaty form or custom) that are considered by the international community as a non-derogable corpus of obligations for states. Although certain *jus cogens* rules operate in the inter-state (and international organizations) level, some of them are equally important to other non-state entities, due to their fundamental character. In essence, non-state

---

226 Similarly *Roberts and Sivakumaran*, 151.

227 Ibid., 138.

228 Actually the emergence of customary law is impressive, since the reference to the Martens clause in the preamble of Protocol II did not even include 'established custom'. On a more extensive discourse on the breadth of customary substantive rules see *infra* sub-chapter *From Numerable Rules to Wider Obligations*, at 99–103.

229 *Kleffner* 2011, 455.

230 *Sesay* Decision [47].

actors are prohibited from breaching the relevant rules,[231] regardless of international subjectivity. The principle of distinction between combatants and non-combatants[232] and the prohibition to 'cause unnecessary suffering to combatants' were deemed as cardinal for the ICJ in *Nuclear Weapons*.[233] As a result of the first principle, attacks against the civilian population and civilians are prohibited,[234] while the same should hold true for individuals not participating in hostilities (*hors de combat* or surrendered).[235] Dieter Fleck[236] has also referred to the obligation to protect medical personnel and units and cultural property, without necessarily determining whether they are binding on the ANSA.[237] Several writers[238] have also referred to the essence of common article 3 as being a *jus cogens* norm, while the prohibition of torture has been picked repetitively[239] as a norm of such nature. The prohibitions on genocide[240] and crimes against humanity[241] are also considered

---

231 See *Meyrowitz*, 171, *Schindler*, 151 and *Miyazaki* 1980, 188. See also *Provost*, 98, using a slightly different language.

232 See also the Turkish National Commission of Inquiry, Report on the Israeli Attack on the Humanitarian Aid Convoy to Gaza on 31 May 2010 (2011) 83–4. Significantly, in the Federal Government Reply, *Sassòli and Bouvier*, 2415–16, art 48 of Protocol I was not perceived to apply to the Chechnya conflict, because it was non-international, nor was a corresponding customary rule mentioned.

233 ICJ Rep 78. See also the Declaration of President Bedjaoui, *Nuclear Weapons*, ICJ Rep 273, 'most of the principles and rules of humanitarian law and, in any event, the two principles, one of which prohibits the use of weapons with indiscriminate effects and the other the use of arms causing unnecessary suffering … '.

234 Dieter Fleck, 'The Protocols Additional to the Geneva Conventions and Customary International Law' (1990) 29 Mil.L. & L. War Rev. 497, 501. See also the *Galic* Judgment [98]: 'the general prohibition of attack on civilians … is a peremptory norm of customary international law … .'

235 Hans-Peter Gasser, 'Determining Customary International Law Relative to the Conduct of Hostilities in Non-International Armed Conflicts' (1987) 2 Am.U.J.Int'l L. & Pol'y 478, 480, with regard to attacks against individuals that have surrendered and are *hors de combat* and Rosemary Abi-Saab, 'Human Rights and Humanitarian Law in Internal Conflicts' in Daniel Warner (ed.), *Human Rights and Humanitarian Law: the Quest for Universality* (Martinus Nijhoff 1997) 121, generally on individuals not participating in hostilities.

236 1990, 501.

237 See also UNCHR, 'Report on the Human Rights Situation in the Islamic Republic of Iran By the Special Representative of the Commission on Human Rights, Reynaldo Galindo Pohl, Pursuant to Commission Resolution 1991/82' (2 January 1992) UN Doc E/CN.4/1992/34, 76, on the prohibition to use chemical weapons.

238 *Veuthey* 1975, 262; *Schindler*, 151; *Baloro*, 461; *R. Abi-Saab*, 121; and Rafael Nieto-Navia, 'International Peremptory Norms (*Jus Cogens*) and International Humanitarian Law' (2001) 1, 25.

239 *Furundzija* [153–7], *Prosecutor v Delalic* (Judgment) ICTY-96- 21-T (16 November 1998) [454] and *Prosecutor v Kunarac* (Trial Judgment) (22 February 2001) [466].

240 Sri Lanka, Lebanon and Uruguay, *1969 Records* First Session, 219, 297 and 303 respectively. See also the positions of the DRC and the Court in *Armed Activities on the Territory of the Congo (New Application: 2002) (Democratic Republic of the Congo v Rwanda)* (Jurisdiction and Admissibility, Judgment) [2006] ICJ Rep 27 and 31 respectively.

241 *Prosecutor v Kupreskic* (Judgment) ICTY-95-16-T (14 January 2000) [520], *Responsibility Commentary*, 85 and *Bassiouni*, 726.

to attract this character, although they are not 'pure' international humanitarian law rules, since they are applicable outside armed conflicts as well.

The *jus cogens* approach as a law which should be respected by anyone, regardless of affiliation to a state or, generally speaking, any specific status, is satisfactory in general, while it could generate responses not only from the injured individual or party to the conflict but also from third states[242] and the international community in general. Nonetheless not all humanitarian law rules are of such quality and therefore it could not cover the whole spectrum of treaty provisions relating to humanitarian law obligations during non-international armed conflicts, although certain states have occasionally claimed that ' ... the humanitarian provisions of the Geneva Conventions are of a super-contractual character ... '[243] and ' ... humanitarian law should be regarded as coming under jus cogens'.[244] These maximalist positions seem justified: since humanitarian law is an implied derogation from normal human rights during peacetime, it appears plausible to consider humanitarian law as a complete code of non-derogable human rights during wartime. However, they appear to be minority considerations up to now.

Moreover the *jus cogens* justification would not explain how ANSAs were bound before certain humanitarian law rules acquired this quality. Consequently it could not be the sole base of ANSA obligations in humanitarian law, but only supplementary and parallel to other justifications.

Some Conclusions

To sum up, none of the above justifications is wholly satisfactory. The legislative jurisdiction treats ANSAs as subordinate to the state, while all other explanations confer a degree of autonomy on ANSAs or some form of status in the sense of being subject directly to international rather than municipal law. Consequently ANSAs would prefer any explanation other than the legislative jurisdiction approach, which is more appealing to states.[245] Nonetheless it is not obvious that all states, chiefly at the negotiating table of Protocol II, accepted its validity; there is a degree of speculation as to whether (subsequent) state practice, as elucidating the ordinary meaning of humanitarian law treaties, lends actual support to this justification, although it attracts the majority of doctrine.

The possibility of an 'extra-territorial' internal armed conflict could show the limits of each justification. As such we describe a conflict of an ANSA with its state of origin on foreign soil. Supposing that this still remains a non-international armed conflict, under the legislative jurisdiction, the ANSA would be bound by the internal laws of the territorial

---

242 Under the state responsibility rules a breach of a peremptory obligation could generate: a) the duty of other states to cooperate so as to bring the cessation of such breach, b) a prohibition of aid or assistance towards the state committing the wrongful act and its recognition. Such effect should pertain to breaches of peremptory norms by entities other than states.

243 Monaco, *1949 Records* Vol. II-B, 79.

244 Syria, *1977 Records* Vol. 5, 193. See also Lebanon's reference to 'the wartime treatment of prisoners and wounded and of the civil population' as part of *jus cogens*, *1969 Records* First Session, 297 and Poland, *1969 Records* First Session, 302, referring to 'some of the rules of land warfare'.

245 For *Kleffner* 2011, 460, the legislative jurisdiction also encompasses more comprehensively the legal framework, while other explanations have a better prospect to induce compliance by ANSAs.

state, while the basis of obligations for the state in conflict with the ANSA will be its own treaty obligations, possibly different from those of the ANSA. The claim of state representation appears weaker in an 'extra-territorial' context, since treaties relevant to non-international armed conflicts are, primarily, destined to apply within the borders of the state in conflict. The effect of treaties for third parties appears more relevant, if both states have ratified the same treaties, depending also on whether the ANSA again accepts the obligations. In that regard, custom and *jus cogens* are more appealing in the sense that they are not spatially limited, although they both cover only a sub-part of the whole of humanitarian rules.

The legislative jurisdiction is probably the best way to explain how humanitarian law was initially binding upon individuals, and, arguably,[246] ANSAs;[247] neither the *travaux préparatoires* nor subsequent state practice seemed to accept unreservedly that *international* law would bind non-state entities and therefore only internal law (as a mirror of international law) would be the source of obligations. Probably the understanding was that only certain ANSAs would be bound, excluding common article 3 ANSAs. Gradually, however, it was supplemented, if not replaced, by a customary rule which automatically binds ANSAs once there is an armed conflict,[248] as the SCSL accepted in the *Sesay* decision. It remains then to examine the temporal (when has this rule emerged) and the material element (the evidence of practice and whether it includes ANSA practice as well).

References to Security Council resolutions, whether under Chapter VII or not, became quite typical in recent years, although they appeared initially in the beginning of the 1990s. The Security Council called upon all parties to the conflict 'to respect strictly the provisions of international humanitarian law' (Res 788 (19 November 1992) [5]) and demanded that 'all parties, movements and factions in Somalia immediately cease and desist from all breaches of international humanitarian law ... '.[249]

The General Assembly seems to have endorsed such possibility at least a decade earlier. In Res 2444 (XXIII) (19 December 1968) [1], it affirms ' ... the following principles for observance by all governmental and other authorities responsible for action in armed conflicts'.[250] In other contemporary resolutions, such as 2677 (XXV) (9 December 1970) and 2852 (XXVI) (20 December 1971) [1], the Assembly is more ambiguous, because on the one hand, it calls upon 'parties to any armed conflict', but on the other hand it seeks

---

246 See also the reluctance of *Boothby* 2009, 318.

247 See *Sivakumaran* 2006, 393: 'under the legislative jurisdiction explanation, all armed opposition groups are bound. Some may not consider themselves bound and therefore not follow the rules but they would remain bound'.

248 The parallel validity of other justifications cannot be excluded, depending on the respective ANSA and the content of the rule.

249 S/RES/794 [4]. See also, indicatively, UNSC Res 771 (13 August 1992) [3], S/RES/814 [13], 820 (17 April 1993) [4], 834 (1 June 1993) [13], 851 (15 July 1993) [18–19], S/RES/864 [13], 950 (21 October 1994) [7], 972 (13 January 1995) [7], 985 (13 April 1995) [6], 1001 (30 June 1995) preamble and [13], 1059 (31 May 1996) [7] and S/RES/1193 [12].

250 For the International Institute of Humanitarian Law, 'Rules of International Humanitarian Law Governing the Conduct of Hostilities in Non-International Armed Conflicts' (1990) 30 IRRC 383, 389 and 408 (hereinafter IIHL 1990), it implies ANSAs as well.

respect for conventions that are unconcerned with non-international armed conflicts, such as the Hague Conventions of 1899 and 1907. In the preamble of A/RES/42/137 on El Salvador[251] it is considered that ' … the parties involved are under an obligation to apply the minimum standards of protection of human rights and humanitarian treatment provided for in article 3 common to the Geneva Conventions of 1949 and in Additional Protocol II thereto, of 1977' and, therefore, the intention is much more evident. The differentiation with regard to UNGA Res 36/155[252] which

> *draws the attention* of all parties concerned to the fact that the rules of international law, as contained in common article three of the Geneva Conventions of 12 August 1949, are applicable to armed conflicts not of an international character and *requests* the parties involved to apply a minimum standard of protection to the affected population (emphasis added)

is fairly evident. Around the same time as A/RES/2444 (XXIII), the Secretary General stated that 'common article 3 of the four Conventions … extends the scope of international rules also to conflicts not of an international character by imposing upon the Parties to such a conflict the duty to observe a minimum, standard of conduct'.[253] More recently the ICJ in *Nicaragua*[254] has also affirmed that 'the acts of the *contras* towards the Nicaraguan government are … covered by the law applicable to conflicts of that character', meaning non-international armed conflicts.

As regards states, the negotiations phase for the Geneva Conventions exhibited a minority number in favour of ANSAs having obligations. The preparatory period of the Protocols shows that the minority grew stronger and it might even have become a majority, including Western states that displayed a different understanding in 1949. The strongly opposing dissent came from non-Western states, mainly Latin American and Asian ones (some of them specially affected). This dissent has eroded with the passage of time. It was during the 1990s that the *opinio juris* of states was evident and elucidated the meaning of relevant treaty rules. For Ecuador 'it is necessary for all the parties … strictly to comply with the rules of humanitarian international law',[255] while Zambia ' … strongly support[ed] the appeal … to … UNITA – to abide by … international humanitarian law',[256] followed by Tanzania's reference to the humanitarian law obligations

251 See also UNGA Res 38/100 (16 December 1983) [7] on Guatemala, 40/137 (13 December 1985) [8] on Afghanistan, A/RES/40/140 [10] on Guatemala, 43/139 (8 December 1988) [9] on Afghanistan, 43/145 (8 December 1988) and 44/165 (15 December 1989) preamble on El Salvador, 48/153 (20 December 1993) [4] on Yugoslavia and A/RES/51/112 [9] on Sudan. The evolution could also be seen in the difference between A/RES/51/117 [15] and A/RES/47/144 [10], since the latter is addressed only to the Burmese government, while the former is 'to other parties to the hostilities' as well.

252 (16 December 1981) [4].

253 UN Doc A/7720, 26.

254 [1986] ICJ Rep 114.

255 UN Doc S/PV. 3138 (19 November 1992) 82.

256 UN Doc S/PV. 3254 (15 July 1993) 78.

of UNITA.[257] Germany's Manual[258] refers to 'each party [that] shall be bound to apply ... the fundamental provisions', while South Korea[259] referred to observation of IHL by Afghan parties. Honduras ' ... appeal[ed] to the Afghan parties ... to abide by international humanitarian law'[260] and Costa Rica ' ... reiterate[d] the obligation of the parties to the conflict to respect international humanitarian law customarily applied to internal armed conflicts'.[261] Slovenia[262] has also stressed the duty of parties to the conflict in Afghanistan to respect IHL. More importantly, the reappearance of the language of common article 3 in Protocol II as Amended on 3 May 1996 and Amended Article 1 to the CCW as well as the Second Protocol to the 1954 Hague Convention could not but mean that humanitarian law was intended to apply to ANSAs equally, while 'dissenters' in the preparatory works of Protocol II as Amended on 3 May 1996 are missing. Even Colombia, which exhibited a different understanding in 1977, has altered its position.[263]

The practice of ANSAs seems equally extensive and it should be accepted that ANSAs have had a role in the emergence of such customary rule: unlike substantive customary rules, which undoubtedly are formed as standards of conduct that states should follow themselves, it would be difficult to see why and how the practice of states alone could form a rule which would be relevant and applicable *exclusively* to non-state entities. In that sense the formation of the customary rule echoes the mechanism of third-party obligations through treaties, which (would) require some form of assent by the third party.

Algeria argued quite early in its conflict with France that common article 3 is applicable.[264] Other non-state parties, such as those in Lebanon (1958) and Cuba (1959) have also accepted their relevant obligations.[265] A similar acceptance was exhibited by several armed groups, such as the Ian Smith regime in Rhodesia (1978),[266] the Moro National Front in the Philippines,[267] the FMLN in El Salvador and the Contras in Nicaragua,[268] the Rwandan

257 Ibid., 84–5. See also Venezuela, 107 and Morocco, 112.

258 In *Fleck* 1995, 47. See also the Reply by the Federal Government to the Written Question Submitted by Bundestag Member Vera Wollenberger and the Parliamentary Party of the Alliance 9O/Greens in *Sassòli and Bouvier*, 2292.

259 UN Doc S/PV. 3705 (16 October 1996) 19.

260 Ibid., 26.

261 UN Doc S/PV. 3765, 20. See also S/PV. 3921 (Resumption) (28 August 1998) 9. See also Portugal in UN Doc S/PV. 3765 (Resumption) (15 April 1997) 13 and S/PV. 3921 (Resumption) 4.

262 UN Doc S/PV. 3921 (Resumption) 12.

263 Statement of Government of Colombia Regarding the Status of FARC, 16 June 1999 (1999) 2 YIHL 441. See also Pakistan's condemnation of IHL violations by the Bosnian Serbs in S/PV. 3200 (18 April 1993) 44.

264 Eldon Van Cleef Greenberg, 'Law and the Conduct of the Algerian Revolution' (1970) 11 Harv.Int'l L.J. 37, 49 and 55.

265 *Veuthey* 1975, 237–8 and *Forsythe* 1978, 275. See also *Veuthey* 1975, 236–7 on Guatemala (1954) and Iraq (1961). Many more, however, did not.

266 David P. Forsythe, 'Comment' (1981–2) 31 Am.U.L.Rev. 833, 834 and *Boister*, 132.

267 *Veuthey* 1983, 92–3.

268 *Kogod Goldman*, 550–51. See also *Rondeau*, 664.

Patriotic Front in Rwanda,[269] the MRTA in Peru,[270] the ELN in Colombia,[271] the SPLM in Sudan,[272] the CPN (Maoist) in Nepal[273] and the NTC.[274] Significantly, express denials by ANSAs did not appear, to the author's knowledge, within the last decades. Much of ANSA practice cited in the CIHL Study (and mostly covering the period from 1980 to 1995) also corroborates the assent of these actors to be bound by (at least specific) humanitarian law rules. More recently, the signatories of Geneva Call's Deed of Commitment accept, in the preamble, that humanitarian law applies to and obligates all parties to armed conflict. Although it is not certain that such acceptances are always a pure exhibition of *opinio juris*, they have become habitual over the years, regardless of the type of ANSAs, and they are too numerous to indicate only policy. Noticeably, even ANSAs who were negative in the past with regard to their own humanitarian law obligations, such as the FARC and NDFP, have changed their minds.[275] Consequently it would appear that the *opinio juris* and the practice of ANSAs[276] were evident around the time period in the beginning of the 1990s. In light of these, it seems difficult to accept nowadays the position of Meron that 'nongovernmental entities that exercise control over people … habitually deny that they are bound by international standards'.[277]

To sum up, it would appear that at present there is a customary international law norm with regard to the applicability of humanitarian law standards to ANSAs. The generality of practice and its consistency, although not necessarily evident in compliance, points towards the existence of such a norm. Yet the content of these standards does not apply for every new convention relevant to non-international armed conflicts. It is mainly applicable to the older treaty law, common article 3 and, arguably,[278] Protocol II. Protocol II as Amended on 3 May 1996, the Second Protocol to the 1954 Hague Convention and the Amended Article 1 to the CCW have to be tested against time, unless they are considered

269 UNCHR, 'Report of the United Nations High Commissioner for Human Rights on His Mission to Rwanda of 11–12 May 1994' (19 May 1994) E/CN.4/S-3/3, 10. The Court in *Akayesu* [627] considered Protocol II as applicable for various reasons including the acceptance of the ANSA's humanitarian obligations.

270 *Sivakumaran* 2012, 122.

271 See the *ELN Declaration*. Colombia became a party to the Protocol this same year.

272 See the *Agreement between the Government of the Republic of Sudan and The Sudan People's Liberation Movement To Protect Non-Combatant Civilians And Civilian Facilities from Military Attack*, art 1.

273 P.J.C. Schimmelpenninck van der Oije, 'International Humanitarian Law from a Field Perspective: Nepal' (2006) 9 YIHL 394, 404.

274 'Frontline Manual' (2011).

275 *Jaramillo*, 189 ff.

276 This is a reference to practice with regard to the core rule, because violations of specific rules have occurred in every armed conflict, without this meaning that there was no overall compliance.

277 Theodor Meron, 'The Humanization of Humanitarian Law' (2000) 94 AJIL 239, 273. See the opposite opinion from *Veuthey* 1975, 262 and Noelle Higgins, 'The Application of International Humanitarian Law to Wars of National Liberation' (2004) Journal of Humanitarian Assistance 5.

278 The above-mentioned acceptances only rarely make an explicit reference to Protocol II. It is more common to refer to IHL in general or common article 3.

in their substantive part as customary law – the CIHL Study suggests that they are, for their most part. Otherwise, new treaty rules should be seen under the legislative jurisdiction, unless any other justification (such as the effect of treaties for third parties) appears more plausible, according to the circumstances of the case. This highly fragmented situation of affairs is partly due to the lack of an accepted status for ANSAs and it can have an impact on their obligations as well as, mainly, their accountability, to which we now turn.

The Obligations of Armed Non-State Actors

The Extent of Obligations: From Numerable Rules to Wider Obligations

The obligations of ANSAs through humanitarian law have evolved considerably since 1949, especially during the last two decades. Common article 3 was applicable for almost 30 years on its own, with the exception of art 19 of the 1954 Hague Convention. Protocol II was bound to apply to a certain segment of ANSAs, while in the 1990s common article 3 ANSAs were expected to apply additional rules regarding the use of weapons and the protection of cultural property. The Rome Statute has solidified the existence of other rules besides the above-mentioned, even if not directly applicable to common article 3 ANSAs. Finally, the (r)evolution of customary law, as initiated by the ICTY jurisprudence, has brought certain norms applicable to international armed conflicts to their internal counterpart. In summation, the regulatory framework for ANSAs contains the following:[279]

a. The treatment of civilians and persons *hors de combat*
b. The principle of distinction
c. Specifically protected persons and objects
d. Specific methods of warfare
e. Weapons.

This legal framework would be so concise,[280] provided that the CIHL Study represents an exact mirror of the customary rules in this regard. This framework is deemed to be applicable to all types of ANSAs. There is, however, controversy on several issues. The method of reliance on written resources rather than actual practice in the field[281] appears

279 The wording of the *CIHL Study* has been deliberately chosen, so that there is a common point of reference.

280 Note though that less than 20 years before the publication of the *CIHL Study* one of its editors, Louise Doswald-Beck, 'The Civilian in the Crossfire' (1987) 24 JPR 251, 258, was concluding that 'the major problems are actually to be found in internal armed conflicts where the regulation of hostilities as such is not covered by customary law'. See also the quote from Professor Melander in UNSG, 'Minimum Humanitarian Standards: Report of the Secretary General' (28 January 1997) E/CN.4/1997/77/Add.1, 22 on the '[i]nadequate protection of the civilian population' within humanitarian law. But see opposite, *Gasser*, 478 ff., also a legal advisor to the ICRC, and *Walker*, 166 ff.

281 Likewise see John B. Bellinger, III and William J. Haynes II, 'A US Government Response to the International Committee of the Red Cross Study Customary International Humanitarian

to be an issue. However, Bothe[282] is right to comment that this 'implies that states do not really mean what they say' and, therefore, written materials are important. Field practice also presents a difficulty to ascertain, if only because states (and ANSAs) are rarely ready to share their conduct. This, of course, should not mean that field practice should be discarded; it should mean, though, that alternate practice should also be taken into account.

The normative weight given to certain practice has also been criticized.[283] These comments reveal a highly state-centred approach to customary law, which is not proper. States should not be the only vehicles for the expression of a certain *opinio iuris* and, in fact, more weight should have been given to the views of ANSAs, not only as one of the principal actors of a non-international armed conflict but also because many of them have a valid representation claim which goes beyond the armed group itself. The views of NGOs, the ICRC and/or human rights bodies should also carry a normative weight, especially since they might express a public world conscience on certain matters that pertain to IHL.

A more valid objection concerns the fact that it is too easily assumed that *opinio iuris* and practice of states reflect customary law, although they have the same obligations under treaty law.[284] This is particularly evident with military manuals which might '... also reflect policy and operational concerns'[285] or, simply, treaty rules.[286] In such cases it might be necessary to examine the overall status of the manual (for example it might be stated that it has been approved by the higher military and political echelons), its uniqueness, the language used (for example any reference to policy) and so on. Depending on circumstances, there might be a need to corroborate the rule with further evidence from other national sources. For example, the passing of a law which merely translates the international treaty would not be particularly significant. An internal law which *adds* content to the international treaty

---

Law' (2007) 89 IRRC 443, 445.

282 Michael Bothe, 'Customary International Humanitarian Law: Some Reflections on the ICRC Study' (2005) 8 YIHL 143, 156–7. See also Iain Scobbie, 'The Approach to Customary International Law in the Study' in Elizabeth Wilmshurst and Susan Breau (eds), *Perspectives on the ICRC Study on Customary International Humanitarian Law* (CUP 2007) 38.

283 As examples see Yoram Dinstein, 'The ICRC Customary International Humanitarian Law Study' in Anthony M. Helm (ed.), *The Law of War in the 21st Century: Weaponry and the Use of Force* (International Law Studies Vol. 82, Naval War College 2006) 102, who rejects the validity of practice by the ICRC or other NGOs and Yutuka Arai-Takahashi, *The Law of Occupation: Continuity and Change of International Humanitarian Law, and its Interaction with International Human Rights Law* (Nijhoff 2009) 516, on reliance on documents from the monitoring bodies of human rights treaties.

284 See *Scobbie*, 32 ff. Obviously an additional step is needed for states that rejected becoming bound by treaty rules.

285 Michael N. Schmitt, 'The Law of Targeting' in in Elizabeth Wilmshurst and Susan Breau (eds), *Perspectives on the ICRC Study on Customary International Humanitarian Law* (CUP 2007) 134 and *Abresch*, 749–50. Abresch also notices, rightly, the assumptions that the manuals 'apply to internal armed conflicts unless explicitly limited to international armed conflicts'.

286 *Bothe* 2005, 156–7.

would appear to be a more significant piece of evidence.[287] With regard to rules which are not expressly to be found in international treaties, but, nevertheless, appear to be included in formal internal sources (for example laws, manuals and so on), the indications are even more serious. Even the steady repetition of certain rules in a variety of national sources cannot but be a serious *indication* that a norm is not only an operational or policy concern.

Several doubts have also been raised with regard to the content of the study.[288] One could reasonably wonder why in the most comprehensive recent statement of the law of non-international armed conflict, the Rome Statute, many of the rules deemed as customary were not included.[289] In addition 'some of its findings remain rather vague due to the absence of convincing practice'.[290] Consequently more gaps exist in the law of non-international armed conflict. These gaps correspond to certain provisions of Protocol II[291] – the non-inclusion of customary law in the Martens clause of Protocol II preamble exhibited the lack of established custom[292] – and, mainly, non-treaty provisions. It is possible that the desire to solidify the humanizing content of IHL has affected the attitudes of the drafters,[293] in a way similar to how it has previously affected judges of international criminal tribunals.

For example it is doubtful, in the least, whether perfidy includes capturing the enemy combatant.[294] Even the references to certain military manuals as supportive of the rule

287 Another possible example would be that of a state which is not party to a particular treaty but, nevertheless, appears to follow that treaty or parts of it.

288 See *Aust* 2010, 237 ' … overstates many claims to customary law status'.

289 See for example the comment of Andreas Zimmermann, 'Commentary on Para. 2 (c)–(f) and Para. 3: War Crimes in an Armed Conflict Not of an International Character' in Otto Triffterer (ed.), *Commentary on the Rome Statute of the International Criminal Court: Observers' Notes, Article by Article* (Nomos 1999) 277, with regard to direct attacks on civilian objects in non-international armed conflict. A possible answer could be the lack of criminality and not that a corresponding IHL rule does not exist. See also the Federal Government Reply in *Sassòli and Bouvier*, 2415–6, also casting doubts on the applicability of such a principle in non-international armed conflicts.

290 Dieter Fleck, 'International Accountability for Violations of the *Ius In Bello*: The Impact of the ICRC Study on Customary International Humanitarian Law' (2006) 11 J.C.& S.L. 179, 197.

291 On several doubts on its customary status see Françoise Hampson, 'Human Rights and Humanitarian Law in Internal Conflicts' in Michael A. Meyer (ed.), *Armed Conflict and the New Law* (British Institute of International and Comparative Law 1989) 68; *L.C. Green*, 320; *Rogers* 2004, 236; *Yihdego*, 45; and *Solis*, 129 as well as UNSG, 'Letter Transmitting the Final Report of the Commission of Experts Established Pursuant to Security Council Resolution 780 (1992)' (27 May 1994) S/1994/674, 15; *Akayesu* [610]; and *Tadic* Appeals Decision [117]. It is not always obvious in the *CIHL Study* that practice pertaining to customized Protocol II provisions was exercised in common article 3 conflicts or by common article 3 ANSAs.

292 Karl Josef Partsch, 'Preamble, Protocol II' in Bothe et al. (eds), *New Rules for Victims of Armed Conflicts: Commentary on the Two 1977 Protocols Additional to the Geneva Conventions of 1949* (Martinus Nijhoff Publishers 1982) 621.

293 But, at times, it has led to lesser protection in customary law, despite a treaty law offering more, see *Sivakumaran* 2012, 69, on works and installations containing dangerous forces.

294 See *IIHL Manual*, Rule 2.3.6; Christopher Greenwood, 'International Humanitarian Law and the Tadic Case' (1996) 7 EJIL 265, 278; *Moir*, 146; and Tamas Hoffmann, 'The Gentle

might not be necessarily proper: apart from the practice of Israel,[295] the Canadian Manual[296] does not state anywhere that a prohibition of perfidy is part and parcel of the law of non-international armed conflict (chapter 17); there is a reference that 'it is CF. policy, however, that the CF. will, as a minimum, apply the spirit and principles of the [law of armed conflict] during all operations other than domestic operations [1702.2]', yet policy is not evidence of *opinio juris*.

Other controversies that arose include (but are not limited to[297]) the distinction between combatants and civilians, the definition of combatants and who can be regarded as a prisoner of war,[298] humanitarian relief,[299] the effect of armed conflict on the environment,[300] reprisals[301] and the use of certain weapons.[302] With regard to the latter, weapons or other materials or methods prohibited in international armed conflicts are not prohibited *ipso facto* in non-international armed conflicts,[303] although there is an opinion to

---

Humanizer of Humanitarian Law – Antonio Cassese and the Creation of the Customary Law of Non-International Armed Conflicts' (2009) 9. On the other hand see *IIHL* 1990, 390; Antonio Cassese, 'The Geneva Protocols of 1977 on the Humanitarian Law of Armed Conflict and Customary International Law' (1984) 3 UCLA Pacific Basin L.J. 55, 78–9; Denise Plattner, 'The 1980 Convention on Conventional Weapons and the Applicability of Rules Governing Means of Combat in a Non-International Armed Conflict' (1990) 30 IRRC 551, 554; and George H. Aldrich, 'Customary International Humanitarian Law – An Interpretation on behalf of the International Committee of the Red Cross' (2006) 76 British YBIL 503, 518.

295 *Dinstein* 2006, 103. But see *Scobbie*, 40.

296 The *CIHL Study* has resorted to a 1999 manual.

297 The obligation to report missing persons, per the *CIHL Study*, Rule 117, might be on the way of becoming a customary rule, see *Sivakumaran* 2012, 285. Similarly *CIHL Study*, Rule 123, see *Sivakumaran* 2012, 295 and Rule 54, see *Aldrich*, 516–17. In addition, the maintenance of graves in Rule 115, is not supported in either treaty law or adequately in practice, as regards non-international armed conflicts.

298 *IIHL Manual*, 5. See also HCJ 769/02 *The Public Committee Against Torture in Israel v the Government of Israel* (14 December 2006) [30], on the position of Israel. Jean Marie Henckaerts, 'Customary International Humanitarian Law – A Rejoinder to Judge Aldrich' (2006) 76 British YBIL 525, 532, accepts that the Commentary is inconclusive on the extent of customization of art 44.3 second sentence.

299 See the quite convincing comments of the US in *Bellinger III and Haynes II*, 448–54 and *Aldrich* 517. The comment of Professor Melander in UN Doc E/CN.4/1997/77/Add.1, 22, with regard to the 'inadequate provisions relating to humanitarian assistance', could show that the Study might be forward-looking rather than freezing the situation as it was at the time of its publication. See also India, S/PV.4046 (Resumption 1) (17 September 1999) 26.

300 See the long-standing opposition of the US in *Matheson*, 424 and *Aldrich*, 514 ff. as well as *Rogers* 2004, 233. The rule of Protocol I was considered to be an innovation, see *Fleck* 1990, 502.

301 *Rogers* 2004, 235 and *Sivakumaran* 2012, 452. See also, indirectly, *de Beco*, 198.

302 See, for example, David Turns, 'Weapons in the ICRC Study on Customary International Humanitarian Law' (2006) 11 J.C.& S.L. 201–37, *Aldrich*, 518 ff. and *Boothby* 2009, 325 ff.

303 See *Turns* 2006, 208 ff. and Steve Haines, 'Weapons, Means and Methods of Warfare' in Elizabeth Wilmshurst and Susan Breau (eds), *Perspectives on the ICRC Study on Customary International Humanitarian Law* (CUP 2007) 262–3. The Declaration of Israel (22 March 1995) as well as the Reservation of France (18 July 2002) to the Convention on Prohibitions or Restrictions on the

the opposite, at least as regards weapons. The International Institute of Humanitarian Law considered almost all weapon prohibitions in international armed conflicts as applicable, equally, in non-international ones.[304] Art 5.3 of the Declaration on Minimum Humanitarian Standards (hereinafter Minimum Humanitarian Standards)[305] attempted to illegalize such uses, but only remained a soft law instrument. The Rome Statute has accepted a limited convergence of corresponding rules, though increasing after the later expansion of the list of prohibited weapons in 2010 with the addition of chemicals and expanding bullets. Consequently the CIHL Study and state practice do not appear to match exactly.

In any case this study is a point of reference[306] as well as a starting point for a debate on the exact content of customary law;[307] it does not necessarily provide conclusive facts. However, Sivakumaran[308] might be right to assert that the existence of the Study and its citations with approval tend to reverse the burden of proof with regard to the existence and content of a customary rule. On the other hand, these controversies make it even more difficult to argue that such rules are applicable to ANSAs, when the primary bearers of obligations and the users of law are denying its content. Regardless of any controversy, though, the overall legal framework is somewhat impressive, if compared to the situation approximately 25 years ago. In fact the obligations of ANSAs are not only termed in the negative, as prohibitions. On the contrary ANSAs are sometimes required to take positive measures: precautionary measures during hostilities mean that the ANSA should act positively prior to attacks, for example by notifying the civilian population of its intentions, in order to minimize civilian losses and damages to civilian objects. Likewise, the obligation to collect and care for the wounded and the sick (common article 3.2) requires action for the benefit of those categories. Protocol II contains more provisions of such quality: art 7.1 requires that 'the wounded, sick and shipwrecked … shall be respected and protected', using language which is broader than that of common article 3.2. Other provisions of Protocol II require the fighting parties to act with due diligence and are reflected, *inter alia*, in arts 5.4 and 8.[309]

Use of Certain Conventional Weapons which May Be Deemed to Be Excessively Injurious or to Have Indiscriminate Effects (adopted 10 October 1980, entered into force 2 December 1983) 1342 UNTS 137, that they will apply the treaty in both international and non-international armed conflicts, specifically illustrates this point.

304 *IIHL 1990*, 395 ff. See also *Kelly*, 107, Frits Kalshoven, 'Applicability of Customary International Law in Non-International Armed Conflicts' in Antonio Cassese (ed.), *Current Problems of International Law: Essays on U.N. Law and on the Law of Armed Conflict* (Dott. A. Giuffrè 1975) 282, *Kogod Goldman*, 559, UNSG, 'Note Transmitting 3rd Report of the Director of the Human Rights Division of ONUSAL' (19 February 1992) A/46/876, 36 and the *Tadic* Appeals Decision [119 ff.].

305 Theodor Meron and Alan Rosas, 'Declaration on Minimum Humanitarian Standards' (1991) 85 AJIL 375–81.

306 See *Bothe* 2005, 176.

307 See UNGA Res 61/30 (18 December 2006).

308 2012, 104.

309 See also arts 4.3, 5.2e and 9.1 of Protocol II.

In recent times it appears that UN organs tend to demand some form of due diligence from ANSAs.[310] For the Security Council 'parties to armed conflict bear the primary responsibility to take all feasible steps to ensure the protection of affected civilians',[311] while they are also requested to prevent violations of IHL.[312] In Res 1894 (11 November 2009) [1], the Council urges parties to conflicts 'to take all required measures to respect and protect the civilian population and meet its basic needs'. In UNCHR Res 63 (2005) [1], parties to the conflict are urged to ' ... comply with their obligations under international humanitarian law, in particular to ensure respect for and protection of the civilian population'. However, it is not obvious what sort of additional obligations these international acts entail.

One step further, a Group of Special Rapporteurs[313] considered that 'those in positions of authority in Gaza have ... a responsibility to ensure that these [international humanitarian] norms are respected by others'. Obviously this is a far-reaching conclusion, but in light of the situation in Gaza, resembling a *de facto* regime, it might be proper and commensurate to the strength of the entity in the ruling position over the territory. It is not certain, though, whether the objective capability of the ANSAs is duly taken into account,[314] and therefore the actual compliance of ANSAs might be put into question, regardless of whether they choose to abide by those rules or not. Maybe we could refer to a general desirability (or a policy principle) that ANSAs exercise some form of diligence, which, of course, relates to the prevailing circumstances each time (control over territory, organization of the ANSA, capability of the state to exercise due diligence and so on). While, however, the extension of obligations appears legitimate, if not required, in certain circumstances in which the law does not provide adequate answers for ANSAs with substantive factual powers and control over territory, it is also debatable whether the extension of obligations took into account the realities of non-international armed conflicts.

---

310 See also the rather unconvincing Rule 139 of the *CIHL Study* Vol. 1, 495–8 and the comments of *Zegveld*, 92–3 and *Somer*, 684.

311 Preambles of S/RES/1674, Res 1738 (23 December 2006), 2109 (11 July 2013) and 2120 (10 October 2013).

312 UNSC Res 1479 (13 May 2003) [8], 1493 (28 July 2003) [8], 1556 (30 July 2004) preamble and S/RES/1738 [6]. See also Res 2173 (27 August 2014) [25] and the demand to prevent the ' ... recruitment and use of children ... '.

313 UNHRC, 'Report of the High-Level Fact-Finding Mission to Beit Hanoun Established under Council Resolution S-3/1' (1 September 2008) A/HRC/9/26, 21–2. See also UNHRC, 'Report of the United Nations Fact-Finding Mission on the Gaza Conflict' (15 September 2009) A/HRC/12/48, 124.

314 See, for example, 'Report of the Independent International Commission of Inquiry on the Syrian Arab Republic' (4 June 2013) A/HRC/23/58, 25, where there is a recommendation towards ' ... anti-Government armed groups' to ' ... compel all groups to respect ... international humanitarian law'.

Between Over- and Under- Regulation: Does One Size Fit All Armed Non-State Actors?

In light of the CIHL Study, it appears that most treaty rules (including those of Protocol II) would apply to ANSAs without any (or substantive) control of territory, that is, common article 3 ANSAs. Would this be a viable solution for ANSAs that have not reached a certain level of effectiveness? Similar fears were expressed at the negotiating table for Protocol I, with regard to national liberation movements,[315] as well as Protocol II, with regard to the respective ANSAs.[316] Common article 3 ANSAs would find even more serious impediments to their effort to respect humanitarian law.[317] For example, will they have the resources for a 'regularly constituted court affording all the judicial guarantees which are recognized as indispensable by civilized peoples' in order to satisfy the relevant provision? This provision could be an indication that either common article 3 was not necessarily intended to bind the ANSAs or, alternatively, that the formulation of humanitarian rules did not take the realities of ANSAs into account. Moreover, would they have the means to record the emplacement of mines, according to Protocol II as Amended on 3 May 1996 (art 9.1)? Yet the international community did not seem to take this potential incapacity of ANSAs into account[318] – in fact it shows a reason why the practice of ANSAs should have played a certain role; at least because it would show the limits of their capacity.[319] There are, though, certain exceptions, evident mainly in Protocol II provisions depending on 'the limits of their capabilities' (art 5.2) and 'to the fullest extent practicable' (art 7.2).[320]

G. Abi-Saab[321] persuasively rejected such difficulties for national liberation movements.[322] He referred, among other factors, to micro-states which are parties to the treaties and to the similarity of the situation to belligerent occupation where resistance movements were not considered to have a problem of adherence. But micro-states still control territory, while certain national liberation movements did not – analogically the same applies with

315 Burundi, *1977 Records* Vol. 5, 116, Israel, *1977 Records* Vol. 6, 42 and Netherlands *1977 Records* Vol. 8, 31.

316 India, *1977 Records* Vol. 8, 309. See also the remarks of Canada and Spain, *1977 Records* Vol. 8, 337 and 362 respectively.

317 *Rubin*, 485, *Dinstein* 1976, 67 and U.O. Umozurike, 'The Application of International Humanitarian Law to Civil Conflicts' (1992) 4 AFJICL 493, 498.

318 *Zegveld*, 34–5.

319 Several other provisions of Protocol II which would appear difficult to implement by common article 3 ANSAs are the ones regarding access to education of children, letters to and from detained people, protection of medical units (as opposed to respect) and art 8.

320 See also art 8, on all possible measures to search for the sick, wounded and the dead whenever circumstances permit (which was abandoned as regards circumstances in the *CIHL Study*, see Rule 115) and art 9.1 on the available help to medical and religious personnel (which was abandoned with regard to availability in *CIHL Study*, see Rule 25).

321 At 383–4 and 432. See also the statement by the Mozambique Liberation Front, *1977 Records* Vol. 8, 32 that '[i]t had been shown in practice that, despite disparities in the resources of the parties involved, nothing prevented the national liberation movements from respecting the principles of humanitarian law', PLO, 34 and Senegal, 45. But see *Boister*, 132.

322 Alternatively, many actors insisted on the relevant willingness of national liberation movements, see Ukraine, *1977 Records* Vol. 8, 35 and Mozambique Liberation Front, 36.

common article 3 ANSAs. Interestingly, though, he concludes that ' … an equivalent modality of implementation, feasible in the conditions of liberation movements, … can always be found'.[323] This is not, though, only a matter of implementation; it impacts severely on accountability as well.

It is possible that certain ANSAs will find themselves unable, at least in the initial stages of the conflict, to act in accordance with their obligations with regard to particular stipulations. The solution to this conundrum is that ANSAs are bound to the extent of their capacity and once they are not able to conduct themselves accordingly, they are precluded from acting in this regard.[324] But is this a valid understanding of the necessities of the conflict? Would it be commensurate to the equality of a belligerent's obligations? This is hardly the case.

The *de facto* erosion of territorial control for the applicability of Protocol II was not well thought-out, probably drawn by an urge to humanize internal conflicts (and in light of the depressing experiences of the 1990s). This is not to suggest that all such provisions cannot be applied by common article 3 ANSAs. But several stipulations regarding fundamental guarantees (for example education of children), restriction of liberty (for example location of internment places and segregation) and, mainly, penal prosecutions require more than most common article 3 ANSAs could logically bear. A fragmentation of the scarce resources of ANSAs into an array of obligations would not help in respecting other core obligations. To a certain extent, instead of widening the obligations, more thought should have been given on how to strengthen the existing framework, by making ANSAs accountable.

In that regard there is a need to restore, to a certain degree, the sliding scale of obligations that existed after the conclusion of Protocol II. The obligations of common article 3 ANSAs should be termed in a more rudimentary form and, whenever there is an increased level of required action, there should be some leniency on the requirements. ANSAs in control of territory should bear an increased level of obligations, (possibly) even beyond the requirements of Protocol II, while *de facto* entities should go far beyond these obligations, if only, because the one-size-fits-all with regard to the obligations of ANSAs might be less than comprehensive for them, taking into account their rather stable control over territory. *De facto* entities could exercise a form of authority which exceeds the scope of the norms of humanitarian law; while the principle of effectiveness would give legal validity to some of their acts, there is hardly any framework that the ANSA will be bound to follow. Thereafter only the Martens clause could give an indication as to how the ANSA and its members should act.[325]

---

323 At 432. Similarly, *Anonymous*, 855.

324 See also *Draper* 1965, 91 and *Meyrowitz*, 173.

325 On the interpretation that the Martens clause limits the general freedom of state action when international law is silent, see G.I.A.D. Draper, 'The Relationship between the Human Rights Regime and the Law of Armed Conflict' (1971) 1 Israel Yrbk Hum Rts 191, 197–8; *Plattner* 1990, 552; the *Canadian Manual* [106.2]; and the Constitutional Court of Colombia, *Sassòli and Bouvier*, 2272–3. It does not seem to create, however, an autonomous source of customary law, *Cassese* 2000, 211–12. Opposite Shigeki Miyazaki, 'The Martens Clause and International Humanitarian Law' in Jean Simon Pictet and Christophe Swinarski (eds), *Études et Essais sur le Droit International Humanitaire et sur les Principes de la Croix-Rouge en l'Honneur de Jean Pictet* (Comité International de la Croix-Rouge 1984) 437 and the Dissenting Opinion of Judge Shahabuddeen, *Nuclear Weapons*, ICJ Rep 406 and 408.

The possible gaps or inadequacies of IHL, besides the above-mentioned controversies on the content of the CIHL Study, include the following:[326]

a) Reasons and procedures for internment – administrative detention,[327] including the release of people deprived of their liberty.[328] Interestingly, Rule 99 from the CIHL Study on the prohibition of arbitrary detention is mostly based on human rights law rather than IHL and it is doubtful whether it is a valid rule[329] applicable to ANSAs. Another viewpoint suggests that the relevant rules and procedures of the law of international armed conflict should be used.[330]
b) Measures for the protection/welfare of the civilian population (public hygiene, provision of foodstuffs, education, public order).
c) Measures relevant to the existing legal order in the territory controlled by ANSAs (law,[331] public officials and, possibly, courts[332]).

---

326 Konstantinos Mastorodimos, 'The Utility and Limits of International Human Rights Law and International Humanitarian Law's Parallel Applicability' (2009) 5 Review of International Law and Politics 129, 132–3.

327 Louise Doswald-Beck, 'Human Rights and Humanitarian Law: Are There Some Individuals Bereft of All Legal Protection?' (2004) 98 Am. Soc'y Int'l. L. Proc. 353, 357, *Somer*, 667 and Françoise Hampson, 'Fundamental Guarantees' in Elizabeth Wilmshurst and Susan Breau (eds), *Perspectives on the ICRC Study on Customary International Humanitarian Law* (CUP 2007) 296–8. See also *Pejic* 2005, 376: 'the protection of the rights of the persons affected by it is insufficiently elaborated'. As a further argument see S/RES/2109 preamble and S/RES/2173 [19], where 'arbitrary arrest and detention' is termed as a human rights violation/abuse and not a humanitarian one. For the opposing position see Ryan Goodman, 'Rationales for Detention: Security Threats and Intelligence Value' in Michael N. Schmitt (ed.), *The War in Afghanistan: A Legal Analysis* (International Law Studies Vol. 85, Naval War College 2009) 371–86 with further references. See also UNHRC, 'Report of the Independent International Commission of Inquiry on the Syrian Arab Republic' (12 February 2014) A/HRC/25/65, 9, condemning arbitrary deprivation of liberty by ANSAs, thus '... violating their obligations under international humanitarian law'. Significantly the non-existence of an '... initial and periodic review of the detention by an independent entity' is mentioned, but it is not explicitly termed a violation.

328 *Fleck* 2008, 628.

329 See also the 'Expert Meeting on Procedural Safeguards for Security Detention in Non-international Armed Conflict' (2009) 91 IRRC 859, 866.

330 See Ashley S. Deeks, 'Administrative Detention in Armed Conflict' (2009) 40 Case W.Res.J.Int'l L. 403, 434, proposing the adoption of the relevant rules of the Fourth Geneva Convention as well as ibid., 864 and 877–8.

331 The representatives of Iraq, *1977 Records* Vol. 8, 355, Argentina, Vol. 9, 314 and Hungary, Vol. 11, 442, have also foreseen this possibility. See also art 6.2(c) and (d) of Protocol II and the interpretations of the term 'law' by Karl Josef Partsch, 'Article 6, Protocol II' in Bothe et al. (eds), *New Rules for Victims of Armed Conflicts: Commentary on the Two 1977 Protocols Additional to the Geneva Conventions of 1949* (Martinus Nijhoff Publishers 1982) 651–2; Sylvie-Stoyanka Junod, 'Article 6, Protocol II' in Sandoz et al. (eds), *Commentary on the Additional Protocols of 8 June 1977 to the Geneva Conventions of 12 August 1949* (International Committee of the Red Cross 1987) 1399; and the *UK Manual* [15.42], as including rebel law.

332 While common article 3 and art 6.2 of Protocol II seem to adopt the possibility of (criminal) judicial mechanisms by ANSAs, only the minimum standards of due process are envisaged.

d) Measures related to private property beyond pillage (for example confiscation, taxes[333] and dues, contributions).[334]
e) Sea warfare.[335]
f) Some rules on the conduct of hostilities (precautionary measures on the effects of attacks[336]) and the use of certain weapons (mines[337]).

In consequence, the question that emerges is how to regulate such situations.

There are a number of possible solutions: the first one is to resort to the context of international armed conflicts and transpose such solutions to the (expected) conduct of ANSAs. Obviously such possibility will not be acceptable for states in the first place because the division between international and non-international armed conflicts serves this purpose among others. Moreover if states wished to do so, they would have already acted accordingly, taking into account that the relevant international law was negotiated for both types of conflicts separately (including also the Rome Statute).[338] However the ICTY, UN Commissions and, ultimately, the CIHL Study have resorted largely to this avenue, when considering such rules that did not even have any corresponding treaty law or only appeared very recently in treaty law as customary.[339] It is ironical, in a way, that the ICTY[340] has claimed that 'this extension has not taken place in the form of a full and mechanical transplant of those rules to internal conflicts' – in fact this is what has happened. Such extension has probably run its course, with the increased possibility of extension for sea warfare measures, internment and the minor rules regarding weapons and the conduct of hostilities. The upper limits of this extension are considered to be the

333 For examples of such measures by ANSAs see Taslim O. Elias, 'The Nigerian Crisis in International Law' (1971) 5 The Nigerian Law Journal 1, 5–7, UN Doc A/46/876, 37 and UNCHR, 'Report of the Independent Expert on the Situation of Human Rights in Afghanistan, M. Cherif Bassiouni' (11 March 2005) E/CN.4/2005/122, 9.

334 With regard to public property, *Fleck* 2008, 628, wrote that 'in a non-international armed conflict the seizure of such equipment is not regulated under international law'. This, however, might not be true in light of art 8.2(e)(xii) of the Rome Statute and Rule 50 of the *CIHL Study*, although the practice of states in the latter does not seem particularly convincing. The seizure of military equipment by the adversary is left unregulated, *CIHL Study* Vol. I, 174.

335 See *Kolb and Hyde*, 253–4, referring to an obligation 'to respect the common core of humanity ... applicable to both international and non-international sea warfare'.

336 See the indeterminacy of Rules 23–4 of the *CIHL Study*. See also *Rogers* 2004, 232. But see the *IIHL Manual*, 44, being positive, with regard to the location of military objectives, as well as *Sivakumaran* 2012, 356 and also, indirectly, UNSG, 'Report of the Secretary-General on the Protection of Civilians in Armed Conflict' (11 November 2010) S/2010/579, 10, UN Doc S/2012/376, 8 and UNHRC, 'Report of the Independent International Commission of Inquiry on the Syrian Arab Republic' (5 February 2013) A/HRC/22/59, 103.

337 See *supra* sub-chapter *Legislative Jurisdiction*, at 79–80.

338 *Daboné*, 422. But, on the other hand, see the extension of the Amended Article 1 to the CCW.

339 See, as examples, the maintenance of graves in *CIHL Study* Rule 115, Rule 43 on conduct of hostilities and the environment and generally the rules on the conduct of hostilities.

340 *Tadic* Appeals Decision [126].

rules on POWs[341] and combatant-like status[342] as well as military occupation. Regardless of whether such considerations are right altogether – as they represent the persisting distinction between international and non-international conflicts – in certain cases it is to be doubted whether the transposition of rules for international conflicts to non-international ones was particularly successful in humanitarian terms. For example the transposition of the rules on conduct of hostilities in all kinds of non-international armed conflicts entails collateral damage having become legalized and, therefore, acceptable. It is possible that the movement to humanize armed conflict is backfiring at this particular instant and that either a human rights-based regime[343] or a merger of humanitarian law with human rights would be more appropriate, predominantly, to these internal conflicts where the ANSA is unable to seriously doubt the supremacy of the government, or where its low-intensity character[344] does not generally make the use of lethal force an absolute necessity.[345] In a similar vein, there is a phenomenon, which is described by Marco Sassòli as over-classification, that reveals the tendency of states in recent years to qualify as conflict situations that fall short of the respective threshold. This ' … is no longer a privilege of the US, but it seems also to be used by some Latin American military to justify more robust methods in fighting social unrest'[346] – a policy which is mentioned in the UK Manual with regard to internal disturbances.[347] The 'benefits' from this approach could include the right of states to act with less restraint than under human rights law[348] and the paradigm of terrorists (with regard to their 'targeted killings' or indefinite detention) under the 'war on terror' is illustrative of this.[349] The difficulty of enforcing IHL against states' violations of

341 But see Emily Crawford, *The Treatment of Combatants and Insurgents under the Law of Armed Conflict* (OUP 2010) 116, ' … the essential content of a considerable number of the obligations in the POW Convention is entirely reflected in the content and accepted interpretations of CA3 and APII'.

342 See such propositions from Michelle L. Mack, 'Compliance with International Humanitarian Law by Non-State Actors in Non-International Armed Conflicts' (2003) 5 and *de Beco*, 194.

343 See *Abresch*, 757 ff. and 767.

344 See a similar comment from *T. Hoffmann*, 20: '[t]he application of certain rules pertaining to international armed conflicts in non international armed conflicts – especially … in low and high-intensity internal conflicts – might be downright disadvantageous to the realization of the aim of protecting the victims of war'. See also David Kretzmer, 'Rethinking the Application of IHL in Non-International Armed Conflicts' (2009) 42 Israel L.Rev. 8, 39 ff.

345 Of course, this could be situation specific, because in a generally low-intensity armed conflict, there will be situations where the use of lethal force will be necessary, see *Abresch*, 759.

346 *Sassòli* 2007, 51. See also Gabor Rona, 'Interesting Times for International Humanitarian Law: Challenges from the "War on Terror"' (2003) 27 Fletcher F.Wld.Aff. 55, 67 as well as the dangers of over-classifying the conflict between Hamas and Israel in *Mastorodimos* 2010, 445–6.

347 *UK Manual* [15.2.1]. It does not seem to endorse it, though – but one can ponder on the reasons for exposing it.

348 Similarly a classification of a non-international armed conflict as international could imply a less prominent role for human rights law, since its extra-territoriality is still not acceptable by all states.

349 This over-classification could even justify *jus ad bellum* use of force, despite the irrelevance between *jus ad bellum* and *jus in bello*. A classification, for example, of a conflict as international

the rules (when compared to human rights law)[350] could be another reason for the tendency to 'over-classify' a certain factual situation. In addition, it could also result in attributing responsibility to an ANSA which does not have the capacity to be a party to the 'conflict'. In the end, the mechanical transplant of rules from international to non-international armed conflicts might serve a similar rationale as over-classification, and even though it may have been well-intended towards humanitarianism, it would fail to acknowledge that the state continued to be bound by a host of human rights treaties.[351] Such transpositions would be particularly welcome by anyone who does not feel comfortable with the applicability of human rights during armed conflicts, because it creates a *lex specialis* which balances humanitarian considerations with military necessity – a balance which is less obvious in the human rights regime.

Another possibility is to resort to a more limited part of the law of international armed conflict, meaning the rules of military occupation, since factual criteria of occupation are similar to control of territory by an ANSA.[352] Similar thoughts pertained to UN peace operations exercising factual authority.[353] Certainly the possibility of application could only take place by analogy and could not constitute a 'full and mechanical transplant', because the rules on military occupation are predicated on the difference of nationality for protected persons, something that is not applicable as such in non-international armed

---

could by implication give a green light to use a certain amount of force in international relations. Politically also 'labelling a situation as an armed conflict might also serve to expand executive power both as a matter of domestic law and in terms of public support', UNHRC, 'Report of the Special Rapporteur on Extrajudicial, Summary or Arbitrary Executions, Philip Alston: Study on Targeted Killings' (28 May 2010) A/HRC/14/24/Add.6, 16.

350 See the Committee on Reparation for Victims of Armed Conflict, 'Draft Declaration of International Law Principles on Reparation for Victims of Armed Conflict (Substantive Issues) in International Law Association Report of the Seventy-Fourth Conference (The Hague, 2010) (International Law Association 2010) 318 (hereinafter *ILA Reparations Committee 2010*), 'The Committee can find no reason why the individual, who already enjoys strong protection under international human rights law, should have a weaker position under the rules of international law applicable in armed conflict. This would create perverse incentives for parties to armed conflict … .'

351 It leaves, though, a lacuna with regard to standards of conduct regarding ANSAs.

352 *Mastorodimos* 2009, 145. For *Fleck* 2008, 628, 'it would not be correct to deny the applicability of occupational law in non-internal armed conflicts altogether'. The opposite opinion from Marco Sassòli, 'The Legal Qualification of the Conflicts in the Former Yugoslavia: Double Standards or New Horizons for International Humanitarian Law?' in Sienho Yee and Wang Tieya (eds), *International Law in the Post-Cold War World: Essays in Memory of Li Haopei* (Routledge 2001) 312 and *Dinstein* 2009, 34, while it was rejected in the *Sesay* Judgment [982 ff.]. For *Sassòli* 2010, 35 '[t]he disadvantage of this proposal is that armed groups would be subject to more restrictions than their enemy, the government, because the latter could certainly not be expected to respect on the territory it controls the restraints applicable to an occupying power. Such a differentiation would be politically delicate and contrary to the principle of equality of the belligerents before IHL'.

353 See, for example, Australia's Government Statement for the Meeting of Contracting Parties to the Fourth Geneva Convention, Geneva, 27–29 October 1998 (1999) 2 YIHL 450, 451–2 and Steven Ratner, 'Foreign Occupation and International Territorial Administration: The Challenges of Convergence' (2005) 16 EJIL 695–719.

conflicts. The differentiation between 'own' and 'occupied' territory would also present some practical difficulties. Furthermore, several provisions of occupation law require the existence of a governmental function, a feature which is not obvious in the majority of ANSAs. On the other hand, a large part of (current) occupation law, namely the Fourth Geneva Convention, carries the same underlying rationale, that of protecting individual rights. Consequently, the analogies are serious enough to necessitate a reconsideration of the non-applicability of occupation law to territories that are under the effective control of an ANSA.

Another option is to examine whether ANSAs could create standards of conduct based on their volition and practice.[354] It has already been noted that their volition has been rejected with regard to the formation of customary law – an incorrect assumption because ANSAs are significant actors in conflicts. If, however, the rationale for this avoidance is to overcome the possibility that ANSAs could contribute to the formation of rules that would apply equally to states, the same fear cannot hold true in this case. In essence, the Geneva Call's Deed of Commitment and the subsequent practice of the signatories could, precisely, evince the creation of certain normative standards with regard to anti-personnel mines, to the extent that the Ottawa Convention cannot be relevant to the conduct of ANSAs *per se*. Such examination, however, is not feasible in the present context and demands a degree of collaboration similar to that which produced the CIHL Study, while its exact outcome could not be predicted in advance.

The last possibility that has been suggested is the applicability of human rights to ANSAs. While this has gained support, unlike any of the two previous propositions, its rationale is not to regulate the conduct of ANSAs where there is a gap regarding rules of conduct; rather than that, it is an attempt to expand the scope of protection for individuals. Certainly, human rights are not formulated with conflict realities in mind. But any solution based on this legal regime would not necessarily be a replicate of the provisions as envisaged in treaties and customary law, but rather an adaptation with some regard to the characteristics of the ANSA as well. An additional argument for the adoption of this solution is that states in a non-international conflict context have the corresponding obligations of human rights.

Undoubtedly, the limited effects of the implied mandate doctrine or an expansive interpretation of the Martens clause could provide some answers in this regard, but they would be indeterminate.[355] In addition, agreements between the parties or civil society-induced unilateral declarations on the part of the ANSAs could fill this void and lead to further developments.[356] In fact those types of ANSAs that usually commit to obligations

---

354 Similarly, *Sassòli* 2010, 23, although with a different rationale.

355 The legal criteria for the validity of the several acts of ANSAs are not obvious under the implied mandate doctrine; it could however be particularly relevant for the validity of acts which do not relate to the armed conflict.

356 See, in this regard, the *Geneva Call's Deed of Commitment*. Furthermore, the understandings or declarations of other ANSAs, see for example the Defence Commission (PKK), 'Rules for the Conduct of Warfare' (2011) which, *inter alia*, rejects the use of weapons of mass destruction, including biological, nuclear and chemical, as well as anti-personnel mines and cluster bombs, could lead to a similar outcome.

are the ones that might need additional regulation concerning their activities. On the other hand, such options offer a local or partial solution to relevant situations rather than a comprehensive solution for all similar ANSAs. All the above-mentioned options are more comprehensive, while, in addition, they have another distinct advantage, quite apart from the transposition of rules from international to non-international conflicts: they are not necessarily confined to the period of violence. The military occupation regime continues to apply despite the lack of violence, while human rights standards are usually not derogated from in periods of armed conflicts. In many respects, the human rights applicability is desirable, not only because the military occupation rules (and the transposition of rules from international armed conflicts to non-international ones) could only cover a sub-set of activities by ANSAs, but also because they assume a state of 'belligerency' with regard to the local population, which is not, in many cases of non-international armed conflicts, usual. The possibility of law creation by ANSAs would probably be dismissed as too progressive. Finally it seems that human rights applicability gains momentum beyond the realm of scholarship and, therefore, appears to be the most promising proposition with regard to the lack of legal regulation.

Even when there is a comprehensive legal framework for the action of the ANSA, there is also a question on the rules of accountability once there are violations of the law, which is to be focused on the following sub-chapter.

Accountability Norms: Problems and Prospects

While the advancement of substantive regulation in non-international armed conflicts was impressive, accountability for breach of humanitarian rules did not necessarily follow at the same pace. Certainly international realities have changed substantially since the 1980s and the lack of supervision and enforcement[357] is not necessarily the reality any more. Apart from the ICRC, several actors on the ground, ranging from international organizations, through its organs (peacekeeping forces, Special Rapporteurs, Commissions), to non-governmental organizations, are scrutinizing ANSAs' conduct. The birth of international criminal law mechanisms has also led to individual accountability for war crimes. Notwithstanding the fact that not all violations of humanitarian law are criminalized, this is a significant evolution, coupled, recently, with a stronger standing for victims. The Rome Statute permits a victim's participation in its proceedings, while it foresees some form of reparation for direct or indirect victims (art 75) as well as the existence of a Trust Fund (art 79), which would provide compensation.[358] But this procedure is relative to the responsibility of individual members and it does not cover the accountability of ANSAs, as it runs parallel to it.

There is no explicit rule within IHL treaties regarding the accountability of ANSAs. But even with regard to states, there is no explicit *treaty* rule regarding responsibility towards individual victims of armed conflict, whether international or non-international. There is,

357 *Cassese* 1981, 419–20.

358 See also ICC, Rules *of Procedure and Evidence* (2nd edn 2013) Rules 94–6 and 97.

roughly, a liability clause regarding compensation in art 3 of the Hague Convention and art 91 of Protocol I,[359] although the reparation's beneficiary is not spelled out. Certainly, even without the existence of the said provisions, states would automatically[360] be obliged to make reparation to other states for an injury caused by a breach of international law (State Responsibility articles 1 and 31), as a general principle of international law.[361]

While international law is primarily a law between states, it is clear that it increasingly regulates conduct between states and non-state actors. As a corollary to regulation, responsibility for violations is owed to non-state actors (particularly individuals) as well. In the same direction, humanitarian law is slowly perceived as a law that does not only confine the conduct of states (and ANSAs) but also attributes rights to its beneficiaries, mainly civilians and secondarily combatants.[362] It has even been claimed that IHL could share ' ... the ultimate goal of enhancing the protection of people and to enable them to enjoy their human rights in all circumstances'.[363] It is certain, though, that if responsibility was only attached towards other subjects of international law, this would exclude citizens of the same state, who actually comprise the majority of victims during a non-international armed conflict. This would impair, in all ways, the meaning and efficacy of IHL.

The way towards the establishment of an individual right to reparation has not been easy. Meron and Kalshoven have argued that the *travaux preparatoires* of article 3 of the Hague Convention show that it was intended to cover individual–state relations rather than inter-state relations.[364] Even if this holds true, past practice, both older and recent, is not

---

359 On its customary status see Jean de Preux, 'Article 91, Protocol I' in Sandoz et al. (eds), *Commentary on the Additional Protocols of 8 June 1977 to the Geneva Conventions of 12 August 1949* (International Committee of the Red Cross 1987) 1053, Tihomir Kamenov, 'The Origin of State and Entity Responsibility for Violations of International Humanitarian Law in Armed Conflicts' in Frits Kalshoven and Yves Sandoz (eds), *Implementation of International Humanitarian Law* (Martinus Nijhoff 1989) 172 and *Armed Activities Case*, ICJ Rep 242. Gravity is not a requirement, Emanuela-Chiara Gillard, 'Reparation for Violations of International Humanitarian Law' (2003) 85 IRRC 529, 534. Another measure of reparation is the restitution of cultural property as in the Second Protocol to the 1954 Hague Convention, art 3.

360 *Gillard*, 532.

361 Ibid., 530.

362 Marten Zwanenburg, 'The Van Boven/Bassiouni Principles: An Appraisal' (2006) 24 NQHR 641, 657. See also UNHRC Res 25/36 (2014) [2] referring to ' ... violations of international humanitarian rights law ... '. But see Christian Tomuschat, 'Reparation in Favour of Individual Victims of Gross Violations of Human Rights and International Humanitarian Law' in Marcelo G. Kohen (ed.), *Promoting Justice, Human Rights and Conflict Resolution through International Law: Liber Amicorum Lucius Caflisch* (Brill 2007) 577.

363 UN Doc A/HRC/12/48, 80.

364 *Meron* 1989, 223 and Frits Kalshoven, 'State Responsibility for Warlike Acts of the Armed Forces: From Article 3 of the Hague Convention IV of 1907 to Article 91 of Additional Protocol I of 1977 and Beyond' (1991) 40 ICLQ 827, 830. Similarly see Elke Schwager, 'The Right to Compensation for Victims of an Armed Conflict' (2005) 4 Chinese JIL 417, 427 and the preamble of UNGA Res 60/147 (16 December 2005), Basic Principles and Guidelines on the Right to a Remedy and Reparation for Victims of Gross Violations of International Human Rights Law and Serious Violations of International Humanitarian Law (hereinafter Basic Principles), where, among

particularly helpful. The possibility that a victim could turn against a party to the conflict in a meaningful and effective manner has been repeatedly denied.[365] The Rapporteur of the ILA's Committee on Reparation for Victims of Armed Conflict[366] was commenting that 'in view of the relevant state practice and taking note of a strong majority among scholars, the Committee came to the conclusion that, *until most recently*, international law did not provide for any right to reparation for victims of armed conflicts' (emphasis added). But we can hardly conclude that the question is settled.

For a start, it is one thing that a right to reparation is not provided to victims by international law due to the deficiency of appropriate procedures, thus designating the lack of an effective remedy,and another thing that individuals do not have a right to reparation at all or, even worse, that the state is not responsible for its own violations. The last scenario is dismissible, since states can demand reparations for and on behalf of their nationals. Furthermore, the reparations granted by a state do not aim towards another state apparatus but, primarily, towards its population. After all, any state apparatus exists for the benefit of its people and not for the sake of its own continuation. In that regard, it could be explained why certain measures of reparation and, particularly, compensation should be distributed and used primarily to the benefit of those that incurred the damages, through a myriad of measures (public services, distribution of goods, development programmes and so on).[367] In addition, the frequent denial of an individual's reparation right by national courts hardly means its inexistence: there are a host of procedural problems that can deny its effectiveness: immunities, statute of limitations, the non-self-executing nature of the right and so on.[368] Therefore, the wealth of negative national jurisprudence constitutes only an indication and not firm evidence on its own.

---

the provisions on the right to a remedy, art 3 of the Hague Convention and art 91 of Protocol I feature prominently. But see Natalino Ronzitti, 'Compensation for Violations of the Law of War and Individual Claims' (2002) 12 Italian YBIL 39, *Zwanenburg*, 658 ff. and *Tomuschat* 2007, 576.

365 See Sangeeta Shah, 'Seeking Remedies for Violations of International Humanitarian Law: *Markovic v Italy*' (2007) 7 H.R.L.Rev. 412, 413. For cases denying the individual right to compensation see Hideyuki Kasutani, 'Correspondent's Report: Japan' (1999) 2 YIHL 389–90, Jann K. Kleffner and Liesbeth Zegveld, 'Establishing an Individual Complaints Procedure for Violation of International Humanitarian Law' (2000) 3 YIHL 384, 394–5, *CIHL Study* Vol. I, 544–5, and *Arai-Takahashi*, 266–7. But, 'none of the courts denied the underlying right to compensation', *Gillard*, 538.

366 *ILA Reparations Committee 2010*, 293.

367 In some reparation mechanisms, the state has acted as the intermediary between the victim and the appropriate forum, see the Committee on Reparation for Victims of Armed Conflict, 'Reparation for Victims of Armed Conflict (Procedural Issues)' in International Law Association Report of the Seventy-Fifth Conference (Sofia 2012) (International Law Association 2012) 599 (hereinafter ILA Reparations Committee 2012).

368 See *Gillard*, 537, *ILA Reparations Committee 2012*, 581 and, more generally, Theo van Boven, 'Victims' Rights to a Remedy and Reparation: The New United Nations Principles and Guidelines' in Carla Ferstman et al. (eds), *Reparations for Victims of Genocide, War Crimes and Crimes Against Humanity* (Brill 2009) 19–40.

At the international level, many UN and private initiatives show a reversal with regard to the existence of a reparation right. A first piece of evidence is the Basic Principles,[369] although concerned only with *serious* violations,[370] while art 3 of the Hague Convention and art 91 of Protocol I feature prominently in its preamble.[371] The Chicago Principles on Post-Conflict Justice[372] (hereinafter Chicago Principles) and the ILA Reparations Committee 2010 (in its Draft Declaration, art 6) also corroborate this change. Further support can be found in the positions of Guatemala and the ICRC,[373] while the ICJ on the *Legal Consequences of the Construction of a Wall in the Occupied Palestinian Territory*[374] recalled the obligation of Israel ' … to make reparation for the damage caused to all the natural or legal persons concerned'. The CIHL Study gives support to its customary status,[375] albeit not unequivocally.[376]

The position of ANSAs in the system of reparations for humanitarian law violations is less evident. The CIHL Study refers only to the state as being responsible for providing reparations. In the commentary it notices some relevant practice from ANSAs, but it concludes that 'it is unclear to what extent armed opposition groups are under an obligation to make full reparation'.[377] The Basic Principles are also unclear, despite a reference to liability of ' … a person, a legal person, or other entity … ' ([15] of the Annex to the resolution). From the way that the Basic Principles are formulated, the existence of a state with a functioning system of justice appears necessary. But ANSAs, in many cases, appear and act outside this system. Presumably the non-binding character of the resolution does not have an effect on the quality of the content since its drafters emphasize ' … that the Basic Principles and Guidelines contained herein do not entail new international or

369 A/RES/60/147. See also A/RES/48/153 [13]. But see the different reading of *Tomuschat* 2007, 579.

370 The *ILA Reparations Committee 2010*, 302 ff., avoids mentioning gravity as an element for reparation. See also *ILA Reparations Committee 2012*, 589–90, on past practice on mechanisms that did not have a gravity threshold regarding law violations, although leaving a choice to ' … policy-makers who actually face the situation … '. Furthermore even the *Basic Principles*, Annex to A/RES/60/147 [26], acknowledge, indirectly, that all victims have a reparation right.

371 See also the *Public Committee against Torture v Government of Israel* [40], mentioning these provisions as well with regard to the right of reparation of an individual.

372 (2007) 29, Principle 3.

373 UNCHR, 'The Right to a Remedy and Reparation for Victims of Violations of International Human Rights and Humanitarian Law, Note by the High Commissioner for Human Rights' (27 December 2002) E/CN.4/2003/63, 29 and 31 respectively. On the other hand see the denial of Germany in UNCHR, 57th Meeting Record, E/CN.4/2005/SR.57, 9.

374 (Advisory Opinion) [2004] ICJ Rep 179. See also *Prosecutor v Thomas Lubanga Dyilo* (Decision Establishing the Principles and Procedures to Be Applied to Reparations) ICC-01/04-01/06 (7 August 2012) [185], '[t]he Chamber accepts that the right to reparations is a well-established and basic human right … '.

375 See Rule 150. See also *Arai-Takahashi*, 267. But see *Turns* 2007, 354.

376 *CIHL Study* Vol. I, 541.

377 Ibid., 550. See also *Turns* 2007, 356.

domestic legal obligations … '.[378] Yet this should not be overstated because the language of the document and the use of the verb 'should', instead of 'shall', suggests that the 'international norm is less mandatory'.[379] And, overall, the resolution is inadequate in terms of modalities and procedures with regard to ANSA accountability. Its contribution could lie in the acknowledgement that ANSAs could be responsible for reparations – a conclusion that is more easily discernible in previous versions of these Principles,[380] the ILA Reparations Committee 2010[381] and the Chicago Principles[382] – as well as in the inspiration that it provides with regard to reparations. Moreover, the Darfur Inquiry[383] mentions the international responsibility of the state-like entity to pay compensation to the victim, while the Secretary General[384] referred to ' … the duty to make reparations for [international humanitarian law] violations … '.

It would be, at the very least, anachronistic to consider ANSAs as not being accountable towards individual victims of the conflict as a matter of international law,[385] especially in an era where the relevant accountability of states, individuals, as *per* criminal law, and non-state actors (corporations) has expanded. The social need to enforce the primary rules points to the necessity of having a corresponding norm on accountability, while there is

378 But see *Zwanenburg*, 667, commenting that 'in some respects they appear to go beyond existing law' and *Tomuschat* 2007, 571.

379 UN Doc E/CN.4/2003/63, 6.

380 UNCHR, 'The Right to Restitution, Compensation and Rehabilitation for Victims of Gross Violations of Human Rights and Fundamental Freedoms: Final Report of the Special Rapporteur, M. Cherif Bassiouni, Submitted in Accordance with Commission Resolution 1999/33' (18 January 2000) E/CN.4/2000/62, 9. See also UNCHR, 'The Right to a Remedy and Reparation for Victims of Violations of International Human Rights and Humanitarian Law, Note by the High Commissioner for Human Rights' (10 November 2003) E/CN.4/2004/57, 5 and 27–8, referring to the ' … emerging concept of the responsibility of non-State actors … ', although, seemingly, confined to ' … groups that assume effective control over a territory and exercise over that territory and the people on that territory the equivalent control exercised by States … '.

381 At 307 ff. See also the Committee on Compensation for Victims of War, 'Report' in International Law Association Report of the Seventy-Third Conference (Rio de Janeiro 2008) (International Law Association, London 2008) 505–6 (hereinafter *ILA 2008 Report*) as well as Professor Furuya in the *ILA Reparations Committee 2012*, 606.

382 At 30, although the language, again, does not denote a hard law obligation. See also art 6, Part IV of the *Philippines Comprehensive Agreement*, which can be construed this way. The *Darfur Peace Agreement*, art 21.199, also refers to an 'inalienable right to have [the] grievances [of war affected persons] addressed in a comprehensive manner'.

383 At 150. See also UN Docs A/HRC/17/44, 9 and A/HRC/22/59, 25 as well as a passing reference in the *Responsibility Commentary*, 52.

384 UN Doc S/2009/277, 15. However in UN Doc S/2010/579, 18–19, while there is a reference to the ' … need to enhance accountability for violations of international humanitarian and human rights law, both for parties to conflict and individual perpetrators' as well as a reference to the right of reparations for victims, the ' … emerging practice of several States, … of acknowledging the harm they cause to civilians and compensating victims' is noted and this practice ' … other parties to armed conflict *might* consider' (emphasis added).

385 See also *Fleck* 2006, 197 and *Dudai*, 792, with further references. Opposite *Tomuschat* 2007, 577.

no apparent reason why, specifically, ANSAs should escape accountability. Furthermore, it is highly improbable that there is any legal system that does not incorporate a principle of law according to which an aggrieved actor cannot hold other actors responsible. Therefore a general principle of law already exists in this regard and hence, even if a particular norm in international law was missing, a general principle of law could fill the void.[386] Any discussion of the sort should not be limited to if, but to what extent and how.

As to the extent of the duty to reparations, this is limited, obviously, by the primary obligations that apply to ANSAs (and not the ones that *should* apply to them) as well as the way that the primary rule becomes an obligation of the ANSA. Only common article 3, Protocol II, arguably, and other customary norms will trigger the *international* accountability of ANSAs. All other norms, to the extent that a national law is the vehicle for the creation of obligations, could trigger a duty to reparations only to the point that it is envisaged in the national legal order, including the certain forms that it will take.

This duty, however, is dependent on attribution of the conduct to the ANSA. But before examining attribution, an exercise that is mostly *lex ferenda*, it is necessary to see how ANSAs are treated in the State Responsibility articles, especially since state responsibility for IHL violations does not seem to escape the general rules.[387] Such exercise would differentiate ANSA conduct as part of state responsibility from equal conduct as part of ANSA accountability.

Non-State Actors Within State-centred International Law

The State Responsibility articles do not escape the general logic of international law as inter-state law. Not only is there an utter lack of any meaningful reference to ANSAs, but, for their most part, the State Responsibility articles also reveal that every 'effort' was undertaken on expanding the notion of the state (and its organs) and attributing all sorts of wrongful conduct to them. Responsibility to the state is attributed: a) when their agents act by exceeding authority or contravening instructions (art 7),[388]; b) when an individual or a group thereof exercises elements of governmental authority in the absence or default of the official authorities (art 9); c) when it adopts and not merely endorses[389] private conduct

---

386 See also *Kleffner* 2009, 259, on the possible role of the rule of law at the international level.

387 Attribution appears to follow the formulation of State Responsibility articles, see *CIHL Study*, Rule 149. IHL is generally not considered to be a 'self-contained system', *Sassòli* 2002, 403–4.

388 Andre J.J. De Hoogh, 'Articles 4 and 8 of the 2001 ILC Articles on State Responsibility, the *Tadic Case* and Attribution of Acts of Bosnian Serb Authorities to the Federal Republic of Yugoslavia' (2002) 72 British YBIL 255, 290: 'the *ultra vires* acts of a controlled person will not be attributable to the state'.

389 See the *Case Concerning United States Diplomatic and Consular Staff in Tehran (United States of America v Iran)* (Merits) [1980] ICJ Rep 29 and 35. Similarly condonement or political approval do not seem sufficient, Stefan Talmon, 'The Responsibility of Outside Powers for Acts of Secessionist Entities' (2009) 58 ICLQ 493, 496. On several other problems on the applicability of the article, see Olivier de Frouville, 'Attribution of Conduct to the State: Private Individuals' in James Crawford et al. (eds), *The Law of International Responsibility* (CUP 2010) 274–5.

as its own (art 11); and d) when the non-state actor acts on the instructions of, or under the direction or control of a state (art 8).[390]

The existence of these basic rules, though, does not mean that different interpretations do not exist on the interrelation between a state and an ANSA. The case of an ANSA constituting a *de facto* organ of the state, because of its complete dependence,[391] could fall under art 8.[392] However, recent jurisprudence[393] suggests a more expansive interpretation of art 4 instead – generally speaking, though, the State Responsibility articles and commentary do not easily fit the category of *de facto* organs within a certain article.[394]

Furthermore, art 9 is a relatively unclear norm, since its first reading would suggest that all non-state entities exercising some sort of governmental functions would necessarily trigger the responsibility of the state.[395] This, however, appears illogical, to the extent that the ANSA is fighting against the state and the latter is unable to counter ANSA conduct. Similarly, it is not evident, even from the *Responsibility Commentary*,[396] whether (and the extent to which) this article would function in the environment of a failed state, as, on the one hand, '[t]he cases envisaged by article 9 presuppose the existence of a Government in office', while on the other ' … the phrase "in the absence or default of " is intended to cover both the situation of a total collapse of the State apparatus … ', two situations which are probably incompatible in themselves.

More importantly, the meaning of the term 'control' under art 8 has created a controversy in international law *fora*. For the ICJ in the *Nicaragua Case*,[397] the USA lacked the direct or effective control of all activities of the Contras, so that the ANSA's conduct was not to be attributed to the state. For the World Court, 'a general situation of dependence and support (which included financing, organising, training, equipping and planning of the operations)' was insufficient in itself to justify attribution.[398] On the contrary, the issuance of specific instructions was needed. The effective control test has sparked significant

390 On its customary status see, *Genocide Case*, ICJ Rep 207.

391 *Nicaragua Case*, ICJ Rep 62–3. See also *Prosecutor v Tadic* (Appeals Judgment) ICTY-94-1-A (15 July 1999) [141] and Theodor Meron, 'Classification of Armed Conflict in the Former Yugoslavia: Nicaragua's Fallout' (1998) 92 AJIL 236, 236–7.

392 See James Crawford, 'First Report on State Responsibility' (1998) YILC Vol. II Part One 1, 40.

393 *Genocide Case*, ICJ Rep 205. See also Luigi Condorelli and Claus Kress, 'The Rules of Attribution: General Considerations' in James Crawford et al. (eds), *The Law of International Responsibility* (CUP 2010) 230.

394 See also Marco Milanovic, 'State Responsibility for Acts of Non-state Actors: A Comment on Griebel and Plücken' (2009) 22 LJIL 307, 312 and 318.

395 See such interpretation in *Cahin*, 335 and, Netherlands in 'State Responsibility – Comments and Observations Received from Governments' (2001) YILC Vol. II Part One 33, 50, referring specifically to unsuccessful insurrectional movements.

396 At 49. *Cahin*, 335, notices also the lack of international practice and jurisprudence.

397 ICJ Rep 64–5. See also *Armed Activities Case*, ICJ Rep 226, regarding training and military support.

398 *Mastorodimos* 2010, 447.

criticism for its high threshold of attribution[399] and led, ultimately, the ICTY to pursue its own interpretation through an 'overall control' test:

> In order to attribute the acts of a military or paramilitary group to a State, it must be proved that the State wields overall control over the group, not only by equipping and financing the group, but also by coordinating or helping in the general planning of its military activity … . However, it is not necessary that, in addition, the State should also issue, either to the head or to members of the group, instructions for the commission of specific acts contrary to international law.[400]

The ILC[401] noted that 'the tribunal's mandate is directed to issues of individual criminal responsibility, not State responsibility, and the question in that case concerned not responsibility but the applicable rules of international humanitarian law', without, however, necessarily rejecting the possibility of future reference to the overall control threshold.[402] More recently, the ICJ rejected the test as unpersuasive for issues of state responsibility, although it conceded that 'insofar as the "overall control" test is employed to determine whether or not an armed conflict is international … it may well be that [it] is applicable and suitable'.[403] Without delving more into this issue, it might be easier for a state to control armed non-state groups rather than other non-state entities (or unstructured groups of individuals),[404] because armed groups are usually based on a system of hierarchy; to the extent that this functions effectively, sufficient control of the state to the leadership of

399 See, indicatively, *Kalshoven* 1991, 855; Dissenting Opinion of Vice-President Al-Khasawneh, *Genocide Case*, ICJ Rep 256; Stephanie A. Barbour and Zoe A. Salzman, 'The "Tangled Web": The Right of Self-Defense Against Non-State Actors in the Armed Activities Case' (2008) 40 N.Y.U.J. Int'l L. & Pol'y 53, 75; and Noam Lubell, *Extraterritorial Use of Force against Non-state Actors* (OUP 2010) 38. *Talmon* 2009, 503, notices that relevant proof will be very difficult to advance.

400 *Tadic* Appeals Judgment [131].

401 *Responsibility Commentary*, 48.

402 For *Momtaz*, 65, State Responsibility art 8 'appears to go beyond even from the Tadic jurisprudence by introducing an element of supplementary flexibility'. The flexibility retained in the article was commented on positively by the Netherlands, (2001) YILC Vol. II Part One 49, while also, Judge Al-Khasawneh, Dissenting Opinion in the *Genocide Case*, ICJ Rep 255, appears to endorse the existence of ' … varying degrees of sufficient control required in specific legal contexts … '.

403 *Genocide Case*, ICJ Rep 210. In the *Application of the International Convention on the Elimination of all Forms of Racial Discrimination (Georgia v Russian Federation)* (Provisional Measures: Order) [2008] ICJ Rep 362–3 and 373, the two states appear to endorse the approach of the ICJ in *Nicaragua*. See also the critique of *Tadic* in *Provost*, 92–3; Marko Milanovic, 'From Compromise to Principle: Clarifying the Concept of State Jurisdiction in Human Rights Treaties' (2008) 8 H.R.L.Rev. 411, 439–40; Eduardo Savarese, 'Issues of Attribution to States of Private Acts: Between the Concept of *De Facto* Organs and Complicity' (2005) 15 Italian YBIL 111, 120; and *Frouville*, 270.

404 States apply stricter control to armies rather than other state officials, *Sassòli* 2002, 406, *Brownlie*, 450 and Emanuele Sommario, 'State Responsibility for Violations of International Humanitarian Law in the Work of the Eritrea-Ethiopia Claims Commission' in Andrea de Guttry, Gabriella Venturini and Harry H.G. Post (eds), *The 1998–2000 War Between Eritrea and Ethiopia: An International Legal Perspective* (T.M.C. Asser Press 2009) 398.

the ANSA might be enough to bring the ANSA under the control of the state and trigger the rules of state responsibility (at least in the event of IHL violations). Condorelli and Kress[405] similarly claim that this justifies a stricter control of attribution of responsibility to states for the acts of their soldiers.

The State Responsibility articles have also foreseen a role for insurrectional movements (art 10).[406] In the event that the movement owes certain primary obligations, responsibility can be attributed to a state if the movement is successful in becoming the new government or creating a new state,[407] thus excluding cession and transfer of territory.[408] This is based on the continuity between the insurrectional movement and the new government/state.[409] Yet there is only scant state practice, especially recently, to support the principle.[410]

But, although this is a rule of attribution, there is little evidence on how to attach responsibility to the movement, which then becomes part of state responsibility. Condorelli and Kress[411] suggest that in a movement that has established state-like institutions, it might be appropriate to look at its internal law; and if the movement is state-like, the existence of *de facto* organs is possible.

The new government of the state would also bear responsibility for the actions and the conduct of the displaced government,[412] unless 'the revolutionary change in the State structures [are] so far-reaching as to affect the very continuity and identity of the State'.[413] There is, however, the possibility that the new government voluntarily accepts

---

405 At 227–8.

406 *Cahin2*, 249, supports its customary character. See also *Akehurst*, 55, mentioning this principle.

407 Significantly liberation movements are only relevant with regard to the second option. Presumably this implies that the category of national liberation movements cannot be relevant in an already existing state.

408 *Responsibility Commentary*, 51. For *Dumberry* 2006, 619–20, this is an incorrect solution.

409 *ILC* 1975, 100. For Eyassu Gayim, 'Reflections on the Draft Articles of the International Law Commission on State Responsibility: Articles 14;15;&19 in the Context of the Contemporary International Law of Self-Determination' (1985) 54 Nordisk Tidsskrift Int'l Ret 85, 96, this is a 'weak and controversial base'. For a more detailed analysis of the underlying theories see *Dumberry* 2006, 609–12.

410 In light of this, *D'Aspremont* 2009, 432, argues that this rule ' ... undoubtedly was primarily designed to fill an accountability gap' a conclusion that could be supported by the acknowledgement in the *Responsibility Commentary*, 50, that the state ' ... is the only subject of international law to which responsibility can be attributed'. But see *ILC* 1975, 102, the statements of arbitral tribunals are less numerous 'but this can be explained specifically by the fact that there is no divergence of views, no doubt whatsoever, as to the validity of the principle in question'. See also *Cahin2*, 247, referring to 'abundant international practice and case-law'.

411 At 231. See also *Cahin2*, 255, implying that only article 4 is relevant to such cases.

412 Eduardo Jimenez de Arechaga, 'International Responsibility' in Max Sorensen (ed.), *Manual of Public International Law* (MacMillan 1968) 564; *Jennings* and *Watts*, 554; *Responsibility Commentary*, 50; and *Cahin2*, 249.

413 *Ago*, 131. For *Atlam*, 51, the victory of a liberation movement is one such paradigm. See also *Cahin2*, 250.

otherwise.[414] It is uncertain what happens when the ANSA is absorbed into the structure of the society of a state or, mainly, its government[415] – the wording of article 10 does not seem to include this scenario. When the insurrection is unsuccessful, it appears that the state evades responsibility in principle,[416] thus not resolving the issue concerning how to proceed thereafter, especially since 'in practice no injured State has ever brought claims against insurrectional movements'.[417]

In view of the perception of the lack of accountability for non-state actors and the actual inexistence of relevant mechanisms, the expansion of state responsibility appears rational. Nonetheless, the fact that the state has lost part of its factual supremacy in international relations and that certain conduct of non-state actors cannot be covered by the above-mentioned rules[418] comprises an additional argument for the need to focus on the accountability of non-state actors *per se*. This exercise will start with an examination of attribution rules. Their importance has a certain impact on the state responsibility context, to the extent that the organs of an insurrectional movement are not defined but are, instead, equated with an ANSA with control over territory, subject to Protocol II. In sequence, the content and procedures of reparations for violations of IHL by ANSAs will be examined.

Attributing Conduct to Armed Non-State Actors

From the evolution of the notion of ANSAs, we can extract one situation where the State Responsibility articles would be applicable: a state of belligerency recognition requires not only that the ANSA is a state-like organization but also that resort should be made to

---

414 See Patrick Dumberry, 'Is a New State Responsible for Obligations Arising from Internationally Wrongful Acts Committed before its Independence in the Context of Secession?' (2005) 43 Canadian YBIL 419, 445–6.

415 Indeed, *Ago*, 146, envisaged that the rule would also apply 'in the case of an agreement between the legitimate government and the insurrectional government under which members of the insurrection are called upon to participate in the government of the State', although noting, at 149, its rare occurrence. Similarly, *Akehurst*, 60 and *Gayim*, 94. But see the *Responsibility Commentary*, 51, which seems to have backed away from this solution and considered that the principle '... should not be pressed too far in the case of a government of national reconciliation, formed following an agreement between the existing authorities and the leaders of an insurrectional movement'.

416 *Ago*, 130, *Kamenov*, 185 and *Responsibility Commentary*, 50. On the reasons why this appears justified, see *O'Connell*, 969.

417 *Cahin2*, 252.

418 For John Cerone, 'Human Dignity in the Line of Fire: The Application of International Human Rights Law during Armed Conflict, Occupation, and Peace Operations' (2006) 39 Vand. J. Transnat'l L. 1447, 1458, 'these standards establish a fairly high threshold of state involvement', while Shabtai Rosenne, 'State Responsibility and International Crimes: Further Reflections on Article 19 of the Draft Articles on State Responsibility' (1997) 30 N.Y.U.J.Int'l L. & Pol'y 145, 165–6, notes that the State Responsibility articles 'do not take sufficient account of the consequences of the breakdown of the traditional State system ..., nor its replacement by a new system which is slowly taking shape before our very eyes ... . International responsibility can be attributed to entities which are not deemed States ... '.

the inter-state rules of attribution, with all the strengths and weaknesses that they carry with them. Consequently, situations of this kind should be treated as if the rules of state responsibility apply directly.

From the basic characteristics of an ANSA (organized armed group), it is obvious that it must have at least a fighting force – common article 3 itself refers to 'members of armed forces' without distinguishing between the parties to the conflict.[419] Common article 3 ANSAs would probably only have an armed force, despite the fact that this common article leaves open the possibility of the existence of a 'judicial' branch. Protocol II allows for the existence of rebel laws[420] as well and, therefore, refers to an advanced level of organization, possibly including a 'legislative' branch. *De facto* entities resemble states, as they have a political/executive branch, apart from the above-mentioned elements. ANSAs with some control over territory appear to subordinate their fighting force to a political structure, which, however, does not necessitate that common article 3 ANSAs could not be organized accordingly. Of course it is not indispensable that different individuals perform these different tasks. But it is likely that the more advanced the organization, the greater the number/range of different individuals performing the variable tasks will be.

Such a scheme might be based on an internal 'law' or regulation,[421] but it might also function as such only in practice. Due to the fact that the ANSA is operating in a rather informal and secretive context it makes sense not to confine its organs, whether individual or collective, only to those that are included in its internal regulation. Unlike states, for which there is an acceptable minimum of organization in international law, the case for ANSAs is not as obvious. For attribution purposes, it might be sufficient that *de facto* organs exist, without being included in an internal regulation.

Of course the existence of such internal regulation or relevant attestations in ANSAs' texts and/or agreements with the 'enemy' could clarify attribution. The Fifteen-Point Programme of the SPLM[422] clearly envisaged that 'the Sudan People's Liberation Army (SPLA) is the military wing of the SPLM' and therefore considers the armed element as integral to its organization. Similarly, the NDFP states in the Organizational Principles and Policies of its Constitution that 'the New People's Army is under the absolute leadership of the Communist Party of the Philippines'.[423] Several other acts that bear the signature

---

419 See also the Global and Inclusive Agreement on Transition in the Democratic Republic of Congo, Pretoria, South Africa, 16 December 2002, art I.2, referring to the armed forces of the parties to this agreement, and, similarly, the Protocol between the Government of the Sudan (GoS), the Sudan Liberation Movement/Army (SLM/A) and the Justice and Equality Movement (JEM) on the Enhancement of the Security Situation in Darfur in Accordance with the N'Djamena Agreement, Abuja, Nigeria, 9 November 2004, art 6 and the UCK (KLA), 'Undertaking of Demilitarisation and Transformation', 20 June 1999 [5a] referring to 'forces'.

420 See arts 6.2(c) and (d) of Protocol II.

421 See also *Sivakumaran* 2012, 360.

422 At [2.1].

423 See also the Administrative Arrangement between the Government of Malaysia and the Communist Party of Malaya Pursuant to the Agreement to Terminate Hostilities, Haadyai, Thailand, 2 December 1989 [2.1], where the Party undertakes to disband its armed units, 'namely the Malayan People's Army (MPA) in Malaysia and Thailand'.

of ANSAs reveal their pledge to control, on the one hand, members of their forces or forces themselves (obviously including their members)[424] and, on the other hand, other individuals or entities under their control.[425] Therefore, it seems that ANSA practice appears to endorse the duality of attribution between individuals or collectivities that form part of it or individuals or collectivities under its control. The CIHL Study uses this scheme in the context of compliance with IHL (Rule 139), in essence copying the State Responsibility articles. There is no explanation as to why it is adopted and where it stems from – probably it is due to the lack of specifically designated rules.[426]

The question of who constitutes the fighting force, which at times equals the ANSA, is not easy to answer. The only context within which the defining element between members and non-members of the group has been discussed is in relation to direct participation in hostilities.[427] However, this notion concerns particularly the legitimate target of lethal force or else the interpretation of arts 51.3 of Protocol I and 13.3 of Protocol II, among others; it does not concern the attribution of the act of an individual to the group. Even this discussion, though, is confusing because there are different schools of thought: members of ANSAs are liable to attack at any time and anywhere,[428] because their function and acts render them continuous combatants. A second line of thought[429] assimilates ANSAs'

---

424 Cessation of Hostilities Framework Agreement between Government of the Republic of Indonesia and the Free Aceh Movement, 9 December 2002, art 2a, *Protocol between the Government of the Sudan (GoS), the Sudan Liberation Movement/Army (SLM/A) and the Justice and Equality Movement (JEM) on the Enhancement of the Security Situation in Darfur in Accordance with the N'Djamena Agreement*, art 6, and the Agreement on a Permanent Ceasefire, Juba, Sudan, 23 February 2008, art 2.3. See also the 'Report of the Panel of Experts Established Pursuant to Resolution 1591 (2005) Concerning the Sudan Prepared in Accordance with Paragraph 2 of Resolution 1713 (2006)' (3 October 2007) S/2007/584, 89.

425 *Darfur Peace Agreement*, art 32.509 and *UCK (KLA) Undertaking of Demilitarisation and Transformation* [5a].

426 *Zegveld*, 227, also notes the lack of attribution principles as being a factor limiting the ANSA's accountability. Her position, 155, is the use of the State Responsibility arts by analogy for state-like ANSAs, while smaller opposition groups might need the composition of other rules. *Kleffner* 2009, 261, seems to favour the same viewpoint.

427 See, indicatively, A.P.V. Rogers, 'Direct Participation in Hostilities: Some Personal Reflections' (2009) 48 Mil.L. & L. War Rev. 143–63; William H. Boothby, 'Direct Participation in Hostilities – A Discussion of the ICRC Interpretive Guidance' (2010) 1 International Humanitarian Legal Studies 143–64; and Jamie A. Williamson, 'Challenges of Twenty-First Century Conflicts: A Look at Direct Participation in Hostilities' (2010) 20 Duke J.Comp.& Int'l L. 457–71.

428 *Boothby* 2010, 152–3 and *Rogers* 2009, 159. See also the *Third Report on the Human Rights Situation in Colombia* chapter 4a [46]. Significantly, the understanding of ANSAs with regard to the enemy state seems to corroborate this approach, see the broad definition of FARC on military objectives, *Jaramillo*, 195, the practice of ELN, *Jaramillo*, 200 ff. and FMLN, 'Note Transmitting the Report on the Situation of Human Rights in El Salvador Prepared by the Independent Expert of the Commission on Human Rights in Accordance with Paragraph 17 of Commission Resolution 1990/77 and Economic and Social Council Decision 1990/242' (22 October 1990) A/45/630, 4.

429 Assembly of the International Committee of the Red Cross, 'Interpretive Guidance on the Notion of Direct Participation in Hostilities under International Humanitarian Law' (2008) 90

members with those that have a 'continuous combat function' and, therefore, they could become targets of lethal force. Once this function stops they cease to be targets. A third approach, stemming from the direct interpretation of the relevant clauses, would submit that the adversaries of states are civilians and they can only be targeted for as long as they participate in hostilities directly.

The possibility of official membership, just like in state armies, is not always an option,[430] not to mention that it might be indicative in state armies as well, in view of the privatization of state functions. By all probabilities, the defining element for attribution must be an inclusion in the organizational chart of the ANSA,[431] wherever this exists. Such inclusion might be easier to prove for lawful entities, such as private military companies, or previously lawful entities, such as dissident armed forces in mutiny. In this case of having an 'official capacity', the conduct of an individual under the colour/appearance of the ANSA's authority could generate the ANSA's accountability, despite being beyond its authority or instructions (*ultra vires*).[432] It is not evident, though, how to treat the case where the conduct in question does not match the function of the individual or collective organ of the ANSA. For instance, in the case where a fighter of an ANSA undertakes the role of a judge, obviously under the guise of the ANSA, should that conduct be attributed to the ANSA? Its 'official capacity' concerns an act beyond its functions. While such conduct appears to come under State Responsibility art 7,[433] it might be questioned whether it is not so removed from its 'official' functions, so that only in a recurrent situation or when the ANSA ought to have knowledge, the act should be attributed to the ANSA.

In the event that there is no (written) official membership status or internal regulation on the organs or individuals that comprise the ANSA, the question of attribution appears more puzzling. The State Responsibility rules envisage the possibility that besides internal law, practice might also be sufficient to attribute an organ to a state. Such scheme should work for ANSAs,[434] even if it is not exceptional and it is the only basis for attribution (in the absence of an internal 'law'); a function within it should be sufficient for attribution purposes. Without such flexibility, there might be a danger of having an organized armed group, predominantly a common article 3 ANSA, to whom no accountability can be attributed. With regard to individuals, specifically, a continuous (functional) link to the command structure (whether as part of it or as subordinate to it, voluntary or involuntary) should be sufficient in order to generate attribution.[435] This link might be easier to prove depending on the type of conduct and its recurring character. Any case of participation

---

IRRC 991, 995. See also the positive assessment of *Solis*, 205–6.

430 *Williamson*, 464.

431 *Zegveld*, 153, refers to the membership approach.

432 See also UN Doc E/CN.4/1996/62, 24, 'SPLA bears responsibility for the violations and atrocities committed in 1995 by local commanders from its own ranks, although it has not been proved that they committed these actions on orders from the senior leadership.'

433 But see *Frouville*, 264.

434 See also *Kleffner* 2009, 263.

435 See the *Tadic* Appeals Judgment [141], on 'the assimilation of individuals to State organs *on account of their actual behaviour within the structure of a State (and regardless of any possible requirement of State instructions)*'.

in hostilities could be attributed to the ANSA in principle, especially since it serves their war aim (which is broadly to overrun the enemy). Examples of such conduct include: shooting or any other attempt to kill, immobilize and/or capture the enemy; attacks on the war material or facilities of the enemy and acts of sabotage; guarding ANSA installations or other military objectives, transfer of weapons or spying. Recruiting, training, financing, propaganda and road construction contribute to the general war effort of ANSAs and could be attributed to the ANSA, at least as a presumption, even if they do not constitute participation in hostilities. The same presumption should apply for high-ranking operatives, who command and control or are involved in decision making and planning processes. Beyond individuals, organs that undertake these or other functions (for example judicial/disciplinary) within the context of an ANSA umbrella should be considered as organs of it, despite the lack of an official status. It is possible, though, that whenever an official status exists for certain individuals or organs, it might be more difficult[436] to attribute the *ultra vires* conduct of an 'unofficial' organ to the ANSA, especially if it is not conducted in the ANSA's name.

If their function is not continuous, attribution might be more problematic and the existence of specific instructions might be necessary.[437] An individual/civilian, who wilfully takes part in a battle alongside an ANSA, although he does not follow instructions nor is part of the command structure of the ANSA, should not be considered as being under the ANSA's control. A case of direct participation in hostilities that is generated randomly and without any instructions from the command of the ANSA should not be attributed to it.[438] It could be different, though, if the individual continues to act in collusion with the ANSA after the disengagement. Generally speaking, it would not make sense to attribute the *ultra vires* conduct of the individual to the ANSA when there are specific instructions, because it directly opposes their existence.[439] A possible due diligence requirement from the ANSA is a different issue.

In the case of direction or control over another individual or group, much would depend on its civilian or military character, regarding its pedigree and functions. The overall control test of the *Tadic* judgment appears more relevant in light of military organizations which are based on hierarchy. However, if the standard in state responsibility is higher, it is questionable why an organization with fewer resources and capabilities than states should be accountable for more than states. Consequently, it is inadvisable to use the overall control, with regard to ANSAs' control over other armed groups, since the standard in state responsibility is higher, so far. On the other hand, it is difficult to sustain that either overall or effective control is sufficient whenever the allegedly controlled group is not organized, at least in the sense of a common article 3 ANSA.[440] It is certain, though,

436 *Cahin2*, 255, rejects such possibility as 'unrealistic'.

437 See also *Tadic* Appeals Judgment [132 ff.].

438 But see the *Tadic* Appeals Judgment [144] assessment, 'that private individuals acting … in collusion with State authorities may be regarded as *de facto* State organs' as well as the paradigm in [141].

439 General instructions, on the other hand, do not appear adequate to absolve a state from responsibility.

440 See also *Tadic* Appeals Judgment [141].

that an advanced and firmly organized ANSA, especially with elements of control over territory, could be in a better position to exercise control over individuals and other groups and generate its accountability for conduct through third parties. In such cases, individuals or groups that do not form part of the ANSA machinery will function under its authority or with its consent, so that there is a minimum administration within this territory.

This last case could bring us to a situation of 'placing at the disposal' of the ANSA. Such a scenario arises, according to the State Responsibility Commentary,[441] when ' ... the organ is acting with the consent, under the authority of and for the purposes of the receiving State'. A similar situation could take place when, for example, in a territory controlled by an ANSA the elements of governmental authority come under the ANSA authority. Although in a state responsibility paradigm the consent of the sending state is required, a situation which will be hardly copied in a state–ANSA relational setting, the principle appears, at least in an initial phase, rational. It is probable, though, that in such a scenario the former elements of governmental authority would become *de facto* organs of the ANSA and, after appointment by law or regulation, *de jure* ones.

This scenario would also fit when a state or an ANSA places a fighting force or, even, individuals at the disposal of an(other) ANSA. Provided that the sending entity does not keep control or sends instructions/directions and, conversely, the receiving ANSA keeps the exclusive control, the conduct of these forces and/or individuals would be attributed to the receiving ANSA. But most commonly, ANSAs act in concert/alliance with other ANSAs[442] or even states, so that their shared responsibility is more usual.

Attribution could also be generated if there is an *ex post facto* adoption of the wrongful conduct,[443] although the chances of this happening are faint.

In sum it would appear that the starting point for attribution would be the internal law/regulation of the ANSA and the category of *de facto* organs. A continuous functional link with the ANSA would satisfy the standard for attribution. The cases of direction or control over individuals or other non-state actors would, probably, appear depending on the level of formal organization of the ANSA and its strength.[444] The remaining bases for attribution (*ex post facto* endorsement and placing at the disposal) would probably be exceptional.

If a certain conduct can be attributed to the ANSA, both the issue of reparation and the procedures for claiming it become important. After all, a substantive right to reparation could be realized only with the parallel existence of an effective remedy.[445] This will be the topic of the following sub-chapters.

---

441 At 44.

442 A relevant example is the SELEKA coalition in the Central African Republic, which has even signed the (Central African Republic) Accord De Cessez-le-Feu, Libreville, Gabon, 11 January 2013.

443 Consider for example an individual that extracted information through torture, which, subsequently, is shared with the ANSA. If the ANSA adopts the act, the latter would be attributable to the ANSA.

444 But see *Sassòli* 2010, 47, 'it is true that the smaller a group is and the less State-like organization and territorial control it has the more important attribution based on effective control over persons will be in practice.'

445 See *ILA Reparations Committee 2012*, 588 and Annex to A/RES/60/147 [11].

Reparations

With regard to the substantive aspect of accountability,[446] three types of reparations appear to be nearer the objective capabilities of ANSAs: restitution,[447] satisfaction[448] and guarantees of non-repetition.[449]

Restitution measures have been envisaged in agreements with ANSAs: in the Somali Agreement on Implementing the Cease-fire and on Modalities of Disarmament,[450] 'all sides agree in principle that properties unlawfully taken during the fighting shall be returned to the lawful owners'.[451] In a way, they constitute the 'easiest' way to rectify a violation, although, depending on each case, it might not be possible to bring the situation as it existed prior to the violation. It is also the means of reparation that has gained a certain primacy between the various available forms.[452]

Satisfaction has also been provided *ad hoc*[453] or in intra-state agreements.[454] The Linas-Marcoussis Agreement[455] foresaw (Annex, art VI.3 and 4) the creation of an 'international board of enquiry to investigate and establish the facts throughout the national territory in order to identify cases of serious violations of human rights and international humanitarian law', which would be later brought to justice. In the Comprehensive Peace

---

446 *Kleffner* 2009, 264 ff. prefers to focus on the analogy to the State Responsibility Articles.

447 Annex to A/RES/60/147 [19], *ILA Reparations Committee 2010*, Draft Declaration, art 7 and *Chicago Principles*, 30.

448 Annex to A/RES/60/147 [22] and *ILA Reparations Committee 2010*, Draft Declaration, art 9. But see *Kleffner* 2009, 265.

449 Annex to A/RES/60/147 [23], *ILA Reparations Committee 2010*, Draft Declaration, art 10 and *Chicago Principles*, 31. In the State Responsibility articles, guarantees of non-repetition are mainly treated as a consequence of a wrongful act, rather than a form of reparation, see, in more detail, Sandrine Barbier, 'Assurances and Guarantees of Non-Repetition' in James Crawford et al. (eds), *The Law of International Responsibility* (CUP 2010) 555–6 and Jann Kerbrat, 'Interaction Between the Forms of Reparation' in James Crawford et al. (eds), *The Law of International Responsibility* (CUP 2010) 573–4, although the *Responsibility Commentary*, 106, accepts that it ' … may also amount to a form of satisfaction'.

450 Addis Ababa, 15 January 1993, art III. See also the Acte d'Engagement, Gaborone, 24 August 2001, art 6 (hereinafter Gaborone Acte) and the *Darfur Peace Agreement*, art 17.97. The release of detainees is another measure of restitution, see the Peace Agreement between the Government of the Republic of Sierra Leone and the Revolutionary United Front of Sierra Leone, Abidjan, 30 November 1996, art 19, the Ceasefire Agreement, Lusaka, 10 July 1999, art III.7 and 8 (hereinafter Ceasefire Agreement in Lusaka) and the *Darfur Peace Agreement*, art 27.364 as well as the return of displaced persons. Note, though, that these are not necessarily hard law obligations under humanitarian law.

451 See also UNSC Res 1083 (27 November 1996) [6] demanding that ANSAs demobilize child soldiers and UNGA Res 49/196 (23 December 1994) [13] and [23].

452 *Responsibility Commentary*, 96–7.

453 See an example in *Gillard*, 535, regarding the ELN and *Dudai*, 792. See also some limited practice in the *CIHL Study* Vol. I, 549–50.

454 See also UNHRC Res 7/28 (2008) [4].

455 Linas-Marcoussis, 23 January 2003.

Agreement Concluded between the Government of Nepal and the Communist Party of Nepal (Maoist)[456] (hereinafter Nepali Peace Agreement) the parties also agreed 'to set up … a High-level Truth and Reconciliation Commission in order to probe into those involved in serious violation of human rights and crime against humanity in course of the armed conflict … '. The Arusha Peace and Reconciliation Agreement for Burundi (arts 6.7 and 6.8 of Protocol I) envisaged the 'erection of a national monument in memory of all victims … ', the 'institution of a national day of remembrance for victims … ' and ' … measures that would facilitate the identification of mass graves and ensure a dignified burial for the victims'.

The issuance of written codes of conduct would be a measure to guarantee non-repetition. In a statement[457] the NTC guaranteed that mistreatment of this class of people ' … would not be repeated'. More importantly, the Security Council has called on ' … parties to armed conflict to make and implement specific and time-bound commitments to combat sexual violence, which should include, inter alia, issuance of clear orders through chains of command prohibiting sexual violence and the prohibition of sexual violence in Codes of Conduct, military field manuals, or equivalent'.[458] As the assurances and guarantees of non-repetition have a mainly preventive role and concern a future act, they might be particularly appropriate in the case of a *jus cogens* norm having been violated.[459]

Rehabilitation, on the other hand, demands a quality of control and effectiveness that only a minority of ANSAs have, while 'monetary compensation may be difficult to implement since affording to all victims compensation that is proportionate to the gravity of the violation may actually bankrupt the … armed opposition group'.[460] Recognized belligerents and *de facto* entities might have the means to provide for these types of reparations; other ANSAs and particularly common article 3 ANSAs would probably not.[461]

The grant of one form of reparation does not, of course, preclude other types of reparation being adopted simultaneously.[462] Much would depend on the nature of the wrongful conduct. ' … [S]atisfaction is a particularly adequate form of reparation for moral or non-material damages, whereas restitution and compensation are more adequate to repair damages which are financially assessable'.[463] The State Responsibility articles

456 Kathmandu, Nepal, 21 November 2006, art 5.2.5.

457 NTC, 'The Treatment of Detainees and Prisoners', Benghazi, 25 March 2011.

458 Res 1960 (16 December 2010) [5]. See also Res 2121 (10 October 2013) [16] and S/RES/2173 [24]. Similarly, the action plans on children would also function as a guarantee of non-repetition.

459 *Barbier*, 558.

460 *Kleffner and Zegveld*, 399. Similarly see *Sassòli* 2003, 18 and *ILA 2008 Report*, 505. However, this would be a problem for states as well.

461 The *ILA 2008 Report*, 504, gives support to this conclusion. See also UN Doc E/CN.4/2004/57, 27–8, further excluding Protocol II ANSAs, but including *de facto* entities. See also the *Darfur Inquiry*, 150, referring to a state-like entity.

462 *Van Boven* 2009, 39.

463 *Kerbrat*, 580.

seem to prioritize restitution over other forms of reparations[464] (and compensation over satisfaction),[465] unless the injured state elects otherwise.[466] However, no such priority is evident in the Basic Principles,[467] although there is no apparent reason why the victim should not able to choose, depending on availability and feasibility. Furthermore, it is suggested in the *Responsibility Commentary*[468] that some type of reparations might be particularly relevant with regard to certain violations. The requirement of reparation effectiveness in the Basic Principles should also lead towards the primacy of a certain reparation scheme in dependence on the wrongful conduct. But it is to be noted that this priority of reparations is not the same as the gravity requirement that leads to accountability.

However, even the prospect of ANSAs' provision of reparations needs to be addressed through an appropriate mechanism/forum which will be the focal point of the section to follow.

Remedies/Reparation Mechanisms

The lack of accountability mechanisms has led, in the recent past, to proposals to institutionalize an IHL committee with the capacity to examine individual complaints against ANSAs as well.[469] The ILA Committee on the 'Compensation for Victims of War' has proposed a Draft Model Statute of an *Ad Hoc* International Compensation Commission.[470] While it allegedly places ANSA accountability within the context of state responsibility,[471] including the case in which the state has not shown due diligence in suppressing the rebellion, it envisages the direct accountability of ANSAs and their obligation to provide reparations in accordance with the Commission's decisions, subject to ANSA's consent.[472] Such a possibility, though, could only come about with the consent of a state; if the ANSA was the adversary, only after the end of the conflict could this consent appear.

---

464 See art 36.1. But see *Kerbrat*, 573 and 581 ff., whose survey reveals that although the ' … existence of the rule is generally affirmed in the reasoning of the decisions, […] it is applied very rarely'. See also Christine Gray, 'The Different Forms of Reparation: Restitution' in James Crawford et al. (eds), *The Law of International Responsibility* (CUP 2010) 589 and 591 and 595.

465 See art 37.1. But see *Kerbrat*, 581, claiming that this is not ' … an expression of positive law: it is not supported either by practice or jurisprudence'.

466 See art 43.2. Several limits are also offered or implied within the State Responsibility articles, as the example of art 35 on restitution shows.

467 Also *Zwanenburg*, 666. The sequence of reparation measures could be used as an indication, though.

468 At 120. See also *Brownlie*, 464 and *Gray*, 354.

469 See *Kleffner and Zegveld*, 384–401. For other similar proposals see *ICRC* 2003, 16 ff. See also the self-assessment of the International Fact Finding Commission of art 90 of Protocol I, on its competence to investigate and make recommendations within the context of non-international armed conflicts, in *Momtaz*, 105.

470 *ILA 2008 Report*, 500 ff.

471 Ibid., 504.

472 Ibid., 515.

The answer to the lack of mechanisms should not necessarily be sought externally: as the state is the first point of reference in cases of individual victims of violations of human and/or humanitarian rights,[473] similarly we might have to consider the option of the ANSA becoming the focal (or, at least, the initial) point of reparations for violations that are attributed to it.[474] After all, law enforcement is significantly stronger at a national rather than at international level;[475] implementation of international law should take place at the national level through the local actors or else it risks no implementation. In fact, this might be a case in which, depending on the fairness and efficacy of the procedures, such enforcement of reparations by ANSAs should be acknowledged as lawful in accordance with the implied mandate doctrine, even if the ANSA disappears in the future. This aspect could be combined with the increasing acknowledgement, pairing with individual victim's right to reparation, of a '... right to access to an effective mechanism to claim reparation'[476]. First of all, as ANSAs are interested in preserving discipline within their ranks, they have adopted acts,[477] regardless of the name given, that define military offences[478] or even other violations pertinent to humanitarian law, which are to be dealt with either by disciplinary committees or even court martial. While the imposition of discipline appears to be an element of an ANSA in control of territory,[479] it is also a sanction[480] with a potential double effect: it does not only provide a measure of satisfaction to the victim but it can also have a deterrent effect so that it functions as a guarantee of non-repetition. The imposition of discipline might also be combined with the duty to investigate.[481] This duty has been repeatedly featured as an element expected from ANSAs.[482] The victim could instigate this duty and demand a follow-up. Certainly disciplinary measures alone would be more appropriate should the violation of an IHL rule be of a minor importance. The duty

473 Although the impartiality of national courts in such cases could be doubted, see Luisa Castagnetti, 'The Claims on Behalf of Individuals before the Eritrea-Ethiopia Claims Commission' in Andrea de Guttry et al. (eds), *The 1998–2000 War Between Eritrea and Ethiopia: An International Legal Perspective* (T.M.C. Asser Press 2009) 411, and, therefore, international procedures could be more appropriate.

474 Also *Sivakumaran* 2009, 490 and 512.

475 See also *Bassiouni*, 793–4.

476 See the Committee on Reparation for Victims of Armed Conflict, 'Draft Procedural Principles for Reparation Mechanisms' in International Law Association Report of the Seventy-Sixth Conference (Washington 2014) (International Law Association 2014) 789 (hereinafter ILA Reparations Committee 2014) as well as the *Basic Principles*, Annex to A/RES/60/147 [11].

477 See The SPLA Act (2003) and the NRA's (Uganda) Code of Conduct.

478 See, for example, arts 20 and 39 of the SPLA Act with regard to property and the NRA's Code of Conduct, A1 and A4 with regard to inhuman treatment and killings.

479 See also S/RES/1894 [7c].

480 See also *La Rosa and Wuerzner*, 334 ff. For such practice see the *Sesay* Judgment [707] and *Sivakumaran* 2012, 446 ff. See also the *Philippines Comprehensive Agreement*, Part IV, art 4.5 and the *1996 NDFP Declaration*.

481 *Tomuschat* 2007, 575.

482 See S/RES/1960 [5], S/RES/2121 [16] and UN Doc A/HRC/17/44, 9.

to investigate, on the other hand, could also lead to evidence of more serious violations which should be treated in a different way, leading, possibly, to court proceedings.

The possibility of court-like mechanisms can be traced in humanitarian law provisions. Once ANSAs choose to create (and make use) of such institutions, certain articles (common article 3 and art 6 of Protocol II) become applicable. While these mechanisms are relevant only for individual criminal prosecutions and constitute a form of satisfaction to victims,[483] there is no reason why they cannot be used by individuals instigating the criminal prosecution of other individuals (for example members of ANSAs liable for criminalized humanitarian law violations), participating in the proceedings as a civil party and thereafter asking for reparations.[484] Of course this is more relevant to individual accountability rather than ANSA accountability, while it presupposes functioning, independent and impartial institutions and local/international criminal laws, which are applied in practice by the courts of insurgent entities. But part of ANSA accountability includes the punishment of the individual whose conduct is attributed to it.[485] This is evident as an obligation of national liberation movements (art 86.1 of Protocol I) and, increasingly, it can be inferred in relation to other ANSAs. The JEM and SLM-Unity have pledged 'to hold to account perpetrators of acts of rape and other forms of gender based violence'.[486] Art 6, Part IV, of the Philippines Comprehensive Agreement envisages prosecution and trial of ' … persons liable for violations of the principles of international humanitarian law … '. An NGO had 'expressed "disappointment" that the FMLN had not made more progress in fulfilling its *obligations under international law* to punish gross abusers'[487] (emphasis added), while a United Nations Fact-Finding Mission has referred to the ' … the obligation of the Gaza authorities to respect international law …, and is of the view that this requires the prevention and prosecution of violations of international law'.[488] More significantly several Security Council resolutions referred to the ' … need to bring to justice those responsible for … serious violations of … international humanitarian law',[489] without identifying the

483 But see Spain, (2001) YILC 2001 Vol. II Part One 63 commenting that ' … the reference to punishment of those responsible for a wrongful act as one of the forms of satisfaction … certainly does not appear to have been confirmed in State practice thus far'.

484 See this possibility as a leeway for the right to compensation in 'Victims' Compensation and Participation', Appendix to 'Letter Dated 2 November 2000 from the Secretary-General Addressed to the President of the Security Council' (3 November 2000) S/2000/1063, 11.

485 UNHRC, 'Report of the Independent International Commission of Inquiry on the Syrian Arab Republic' (22 February 2012) A/HRC/19/69, 23, UNHRC, 'Report of the Independent International Commission of Inquiry on the Syrian Arab Republic' (16 August 2012) A/HRC/21/50, 24 and UN Doc A/HRC/22/59, 25.

486 Statement by the Opposition Movements (JEM and SLM-Unity). See also the Defence Commission (PKK), 'Rules for the Conduct of Warfare' that ' … extra judicial executions shall be investigated and shall be accounted for'.

487 See this assessment by Americas Watch in Human Rights Watch, 'World Report 1992: El Salvador'.

488 UN Doc A/HRC/12/48, 471. See also Council of Europe's Parliamentary Assembly, Recommendation 1444 on the Conflict in Chechnya (2000) [11].

489 See indicatively S/RES/1479 [8] and 1509 (19 September 2003) [10].

party that would proceed accordingly. Yet in a number of resolutions the same organ '*emphasize[d]* the responsibility of States to comply with the relevant obligations under international law to end impunity and to prosecute those responsible for serious violations of international humanitarian law'.[490] Furthermore, the CIHL Study (Rule 158) refers only to states as having a customary law obligation to investigate and prosecute.

Beyond ANSAs' criminal prosecutions, the existence of Commissions or courts to deal with a victim's (civil) claims might not only be desirable but indeed indispensable. Certainly the general existence of 'justice' structures outside the state is not to be particularly welcomed;[491] yet it is a more pragmatic solution as to how to put the accountability of ANSAs into operation. Actually, *de facto* entities, at least, and some ANSAs in control of territory create institutions that concern themselves with issues of law, order and justice[492] in the territory they control and, according to the implied mandate doctrine, the effects of actions by (some of) such institutions is (or should be) occasionally acknowledged and validated,[493] at least to the extent that they contribute to respect for international law norms. In such cases, even the extent of reparations could increase (including rehabilitation and/or compensation), while the representativeness or legitimacy of the ANSA, whether on the inside or the outside of its 'jurisdiction', could enhance its relevant efforts, too. La Rosa[494] is right to comment that '[t]he size of the group, the intensity and the length of time during which control is exercised over a territory are factors which are crucial to the establishment of institutions similar to those that the states are obliged to set up'.

One situation in which an ANSA would be expected to set up mechanisms and provide reparations is that of belligerency recognition . Although this scenario falls under the State Responsibility articles, it simultaneously raises the problems of accountability towards other subjects of international law as well as in the situation arising from a conflict that comes to an end.

Reparations and Remedies: Further Prospects

ANSA accountability in its relations with the 'enemy' state, third states, international organizations or even the international community would more or less encounter the same problems, with regard to reparations and remedies, especially if the latter are sought during the armed conflict period.[495] The animosity between the conflicting parties would barely leave any communication point that could subsequently become a channel for reparations.

---

490 S/RES/1674 [8], S/RES/1738 [7] and S/RES/2173, preamble, using a similar language. In a similar vein see Res 2100 (25 April 2013) [27] and S/RES/2109 [22]. See also UN Doc S/2010/579, 20.

491 *Sivakumaran* 2009, 489.

492 See one such attempt in *Walker*, 165.

493 See also *Sivakumaran* 2009, 511.

494 Anne-Marie La Rosa, 'Sanctions as a Means of Obtaining Greater Respect for Humanitarian Law: A Review of Their Effectiveness' (2008) 90 IRRC 221, 236.

495 *Atlam*, 50, notes the lack of precedent with regard to claims against national liberation movements during the course of fighting.

Furthermore, past experiences in armed conflicts[496] have shown that only after their effective end will it be possible to establish reparation mechanisms. This is also obvious in the criminal law mechanisms: with the exception of the permanent ICC, all other criminal mechanisms functioned after the effective termination of the respective conflicts. However, there is no obvious reason why third states or international organizations should not pursue the accountability of ANSAs, even during an armed conflict period.[497] After all, natural or legal persons of a state might be subjected to the authority of an ANSA, while it is possible that elements of international organizations come into direct contact with ANSAs.

Roberto Ago concluded approximately 40 years ago that reparations during an armed conflict are an uncertain prospect,[498] while noting the insecurity as to the final solution of the conflict and the subsequent place of the ANSA within or outside the existing system of states, as well as the timely character of reparations. Much would depend also on the 'extent and size of the insurrectional movement' and the 'territory over which it exercises authority' as well as on its ownership of 'property which, when the need arises, could afford a means of compensation'. However, since reparations have a broad meaning, the uncertainty with regard to their prospect during an armed conflict should not, by itself, detract from the raising of relevant claims.

Compensation could also be granted indirectly, if, for example, the ANSA was designated as a terrorist organization and some of its (frozen or confiscated) funds were used towards the aim of reparations (compensation). A similar mechanism could function against ANSAs irrespective of the designation as a terrorist organization, as already proposed by the UN Secretary General.[499] But, so far, targeted sanctions usually refer to individuals rather than collectivities,[500] while frozen assets cannot be directed towards compensation, unless there is a lien or judgment entered *prior* to the imposition of sanctions.[501] Therefore,

---

496 See, for example the various Commissions in *ILA 2008 Report*, 502.

497 See, as examples, S/RES/1059 [6] and Res 1071 (30 August 1996) [8].

498 *Ago*, 130. See also *Jennings and Watts*, 553.

499 UNSG, 'The Causes of Conflict and the Promotion of Durable Peace and Sustainable Development in Africa: Report' (13 April 1998) A/52/871, 11 and 'Report of the Secretary-General to the Security Council on the Protection of Civilians in Armed Conflict' (8 September 1999) S/1999/957, 9. It received some positive reactions from Canada and Slovenia, UN Doc S/PV.4046 (16 September 1999) 8 and 9 respectively. See also *Cahin*, 340 and the Committee on Non-State Actors, 'Third Report' in International Law Association Report of the Seventy-Sixth Conference (Washington 2014) (International Law Association 2014) 699 (hereinafter ILA Committee on Non-State Actors 2014). The SG has repeated his proposal only very recently, see UN Doc S/2012/376, 17.

500 See the Sanction Committees on Sudan, Liberia and DRC in <http://www.un.org/sc/committees/>. Whenever entities under an individual's control are covered, they usually do not relate to the ANSA but to companies, NGOs and so on. Al-Shabab in Somalia constitutes the exception. See also *Constantinides*, 106 ff.

501 See the Security Council Committee Established Pursuant to Resolution 1521 (2004) Concerning Liberia, 'Guidelines of the Committee for the Conduct of Its Work', 30 March 2010, 14; and the Security Council Committee Established Pursuant to Resolution 1533 (2004) Concerning the Democratic Republic of the Congo, 'Guidelines of the Committee for the Conduct of Its

current practice hardly endorses a compensatory scheme against ANSAs. In addition such attempts might also have a negative impact: since ANSAs need material resources for their recourse to violence, their financial strangulation could end up in violation of humanitarian law provisions – but this is a possible outcome of similar measures against a state. Satisfaction, restitution and guarantees of non-repetition should be given priority during the armed conflict.

The post-conflict position of the ANSA will be a crucial element in the possibility of reparations, whether towards individuals or international subjects. If the conflict finishes up with the ANSA's defeat and extinction, it would be difficult to see how the accountability of the ANSA could materialize, outside (the concurrent) individual criminal and/or civil responsibility. If there is a kind of agreement between the adversaries, that could be the first medium for putting ANSA accountability into practice. However, the issue of post-conflict reparations has the potential to stall a peace process. Furthermore, while peace agreements are sometimes concerned with forms of reparations towards individuals,[502] the specific accountability of ANSAs is usually not embossed in their texts and it is absorbed, operationally, from the *de jure* government that emerges thereafter.[503] Consequently after its signature and successful implementation, the only possibility for individuals or other injured actors to claim specifically for reparations from ANSAs would depend on their place in the post-conflict society, national or international. In the case of a new state formation, the ANSA accountability becomes part of the new state responsibility. In the case of national reconciliation governments, the accountability of the ANSA seems to 'disappear', but it might be possible to consider the successor entity as liable for previous wrongdoings.[504] The same could apply whenever the reconciliation government does not only draw elements from the ANSA; on the contrary, it draws elements from the existing authority and consists mainly of ANSA members, a rare occurrence in any case. In the same vein, it is to be questioned why accountability disappears after elections that brought a former ANSA into the governmental place. If the usually invoked immunity is the answer, is it necessary to include immunity from civil responsibility? On the other hand, if the actual conflict ends at a standstill (as in the case of *de facto* entities) or in a sort of legal limbo (for example Southern Sudan between the conclusion of the peace agreement and its emergence as a new state), individuals and/or subjects of international law could present claims for injuries and, in principle, ANSAs should (and could) satisfy them.

Work', 6 August 2010, 16; and the Security Council Committee Established Pursuant to Resolution 1591 (2005) Concerning the Sudan, 'Guidelines of the Committee for the Conduct of Its Work', 23 December 2013, 15. There is no similar procedure for Somalia.

502 For such examples see the sub-chapter on *Reparations*, at 127, and Chapter 4, sub-chapter on *Putting the Accountability of Armed Non-State Actors into Operation*, at 202.

503 See the Agreement between the Government of the Republic of South Sudan (GRSS) and the South Sudan Democratic Movement/Army (SSDM/A), 27 February 2012, point 7, on the provision of compensation and reparations by the government through social services delivery. The *(Central African Republic) Accord De Cessez-le-Feu*, art 5, envisages rehabilitation of affected zones, implicitly by the government.

504 See the examples of the ANC and Irish Republican Army in *Dudai*, 796 ff., which offered some limited reparations beyond the conflict period.

Along with the practice of peace agreements, it is possible to discern a tendency (and certainly not an established norm) to have the state substitute in cases where the ANSA is unable or unwilling to provide reparations, therefore potentially including those cases of a reconciliation government or total defeat of the ANSA. The Basic Principles[505] envisaged that possibility, while the drafters of the Chicago Principles similarly claimed that 'where these [non-state] actors are unable or unwilling to meet their obligations, States should assume this responsibility, especially where a State was either partially complicit or failed to take adequate preventative action'.[506] We have to note though that both these instruments are concerned with ANSA accountability towards individuals and imply a soft law obligation; otherwise the usual rules of state responsibility apply and reparations can be sought from the government for acts of the ANSA, only to the extent that it was not diligent in prevention of the ANSA act.

But even this substitution could not be a panacea. Practical considerations would probably bar full remedies, as could be easily demonstrated by the post-conflict situation in Rwanda.[507] Similarly, reparations through the court system would be near-impossible and therefore alternatives would have to be found.[508] In fact there might be a need to prioritize reparations for certain rights violations (or violations suffered by certain classes of people), if not with regard to gravity at least with the aim of post-conflict reconstruction of the national society and certainly not at the expense of the needs of the local population.[509] In the same vein, it might be important ' ... to look beyond individual victims and also consider affected communities as recipients of reparations'.[510]

The proposal of the ILA[511] for the creation of a special fund, ' ... in order to secure payments from non-state actors' could also be seen to go along the same way of substitution. However the creation of such fund could also be combined with the possibility to use frozen assets, following sanctions, for this same cause of granting reparations to the victim.

Zegveld concluded more than 10 years ago that 'the international accountability of armed opposition groups is primitive and the prospects for further development are limited'.[512] The first part of her conclusion remains largely true, although the increasing

505 Annex to A/RES/60/147 [16] and UN Doc E/CN.4/2000/62, 10. See also *Tomuschat* 2007, 578.

506 At 30.

507 UNCHR, 'Report of the Independent Expert on the Right to Restitution, Compensation and Rehabilitation for Victims of Grave Violations of Human Rights and Fundamental Freedoms, Mr. M. Cherif Bassiouni, Submitted Pursuant to Commission on Human Rights Resolution 1998/43' (8 February 1999) E/CN.4/1999/65, 21. See also *ILA Reparations Committee 2010*, 320 and, on Liberia see Cecily Rose, 'An Emerging Norm: The Duty of States to Provide Reparations for Human Rights Violations by Non-State Actors' (2010) 33 Hastings Int'l & Comp.L.Rev. 307, 336.

508 See the *Sierra Leone Truth and Reconciliation Report*, 229.

509 See the *ILA Reparations Committee 2010*, 321–2 ff. about practice acknowledging such principle.

510 UN Doc S/2012/376, 17.

511 *ILA Reparations Committee 2014*, 808.

512 At 229. But see *Kleffner* 2009, 258.

debate, when compared to the period of the quote, is evident. Certainly, there are good reasons to pursue accountability, especially since we cannot associate all humanitarian law violations with individual criminal responsibility. A 'body of law is strengthened if a breach thereof gives rise to an entitlement to reparation'[513] and there are certain prospects that accountability would create a culture of compliance.[514] As regards the second part of her conclusion, certainly the values of justice are given more leeway in peace agreements. In addition, the prospect of operationalization of the ANSA accountability might come from the ANSA itself and the strengthening of its procedural capacity to provide several forms of reparation, at least during the conflict period. Furthermore, accountability could be pursued towards the successive entity to ANSAs in the post-conflict period. The possibility of compensation through targeted measures against the assets of the ANSA could also give a practical way to hold ANSAs accountable. Of course, their respective capacity would be subject to its actual capabilities, which will be reduced for common article 3 ANSAs and increased for *de facto* entities. It is probably the accountability of ANSAs towards international law subjects which does not have, in the current phase of international law, more prospects of development. Not only does a victim-orientated approach militate towards the increased importance of their accountability to individuals rather than international law subjects; in addition the latter would also be hesitant to present claims towards them, in the fear of conferring some sort of legitimacy. To the extent that states, primarily, and other international law subjects do not overcome this fear, accountability of ANSAs to them will not become operational.

Concluding Remarks

In this chapter the obligations and accountability of ANSAs under IHL have been examined. Despite the fact that a little more than half a century ago, it was not so obvious that ANSAs even had obligations under humanitarian law – let alone their international character – it appears that in the last 20 to 30 years a relevant consensus[515] has emerged, from international organs, states and ANSAs. The mechanism that made it possible to bind a non-contracting party has moved from the state and the latter's volition is not the only single criterion any more. While the legislative jurisdiction was, probably, the pedigree of how ANSAs were bound by humanitarian law, absent a better explanation for specific cases, nowadays it is possible to claim persuasively that there is a customary rule on the existence of certain humanitarian law obligations for ANSAs. This norm materialized with the participation of ANSAs, although, again, the role of states and the international community was also significant. In addition, ANSAs have signed agreements with states or other actors and have made unilateral declarations, which, in varying degrees, create obligations either for them (exclusively) or for the contracting party as well (in the

513 *Gillard*, 530.

514 *Vasquez*, 955: '[t]hese theories suggest that international legal norms addressed to non-state actors are far less likely to be observed in the absence of effective enforcement mechanisms'.

515 The consensus in the academic community and the civil society realized well before.

case of agreements). Consequently their (limited) participation in law-making processes, although denied, wrongly, with regard to substantive customary law rules, could evince that, at least for humanitarian law purposes, they possess a certain degree of international personality. This status, apart from the rights and/or obligations that it entails (and which in fact precede, in certain cases, the acquirement of personality), should also lead to the *international* accountability, if not *responsibility*, of ANSAs.

The extent of obligations and the practical aspects for the accountability of the ANSA appear, up to some point, prisoners of the statist approach to international law. On the one hand, the substantive obligations, applicable both to states and ANSAs, were created with the state in mind and ANSAs feature only incidentally, if at all, in this equation. The outcome is that, while in some parts the law is over-comprehensive, in other parts there is a normative gap which needs to be addressed elsewhere.[516] Secondary rules on accountability, on the other hand, are under-developed, although state responsibility rules cannot provide all the answers in every case of ANSA conduct. This under-development is obvious in attribution principles and the available remedies. At least there is an increasing acknowledgement that ANSAs are accountable for violations of humanitarian law and that certain reparations should be provided by them.[517] It is proper to pursue accountability of ANSAs through their own organs, peace agreements or, at least, through collective measures by the international community; otherwise the existence of obligations would (continue to) be only a matter of compliance rather than actual accountability. Nevertheless, compliance might be decreased if accountability is pursued only through criminal and state responsibility: it is not at all obvious that the proliferation of international criminal law or that the elucidation of the state responsibility rules have led to better compliance from ANSAs. The latter, as responsible entities that seriously affect the rights and interests of individuals and states alike, should take positive steps to carry the burden of their obligations and accountability. Certainly not every type of ANSA is capable of providing all means of reparations. In particular common article 3 ANSAs will not have the adequate capabilities to operationalize accountability in all its forms and aspects. But this is different from discounting all forms of accountability[518] and leaving individual and state responsibility rules to fill in the gap.

The less than comprehensive legal obligations and the lack of operational accountability mechanisms could also beg the question whether the (relative to humanitarian law) human rights regime could provide a certain alternative. The rest of the book will be dedicated to this prospect.

---

516 See *Roberts and Sivakumaran*, 139: 'the practice of armed groups may demonstrate the inadequacies of international humanitarian law taking a "one size fits all" approach in all circumstances and might support the recognition of different standards for states and armed groups, or for different types of states and armed groups, in certain circumstances.'

517 Yet 'the Security Council has not gone … so far as to impose on non-State entities the same duty it has imposed on States, namely the obligation to make reparation for the damage caused by their actions', *Cahin*, 340.

518 Also *Dudai*, 785–6.

Chapter 4
Obligations and Accountability of Armed Non-State Actors in International Human Rights Law

In Chapter 3, the sub-chapter *Between Over- and Under Regulation: Does One Size Fit All Armed Non-State Actors?* we have contended that the humanitarian law applicable to ANSAs does not cover all their possible conduct (as well as the implications of ANSA conduct towards individuals) and we have pondered briefly on a number of solutions including the question as to whether the (additional) regime of human rights could provide a legal framework. It is beyond doubt that both an armed conflict and the existence of the ANSA denote an abnormal situation where the state loses effective control, to varying degrees, and human rights are particularly endangered by non-state actors. Consequently an examination of whether these entities are bound by the relevant international law obligations is both pertinent and necessary. It is pertinent because IHL, the principal legal regime which is applicable to ANSAs, is increasingly concerned with the protection of individuals, which is an aim commonly shared with human rights law.[1] It is also necessary because the state might not be able to protect its citizens from human rights violations, although this is one of its principal targets.

In terms of structure, it will firstly be explained why the obligations and accountability of ANSAs in human rights law are needed, before turning to the possible legal bases for obligations and how international actors react to this topic. The remaining part will be devoted to an examination of the circumstances of human rights applicability, since international doctrine (and practice) has only tackled, at best, the basic question of regulation: neither the types of actors bound nor the extent of their responsibilities has undergone any significant scrutiny. The last part will examine the issue of how to put accountability into operation.

1 The ICTY in *Furundzija* [183] noted that 'the general principle of respect for human dignity is the basic underpinning and indeed the very *raison d'être* of international humanitarian law and human rights law', while in *Kunarac* [467], it referred to the 'resemblance, in terms of goals, values and terminology'. See also *Provost*, 133 and UNCHR (Sub-Commission), 'Working Paper on the Relationship between Human Rights Law and International Humanitarian Law by Françoise Hampson and Ibrahim Salama' (21 June 2005) E/CN.4/Sub.2/2005/14, 4.

Accountability in Human Rights Law: Justification, Theory and Practice

There is ample support for the thesis that human rights and humanitarian law co-apply during armed conflicts. Without entering into this discussion,[2] it appears that in recent years only the extra-territorial applicability of human rights *treaties* is contested, while the applicability of human rights law during armed conflicts is not. Since the majority of conflicts with ANSA participation are internal in nature, even extra-territoriality would not normally pose any problem.

If, however, a state is bound to apply both legal regimes during an armed conflict, the situation is less settled for ANSAs. Unlike IHL, which acknowledges the existence of non-state parties and has progressively developed a customary rule that binds ANSAs, human rights treaties are not in principle relevant: they were designed to protect individuals from their state and not from other individuals or non-state entities.[3] Yet this approach is not necessarily considered satisfactory any more. Present-day realities have shown that ANSA conduct can have a serious impact on human rights (beyond the scope of humanitarian law)[4] and, as the UN Secretary General admitted, the conception of human rights as endangered only by states 'has never provided a fully adequate description of the scope of international human rights concern'.[5] The 'values underlying the fundamental rights

---

2 For some writings, in this regard, see Michael J. Dennis, 'Application of Human Rights Treaties Extraterritorially in Times of Armed Conflict and Military Occupation' (2005) 99 AJIL 119, 139. See also Major Michelle A. Hansen, 'Preventing the Emasculation of Warfare: Halting the Expansion of Human Rights Law into Armed Conflict' (2007) 194 Mil.L.Rev. 1, 2; Sean MacBride, 'Human Rights in Armed Conflicts: The Inter-Relationship between the Humanitarian Laws and the Law of Human Rights' (1970) 9 Mil.L. & L. War Rev. 373–91; Aristidis Calogeropoulos-Stratis, 'Droit Humanitaire – Droits de l'Homme et Victims des Conflits Armés' in Jean Simon Pictet and Christophe Swinarski (eds), *Études et Essais sur le Droit International Humanitaire et sur les Principes de la Croix-Rouge en l'Honneur de Jean Pictet* (Comité International de la Croix-Rouge 1984) 654–62; Ralph Wilde, 'The Applicability of International Human Rights Law to the Coalition Provisional Authority (CPA) and Foreign Military Presence in Iraq' (2005) 11 ILSA J.Int'l & Comp.L. 485, 489 ff., *Cerone*, 1507 and Christian Tomuschat, *Human Rights: Between Idealism and Realism* (2nd edn, OUP 2008) 126 ff.

3 For an expression of this position see the statement of the German Democratic Republic in UN Doc E/CN.4/1986/40, 5 and the UN Human Rights Committee, 'General Comment No 31' (26 May 2004) CCPR/C/21/Rev.1/Add.13, 3.

4 For an acknowledgement of the impact that ANSAs can have in the protection of human rights see Council Directive (EC) 2004/83 on Minimum Standards for the Qualification and Status of Third Country Nationals or Stateless Persons as Refugees or as Persons Who Otherwise Need International Protection and the Content of the Protection Granted [2004] OJ L304/12, art 6. ANSAs can be the actors of persecution which could trigger the protection of refugee law. Depending on interpretation, ANSAs can also be actors of protection, according to art 7, so that asylum by third states is not necessary.

5 UNSG, 'Minimum Humanitarian Standards: Analytical Report of the Secretary General Submitted Pursuant to Commission on Human Rights Resolution 1997/21' (15 April 1998) E/CN.4/1998/87, 15.

are such that they should be respected by all bodies, both private and public'.[6] Actually, the tendency to seek accountability of non-state actors in general for violations of human rights has become fairly evident on the international plane.[7]

The reasons for this tendency should be attributed to the following: firstly to the importance of human rights worldwide and the increase of power sources outside the state.[8] This is almost self-evident and will not be pursued any more, as even the evolution of international humanitarian law was triggered, to a certain extent, by this reality. The second relates to the inability of the state responsibility paradigm to provide answers in every instance of human rights violation. Lastly the inherent limits of humanitarian law also reveal that confinement of ANSA's accountability to this legal regime might be inadequate in light of the range and circumstances of endangered human rights.

Why Should Armed Non-State Actors be Held Accountable under Human Rights Law?

The lack of accountability of non-state entities and individuals on the international plane has led to the development of the concept of due diligence, in the law of state responsibility, in general (which is addressed only to aliens), and human rights law, in particular, (which is addressed to individuals in general) as 'each State Party to the present Covenant undertakes to respect and to ensure to all individuals … the rights recognized … '[9]. As the European Court of Human Rights explains, apart from the 'primary duty on the State to secure the [human] right … by putting in place effective criminal-law provisions to deter the commission of offences against the person, backed up by law-enforcement machinery for the prevention, suppression and punishment of breaches of such provisions',[10] the

6 Evert Albert Alkema, 'The Third-Party Applicability of "Drittwirkung" of the European Convention on Human Rights' in Franz Matscher and Herbert Petzold (eds.), *Protecting Human Rights: the European Dimension* (2nd edn, Karl Heymanns 1990) 34.

7 See UN Docs E/CN.4/Sub.2/2005/40 and A/HRC/8/5 and, in the academy, Jordan Paust, 'Human Rights Responsibilities of Private Corporations' (2002) 35 Vand.J.Transnat'l L. 801–25; Christian Tomuschat, 'The Applicability of Human Rights Law to Insurgent Movements' in Horst Fischer et al. (eds), *Krisensicherung und Humanitärer Schutz – Crisis Management and Humanitarian Protection: Festschrift für Dieter Fleck* (Berliner Wissenschafts-Verlag 2004) 573–5; *Alston* (ed.) 2005; and *Clapham* 2006.

8 See August Reinisch, 'The Changing International Legal Framework for Dealing with Non-State Actors' in Philip Alston (ed.), *Non-State Actors and Human Rights* (OUP 2005) 74 and Manisuli Ssenyonjo, *Economic, Social and Cultural Rights in International Law* (Hart 2009) 145.

9 Art 2.1 of the ICCPR. See also art 1 of the Convention for the Protection of Human Rights and Fundamental Freedoms (adopted 4 November 1950, entered into force 3 September 1953) 213 UNTS 221 (hereinafter European Convention) and the American Convention on Human Rights (adopted 21 November 1969, entered into force 18 July 1978) 1144 UNTS 143 (ACHR) as well as art 2.1 of the Convention on the Rights of the Child (adopted 20 November 1989, entered into force 2 September 1990) 1577 UNTS 3.

10 *Osman v United Kingdom* (App no 23452/94) ECHR 1998-VIII [115]. Art 2.1d of the Convention on the Elimination of All Forms of Racial Discrimination (adopted 21 December 1965, entered into force 4 January 1969) 660 UNTS 195 (CERD) and arts 2(e) and 16 the Convention

state has in certain cases 'a positive obligation ... to take preventive operational measures to protect an individual ... from the criminal acts of another individual'.[11] The lack of effective control within a part of national territory does not exclude the jurisdiction of the territorial state and its due diligence duty. In fact the European Court seems to have raised the duties of states to a considerable threshold since there is an 'obligation ... to take the diplomatic, economic, judicial or other measures that it is in its power to take and are in accordance with international law to secure to the applicants the rights guaranteed by the Convention', and a duty to 'endeavour, with all the legal and diplomatic means available to it vis-à-vis foreign States and international organisations, to continue to guarantee the enjoyment of the rights and freedoms guaranteed by the Convention',[12] although acknowledging that 'in the absence of control over ... territory' some measures would be ineffectual.[13] Even as such, it is doubtful whether states are able (or depending on circumstances, even willing[14]) to prevent all conduct that violates human rights by third parties. As due diligence is a relative concept,[15] based on reasonableness and being an obligation of conduct, not result,[16] in the end, the state might not be held responsible.

A situation of armed conflict is probably the exemplary paradigm where the state would not in principle be able to act diligently and effectively. Certainly the criminal law provisions do not have the intended deterrent effect and the rise of the ANSA is a relative and adequate proof in this regard. To make matters worse, the usual avenues of national courts for redress of violations of private rights, which can correspond to human rights violations by private actors, might not be available.[17] In addition, when the ANSA ' ... ha[s] de facto control over at least some of the territory of the State ... only the opposition

---

on the Elimination of All Forms of Discrimination Against Women (adopted 18 December 1979, entered into force 3 March 1981) 1249 UNTS 13 are more explicit in requiring criminal measures. In that sense, human rights law provides indirect obligations upon individuals and this has been the first line of argumentation for the applicability of human rights to non-states, see Marc-André Eissen, 'The European Convention on Human Rights and the Duties of the Individual' (1962) 32 Nordisk Tidsskrift Int'l Ret 230, 233–4.

11 See also UN Human Rights Committee, 'General Comment No 31', 3–4, the *Velasquez Rodriguez Case* (Judgment) Inter-American Court of Human Rights Series C No 4 (29 July 1988) [166] and [174–5] and the *Zimbabwe Human Rights NGO Forum Case* [142 ff.]. However, these positive obligations do not seem to cover all substantive human rights, *Hessbruege*, 75 ff.

12 *Ilascu and Others v Moldova and Russia* (App no 48787/99) ECHR 2004-VII [331] and [333]. See also *Commission Nationale des Droits de l'Homme et des Libertés v Chad*, 74/92, African Commission on Human and Peoples' Rights, 11 October 1995 [22], on the general failure of the state ' ... to provide security and stability in the country, thereby allowing serious and massive violations of human rights'.

13 At [347].

14 *Ssenyonjo*, 114.

15 See *Kilic v Turkey* (App no 22492/93) ECHR 2000-III [63], the *Zimbabwe Human Rights NGO Forum Case* [155–6], the *Genocide Case*, ICJ Rep 221 and Olivier de Schutter, *International Human Rights Law: Cases, Materials, Commentary* (CUP 2010) 423.

16 John H. Knox, 'Horizontal Human Rights Law' (2008) 102 AJIL 1, 22.

17 Similarly, *van den Herik and Cernic*, 726, refer to the potential enforcement gap (at the domestic level) in order to explain the need to resort to human rights for the accountability of corporations.

group can protect the human rights of the persons living there … '.[18] Although this would be a matter of assessment in each case, normal measures, short of armed violence, would probably be inadequate to discharge effective prevention of human rights abuses. It is needless to say that, even lawful, violence has a potential destructive effect on human rights.

Moreover in situations of a failed state the possibility that the government acts as a guarantor of human rights decreases further.[19] Resort to State Responsibility art 9 will not necessarily save the case, because ANSAs do not always undertake state functions; even if they do, in instances of partial collapse of the state apparatus, it would be somewhat absurd to attribute to the state the actions of an ANSA which fights against the central government.[20] Moreover, if state failure persists in time, the responsibility of the state will become a fiction,[21] unless the ANSA undertakes the position of a *de facto* government.[22] The paradigm of state failure (in combination with an armed conflict period) is also significant in the sense that it limits the substantive obligations of ANSAs under international humanitarian law, since Protocol II does not apply.

Apart from expectations of due diligence, it appears that the threshold of attribution of ANSA conduct to states is lowered in comparison with general public international law standards.[23] The European Court of Human Rights in *Loizidou*[24] attached responsibility ' … even if no detailed control is exercised over the policies and actions of the local administration', while in *Ilascu* it implied that 'the decisive influence, of the Russian Federation'[25] to Transdniestria might be sufficient (in combination with other factors) for bringing the applicant under Russia's jurisdiction. Yet even with such a low level of attribution, it is not self-evident that all ANSAs will be under the control of a state. Therefore the state responsibility paradigm still remains insufficient for the protection of human rights by all types of ANSAs.

---

18 UNCHR (Sub-Commission), 'Terrorism and Human Rights: Final Report of the Special Rapporteur, Kalliopi K. Koufa' (25 June 2004) E/CN.4/Sub.2/2004/40, 20.

19 *Constantinides*, 94.

20 See also *Ryngaert* 2008, 360–61 and *Rudolf*, 143. However, see UNCHR, 'Report of the Representative of the Secretary-General on the Human Rights of Internally Displaced Persons, Walter Kälin: Addendum' (24 March 2006) E/CN.4/2006/71/Add.7, 5, which attributed certain human rights obligations to Georgia for the acts of the *de facto* authorities.

21 *Rudolf*, 127.

22 The case of the UN Committee Against Torture, *Sadiq Shek Elmi v Australia* (25 May 1999) CAT/C/22/D/120/1998, appears to be one of (indirect) attribution to the (failed) state of the (potential) activities of the non-state actors. To an extent, it also goes beyond the (disputable) content of State Responsibility art 9.

23 *Cerone*, 1483, *Talmon* 2009, 508 ff. and Anthony Cullen and Steven Wheatley, 'The Human Rights of Individuals in *De Facto* Regimes under the European Convention on Human Rights' (2013) 13 H.R.L.Rev. 691, 704.

24 At [56]. For *Frouville*, 269, the Court has rather classified the TRNC, not as a *de facto* organ but as an administration falling under article 4 of State Responsibility Rules.

25 At [392]. Also *Catan and Others v Moldova and Russia* (Apps nos 43370/04 et al.) ECHR 2012 [122]. Yet see Russia's assessment on the standard of imputability to private parties in *Catan and Others* [96], recalling the approach of the ICJ in the *Genocide Case*.

Other supportive arguments for the need of human rights law's applicability to ANSAs derive from the subject matter of humanitarian law in a two-way direction. On the one hand international humanitarian law resembles human rights law in the sense that most humanitarian rules are nothing more than protection of particular human rights in armed conflicts, albeit with a different formulation. Consequently it is questionable why there should be a distinction depending on the source of obligation and the existence of an armed conflict.[26] George J. Andreopoulos[27] similarly notes 'the increasing emphasis on the nature of the conduct rather than its source'.

On the other hand, certain aspects of human rights are not covered by IHL or are covered only incidentally, such as the right to property or freedom of opinion.[28] A denial of protection during armed conflicts can certainly not be acceptable in view of the fact that individuals are not deprived, in principle, of their rights at any time. Moreover, certain prolonged armed conflicts where the ANSA is in control of territory would also reveal the inadequacy of humanitarian law to provide all answers with regard to the issues that would arise in that territory.

In addition, the trigger for humanitarian law's applicability might be missing, because the conflict is a low-intensity one.[29] Consequently if we do not want to leave a *carte blanche* as to how an ANSA will behave, certain provisions should be made applicable. Furthermore, in the case of an armed conflict, it is not certain whether the lack of violence[30] or peaceful settlement[31] marks its end; regardless of the answer, it is absurd to apply international humanitarian law in frozen conflicts (the law of armed conflict in a non-violent situation), unless the latter is sufficiently informed by human rights standards. But if it does not apply, it would be necessary to provide for adequate protection in between lack of armed violence (either as a result of fatigue or a ceasefire agreement) and peaceful settlement.

Moreover, even peaceful settlement (in the form of an agreement) does not necessarily mean that the potential danger that an ANSA presents to human rights disappears. There is always the possibility that the agreements are inadequate (non-comprehensive)[32]

26 See also *Cullen and Wheatly*, 715–6. Similarly, the emergence of modern IHL and human rights law had the ' … aim of committing governments to protect the most basic notions of humanity', Jonathan Horowitz, 'Human Rights, Positive Obligations, and Armed Conflict: Implementing the Right to Education in Occupied Territories' (2010) 1 International Humanitarian Legal Studies 304, 305.

27 'The International Legal Framework and Armed Groups' (2010) 11 Human Rights Review 223, 224.

28 *ICHRP 2000*, 64;, *Constantinides*, 94; and Yael Ronen, 'Human Rights Obligations of Territorial Non-State Actors' (2013) 46 Cornell Int'l L.J. 21, 23.

29 *Tomuschat* 2004, 589 and *Clapham* 2006, 47.

30 See also *Duffy*, 223 and *Boškoski* [293].

31 *Tadic* Appeals Decision [70]. See also *Delalic* Judgment [183]; *Haradinaj* [37]; *Akayesu* [619]; *Sesay* Judgment [99]; and the *Mission to Caucasus Report*, 299.

32 It is obvious, though, from UNHRC, 'Final Report on the Situation of Human Rights in Darfur Prepared by the Group of Experts Mandated by the Human Rights Council in its Resolution 4/8' (28 November 2007) A/HRC/6/19, that the Special Rapporteurs held Sudan accountable for violations of human rights by the ANSA that signed the peace agreement on Darfur. Consequently

or that low-intensity violence, short of an armed conflict, erupts; in such situations the agreement or humanitarian law might not provide any standard of conduct. Consequently the applicability of human rights law to ANSAs can provide one, especially in light of the (possible) inability of the state to act with due diligence and/or enforce relevant criminal law provisions. Even if peace agreements are duly implemented, there is a period between signature and formal dissolution of the ANSAs and/or effective demobilization of its armed elements, during which the applicability of human rights law could prove crucial, even if it functions at the rear, as supportive of the peace agreement.[33]

The main counter-argument on the human rights applicability to ANSAs is that 'giving terrorist groups the quality of violators of human rights would be dangerous', because it could and has 'amount[ed] to a sort of justification of human rights violations committed by Governments';[34] therefore a 'distinction should be made between citing such groups as human rights violators and the adverse effects their action might have on the enjoyment of human rights'.[35] A similar argumentation was made with regard to the direct human rights accountability of transnational corporations when the 'Norms on the Responsibilities of Transnational Corporations and Other Business Enterprises with Regard to Human Rights'[36] were presented.[37] Nonetheless our experiences from the so-called 'war on terror' have shown that states remain the main focus of human rights concerns and, therefore, this is an exaggerated fear. In fact it has equally been advanced that the failure to criticize the activities of non-state actors might lead to 'toleration of human rights abuses committed by the government' or to a perception of bias towards the government.[38] Similarly the failure of states to live up to their human rights obligations might entail that ANSAs should carry a certain burden and that states and ANSAs should share responsibility for human rights.

Legal and policy arguments in themselves point to the need to hold ANSAs accountable in the international law on human rights. After all 'if a legal system does not take into account social realities, it loses the moral basis for its claim to be respected'.[39] It is then

---

after the successful implementation of peace agreements, responsibility could devolve with the state, although this should be a matter of assessment each time.

33 Some peace agreements make reference to human rights as a basis of the ANSA's framework of conduct, see *infra* sub-chapter *The Approach of States and Armed Non-State Actors*, at 181.

34 UNCHR, 'Note by the High Commissioner for Human Rights Transmitting Report of the Meeting of Special Rapporteurs/Representatives/Experts and Chairpersons of Working Groups of the Special Procedures of the Commission on Human Rights and of the Advisory Services Programme, Geneva, 28–30 May 1996' (30 September 1996) E/CN.4/1997/3, 12 and UN Docs E/CN.4/1998/87, 16 and E/CN.4/Sub.2/2004/40, 19. Similarly see *Kooijmans*, 245.

35 UN Doc E/CN.4/1997/3, 12.

36 UN Doc E/CN.4/Sub.2/2003/12/Rev.2.

37 Larry Catá Backer, 'On the Evolution of the United Nations' "Protect-Respect-Remedy" Project: The State, the Corporation and Human Rights in a Global Governance Context' (2011) 9 Santa Clara J. Int'l L. 37, 46.

38 Ravi Nair, 'Confronting the Violence Committed by Armed Opposition Groups' (1998) 1 Yale Hum. Rts. & Dev.L.J. 1, 8 and 10 and *Ronen*, 49.

39 *Rudolf*, 127.

needed to assess whether international law provides any substantive legal basis in order to create obligations for ANSAs or whether we should resort to practice indicating the existence of a corresponding customary rule.

Legal Basis for Obligations Under Human Rights Law

Preliminaries

In the sub-chapter on *Indirect Obligations of Armed Non-State Actors*, we have examined several possible legal bases with regard to the IHL obligations of ANSAs. However, in light of the fact that humanitarian law explicitly refers to parties to the armed conflict in the relevant treaties it would not be possible to claim that states intended to widen the effect of human rights *treaties* to ANSAs as third parties. The legislative jurisdiction is equally weak, because the treaties foresee only the role of states as guarantor of human rights.[40] Several peace agreements could be construed towards both justifications: in the Darfur Peace Agreement (arts 1.7. and, especially, 3.24)[41] 'the Parties reiterate their commitment to respect and promote human rights and fundamental freedoms as detailed below and in international human rights covenants ratified by the GoS'. To the extent that the human rights covenants have been transposed to internal legislation, this is an acceptance that the state's legislation relevant to human rights is applicable to the ANSA, after the latter has given its consent through the peace agreement. Alternatively it could be a sign of acceptance for these covenants by the ANSAs as third parties.[42] However, the intention of the contracting state parties was different, while the automatic effect of the legislative jurisdiction could not be reconciled with the consent of the ANSA.

The claims of representation of the state[43] could cover only certain ANSAs based on their representativeness, effectiveness (which should somehow overcome that of the central government) and legitimacy and it could leave a gap with regard to how the government is bound by human rights. The *jus cogens* justification[44] could only play a residual role, as it would only be useful for specific and limited rules.[45] Finally the customary international

---

40 However, see the position of David Matas, 'Armed Opposition Groups' (1996–7) 24 Manitoba L.J. 621, 630, 'that treaties made on behalf of the state bind' the insurgent community as well. In the preamble of the UN Doc E/CN.4/Sub.2/2003/12/Rev.2, several human rights treaties are mentioned as if they have a direct effect on corporations. This preamble could also be seen as a direct acceptance of the validity of legislative jurisdiction. See also UN Doc E/CN.4/S-3/3, 5.

41 See also the *Eastern Sudan Peace Agreement*, art 6.13. The *Liberia Peace Agreement*, art XII.1a, seems to be based exclusively on the legislative jurisdiction.

42 It is also possible that the covenants are only a source of inspiration for the content of this article.

43 See *Tomuschat* 2004, 587.

44 *ILA Committee on Non-State Actors* 2010, 652 and UN Doc A/HRC/19/69, 20. See also the Concurring Opinions of Judge Cancado Trindade and Judge Herna Salgado Pesantes in the *Juridical Condition and Rights of the Undocumented Migrants*, Advisory Opinion OC-18, Inter-American Court of Human Rights Series A No 18 (17 September 2003).

45 These rules appear to include: a) the principle of equality and non-discrimination, see Sierra Leone, *1969 Records* First Session, 300; *William Andrews v United States*, Case 11.139, Report

law justification, despite gaining acceptance,[46] requires a corresponding legal status for ANSAs. Even if *de facto* entities have a sort of legal personality, the case for other types of ANSAs (with control over territory or common article 3 ones) appears weaker; and even if accepted, it might only be relevant for the applicability of humanitarian law and not other legal regimes.[47]

There is, however, one (weak) exception to the rule that human rights treaty law does not provide a role for ANSAs. The Optional Protocol (art 4.1) could imply certain obligations for ANSAs. The language used in it is suggestive ('should' instead of 'shall' as in art 4.3.c of Protocol II),[48] since the 'drafters had wished to differentiate between the obligations of non-State actors and those bestowed upon States'.[49]

No. 57/96; Inter-American Commission on Human Rights, OEA/Ser.L/V/II.95 Doc. 7 rev. at 570 (1997) [21]; and *Juridical Condition and Rights of the Undocumented Migrants*, operative [5]; b) the prohibitions of cruel, inhuman or degrading treatment or punishment, see UN Human Rights Committee, 'General Comment No 29' (31 August 2001) CCPR/C/21/Rev.1/Add.11 [11]; UNCHR, 'Report of the Special Rapporteur, Sir Nigel Rodley, Submitted Pursuant to Commission on Human Rights Resolution 2001/62' (27 December 2001) E/CN.4/2002/76, 14; and the *Darfur Inquiry*, 44; c) the prohibition on racial discrimination, Ghana and Uruguay, *1969 Records* First Session, 301 and 303 respectively; DRC, *Armed Activities on the Territory of the Congo (New Application: 2002) (Democratic Republic of the Congo v Rwanda)* (Jurisdiction and Admissibility) [2006] ICJ Rep 34; and the *Responsibility Commentary*, 85; d) the prohibition of slavery, Sri Lanka and Lebanon, *1969 Records* First Session, 219 and 297 respectively; Separate Opinion of Judge ad hoc Dugard in *Armed Activities on the Territory of the Congo (New Application: 2002)* [2006] ICJ Rep 89; the *Responsibility Commentary*, 85; and UNCHR (Sub-Commission), 'Systematic Rape, Sexual Slavery and Slavery-like Practices During Armed Conflict – Final Report Submitted by Ms. Gay J. McDougall, Special Rapporteur' (22 June 1998) UN Doc. E/CN.4/Sub.2/1998/13, 9; and e) the torture prohibition, UNGA 63/166 (18 December 2008) preamble, *Report on Terrorism and Human Rights*; Inter-American Commission on Human Rights, OEA/Ser.L/V/II.116 Doc. 5 rev. 1 corr. (2002) [155]; *Ould Dah v France* (App no 13113/03) ECHR 2009; and UN Doc A/HRC/19/69, 20.

46 Tom Hadden and Colin Harvey, 'The Law of Internal Crisis and Conflict: An Outline Prospectus for the Merger of International Human Rights Law, the Law of Armed Conflict, Refugee Law, and the Law on Humanitarian Intervention' (1999) 81 IRRC 119, 130 and *Heintze* 2009, 268 as well as UN Doc E/CN.4/1991/14, 39, UNHRC, 'Report of the Commission of Inquiry on Lebanon Pursuant to Human Rights Council Resolution S-2/1' (23 November 2006) HRC/3/2, 24 and UN Doc A/HRC/21/50, 47. See also the Agreement on the Implementation of Principles Governing the Protection and Provision of Humanitarian Assistance to War Affected Civilian Populations, Geneva, Switzerland, 15 December 1999, Part 3, where ' … the SPLM and the other Parties to this Agreement recognize that the SPLM is legally bound by customary human rights law … '. Note also that several intra-state peace agreements refer to the UDHR as a standard of conduct.

47 See the disagreement of *Schoiswohl* 2001, 52.

48 For Daniel Helle, 'Optional Protocol on the Involvement of Children in Armed Conflict to the Convention on the Rights of the Child' (2000) 82 IRRC 797, 806, it seems to impose a moral, as opposed to a legal, obligation under international law. See also *Ryngaert* 2008, 364 and *Sivakumaran* 2012, 237 and 324. Opposite *Clapham* 2006, 75 and *Heintze* 2007, 164.

49 UNHRC, 'Outcome of the Expert Consultation on the Issue of Protecting the Human Rights of Civilians in Armed Conflict: Report of the United Nations High Commissioner for Human Rights' (4 June 2009) A/HRC/11/31, 12.

In combination with paragraph 2 of the same article, providing for the criminalization of the relevant conduct by the respective state, this becomes prohibited through national rather than international law.[50] Yet a look at the practice of UN organs would suggest that this stipulation is considered as binding for ANSAs as a matter of international law[51] and not only its individual members. There is a possibility that subsequent to the treaty's conclusion, states have tried to impose their *opinio juris* on ANSAs; yet it would be difficult to see how a norm could acquire customary law status for third parties when the practice of states formulates a norm which would not apply to them.[52] It is the increasing acceptance by ANSAs of their obligations not to recruit/use child soldiers either indirectly[53] or directly[54] (unilateral commitments or the signature of action plans) that suggests a move of international customary law in this direction.

Besides this limited example, suggestions for the duty-creating mechanisms which could explain the accountability of ANSAs could be as follows.

Prohibition of Destruction of Rights

According to art 30[55] of the UDHR, 'nothing in the present Declaration may be interpreted as implying for any State, group or person any right to engage in any activity or perform any act aimed at the destruction of any of the rights and freedoms set forth herein'. The contention is that the group's obligation to respect human rights implicitly derives from the obligation to refrain from destructive acts.[56]

---

50 Ibid., 'parties to the negotiation clearly decided that it was a human rights provision rather than a humanitarian law rule'. This conclusion, however, seems to contradict partially paragraph 3 of the same article which is taken *verbatim* from paragraph 4 of common article 3.

51 See, indicatively, S/RES/1314 [3], S/RES/1379 [8a], S/RES/1998, preamble and Res 2143 (7 March 2014) preamble and [1] as well as UNCHR Res 44 (2005) [39c] and 82 (2005) [3i]. But see the approach in UN Doc A/HRC/17/44, 74–5, avoiding any reference to obligations of the armed groups beyond the Rome Statute and Protocol II.

52 For *Helle*, 807–8, ' … it is uncertain whether non-State entities will feel bound by and thus respect the provision'. The practice of the UN Secretary-General's Special Representative on Children and Armed Conflict could be seen under the dubious obligatory force of this stipulation.

53 See, for example, JEM, Command Order on Recruitment and Use of Child Soldiers, 15 September 2012.

54 See the Chin National Front's Perspective on Child Protection in Armed Conflict (2010). Furthermore, more than 10 ANSAs have signed a Deed of Commitment by Geneva Call relating to the protection of children in armed conflict.

55 See also arts 5.1 of ICCPR and ICESCR, 17 of the European Convention, 29(a) of the ACHR, 31 of the Commonwealth of Independent States Convention on Human Rights and Fundamental Freedoms (adopted 26 May 1995, entered into force 11 August 1998), Council of Europe Doc. (H)95 7 Rev. (hereinafter CIS Convention) and 54 of Charter of Fundamental Rights of the European Union (adopted 7 December 2000, entered into force 1 December 2009) (2001) 40 ILM 266 (hereinafter EU Charter). Note that the human rights treaties are concerned not only with the destruction of rights but also with 'their limitation to a greater extent than is provided for … '.

56 *Matas*, 632, Brice Dickson, 'The Horizontal Application of Human Rights Law' in Angela Hegarty & Siobhan Leonard (eds), *Human Rights: An Agenda for the 21st Century* (Cavendish Publishing Ltd 1999) 71 and *Paust* 2002, 812–13. See, on the other hand, the disagreement of *Hessbruege*, 33–4.

The relevance of this provision to ANSAs is doubtful. The drafters of the Declaration did not have ANSAs in mind when they used the term 'groups' and ANSAs as such do not have human rights; it is possible though to interpret this term accordingly. In any case, even if armed groups are not implied, most of them are affiliated with some sort of associations, political parties or groups (minorities, peoples), of ethnic, religious, political or other character, and therefore they could be covered. For Philip Alston,[57] the aspiration of the LTTE 'to represent a people before the world', is the reason that 'the international community will evaluate their conduct' under human rights. This could place a variety of ANSAs, which are affiliated ethnically with segments of a country's population, under the scrutiny of the international community. Much, of course, would depend on the actual interrelation between the ANSA and the entity, if it is possible to make this differentiation at all. The case that the ANSA is a part of the group or is controlled by one (as the example of the New People's Army in the Philippines) would be quite clear.

The reference to 'acts and activities' was intended to distinguish them from mere opinions, which are not sufficient for triggering application of this article in themselves.[58] These terms must be wider in scope than rights-practising acts, since this provision is addressed to states equally. If it included only such acts, it would have been possible to refer to the exercise of rights and avoid the terms 'activities' or 'acts'. Alternatively, it could simply evoke the rights of others as limitations, a formulation which is quite common, as in arts 32.2 of the ACHR as well as 9.2 and 10.2 of the European Convention.

The beginning of the article ('nothing in the present Declaration') would suggest that the acts or activities should be justifiable specifically on the text of the document. Therefore this provision implies a sort of obligation of conduct for whatever is included in the Declaration. The provisions which could have this potential destructive effect for human rights are the derogation or limitation clauses. Besides the possibility that ANSAs are affiliated with an entity that has a certain right[59] and therefore the limitation clauses might be relevant, it is mostly the use of violence, as recognized implicitly[60] in the UDHR[61] which can have serious repercussions for human rights. Consequently, it is possible to

57 UNCHR, 'Extrajudicial, Summary or Arbitrary Executions: Report of the Special Rapporteur, Philip Alston, Addendum: Mission to Sri Lanka' (27 March 2006) E/CN.4/2006/53/Add.5, 11.

58 Thomas Buergenthal, 'To Respect and to Ensure: State Obligations and Permissible Derogations' in Louis Henkin (ed.), *The International Bill of Rights: The Covenant on Civil and Political Rights* (Columbia University Press 1981) 89.

59 Ibid., 88, noticing the example of a terrorist organization which is outlawed and which cannot invoke the right of association or the freedom of assembly.

60 See the reference to the preamble to 'rebellion against tyranny and oppression'.

61 On the other hand, self-determination of peoples sought by force would probably not be covered, because the ICCPR and the ICESCR do not, even by implication, make reference to any such 'right'. The use of force by peoples has its origins outside human rights law. See also *McCorquodale* 1994, 876 ff. For this reason, examination of UDHR's article instead of the similar ones in human rights treaties is preferred.

consider that ANSAs, even when they exercise legitimate violence,[62] should not destroy human rights, thus having a corresponding obligation under the Declaration. The wording of UNGA Res 49/60,[63] referring to 'acts, methods and practices of terrorism ... aim[ing] at the destruction of human rights ... ' is an indirect acceptance of the effect of the use of force on human rights.

The prospect of sustaining the above-mentioned theoretical construction, even with these limitations, is problematic for a number of reasons. The purpose of the article was mainly to stop parties with subversive ideologies (fascist and so on) from using their freedoms (of opinion, assembly and so on) in order to abolish the rights of others.[64] The reference to states and groups was inserted at a later stage of the negotiations and changed the scope of the article quite substantially,[65] but not in the sense envisaged above. For a start it is continuously supported that it is relevant only with regard to rights-practising activities[66] – this appears to be the understanding of the states negotiating the UDHR. There is also an opinion that only certain rights are covered and not all of them.[67] The inclusion of other interests is rejected.[68] Obviously any reliance on it in international adjudication[69] – itself rare – is bound to remain limited, because ANSAs cannot be directly

62 Although, generally, 'the use of violence in pursuit of political aims' is rejected, see the preambles of UNHRC Res 8/9 (2008) and UNCHR Res 56 (2005), it is considered as legitimate in instances of foreign/military occupation. In UNCHR, 'Report of the Human Rights Inquiry Commission Established Pursuant to Commission Resolution S-5/1 of 19 October 2000' (16 March 2001) E/CN.4/2001/121, 18, the Commission refers to 'a Lebanon-style war of attrition of the sort successfully waged by Hezbollah in the 1990s' as legal. See also UNHRC, 'Report of the Special Rapporteur on the Situation of Human Rights in the Palestinian Territories Occupied since 1967, Richard Falk' (11 February 2009) A/HRC/10/20, 18 as well as the Separate Opinion of Vice-President Ammoun in the *Namibia* Opinion [1971] ICJ Rep 79.

63 (9 December 1994) Annex I.2. Similarly see Res 53/144 (9 December 1998) Annex, art 12; UNCHR Res 46 (1994) preamble; and UNHRC Res 18/10 (2011) [4].

64 See *Zdanoka v Latvia* (App no 58278/00) ECHR 17 June 2004 [109]; *Eissen*, 235; and Torkel Opsahl and Vojin Dimitrijevic, 'Articles 29–30' in Gudmundur Alfredsson and Asbjørn Eide (eds), *The Universal Declaration of Human Rights: A Common Standard of Achievement* (Nijhoff 1999) 649.

65 *Buergenthal*, 87.

66 International Council on Human Rights Policy, *Taking Duties Seriously: Individual Duties in International Human Rights Law* (1999) 46 and Yutaka-Arai, 'Prohibition of Abuse of the Rights and Freedoms Set Forth in the Convention and of their Limitation to a Greater Extent than is Provided for in the Convention' in Pieter Van Dijk (ed.), *Theory and Practice of the European Convention on Human Rights* (4th edn, Intersentia 2006) 1084 and 1088. Buergenthal's example with regard to the terrorist organisation is also instructive.

67 Nigel Rodley, 'Can Armed Opposition Groups Violate Human Rights?' in Kathleen E. Mahoney and Paul Mahoney (eds), *Human Rights in the Twenty-First Century: A Global Challenge* (Nijhoff 1993) 308. Similarly *Yutaka-Arai* 2006, 1084.

68 David John Harris, Michael O'Boyle and Colin Warbrick, *Law of the European Convention on Human Rights* (2nd edn, OUP 2009) 649. Implicitly, Andrew Clapham, *Human Rights in the Private Sphere* (Clarendon Press 1993) 168.

69 See some examples in Manfred Nowak, *U.N. Covenant on Civil and Political Rights: CCPR Commentary* (2nd edn N.P. Engel 2005) 116–17.

accountable under human rights treaties and invocation of this article (by the state) is bound to be connected with a rights violation complained of by an individual or group.

A more significant reservation on the validity of this justification stems from the ordinary meaning of this provision as an interpretation tool[70] rather than a duty-creating norm. If the article was formulated as 'no State, group or person shall engage in any activity or perform any act aimed at the destruction of any of the rights and freedoms set forth herein', it would be easier to consider it as a clause creating accountability for ANSAs in particular and non-state actors in general.

In addition, the act or activity should have (at least) a principal aim of destruction[71] and the use of force by ANSAs is usually not an end in itself. Moreover, we would have to ascertain the customary and binding status of the preamble, something that is less than self-evident,[72] as well as the binding character of the article with regard to ANSAs.[73]

To sum up, it seems highly improbable that art 30 can be viewed as a comprehensive legal basis for the accountability of ANSAs.[74] At best it could cover only ANSAs who represent peoples or that are essentially linked with or even controlled by lawful non-state groups and only with reference to specific rights. Or it could pose some limitations to the exercise of violence. Consequently it seems logical to resort to other justifications in order to find a more convincing basis for the accountability of ANSAs in human rights law.

Preamble of the Universal Declaration of Human Rights

Another justification is a reference in the preamble of the UDHR that 'every individual and every organ of society ... shall strive by teaching and education to promote respect for these rights'.[75] Consequently if they have to promote respect, this presupposes

70 See, indicatively, Erica-Irene A. Daes, *Freedom of the Individual under Law: An Analysis of Article 29 of the Universal Declaration of Human Rights* (United Nations 1990) 17 and 174; *Rodley*, 308; and *Nowak* 2005, 111. For *Ssenyonjo*, 125, while the article is a mere guideline, it is not without legal implications.

71 The proposition of Ecuador, UNGA Third Committee, 155th Meeting (1947) A/C.3/SR.155, 667, to include activities which might destroy rights was not accepted in the end.

72 See this discussion at sub-chapter *Preamble of the Universal Declaration of Human Rights*, at 153. David Kinley and Junko Tadaki, 'From Talk to Walk: The Emergence of Human Rights Responsibilities for Corporations at International Law' (2004) 44 Va.J.Int'l L. 931, 949, doubt also the customary status of this provision, while Torkel Opsahl, 'Articles 29 and 30: The Other Side of the Coin' in Asbjørn Eide and Theresa Swinehart (eds), *The Universal Declaration of Human Rights: A Commentary* (Scandinavian University Press 1992) 469, doubts claims on its universality.

73 See *Ronen*, 36, commenting that 'even if the UDHR addresses the obligations of NSAs, those obligations remain within the UDHR's original, aspirational ambit'.

74 See also *Clapham* 1993, 169. Maybe it could justify the illegitimation of a use of force by ANSAs, which was previously considered legitimate. But see Chile in UNGA Third Committee, 156th Meeting (1947) A/C.3/SR.156, 671.

75 See UNHRC, 'Mission to Lebanon and Israel (7–14 September 2006): Report of the Special Rapporteur on Extrajudicial, Summary or Arbitrary Executions, Philip Alston; the Special Rapporteur on the Right of Everyone to the Enjoyment of the Highest Attainable Standard of Physical and Mental Health, Paul Hunt; the Representative of the Secretary-General on Human Rights of Internally Displaced Persons, Walter Kälin; and the Special Rapporteur on Adequate

(prior) respect for human rights; the reference to an organ of society is considered as all-encompassing of non-state actors, including armed opposition groups and related entities. Similar language is used in the preamble of the ICCPR, as ' ... the individual ... is under a responsibility to strive for the promotion and observance of the rights recognized in the present Covenant'.[76] Obviously the language is somewhat clearer, since it refers to promotion and observance. However, only the UDHR refers to collective entities and therefore it appears more relevant with regard to the (prospect of) obligations by ANSAs.

The originally non-binding character of the Declaration is beyond doubt;[77] this is the reason that it has achieved a more or less consensual adoption. However, with the passage of time, its importance and authority has grown;[78] it is possible that an international instrument would take a course of its own, regardless of the original intent behind its adoption. Apart from constituting 'a common standard of achievement for all peoples and all nations as well as the source of inspiration and a basis of subsequent progress in the field of human rights',[79] there is considerable support that it constitutes customary law and, as such, it binds all states.[80] The frequent reference to the UDHR in intra-state agreements[81] seems to fortify the argument. In the preamble of the Ceasefire Code of Conduct Agreed

---

Housing as a Component of the Right to an Adequate Standard of Living, Miloon Kothari' (2 October 2006) A/HRC/2/7, 7, although using a slightly different formulation on the obligations of Hezbollah, ' ... that every organ of society respect[s] and promote[s] human rights'. See also Louis Henkin, 'The Universal Declaration at 50 and the Challenge of Global Markets' (1999) 25 Brook.J. Int'l L. 17, 25, *Paust* 2002, 813 and 819, UN Doc E/CN.4/Sub.2/2003/12/Rev.2, preamble and Douglas Hodgson, *Individual Duty within a Human Rights Discourse* (Ashgate 2003) 89.

76 For the ICHRP 1999, 28 'it is clear from the language used in the preambles that at least one such duty on individuals is to promote and observe human rights'.

77 See the statements by the US, New Zealand, Norway and Argentina in UNGA Third Committee, 89th Meeting (1947) A/C.3/SR.89. See also Ian Brownlie and Guy Goodwin-Will, *Basic Documents on Human Rights* (4th edn, OUP 2002) 18.

78 UN Doc A/8052, 88.

79 UNGA Res 53/168 (10 December 1998) preamble.

80 See, indicatively, Asbjørn Eide, 'Internal Disturbances and Tensions' in *International Dimensions of Humanitarian Law* (Henry Dunant Institute 1988) 244–5, as well as several instances of international practice in Bertrand Ramcharan, 'The Legal Status of the International Bill of Human Rights' (1986) 55 Nord.J.Int'l.L. 366, 367 ff. See also, indicatively, UNGA 2546 (XXIV) (11 December 1969) [4], the *Case Concerning United States Diplomatic and Consular Staff in Tehran* [1980] ICJ Rep 42, a statement by Jordan in UN Doc S/PV.6061 (6 January 2009) 29 as well as UNCHR, 'Report on the Human Rights Situation in the Islamic Republic of Iran by the Special Representative of the Commission, Mr. Reynaldo Galindo Pohl, Appointed Pursuant to Resolution 1986/41' (28 January 1987) E/CN.4/1987/23, 4, UNCHR, 'Report by the Independent Expert, Mrs. Mónica Pinto, on the Situation of Human Rights in Guatemala, Prepared in Accordance with Commission Resolution 1994/58' (20 December 1994) E/CN.4/1995/15, 5 and the preamble of UNHRC Res 17/21 (2011). It should be noted that the Universal Periodic Review Mechanism in the Human Rights Council uses the Declaration as a basis of the review.

81 See also the Abkhazia and Somaliland Constitutions in sub-chapter *The Approach of States and Armed Non-State Actors*, at 179, as well as the *NDFP's Children Declaration*.

between the Government of Nepal and CPN (Maoist),[82] the parties 'remain … committed towards the Universal Declaration of Human Rights – 1948 … ', while in Annex 8 (art A.I.10) of the Lusaka Protocol, 'the Government and UNITA commit themselves to implement …, respecting … the general principles of internationally recognised human rights, more particularly, the Universal Declaration of Human Rights … '.

However, it is far from certain that all the Declaration's text is customary and this is acknowledged by doctrine as well.[83] In general to consider every word of the Declaration as customary 'is an oversimplification, since there is a lack of a relevant point of reference, as for example the customary humanitarian law study … '.[84] It is probable, though, that aspects of almost every substantive right have become customary.[85]

Regardless of the exact status of the UDHR, preambles are not legally binding as such.[86] In fact they tend to be the disposable place of materials that were left out of the main treaty.[87] Instead they are considered as part of the contextual interpretation of a treaty (art 31.2 of the VCLT). Yet creating duties through the preamble (and of a Declaration, particularly) is far-fetched, while a responsibility to *strive* to *promote* respect *by teaching and education* is different from an obligation to respect human rights.[88] In addition, 'a contention that an ANSA is an 'organ of society' is at least doubtful, although the position could be different for ANSAs which constituted a political party'[89] (or another form of association) before the outbreak of the conflict, or are controlled by one.[90] Furthermore, they could constitute organs of the society in a wider sense to the extent that peoples, or an ethnic or other group, are represented by an ANSA, as most of them have distinct ties with parts of a country's population. The preambles of human rights treaties use stronger language and, despite the reference to individuals only, it would make sense to include groups as bearers of such responsibility, since they are in a far more powerful position to

82 Gokarna, 25 May 2006.

83 *Brownlie and Goodwin-Gill*, 18; *Kinley and Tadaki*, 949; and *Lubell*, 233. The Committee on the Enforcement of Human Rights Law, 'Final Report on the Status of the Universal Declaration of Human Rights in National and International Law' in International Law Association Report of the Sixty-Sixth Conference (Buenos Aires, 1994) (International Law Association, 1994) 544, concludes that 'those who urge acceptance of the Declaration *in toto* as customary law are in a clear minority, and there is insufficient state practice to support such a wide-ranging proposition at this date'.

84 *Mastorodimos* 2009, 135.

85 See UN Doc E/CN.4/1987/23, 4, UNCHR, 'Report on the Situation of Human Rights in Kuwait under Iraqi Occupation Prepared by Mr. Walter Kâlin, Special Rapporteur of the Commission on Human Rights, in Accordance with Commission Resolution 1991/67' (16 January 1992) E/CN.4/1992/26, 13 and UN Doc E/CN.4/1995/15, 5.

86 Christina M. Cerna, 'Reflections on the Normative Status of the American Declaration of the Rights and Duties of Man' (2008–9) 30 U.Pa.J.Int'l L. 1211, 1212.

87 Martii Koskienniemi, 'Preamble' in Gudmundur Alfredsson and Asbjørn Eide (eds), *The Universal Declaration of Human Rights: A Common Standard of Achievement* (Nijhoff 1999) 27.

88 *Rodley*, 305. See also *Hessbruege*, 35 and *Kinley and Tadaki*, 948.

89 *Mastorodimos* 2009, 139.

90 See the position of India in a similar context, UN Doc E/CN.4/1986/40, 11, while UN Doc A/HRC/2/7, 7 with regard to Hezbollah supports this interpretation.

do so, when compared to individuals. But again the choice of language (responsibility to strive) denotes an aspiration rather than a positive obligation.

Finally this part of the preamble continues with the following reference: ' ... and by progressive measures, national and international, to secure their universal and effective recognition and observance'. It would be difficult to see how an individual can take progressive measures to this end, especially since the 'individual natural person does not possess the capacity to create law unless it is part of a group'.[91] Even assuming that the organs of society could take these measures, presumably at the national level, this part of the preamble could at best be considered as an invitation to societal organs to form strategies for the future observance of the rights in the Declaration; such interpretation hardly denotes prior existing obligations.[92]

Overall, while this part of the preamble could give a hint towards certain responsibilities of ANSAs,[93] it would seem a leap of logic to base their overall obligations on it, since its language is quite restrictive, while it might not cover all types of ANSAs.

Language of Duties in Human Rights Instruments

Quite apart from the preamble of the UDHR and human rights treaties, the language of duties appears in these and other human rights instruments.[94] Art 29 of the UDHR provides that 'everyone has duties to the community ... '.[95] The preambles of ICCPR and ICESCR, alongside the responsibility to strive for the observance of rights, acknowledge the existence of individual's ' ... duties to other individuals and to the community to which he belongs ... '.[96] A general reference exists in the ACHR, since 'every person has

91 *Gal-Or*, 137.

92 See also the interpretation of *Vasquez*, 942, for whom ' ... legal obligations bind corporations only to the extent that further "national and international measures" are taken'.

93 For *Hessbruege*, 35, it contains a duty not to cooperate with states in such a way as to further their violations.

94 An argument is also made to the extent that many of the rights provided in human rights instruments do not specify public parties as their potential exclusive violators, *Eissen*, 237–8; Karel Vasak, 'The European Convention on Human Rights: A Useful Complement to the Geneva Convention (1965) 5 IRRC 399, 410; *Paust* 2002, 810; David Weissbrodt, 'Human Rights and Responsibilities of Individuals and Non-state Entities' in Gudmundur Alfredsson and Maria Stavropoulou (eds), *Justice Pending: Indigenous People and Other Good Causes: Essays in Honour of Erica-Irene A. Daes* (Martinus Nijhoff 2002) 244 and 246; and *Hodgson*, 95 ff. In that regard they appear to be permissive towards the imposition of duties, although the impossibility of judicial enforcement through the human rights treaties would suggest that such obligations are imperfect.

95 On the importance attached to this article, see the comments of Brazil and Greece, UNGA Third Committee, 153rd Meeting (1947) A/C.3/SR.153, 646–7 and 649 respectively.

96 This was judged as a re-affirmation of art 29 of the UDHR, UNSG, 'Annotations on the Text of the Draft International Covenants on Human Rights' (1955) A/2929, 12. See also UN Committee on Economic, Social and Cultural Rights, 'General Comment No 12' (12 May 1999) E/C.12/1999/5, 6, ' ... all members of society – individuals, families, local communities, non-governmental organizations, civil society organizations, as well as the private business sector – have responsibilities in the realization of the right to adequate food' and, similarly, UN Committee on Economic, Social and Cultural Rights, 'General Comment No 14' (11 August 2000) E/C.12/2000/4, 12.

responsibilities to his family, his community, and mankind' (art 32), while the EU Charter accepts, in the preamble, that 'enjoyment of these rights entails responsibilities and duties with regard to other persons, to the human community and to future generations'. The title of the American Declaration of the Rights and Duties of Man (hereinafter American Declaration)[97] is instructive, while it contains a separate chapter concerning specific obligations, most of them owed to the state,[98] along with similar inferences in the preamble. The African Charter contains also a separate chapter on duties, some of them owed to other individuals/groups and others to the state.[99] Consequently all human rights instruments[100] make some form of reference to human duties. A strong opinion was thus formulated or, to a certain extent, resurrected,[101] not only towards the existence of individual duties (with the cumulative invocation of the preambles or the prohibition of destruction of rights as well),[102] but also in the direction of creating an instrument which would elaborate the specific.[103] In the context of the United Nations two instruments are worthy of reference. The first one is the Declaration on the Right and Responsibility of Individuals, Groups and Organs of Society to Promote and Protect Universally Recognized Human Rights and Fundamental Freedoms,[104] although seemingly unrelated because it concerns human

---

97 Res. XXX, Final Act of the Ninth International Conference of American States (Pan American Union), Bogota, Colombia, Mar. 30–May 2, 1948.

98 *Knox*, 4.

99 Arts 27–29. See also art 19, 'nothing shall justify the domination of a people by another'. On the conception of duties from African scholars see Annemarie Devereux, 'Should Duties Play a Larger Role in Human Rights – A Critique of Western Liberal and African Human Rights Jurisprudence' (1995) 18 UNSWLJ 464, 473 ff. Yet in *Ilesanmi v Nigeria*, 268/03, African Commission on Human and Peoples' Rights, 11 May 2005, the complaint for violations of arts 27 and 29, with regard to smuggling activities exercised by non-state actors and tolerated by public authorities, was manifestly unsuccessful.

100 See also arts 10.2 (freedom of expression) of the European Convention and 11.2 of the CIS Convention: 'the exercise of these freedoms, since it carries with it *duties and responsibilities* … ' (emphasis added). Art 1c of the Arab Charter on Human Rights (adopted 22 May 2004, entered into force 15 March 2008) (hereinafter Arab Charter) also makes a reference to the ' … interdependence between awareness of rights and commitment to duties … '.

101 See the proposal of Egypt, 95th Meeting (1947) A/C.3/SR.95, 83 and the stance of China, 87 and Argentina, 88.

102 *Daes* and Jordan Paust, 'The Other Side of Right: Private Duties under Human Rights Law' (1992) 5 Harv. Hum. Rts. J. 51–63. See also *Eissen*, 231 ff; *Clapham* 1993, 96–7; *Hodgson*, 91; and David Weissbrodt and Muria Kruger, 'Human Rights Responsibilities of Businesses as Non-State Actors' in Philip Alston (ed.), *Non-State Actors and Human Rights* (OUP 2005) 330. On the other hand *Opsahl*, 450, rejects the notion of fundamental human duties, while *Devereux*, 470 ff., notices several opinions on the inferiority of duties to rights.

103 See such private initiatives with commentary in Ben Saul, 'In the Shadow of Human Rights: Human Duties, Obligations, and Responsibilities' (2001) 32 Colum.Hum.Rts.L.Rev. 565, 571 ff. and 604 ff.

104 A/RES/53/144. This instrument is also referred to in the preamble of UN Doc E/CN.4/Sub.2/2003/12/Rev.2.

rights defenders. Two articles seem particularly relevant.[105] Art 10 provides that 'no one shall participate, by act or by failure to act where required, in violating human rights and fundamental freedoms ... ', while art 18.2 stipulates that ' ... individuals, groups, institutions and non-governmental organizations have an important role to play and *a responsibility in* safeguarding democracy, *promoting human rights and fundamental freedoms* and contributing to the promotion and advancement of democratic societies, institutions and processes' (emphasis added).[106] The initial discussions envisaged stronger language, similar to that used in the preambles of the Covenants.[107] The language of the Declaration, apart from art 18.1, mostly refers to a form of responsibility for the non-state actor when acting in collusion with the state towards rights violations rather than indicating an autonomous source of human rights obligations. However, the understanding of the relevant Special Rapporteur seems different: since '[n]on-State actors are thus included and therefore have a responsibility to promote and respect the rights enshrined in the Declaration',[108] it might be understood, as a minimum, that the rights enumerated within (assembly, association and so on) form part of the obligations of non-state actors.

A UN Special Rapporteur has also drafted a Declaration on Human Social Responsibilities.[109] Could all these instruments cumulatively denote the existence of a general duty to respect human rights, applicable to individuals and collective entities?[110]

For a start, duties are not owed to other individuals only. Many of them relate to the state[111] and, therefore, they would hardly seem to impose obligations to respect human

105 See also the preamble and arts 17, 18.1 and 19.

106 See though the reaction of Brazil ' ... that while individuals could properly contribute to the promotion and protection of human rights, they could not protect human rights per se, that was the sphere of States', UN Doc E/CN.4/1986/40, 4.

107 UNCHR, 'Report of the Working Group on a Draft Declaration on the Right and Responsibility of Individuals, Groups and Organs of Society to Promote and Protect Universally Recognized Human Rights and Fundamental Freedoms' (9 March 1987) E/CN.4/1987/38, 8 and 11–12. See also the comments of *Knox*, 35.

108 UNSG, 'Note Transmitting the Report of the Special Rapporteur on the Situation of Human Rights Defenders' (4 August 2010) A/65/223, 3. See also UNHRC, 'Report of the Special Rapporteur on the Situation of Human Rights Defenders, Margaret Sekaggya' (30 December 2009) A/HRC/13/22, 9: '[n]on-State actors and private entities should therefore also abide by the Declaration and refrain from endangering the safety of defenders and/or impeding their work'.

109 UNCHR, 'Human Rights and Human Responsibilities, Final report of the Special Rapporteur, Miguel Alfonso Martínez, on the Study Requested by the Commission in its Resolution 2000/63, and Submitted Pursuant to Economic and Social Council Decision 2002/277' (10 November 2003) E/CN.4/2003/105. We should also make a reference to the study by *Daes*, 53–64, as being the first catalogue of human duties, coming also from the UN. So far, though, the American Declaration remains the most credible source of specific obligations.

110 For Michael Bothe, 'International Legal Aspects of the Darfur Conflict' in August Reinisch and Ursula Kriebaum (eds), *The Law of International Relations: Liber Amicorum Hanspeter Neuhold* (Eleven International Publishing 2007) 5, this appears to be the right approach.

111 *Knox*, 2, makes this important differentiation, noting that duties owed to the state have the prospect of undermining human rights protection, while only duties owed to individuals are 'truly horizontal'.

rights. Furthermore, individual duties are judged as adverse to individual human rights and specific rights-holders would owe corresponding duties, at least in principle.[112] The consequence, however, of this approach is that group conduct appears irrelevant in this regard and ANSAs could not be covered. Even in the provisions where there is a reference to groups, or where the groups are objectively in a position to fulfil the same duties as the individual, it is doubtful whether ANSAs featured in the mind of the drafters[113] and whether they could be included, unless they are associated with or controlled by a people, ethnic or other groups and/or other collectivities within a state.

Assuming that ANSAs are holders of rights, duties could not correspond to every human right,[114] since some of them can only be protected against state action, according to treaty provisions.[115] It is significant, also, that the universal human rights instruments have refrained from specifying the extent of obligations,[116] despite the efforts of certain delegations to do so in the UDHR.[117] The generality of language denotes, probably, a differentiated opinion of states, if not towards the existence of specific human duties, at least with regard to the need for an international instrument to deal with such issues.[118] The Declaration on Human Social Responsibilities revealed the north–south divide in this regard, as the latter advocated in favour while the former vehemently opposed. The fact that the African Charter offers the most extensive list of human duties (especially in comparison to the European Convention) is also instructive. Such negative state attitudes could reveal

> ... the fear that insisting on pinning down the social duties (or responsibilities) of the individual, or advocating the usefulness of producing an international standard in this

---

112 See, in this regard, the preambles of the American Declaration, the African Charter and the EU Charter. In fact we could refer to a general duty to limit the exercise of a right so as not to disturb the rights of others.

113 The disregard of ANSAs in *General Comments Nos 12 and 14* of the UN Committee on Economic, Social and Cultural Rights is instructive.

114 *Devereux*, 469 and *Hodgson*, 29, notice that this is the opinion of the majority of Western liberal theorists, while *Saul*, 586–7, also concurs. For *Hodgson*, 131, the African Charter 'extends to the recognition of imperfect or non-correlative or freestanding duties'. Opposite, UN Doc A/2929, 12 'it was generally agreed that rights and duties were correlative and that every right carried with it a corresponding duty', Cuba, UN Doc A/C.3/SR.155, 665, ' ... the possession of each right implied a corresponding duty' and UN Doc E/CN.4/2003/105, 13. See also the American Declaration's preamble that '[r]ights and duties are interrelated in every social and political activity of man', while the African and the EU Charter could be construed towards this direction.

115 See for example the *Protocol to the Convention for the Protection of Human Rights and Fundamental Freedoms*, arts 2–3, where the State and the High Contracting Parties are the direct addressees of the rights to education and free elections respectively, while the ICESCR contains many similar provisions.

116 *Hodgson*, 94.

117 See Cuba in UNGA Third Committee, 90th Meeting (1947) A/C.3/SR.90, 38. See also UN Doc A/C.3/SR.95, 83, 87–8.

118 See *Opsahl*, 454 and *Tomuschat* 2008, 5. For Richard Gittleman, 'The African Charter on Human and Peoples' Rights: A Legal Analysis' (1981–2) 22 Va.J.Int'l L. 667, 677, vagueness was intentional on the part of the drafters.

regard, could lead to an instrument that Governments would utilize to limit the exercise of the recognized rights and freedoms of persons under their jurisdiction.[119]

But it is possible that states might have a legitimate interest not to limit the scope of individual obligations with an international instrument, because the option of imposing more extended duties at the domestic level might be questioned.

The vagueness of most human rights instruments appeared also in the latest Declaration on Human Social Responsibilities,[120] while the legal nature of responsibilities can be doubted, since 'the creation of new extralegal perspectives [is] based on morality, human solidarity and equity ... '.[121] Furthermore, even the references in the African Charter and the American Declaration are not clear enough on the scope of human duties.[122] Not surprisingly, the references of the UN Committee on Economic, Social and Cultural Rights in General Comments Nos 12 and 14 (regarding the rights to food and health, respectively) to responsibilities of non-state entities are vague and barely mark their extent. Consequently this ambiguity would imply, at the very least, that duties cannot be effectively enforced,[123] if they are not altogether different from legal obligations.

With regard to instruments enumerating specific duties, such as the American Declaration, it could be implied that there is no general duty to respect human rights, at least originating from international law.[124] The references to individual duties in preambles are obviously not boosting the argument,[125] while the universality[126] and/or the norm-creating character[127] of UDHR's art 29, specifically, is seriously doubted.

Overall it appears that the language of duties is not particularly relevant or adequate for ANSAs. In essence the Minimum Humanitarian Standards was an effort to impose human duties on individuals and non-state actors, including ANSAs. The failure to transpose them into a binding legal instrument is further evidence of the limited normative reach of the

119 UN Doc E/CN.4/2003/105, 8. Significantly, the Annex to this Report is considered a Trojan horse for human rights protection by *Knox*, 2 and 34.

120 Also *Knox*, 32.

121 Preamble. See also UN Doc E/CN.4/2003/105, 3. On the other hand art 5 of the Declaration states that rights and responsibilities have an 'equal value and importance to life in society'.

122 Ebow Bondzie-Simpson, 'A Critique of the African Charter on Human and Peoples' Rights' (1988) 31 Howard L.J. 643, 657 and *Saul*, 593.

123 *Bondzie-Simpson*, 657–8. *Hodgson*, 238–9, dismisses the argument on the ground that human rights might also be formulated vaguely while noting, at 247, some exceptions from the African Charter (art 29.3, 5 and 6).

124 While UN Doc E/CN.4/Sub.2/2003/12/Rev.2 contains specific duties, it also makes a reference to ' ... respect [of] economic, social and cultural rights as well as civil and political rights ... '. The African Charter refers to an individual duty to respect fellow beings (art 28).

125 *Hodgson*, 93 'the preambular provisions ... [do ...] not purport to impose any legally binding duties on individuals. The duties are rather, at best, aspirational and moral in nature'. See also *Knox*, 14.

126 *Opsahl*, 469. *Kinley and Tadaki*, 949, also reject that it constitutes a customary norm.

127 *Rodley*, 306 and *Provost*, 64.

above-mentioned instruments which could, at best, be confined to certain types of ANSAs, because of their affiliation with other groups, and, consequently, lead to limited obligations.

Third Parties' Obligations (Drittwirkung)

An alternative justification is the German public law theory of Drittwirkung,[128] which literally means the 'effect on third parties' and designates, among others,[129] the obligation of private parties to respect the human rights of others.[130] The need for such protection was initiated by the fact that '[s]tructural innovations in contemporary society have in many instances obliged states into sharing their power with influential groups of individuals, large-scale private organizations which hold considerable economic and/or political power (for example corporations, trade unions, political parties) and other institutions'.[131] Further arguments for its evolution rested on the fundamental character of rights[132] or that basic rights '... constitute an objective order of values' that should be preserved.[133] Thus its *raison d'être* coincides partly with the rationale for applying human rights obligations to ANSAs.

This theoretical construction has taken two variations. The first and majority one supports the indirect horizontal effect of basic rights, which are enforced to private parties primarily through general clauses within private law. The second variation supports the direct horizontal effect of human rights. The doctrine itself depends 'rather on the constitutional arrangements of the State concerned'[134] and features now in the positive internal law of several states, but it is debatable whether it has been transposed to international law so far.[135] The intention of human rights treaties drafters was certainly not to bind third parties.[136] As such, this theory is useful in its second variation and it should be distinguished from the internal criminalization and/or prohibition of human rights violations by the state. Although internal (criminal or civil) law complements the law of human rights and it might also be a positive obligation of the state concerned,[137] the issue examined is whether this theory creates *international* legal obligations based on human rights law. This theory (*Drittwirkung*) should also be differentiated from individual responsibility under international criminal law, since accountability for human rights violations is not

---

128 See the *ILA Reparations Committee 2010*, 308, referring to this theory. But see *Clapham* 1993, 181.

129 See Eric Engle, 'Third Party Effect of Fundamental Rights (Drittwirkung)' (2009) 5 Hanse L.Rev. 165.

130 See also Andrew Drzemczewski, 'The European Human Rights Convention and Relations Between Private Parties' (1979) 26 NILR 163.

131 Ibid., 164.

132 *Engle*, 170.

133 Ralf Brinktrine, 'The Horizontal Effect of Human Rights in German Constitutional Law: the British Debate on Horizontality and the Possible Role Model of the German Doctrine of "Mittelbare Drittwirkung der Grundrechte"' (2001) 4 E.H.R.L.R. 421, 424.

134 *Clapham* 1993, 165.

135 See the rejection of *Harris* et al., 20.

136 *Drzemczewski*, 168.

137 An example of such an approach is evident in art 2(d) of CERD, regarding racial discrimination by non-state actors within a state.

necessarily linked with criminal sanctions. Moreover, international criminal law is largely unconcerned with the accountability of collective entities.

As the origin of this theory is European, it is mainly publicists at the European level that have shown positive inclination towards its validity. The European institutions have occasionally made reference to the concept, but they avoided giving a green light to its validity. In *X and Y v Netherlands*,[138] the European Commission on Human Rights rejected the applicability of art 8 among third (private) parties, because 'its contents are [not] unequivocal' and because there was 'a divergence of opinion in the different Member States'.[139] Yet, a judge in the Inter-American Court of Human Rights (A. Cancado Trindade)[140] is the most consistent voice in this regard, claiming that ' ... the protection of human rights determined by the American Convention, to be effective, comprises not only the relations between the individuals and the public power, but also their relations with third parties (clandestine groups, paramilitary, and other groups of individuals)'.[141] In his opinion, situations of armed conflict 'clearly require [...] the recognition of the effects of the American Convention *vis-à-vis* third parties (the *Drittwirkung*), without which the conventional obligations of protection would be reduced to little more than dead letter'. The Inter-American Court took notice of the theory,[142] but it was concerned mostly with the positive obligations of the state during private threats or violations of human rights rather than any obligations of non-state parties. Moreover, in the operative part of the judgment in the same case, the Court was not very clear on the effect of peremptory norms to third parties, as they 'generate effects' for them, unlike their binding character for states.

Judge Trindade in his Concurring Opinion reiterated his approach, referring to ' ... a vertical dimension, [where] the obligations *erga omnes* of protection bind both the organs

---

138 (App 8978/80) (1983) [56].

139 Interestingly the Dutch Government admitted, at [60], that the specific article would apply to a limited extent amongst third persons. See also the Partly Dissenting Opinion of Judge Jambrek in *Gustafsson v Sweden* (App no 15573/89) Reports 1996-II 'on the interpretation and application of Article 11 ... in the light of the Drittwirkung doctrine. In my view, the industrial action giving rise to the applicant's complaint must be subject to the very same restrictions as would apply to direct interference by the State', while the Dissenting Opinion of Judge Walsh referred to 'breaches of the Convention ... caused by private parties'. See also *VgT Verein Gegen Tierfabriken v Switzerland* (App no 24699/94) ECHR 2001-VI [46], where '[t]he Court does not consider it desirable, let alone necessary, to elaborate a general theory concerning the extent to which the Convention guarantees should be extended to relations between private individuals *inter se*'.

140 Concurring Opinions in *Matter of the Peace Community of San José de Apartadó* (Provisional Measures) Inter-American Court of Human Rights Series E (18 June 2002) [13–14], *Communities of the Jiguamiandó and the Curbaradó* (Provisional Measures) Inter-American Court of Human Rights Series E (6 March 2003) [4] and *Matter of Pueblo Indígena Sarayaku* (Provisional Measures) Inter-American Court of Human Rights Series E (6 July 2004) [5–8].

141 The tradition of the Inter-American system of human rights protection towards the existence of human duties might not be irrelevant with the discussion on the horizontal effect of human rights.

142 *Juridical Status and Rights of Undocumented Migrant Workers* [140]. See also the *Mapiripán Massacre Case* (Judgment) Inter-American Court of Human Rights Series C No 134 (15 September 2005) [112].

and agents of (State) public power, and the individuals themselves (in the inter-individual relations)'.[143] And he continues that

> … as to the vertical dimension, the general obligation, set forth in Article 1(1) of the American Convention, to respect and to ensure respect for the free exercise of the rights protected by it, generates *erga omnes* effects, encompassing relations of the individual both with the public (State) authorities as well as with other individuals (*particuliers*).

Although the judge is referring mainly to individuals rather than groups, it is more logical to consider the latter as addressees of the obligation to respect and ensure respect for human rights. However, the extension of such wide-ranging obligation for individuals seems unrealistic; possibly even common article 3 ANSAs will not be able to ensure respect for human rights in general. It is also not certain whether the judge envisages the possibility of applications to the Commission where the respondent would be a private party as opposed to the state.[144] The European Convention in itself does not allow for international adjudication against private parties and therefore the legal effects of Drittwirkung in the international sphere seem uncertain. Despite this significant shortcoming though, it appears that such a concept is more convincing than the references to the destruction of rights or the preamble of the UDHR, but still inadequate to explain the obligations of ANSAs on a comprehensive basis.

Devolution of Human Rights Obligations

Another possibility is that the territorial state's human rights obligations devolve to the ANSAs, after displacement of governmental authority, because territorial control is attached to certain responsibilities.[145] This justification presents a parallel with the rationale for the succession of states to human rights treaties: consideration of human rights as deserving continuous protection despite changes in the actor in control. Thus there is strong support that, regardless of the exact character of the new state formation (between cession, dissolution, unification or secession), human rights treaties are considered as objects of automatic responsibility for the successor state.[146] Of course, succession refers

143 At [78]. See also the Concurring Opinion of Judge Pesantes. Similarly see the Concurring Opinion of Judge A.A. Cancado Trindade in *Matter of Pueblo Indígena de Kankuamo* (Provisional Measures) Inter-American Court of Human Rights Series E (5 July 2004).

144 About the relevant procedural and jurisdictional problems see *Provost*, 65.

145 See also *Tomuschat* 2004, 588 and *Rudolf*, 139–40.

146 UN Human Rights Committee, 'General Comment No 26' (8 December 1997) CCPR/C/21/Rev.1/Add.8/Rev.1, 2; Separate Opinion of Judge Weeramantry, *Application of the Convention on the Prevention and Punishment of the Crime of Genocide (Bosnia and Herzegovina v Serbia and Montenegro)* (Preliminary Objections: Judgment) [1996] ICJ Rep 640 ff.; *Kamminga*, 469–84; and Fausto Pocar, 'Some Remarks on the Continuity of Human Rights and International Humanitarian Law Treaties' in Enzo Cannizzaro (ed.), *The Law of Treaties Beyond the Vienna Convention* (OUP 2011) 290–92. *Shaw*, 889; Andreas Zimmerman, 'Secession and the Law of State Succession' in Marcelo G. Kohen (ed.), *Secession: International Law Perspectives* (CUP 2006) 217–20; and *Schutter*, 57, are much more reluctant. *Rasulov*, 167 ff. and *Aust* 2010, 366 are opposite. The Committee on Aspects of the

to a permanent form of devolution and therefore the use of this term in the context of ANSAs is improper. Yet the fact that certain non-state actors will become new governments or form new states suggests that the term *de facto* (or functional) succession could equally be used or, at least, devolution of international human rights law responsibilities.

When certain territory falls outside the control of the territorial state, the latter ceases to have responsibility, in principle, for violations of international law norms.[147] Who, then, becomes responsible for acts that violate international law norms? If it is not another state, indirectly (through attribution), then, logically, it is the ANSA who should be held accountable for whatever happens in the territory. The ICJ's reference to 'physical control of a territory and not sovereignty or legitimacy of title [as] the basis of State liability for acts affecting other States'[148] must find application to ANSAs as well.

For the UN Human Rights Committee[149]

> once the people are accorded the protection of the rights under the Covenant, such protection devolves with territory and continues to belong to them, notwithstanding change in Government of the State party, including dismemberment in more than one State or State succession or any subsequent action of the State party designed to divest them of the rights guaranteed by the Covenant.

Should the situation be different when authority and effective control changes from the *de jure* government to an ANSA which competes with it for control? The answer should be negative, because it would accord or negate the human rights of those under effective control depending solely on the status of the ruling entity. From a humanitarian perspective (and not a strict positivist one), this is unacceptable and certainly an unnecessary effect of the statist approach to international law.

The ICJ has opined[150] that states should continue to honour multilateral treaties of a humanitarian nature, because 'non-performance … may adversely affect the people of Namibia'. It makes even more sense (for the sake of the relevant people) that performance of these treaties is a legal necessity, by whichever entity exercises control and irrespective of its status. The implied mandate doctrine could also be said to include performance of human rights obligations.[151] Otherwise its normative content would remain very limited. The reference to this doctrine in the Cypriot cases in front of the European Court of Human Rights might also serve as evidence that its relevance extends to non-state

---

Law of State Succession, 'Final Report' in International Law Association Report of the Seventy-Third Conference (Rio de Janeiro 2008) (International Law Association, London 2008) 361–2, has concluded that international practice is not homogenous and therefore general rules on state succession apply, while *Rasulov*'s inquiry, 159 ff., points in the same direction.

147 See *Babiker*, 100 ff.

148 *Namibia* Opinion [1971] ICJ Rep 54.

149 'General Comment No 26', 2 and *Bijelic v Montenegro and Serbia* (App no 11890/05) ECHR 2009 [69]. But see some practice from UN organs, in *Rasulov*, 157, that can be construed in a way that it does not favour automaticity.

150 *Namibia* Opinion [1971] ICJ Rep 55.

151 See *Schoiswohl* 2004, 276 ff.

actors.[152] Even if Turkey was not responsible and the Court could not hold TRNC directly accountable, it would seem at odds to suggest that the latter would not be bound by certain human rights norms.

Obviously such devolution might be temporary and provisional, depending on the fate of the conflict, and does not absolve the state from its responsibility, although it might be reduced to standards of due diligence only. Devolution of obligations will become permanent if the ANSA becomes the sole government of the state and, arguably, if a new state is created.

The United Nations Fact-Finding Mission on the Gaza Conflict[153] was based on the performance of 'government-like functions over a territory' along with the ensuing control in order to affirm the existence of human rights obligations.

Similarly, certain writers have affirmed the obligations of ANSAs on this ground[154] and it has even been suggested that a relevant customary rule might have emerged.[155] The Security Council[156] held RCD-Goma ' … responsible to bring to an end all extrajudicial executions, human rights violations and arbitrary harassment of civilians in Kisangani, and all other areas under RCD-Goma's control', based on the fact that it constituted a 'de facto authority', while, in other regions it called on 'the de facto authorities … to ensure the protection of civilians and the rule of law'.

The above-mentioned views would, logically, cover not only *de facto* entities, but also common article 3 ANSAs and ANSAs in control of territory, at least because they might

---

152 See particularly *Cyprus v Turkey* [98].

153 UN Doc A/HRC/12/48, 80. See also UN Doc S/25500, 20; UNHRC, 'Human Rights Violations Emanating from Israeli Military Attacks and Incursions in the Occupied Palestinian Territory, Particularly the Recent Ones in the Occupied Gaza Strip: Report of the High Commissioner for Human Rights on the Implementation of Human Rights Council Resolution 7/1' (6 June 2008) A/HRC/8/17, 6–7 and 21; UNHRC, 'Report of the Special Rapporteur on Extrajudicial, Summary or Arbitrary Executions, Philip Alston: Addendum, Mission to Philippines' (16 April 2008) A/HRC/8/3/Add.2, 6; UNHRC, 'Human Rights Situation in Palestine and Other Occupied Arab Territories: Combined Report of the Special Rapporteur on the Right of Everyone to the Enjoyment of the Highest Attainable Standard of Physical and Mental Health, the Special Representative of the Secretary-General for Children and Armed Conflict, the Special Rapporteur on Violence against Women, its Causes and Consequences, the Representative of the Secretary-General on the Human Rights of Internally Displaced Persons, the Special Rapporteur on Adequate Housing as a Component of the Right to an Adequate Standard of Living, and on the Right to Non-discrimination in this Context, the Special Rapporteur on the Right to Food, the Special Rapporteur on Extrajudicial, Summary or Arbitrary Executions, the Special Rapporteur on the Right to Education and the Independent Expert on the Question of Human Rights and Extreme Poverty' (20 March 2009) A/HRC/10/22, 10. In UN Docs E/CN.4/2005/7, 21 and A/HRC/2/7, 7, a slightly different formulation was used, which could designate the same outcome: it is 'especially appropriate and feasible to call for an armed group to respect human rights norms when it exercises *significant* control over territory and population and has an *identifiable political structure*' (emphasis added).

154 *Schoiswohl* 2001, 79. See also *Rodley*, 298 and *Zegveld*, 52 ff.

155 *Hessbruege*, 39–41 and 88 and *Constantinides*, 102–3. Opposite *Ronen*, 50.

156 UNSC Res 1417 (14 June 2002) [4] and [5].

have some institutions, such as courts or prisons, which are in essence governmental functions. Conversely, it would appear that ANSAs, generally, without performance of governmental functions could not be covered. However, primarily the exclusiveness of control, evidenced in a Protocol II situation, would suggest that ANSAs in comparable situations should also be included, while there is also modest relevant support. For the former Special Rapporteur on Terrorism and Human Rights ' … the international community increasingly requires non-State actors engaged in armed conflicts to promote and protect human rights in the areas over which they exercise de facto control'.[157] Assuming that 'de facto control' equals displacement of governmental authority but without, necessarily, the assumption of the relevant full function by ANSAs, it could be argued that effectiveness alone creates obligations for ANSAs, including human rights. It could also be argued that in the case of competing authorities and to the extent that the (common article 3) ANSA is able to affect human rights directly, it should also be bound by human rights, within its sphere of influence/jurisdiction, although the extent of obligations might differ significantly. Otherwise we would again create a legal black hole which is unjustified from a humanitarian perspective and is undesirable as well.

It is not evident whether devolution of obligations is automatic or if there should be some proof of ANSA acceptance.[158] Obviously, only automaticity would serve the goal sought by this justification, unless ANSAs regularly commit to human rights responsibilities. On the other hand, automaticity does not necessarily lead to compliance, as the volition of the ANSA is, usually, a significant factor.

In matters of state succession to treaties the situation is less than settled, although it appears that a relevant notification is necessary, at least as confirmation.[159] In matters of ANSAs controlling territory, it does not appear that their volition was regularly considered a significant factor for their human rights obligations.[160] Even if it was significant, since they have exhibited a relevant commitment in various forms (*de facto*, through unilateral declarations or agreements), their practice does not seem to envisage devolution of human rights responsibilities particularly, with the exception of Somaliland. Its Constitution[161] provides that 'the Republic of Somaliland shall observe all treaties and agreements entered into by the former state of Somalia with foreign countries … provided that

157 UN Doc E/CN.4/Sub.2/2004/40, 24. See also UNCHR, 'Report of the Workshop on Internal Displacement in Africa (Addis Ababa, 19–20 October 1998)' (15 January 1999) E/CN.4/1999/79/Add.2, 9 and UN Doc E/CN.4/2006/71/Add.7, 5. See also UN Docs S/2007/584, 89 and A/HRC/17/44, 33. From doctrine, only *Constantinides*, 102–3 would seem to imply that control of territory is sufficient. See also UN Committee on the Rights of the Child, 'Consideration of Reports Submitted by State Parties under Article 44 of the Convention, Concluding Observations: Nepal' (21 September 2005) CRC/C/15/Add.261, 2–3, referring to *de facto* control by non-state actors and respect of child rights in areas that they operate.

158 For *Tomuschat* 2004, 587, 'the rule that any obligation requires the consent of the party concerned has long been abandoned'.

159 But see *Pocar*, 285.

160 See the practice of international organs in sub-chapter *Are Armed Non-State Actors Bound by Human Rights? Evaluating Practice.*

161 Constitution of the Republic of Somaliland (1997) art 10.1.

these do not conflict with the interests and concerns of the Republic … '. There is a good argument for automaticity, though, under this justification: unless there is a strong claim of representativeness and/or effectiveness, usually combined with recognition (as a government and/or a state), the ANSA will not be able to change the international obligations of the parent state (in the same way that a newly emerging state does), including its human rights obligations. Therefore in between the outbreak of a conflict and until the final solution, it is bound to move within the same normative standards as the parent state, unless it elects to bind itself to an increased standard.

Overall, the lack of (known) practice and the uncertainty with regard to the extent of ANSA coverage (especially as to common article 3 ANSAs) might suggest that this justification is not wholly satisfactory. The last possibility that will be examined refers back to the principal legal regime applicable to ANSAs and the possibility of indirect application of human rights law.

Applying Human Rights Law Through Humanitarian Law

It is beyond doubt that human rights law constitutes an interpretive tool of humanitarian law.[162] Notions such as torture and degrading treatment are mostly defined by reference to human rights law.[163] The ICTY has explained that '[b]ecause of the paucity of precedent in the field of international humanitarian law, the Tribunal has, on many occasions, had recourse to instruments and practices developed in the field of human rights law … '.[164] Other 'loans' from international human rights law appear indispensable as Meron[165] notes:

> [t]he reference in common Article 3 to a 'regularly constituted court affording all the judicial guarantees which are recognized as indispensable by civilized peoples' with regard to trials in non international armed conflicts … should inevitably be interpreted and applied by drawing on human rights.

Apart from cases where similar or identical terms are used in both branches, the open-ended language in IHL treaties could accommodate the indirect applicability of other human rights standards. Humanitarian law is framed, in many instances, by references to certain paradigms, while leaving the possibility for additional safeguards which are not expressly laid out in the treaties. For example, the reference of art 4.1 (Protocol II) to

---

162 *Moir*, 196 and *Kolb and Hyde*, 271.

163 See the *Delalic* Judgment [459]; *Furundzija* [159–60]; and Robert Cryer, 'The Interplay of Human Rights and Humanitarian Law: The Approach of the ICTY' (2010) 14 J.C. &S.L. 511, 517 ff. This has become circular, since in *Ould Dah*, the Court mentions common article 3 and the jurisprudence of the ICTY with regard to torture and in *Zontul v Greece* (App no 12294/07) ECHR 2012 [60–64], it mentions the jurisprudence of the ICTY and the ICTR on rape.

164 *Kunarac* [467].

165 *Meron* 2000, 266. The same applies for art 6.2 of Protocol II on the indicative 'essential guarantees of independence and impartiality' for penal prosecutions. In UN Doc A/46/876, 29, the UN Basic Principles on the Independence of the Judiciary were used in order to interpret the relevant provision. *Arai-Takahashi*, 512, takes a more restrictive view, suggesting that customary law (of human rights) should be the point of reference.

respect for their person, honour, convictions and religious practices, as well as humane treatment in all circumstances is not necessarily confined to the prohibited acts of paragraph 2;[166] human rights treaties prohibit other acts, such as harassment and insults, which can be included in the protective scope of the article.[167] Furthermore art 4.3 of Protocol II provides for certain measures for the benefit of children,[168] yet these are understood as being minimum standards. The 'care and aid required' could include other indispensable measures which are laid down in the Convention of the Rights of the Child or other human rights treaties.[169] The references of arts 54 (Protocol I) and 14 (Protocol II) to 'objects indispensable to the survival of the civilian population' are indicative and could also accommodate other objects relevant to social rights. The right to health of those who are 'wounded, sick and shipwrecked' can be interpreted with regard to the relevant human rights treaties,[170] since the language used in parts of the Conventions or the Protocols is only indicative. Similarly, art 5.1 of Protocol II enumerates the minimum guarantees for persons whose liberty has been restricted, thus leaving the door open for a more extended reading of them.

The applicability of human rights standards could also become realized through the effect of local laws, in combination with the analogical application of military occupation rules to ANSAs in control of territory. The references in art 51 of the Fourth Geneva Convention as well as art 5.1(e) of Protocol II, relevant to compulsory labour, will be interpreted in accordance with local laws, which could include relevant human rights treaties as well as the International Labour Organization conventions.[171] Similarly, art 5.1(b) of Protocol II requires that detained people should be provided with certain assets, relevant to the right to health and food, 'to the same extent as the local civilian population'. This reference could imply a factual threshold, a legal threshold (possibly including human rights treaties applicable in the territory[172]) or both. More importantly, the reference of art 43 of the Annex to the Hague Convention to respect for local laws can be understood as creating obligations through the human rights treaties which bind the occupied state[173] and the ANSA as well, if military occupation rules would be applicable

166 See also R. *Abi-Saab*, 114 on common article 3.

167 See also art 4.2(e) of Protocol II on the indicative reference to 'outrages upon personal dignity'.

168 Look also arts 24.1, 26, 38 and 50 of the Fourth Geneva Convention.

169 With regard to education, see the relevant art 13 of the ICESCR. See, similarly, for military occupation, *Horowitz*, 322.

170 In a similar vein see Sylvain Vité, 'The Interrelation of the Law of Occupation and Economic, Social and Cultural Rights: The Examples of Food, Health and Property' (2008) 90 IRRC 629–51.

171 Similarly, *Arai-Takahashi*, 356.

172 Note though that neither of the two commentaries to the Protocols support such an interpretation. But see *Moir*, 222.

173 See a relevant comment from Theodor Meron, 'Applicability of Multilateral Conventions to Occupied Territories' (1978) 72 AJIL 542, 550, with regard to ILO Conventions. Michael Dennis, 'Application of Human Rights Treaties Extraterritorially to Detention of Combatants and Security Internees: Fuzzy Thinking all Around?' (2005–6) 12 ILSA J.Int'l & Comp.L. 459, 470–71, seems

by analogy. Consequently it would seem that, indirectly, human rights can be applicable through humanitarian law treaties.

It is obvious, though, that any imaginative interpretation of humanitarian law through human rights law lenses could not cover all its aspects, because certain rights are not considered as relevant by the treaties (such as freedom of demonstration or association). Nonetheless, this is where the Martens clause could come in; although there is hardly any agreement on what 'the principles of humanity and the dictates of the public conscience' entail and its usual interpretation of content borrows from humanitarian (mainly treaty) law,[174] it is possible that certain human rights or aspects thereof[175] could be included. Certainly, though, reliance on interpretation rather than actual stipulations could come at the expense of legal certainty, while humanitarian law (besides military occupation rules) could not cover the period where there is no armed conflict.

Obviously, the analogical application of military occupation rules could be relevant only for ANSAs in control over territory, probably also with a governmental function. Moreover, any flaw in the implementing legislation would cripple the application of human rights. So if, in a dualist state, the international treaty has not been transposed into a piece of national law, the analogical application of military occupation rules would be fruitless, with the exception of self-executing human rights norms. Consequently even this justification is bound to generate limited results for certain types of ANSAs.

Concluding Remarks

Overall, it would appear that all possible legal bases have certain advantages and drawbacks.[176] Both references to the text of the UDHR (or human rights treaties where comparable provisions exist) as well as the language of duties will hardly encompass all types of ANSAs or range of human rights, apart from not being particularly convincing as theories. Devolution of human rights obligations from the territorial state seems more

---

to imply the same, while *Cerone*, 1477 considers also this possibility in brief. See also *Horowitz*, 326, mentioning a relevant example from the 2003 occupation of Iraq. John Quigley, 'The Relation between Human Rights Law and the Law of Belligerent Occupation: Does an Occupied Population Have a Right to Freedom of Assembly and Expression?' (1989) 12 B.C.Int'l & Comp.L.Rev. 1, 2, mentions this possibility, which, however, he considers anachronistic.

174 See UN Doc E/CN.4/1992/26, 11; *Cassese* 2000, 202 ff.; and Steven R. Ratner, 'Revising the Geneva Conventions to Regulate Force by and against Terrorists: Four Fallacies' (2003) 1 IDF L.Rev. 7, 8–9.

175 A similar understanding from *Arai-Takahashi*, 657 ff. See also UN Doc E/CN.4/ Sub.2/2005/14, 7. The use of the clause in the preamble of *Minimum Humanitarian Standards* shows that its drafters considered it as *adding* content to humanitarian and human rights law; similarly Vesselin Popovski, 'Protection of Children in International Humanitarian Law and Human Rights Law' in Roberta Arnold and Noëlle N.R. Quénivet (eds), *International Humanitarian Law and Human Rights Law: Towards a New Merger in International Law* (Nijhoff 2008) 398. Opposite *Hansen*, 20.

176 In light of these drawbacks it is difficult to accept the comment in UN Doc E/CN.4/ Sub.2/2005/40, 3, on the sustainability, in theory, of a ' … a general obligation to respect human rights and implement international human rights instruments accordingly … ' for ' … States, non-State actors and individuals … '.

convincing, although it appears to demand a certain link of ANSAs with territory, if not (also) the performance of governmental functions.[177] The same problem would arise from the analogous application of military occupation rules, while the extension of human rights law through an extended reading of humanitarian law only has certain potential. The third-party obligations of *Drittwirkung* seem intellectually sound, although it has not received much support in practice. For an advocate of human rights there might be a need to resort to any of these justifications, depending on the context, actor and so on.[178] It is proper, at this point, to examine how various actors address this issue in order to affirm or deny the obligations of ANSAs in human rights law; after all, even within IHL, there is substantial disagreement on the legal basis, although this has led with the passage of time to an implied agreement (and an emergence of a customary rule) that the relevant armed groups bear certain obligations. The examination of these opinions could also elucidate whether there is a customary law rule that ANSAs are bound by human rights law.

Are Armed Non-State Actors Bound by Human Rights? Evaluating Practice

The proliferation of armed conflicts and the need to advance the protection of people has given ample opportunities to a variety of actors to express views on the applicability of human rights standards. This sub-chapter will address (non-exhaustively) opinions and practice from the UN primary organs (with emphasis on the Security Council), human rights (and other) organs (with emphasis, again, on the UN), states and ANSAs in order to discern tendencies with regard to human rights obligations and the responding accountability of ANSAs.[179] In this regard the *opinio juris* of states is less important when compared with humanitarian law, especially on substantive rules. In humanitarian law,

177 This approach is, again, state-centred, to the extent that an analogy with the state is considered necessary.

178 For example an ANSA that rejects human rights law but accepts IHL obligations might be convinced by an argument relating to the existence of human rights law obligations through IHL treaties.

179 The writing of publicists seems divided. See, indicatively, in favour *Walker*, 153; *Matas*, 630; *IDI 1999 Resolution*, *L.C. Green*, 67; *Tomuschat* 2004, 587; *Clapham* 2006, 271 ff.; *Fleck* 2008, 609; *Ssenyonjo*, 121; and *Cullen* and *Wheatley*, 727. *Rodley*, 298, includes armed opposition groups exercising effective power over a significant segment of the population and conducting sustained, organized armed hostilities, while he excludes ANSAs below this level. *Zegveld*, 52 ff., and *Bellal* et al., 23 ff. seem also to adopt this middle approach. On the other hand it should be remembered that the movement in favour of *Minimum Humanitarian Standards* was aimed, *inter alia*, at countering the non-applicability of human rights to ANSAs, see UN Doc E/CN.4/1998/87, 5. For other negative opinions see *Kogod Goldman*, 543; *Kooijmans*, 245; Theo Van Boven, 'Reliance on Norms of Humanitarian Law by United Nations' Organs' in Astrid J.M. Delissen and Gerard J. Tanja (eds), *Humanitarian Law of Armed Conflict Challenges ahead: Essays in Honour of Frits Kalshoven* (Nijhoff Publishers 1991) 511; *Moir*, 44 and 194; Kenneth Watkin, 'Controlling the Use of Force: A Role for Human Rights Norms in Contemporary Armed Conflict' (2004) 98 AJIL 1, 30;, *Cerone*, 1455; *Babiker*, 143; *Ryngaert* 2008, 366–7; *Kretzmer*, 37; and 'Expert Meeting on Procedural Safeguards for Security Detention in Non-international Armed Conflict', 861.

state's *opinio juris* and practice formulate the law regarding their own conduct, primarily and, ultimately, the conduct of ANSAs. In contrast the formulation of customary rules with regard to the substantive obligations of ANSAs cannot solely depend on the practice or consent of states. Such obligations do not relate to their own conduct but that of third parties and states already have certain customary and treaty law obligations on human rights. Consequently the practice (and *opinio juris*) of ANSAs could be relevant not only with the foundation rule (that a customary law rule obliges ANSAs to respect human rights)[180] but also with the substantive content of the obligations.

The Approach of United Nations Primary Organs, with Emphasis on the Security Council

The Security Council appears to be one of the most common supporters of human rights applicability to ANSAs.[181] In the vast majority of cases, its resolutions are situation specific. For example, Res 1814 (15 May 2008) [16] '*condemns* all and any violations of human rights … [and] *calls upon* all parties in Somalia to respect fully their obligations in this regard … '; this is only one out of a dozen similar, such as Res 1214 (8 December 1998) [12] '*demand[ing]* that the Afghan factions put an end to discrimination against girls and women and other violations of human rights' and Res 1216 (21 December 1998) [5], on Guinea-Bissau, '*call[ing]* upon all concerned, including the Government and the Self-Proclaimed Military Junta, to respect strictly relevant provisions of international law, including … human rights law'.[182] In some of these resolutions, the Council does not differentiate between the obligations of the government and the ANSA, revealing that they share responsibility for the overall human rights situation. The quality of the ANSA and its characteristics (organization, effectiveness and so on) do not appear to play a role, at least according to the text of resolutions. Notably such practice appeared (and flourished) rather recently.

In other resolutions there is a discernible tendency of the Security Council to expect the fulfilment of wider obligations by ANSAs: in S/RES/1772 [19] the Council ' … *stresses* the responsibility of all parties and armed groups in Somalia to take appropriate steps to protect the civilian population in the country, consistent with … human rights and refugee

180 But see *Reinisch*, 87, that the volition of states is the key factor for the direct accountability of non-state actors under human rights law. True as it is, though, it is not the only factor.

181 *Tomuschat* 2004, 586, has also examined whether the Security Council could create human rights obligations for ANSAs and after reviewing practice he comes to the conclusion that 'the Security Council does not intend to create new obligations. It just draws the attention of the addressees to the obligations incumbent upon them under international human rights law, as interpreted by it'.

182 See also S/RES/1193 [14] '*urg[ing]* the Afghan factions to put an end to the discrimination against girls and women and to other violations of human rights', 1213 (3 December 1998) [7], 1231 (11 March 1999) [3] and [4], Res 1378 (14 November 2001) [2], S/RES/1493 [10], S/RES/1509 (2003) [10], Res 1592 (30 March 2005) preamble, Res 1662 (23 March 2006) [12], Res 1746 (23 March 2007) [25], Res 1974 (22 March 2011) preamble, Res 2003 (29 July 2011) preamble and [14], Res 2011 (12 October 2011) preamble, Res 2031 (21 December 2011) [13–14], Res 2051 (12 June 2012) [11], S/RES/2096 preamble and [42] and S/RES/2120, preamble.

law'. Similarly, in S/RES/1493 [8], on DRC, the Council '*urges* all parties, including the Government ..., to take all necessary steps to *prevent* further violations of human rights ... ' and in Res 1565 (1 October 2004) [19], on DRC, there is a demand ' ... to ensure respect for human rights ... as well as to guarantee the security and well-being of the civilian population'.[183]

Obviously the reference to refugee law and the implication of positive measures by the resolutions are burdensome. As noted before,[184] the capacity of certain armed groups to uphold humanitarian law standards, as implied by several Security Council resolutions, is rightly doubted. It would be even more difficult to expect ANSAs to uphold human rights law standards under due diligence. However it has been suggested that the Security Council does not 'legislate' blindly and 'whenever an appeal is made to an entity to observe and respect human rights and IHL, the Security Council proceeds from the assumption that it is confronted with a reliable interlocutor able to keep its forces under some kind of control'.[185] For the time being, it is sufficient to comment that these resolutions are a positive proof that ANSAs can (and do) incur human rights obligations.

At times the Council made specific references to armed groups. In S/RES/1417 [4], ' ... it holds the Rassemblement Congolais pour la Democratie-Goma ... responsible to bring to an end all ... human rights violations ... of civilians in Kisangani, and all other areas under RCD Goma's control', while in the preamble of Res 1804 (13 March 2008),[186] it '*deplor[ed]* the persistence of violations of human rights ... carried out by ... the Forces démocratiques de libération du Rwanda (FDLR), ex-Rwandan Armed Forces (ex-FAR)/ Interahamwe ... '. Such resolutions are relatively rare. Of course it is the government that bears the primary responsibility and this is stressed in the preambles to many resolutions.[187]

In thematic resolutions, such as S/RES/1265 [4] on the protection of civilians on armed conflict, the Council '*urge[d]* all parties concerned to comply strictly with their obligations under ... human rights and refugee law ... '. In one of the most recent resolutions in this regard,[188] the difference in language and tone is evident, since the Council '*demands* that parties to armed conflict comply strictly with the obligations applicable to them under ... human rights and refugee law ... '. However, it should not be assumed that the practice of the Security Council is always towards the applicability of human rights to ANSAs. Sometimes it has 'skipped' references to obligations under human rights law, focusing only on humanitarian law obligations instead, as in S/RES/1574 '*demand[ing]* that Government and rebel forces ... ensure that their members comply with international

183 See also S/RES/1314 [6] urging ' ... parties to armed conflict to provide protection and assistance to refugees and internally displaced persons, as appropriate ... ', S/RES/1379 [8a], S/RES/1417 [5], Res 1464 (4 February 2003) [7], S/RES/1479 [8] and the preamble of S/RES/1556. Notably such resolutions were not repeated in recent years.

184 See Chapter 1 sub-chapter on *Common Article 3 to the Geneva Conventions of 1949*, at 16–17.

185 *Tomuschat* 2004, 585.

186 See also S/RES/1216 [5] and Res 1574 (19 November 2004) preamble.

187 Indicatively see S/RES/1556, S/RES/1574, Res 1756 (15 May 2007) and 1861 (14 January 2009).

188 S/RES/1894 [1]. See also Res 2175 (29 August 2014) [1].

humanitarian law … ',[189] In more recent years, starting with Res 1653,[190] the Council has regularly condemned the commission of human rights abuses by specific ANSAs. The reference to abuses instead of violations does not imply that ANSAs do not have human rights obligations:[191] it rather differentiates between government and ANSAs for political rather than legal reasons.[192] It is possible, also, that this language was simply used as the lowest common denominator on the insistence of a state member of the Council and in order to arrive at consensus. Therefore, it could imply that there continues to be a division between states, even if it is not always evident that the language of abuses refers specifically to the ANSAs.

The General Assembly's practice is not as extensive, since its role is residual in the maintenance of international peace and security. However, in a number of resolutions, such as 48/152 (20 December 1993) and 52/145 (12 December 1997),[193] human rights feature as part of the obligations of ANSAs. But then in A/RES/51/112,[194] the Assembly clearly differentiated between the human rights obligations of Sudan and the humanitarian law obligations of the ANSA.

The Secretary General has painted a more nuanced picture. In the 2009 Report on the protection of civilians in armed conflict,[195] 'armed groups are bound by international humanitarian law and must refrain from committing acts that would impair the enjoyment of human rights', while later he refers to ' … the responsibility of parties to conflict to comply with international humanitarian law and human rights law'.[196] In 2004 his view was that 'armed groups … blatantly violate international humanitarian law and human rights standards'.[197]. In an older Report[198] the repeated use of human rights abuses instead of violations is noticeable, while acknowledging that targeting only states for human rights violations 'has never provided a fully adequate description of the scope of international human rights concern'. In another Report, he refers only to humanitarian law as a standard

189 [11]. See also S/RES/771 [1–2], S/RES/814 [13], S/RES/1738 [6], 1765 (16 July 2007) [4], S/RES/1861 [22] and Res 2158 (29 May 2014) preamble and [14].

190 (27 January 2006) [8]. See also Res 1991 (28 June 2011) [13], 2021 (29 November 2011) [13], 2042 (14 April 2012) preamble, 2043 (21 April 2012) preamble, Res 2098 (28 March 2013) preamble and [8], S/RES/2100 preamble, S/RES/2109 [14], 2132 (23 December 2013) preamble, 2136 (30 January 2014) preamble and [6], Res 2155 (27 May 2014) preamble and [18] and S/RES/2173 preamble, [17] and [19].

191 See UN Doc A/HRC/21/50, 47 and S/RES/2173 preamble and [17].

192 *Clapham* 2006, 49.

193 At [9] and [5–6] respectively. See also A/RES/48/153 [4], Res 64/11 (9 November 2009) preamble, [26] and [28] and 65/8 (4 November 2010) preamble and [31]. See also Res 68/152 (18 December 2013) [7], ' … not[ing] that private military and security companies and their personnel are rarely held accountable for violations of human rights'.

194 Similarly in A/RES/52/140.

195 UN Doc S/2009/277, 8 and 15 respectively.

196 Also UN Doc S/2012/376, 1 and, similarly, S/2010/579, 5.

197 'Report of the Secretary-General to the Security Council on the Protection of Civilians in Armed Conflict' (28 May 2004) S/2004/431, 13. See also UN Doc S/1999/957, 1.

198 UN Doc E/CN.4/1998/87.

of conduct for armed groups, but recommends dissemination of human rights law to armed groups.[199]

Overall it appears that there is a growing, if not firm, acceptance of ANSAs' obligations under human rights, but without total consistency, so far. In terms of numbers, the resolutions are too many to suggest that human rights obligations are only a matter of political accountability, in light of the (mainly political) character of these organs.

The Approach of Other International Organs, with Emphasis on United Nations Secondary Organs

The practice of the Human Rights Council appears to follow the path of the Security Council, although it does not refer to human rights as a standard of ANSAs' conduct at every relevant occasion. In Res 7/1 (2008) it urged 'all parties concerned to respect the rules of international human rights law … '.[200] In Res 6/1 (2007), on the other hand, it ' … strongly urge[d] all parties to an armed conflict to strictly observe and respect, as applicable, the rules of international humanitarian law during armed conflicts, and to respect the rules on the protection of cultural property'.[201] Lately, it appears to be using the language of 'abuses'. However, it is not *always* evident that this reference is devoted exclusively to ANSAs and, certainly, it does not seem to imply that human rights law does not carry obligations for the perpetrators of abuses.[202]

Its predecessor, the Commission on Human Rights, was also '*seriously concerned* at the gross violations of human rights perpetrated by terrorist groups' and '*strongly condemn[ed]* the violations of the right to life, liberty and security',[203] while in E/CN.4/RES/2005/63 it '*urges* all parties to armed conflicts to comply with their obligations under international humanitarian law … and also urges all States to comply with their human rights obligations

199 'Report of the Secretary-General to the Security Council on the Protection of Civilians in Armed Conflict' (30 March 2001) S/2001/331, 2 and 11. In the same vein see UNSG, 'Report of the Secretary-General on the Protection of Civilians in Armed Conflict' (22 November 2013) S/2013/689, 9.

200 [6]. See also UNHRC Res 7/35 (2008) [2], S-8/1 (2008) [1–2], S-9/1 (2009) [10], 10/19 (2009) [10], 14/15 (2010) [3], 17/17 (2011) [4], 18/16 (2011) [8], 20/17 (2012) [3–4], 23/1 (2013) [2], 27/10 (2014) [7] and the Decision 2/115 (2006) [2] on Darfur.

201 [1]. See also UNHRC Res S-3/1 (2006) [6], 20/21 (2012) [2 and 11] and the ambiguous Res 18/4 (2011) [6] and [16].

202 See UNHRC Res 21/25 (2012) [1] and [3], 23/26 (2013) [11], 24/22 [3] and [7], A/HRC/RES/25/23 [4], [6] and [11], 25/26 [5] and [8], A/HRC/RES/25/36 [2] and 27/16 [3] and [11].

203 UNCHR Res 37 (2003) [2]. Notably in Res 44 (2004), with the same subject matter, this concern was moved to the preamble, while the condemnation was also accompanied by a reaffirmation that ' … every person has a right to protection from terrorism'. See also Res 59 (1994) [5], 81 (1994) [3], 74 (1995) [12], E/CN.4/RES/1998/59 [3], Res 15 (1999) [3a], Res 78 (2003) [6c] and [8k], 80 (2004) [12b], E/CN.4/RES/2005/82 [3e] and [3i] and Res 85 (2005) [5]. See also the older Res 7 (1990) [16]: 'Further requests the Special Rapporteur to develop further the position that mercenary acts are *means of violating human rights* and thwarting the self-determination of peoples'. *Babiker*, 141, considers this practice as potentially 'attributable to the fact that it was influenced by the need to adopt a balanced approach in reporting human rights violations and does not want to be seen as a biased body whose only purpose is to impose obligations on States'.

in this context'.[204] E/CN.4/RES/2005/78 deserves a special note, since it is excessively careful to address human rights violations of the ANSA in terms of criminal and humanitarian law, while it repeatedly addresses individual members of the ANSA only. It is obvious that the ANSA (CPN (Maoist)) is discredited and denied any legitimacy, although later it gained the governmental position by way of elections. Even this resolution, though, is partly ambiguous[205] since it '*calls upon* all parties to the conflict to respect human rights and international humanitarian law … '. A similar stance was adopted in a Chairperson's Statement regarding Colombia,[206] which ' … notes that, in 2004, illegal armed groups were responsible for a vast majority of the breaches of international humanitarian law and criminal acts' and

> … condemns all acts of terrorism and other criminal attacks, such as attacks against life, physical integrity and personal liberty and safety, committed by the illegal armed groups. It strongly urges all illegal armed groups to comply with international humanitarian law and to respect the legitimate exercise by the population of their human rights.

The approach of the lower echelons of UN (human rights) bodies corroborates also the increasing tendency towards the applicability of human rights to ANSAs. Already in the beginning of the 1990s a UN Special Rapporteur[207] was writing that ' … not only do these irregular armed groups or gangs of drug traffickers or mercenaries commit acts that are contrary to international and national law but they *must* be branded as *violators of human rights* … ' (emphasis added). For the Salvadorian Truth Commission ' … when insurgents assume government powers in territories under their control, they too *can be* required to observe certain human rights obligations that are binding for the State under international human rights law … ' (emphasis added).[208]

O'Donnell[209] was right in concluding that in the late 1990s most UN human rights mechanisms shared the view that human rights law is binding only on states; even the

---

204 [2]. See also the older Res 75 (1990) [1], expressing 'its deep concern at the adverse effects on the enjoyment of human rights of the crimes and atrocities committed in many countries by irregular armed groups, regardless of their origin' and 42 (2003) [7]. Similarly see the differentiation between the obligations of Russia and the Chechen rebels in Res 24 (2001) [3–4].

205 [7]. See also Res 83 (2005) [7b] and [9a] as well as Res 24 (2000) [3a] and [5b], that can be read both ways.

206 1 (2005) [5] and [24].

207 UN Doc E/CN.4/1991/14, 39.

208 UN Doc S/25500, 20. See also UNSG, 'Note Transmitting Report of the Secretary-General's Fact-Finding Mission to Investigate Human Rights Violations in Abkhazia, Republic of Georgia' (17 November 1993) S/26795, which used almost exclusively human rights language for violations from the Abkhaz authorities and 'Note Transmitting the Report of the Director of the United Nations Mission for the Verification of Human Rights and of Compliance with the Commitments of the Comprehensive Agreement on Human Rights in Guatemala' (29 June 1995) A/49/929, 6.

209 Daniel O'Donnell, 'Trends in the Application of International Humanitarian Law by United Nations Human Rights Mechanisms' (1998) 38 IRRC 481, 487.

language of the abovementioned quotes reveals a degree of incertitude. Yet it is difficult to state categorically that this holds true nowadays. In fact it could seem possible to discern several approaches. Explicit denial of human rights applicability is relatively rare: a Group of UN Rapporteurs and Experts commented that terrorist groups should not be cited as human rights violators, since '… states were responsible for human rights violations and were the addressees of the international human rights standards; a difference should be made between "human rights violations" and "crimes"'.[210] Lack of references to human rights law with regard to the conduct of the ANSA is more common in such documents. Therefore, they can be construed as implicitly denying applicability. In the 'Report of the Special Rapporteur on Violence against Women, its Causes and Consequences, Ms. Radhika Coomaraswamy, Submitted in Accordance with Commission Resolution 1997/44' it was explained that 'non-State actors waging war on the State … are bound by international humanitarian law'.[211]

Several reports are fairly ambiguous and can be read both ways. For the High Commissioner for Human Rights, 'under the international system, the insurgent groups in Colombia can only be responsible for breaches of international humanitarian law'; however she then refers to violations of human rights by ANSAs or urges respect for the Convention of the Rights of the Child by armed groups.[212]

---

210 UN Doc E/CN.4/1997/3, 12.

211 (26 January 1998) E/CN.4/1998/54, 21. See also UNSG, 'Note Transmitting Report on the Situation of Human Rights in El Salvador Prepared by the Independent Expert of the Commission on Human Rights in Accordance with Paragraph 12 of Commission Resolution 1992/62 of 3 March 1992 and Economic and Social Council decision 1992/237 of 20 July 1992' (13 November 1992) A/47/596, 28 ff.; UNCHR, 'Report by the Independent Expert, Mrs. Mónica Pinto, on the Situation of Human Rights in Guatemala, Prepared in Accordance with Commission Resolution 1995/51' (5 December 1995) E/CN.4/1996/15, 34; UNCHR, 'Report of the United Nations High Commissioner for Human Rights on the Human Rights Situation in Colombia' (8 February 2001) E/CN.4/2001/15, 10 and UN Docs E/CN.4/2006/9, 9 and A/HRC/9/26, 21–2. See also UN Docs A/HRC/24/46 and A/HRC/25/65, which, apart from very minor references to human rights law, relied heavily on IHL, thus being in contrast to previous Reports of the Commission of Inquiry on Syria.

212 UNCHR, 'Report by the United Nations High Commissioner for Human Rights' (9 March 1998) E/CN.4/1998/16, 7. See also UNSG, 'Letter Transmitting the Executive Summary, Conclusions and Recommendations of the Report of the Commission for Historical Clarification' (27 April 1999) A/53/928, 29 ff. and UN Doc S/2007/584, 66–8 and 86. See also UNCHR, 'Joint Report of the Special Rapporteur on the Question of Torture, Mr. Nigel S. Rodley, and the Special Rapporteur on Extrajudicial, Summary or Arbitrary Executions, Mr. Bacre Waly Ndiaye, Submitted Pursuant to Commission on Human Rights Resolutions 1994/37 and 1994/82: Visit by the Special Rapporteurs to the Republic of Colombia from 17 to 26 October 1994' (16 January 1995) E/CN.4/1995/111, 12 and 18; 'Report of the High Commissioner for Human Rights on the Situation in the Republic of Chechnya of the Russian Federation' (20 February 2001) E/CN.4/2001/36, 16; 'Report of the United Nations High Commissioner for Human Rights' (28 September 2001) A/56/36, 1–3; and *Darfur Inquiry*, 50.

Other Reports use the language of abuses when it comes to ANSAs[213], while several recent reports condemn human rights violations by ANSAs[214] or highlight human rights law as a tool for the obligations and/ or responsibility of ANSAs[215]. Some reports dedicate a few more words in order to explain how an ANSA becomes subject to human rights obligations. A few of them have adopted a language indicating that the ' ... non-State actor ... remains subject to the demand of the international community ... [to] respect and promote human rights ... '.[216] In more recent reports,[217] its authors unequivocally and more forcefully state that ' ... with respect to Hamas, it is worth recalling that non-State actors that exercise government-like functions and control over a territory are obliged to respect human rights norms when their conduct affects the human rights of the individuals under their control'.

The difference in the language with regard to the previous set of reports is evident. In the same vein, the United Nations Fact-Finding Mission on the Gaza Conflict[218] has upheld that ' ... non-State actors that exercise government-like functions over a territory have a duty to respect human rights', although it seems to give significant value to public undertakings by Palestine and the Gaza authorities.[219] For Hamas it also notes that the

213 UNCHR, 'Situation of Human Rights in the Sudan Report of the Special Rapporteur, Mr. Gáspár Bíró, Submitted in Accordance with Commission on Human Rights Resolution 1993/60' (1 February 1994) E/CN.4/1994/48, 7 and 37 ff. and United Nations Office of the High Commissioner for Human Rights in Nepal, 'Human Rights Abuses by the CPN-M: Summary of Concerns' (2006). See also UNSG, 'Note Transmitting the Interim Report of the Special Rapporteur of the Commission on Human Rights on the Situation of Human Rights in the Sudan' (7 September 2001) A/56/336, 4, 6 and 14, using a mixed language.

214 UNHRC, 'Report of the United Nations High Commissioner for Human Rights on the Situation of Human Rights in the Darfur region of the Sudan' (7 May 2004) E/CN.4/2005/3, 14–15 and 'Report of the United Nations High Commissioner for Human Rights on the Situation of Human Rights in Mali' (7 January 2013) A/HRC/22/33, 9 ff. This last Report is commendable to the extent that there is barely any reference to IHL; at the same time it avoids addressing the ANSAs or making positive statements on their human rights obligations.

215 UN Doc A/HRC/3/2, 24 and UN Doc CRC/C/15/Add.261, 2–3. See also UN Doc E/ CN.4/S-3/3, 5, UNHRC, 'Report of the Independent International Commission of Inquiry on the Syrian Arab Republic' (23 November 2011) A/HRC/S-17/2/Add.1, 22 and UN Docs A/ HRC/19/69, 21 and 23 and A/HRC/22/59, 13 and 25.

216 UN Doc A/HRC/2/7, 7. This approach was previously espoused by Philip Alston, UN Doc E/CN.4/2006/53/Add.5, 11. It was also quoted and adopted *verbatim* in the *Mission to Caucasus Report*, 313. For *Ronen*, 46, '[t]his statement carefully remains within the political sphere'.

217 UN Doc A/HRC/8/17, 6–7 and 21. See also UN Docs A/HRC/8/3/Add.2, 6 and A/HRC/10/22, 10, UNHRC, 'Report of the United Nations High Commissioner for Human Rights on the Implementation of Human Rights Council Resolution S-9/1' (19 August 2009) A/ HRC/12/37, 4–5 and *Parliamentary Assembly Recommendation 1444* [10–11].

218 UN Doc A/HRC/12/48, 80.

219 *Ibid.* The tendency to give significant probative value on unilateral undertakings is obvious also in UN Docs E/CN.4/2006/53/Add.5, 12, A/HRC/8/17, 7 and A/HRC/12/37, 4–5. At other situations, significance was given to the agreements signed by the fighting parties, see UNCHR Res 16 (2003) [7] and *Darfur Inquiry*, 50. It might be argued that this tendency shows some insecurity on

internal law (Palestinian Basic Law) is a source of obligation.[220] The Commission of Inquiry on Libya[221] has, similarly, stated that ' … where non-state groups exercise de facto control over territory, they must respect fundamental human rights of persons in that territory', although, again, referring to a public undertaking by the NTC. A special note should be reserved to the African Commission on Human and Peoples' Rights which commented that 'States as well as non-state actors, have been known to violate the right to life',[222] while in the duration of the civil war in Rwanda it has[223] 'called on all parties to respect the African Charter on Human and Peoples' Rights'. Finally, the proposed preamble to a 'Draft of a possible Convention on Private Military and Security Companies (PMSCs)',[224] '*consider[s]* that responsibility for violations of … human rights may be imputable not only to States but also to … non-State actors, including private military and security companies (PMSCs) … '.

In light of the above[225] it seems safe to conclude that, despite .the lack of uniformity, categorical denials of applicability of human rights law to ANSAs, as expressed by the Inter-American Commission on Human Rights,[226] are becoming fairly uncommon.

---

the validity of justification. It could equally be based on the eagerness to show that accountability is not only a theoretical possibility; evaluation of the ANSAs conduct has their consent as well.

220 UN Doc A/HRC/12/48, 80.

221 UN Doc A/HRC/17/44, 33. See also UN Doc A/HRC/21/50, 47.

222 *Sudan Human Rights Org Case* [148]. See also the assessment in *Zimbabwe Human Rights NGO Forum Case* [186], that 'these individuals and organizations can, *under international law*, be held personally liable for human rights violations … ' (emphasis added), a reference to political parties and associations.

223 African Commission on Human and Peoples' Rights, Resolution on the Situation in Rwanda, ACHPR/Res 8 (XV) 94 [3], Resolution on South Africa, ACHPR /Res 9 (XV) 1994 [3], Resolution on the Human Rights Situation in the Republic of Somalia, ACHPR/Res 129 (Ext.OS/IV) 2008 [2] and Resolution on the Human Rights Situation in the Democratic Republic of the Congo (DRC), ACHPR/Res 139 (XXXXIV) 2008 [2]. See also the position of the European Union in UN Doc S/PV. 3705, 33, S/PV. 3921 (28 August 1998) 3 and UN Doc S/PV.4046 (Resumption 1) 8. Similarly Parliamentary Assembly Recommendation 1444 [10] and Parliament Resolution (EC) on the Situation in Sri Lanka [2006] OJ C305/258 [3].

224 UN Doc A/HRC/15/25, 22. See also UN Doc A/HRC/18/32, 15 and 18–19, adopting a more nuanced approach.

225 See also the evolution of this approach with regard to extrajudicial executions in UNSG, 'Extrajudicial, Summary or Arbitrary Executions, Note Transmitting the Interim Report of the Special Rapporteur' (16 August 2007) A/62/265, 13–15.

226 *Third Report on the Human Rights Situation in Colombia*, chapter IV [14]. See also *Fourth Report on the Situation of Human Rights in Guatemala*, Inter-American Commission of Human Rights, OEA/Ser. L/V/ II.83 Doc. 16 rev 1 (1993), chapter XI, where the Commission has condemned 'the crimes and terrorism of insurgent groups'. But see also the *Annual Report 1992–3*, Inter-American Commission on Human Rights, OEA/Ser./L/V/II.83 Doc. 14 corr. 1(1993) chapter V, referring to the 'increasing concern in international and regional human rights organizations with activities that constitute violations of internationally guaranteed human rights by armed groups that operate over a period of time and control, in varying degrees, the territory in which they operate'. See more explicitly the ICTY in *Kunarac* [470], that 'human rights law generally applies to only one party …

In terms of numbers and frequency of appearance, it would seem that the situation has more or less reversed. The shift is evident in the language used: initially condemning abuses or violations of human rights law, but increasingly making positive and explicit statements on the applicability of human rights standards. What seems to be missing though is the practical application with regard to specific human rights, as it is relatively rare to examine compliance specifically.[227]

The Approach of States and Armed Non-State Actors

As regards states,[228] there is also a discernible trend to accept and invoke the human rights obligations of ANSAs. Poland supported that ' ... the parties concerned throughout Afghanistan should respect the human rights of their people',[229] along with Costa Rica referring to ' ... the obligation of the parties to the conflict to respect ... the human rights of civilians in areas under military control'. Slovenia[230] also 'call[ed] upon the parties to respect ... human rights'. The same approach was adopted, during the discussion on the protection of civilians in armed conflict, by Botswana[231] and Bahrain.[232] Australia's understanding[233] is on the 'dissemination of information on ... human rights law to all armed groups, with a clear expectation that they are required to respect such standards'. Ireland, during the Afghan conflict in 2001, appealed to 'all sides involved in the conflict to respect human rights.[234]

Burkina Faso[235] referred to respect for human rights from the non-state authorities in the 2008 Caucasus conflict, while the representatives of Austria[236] and Vietnam[237] affirmed that the parties to the conflict in Gaza (including Hamas) should respect human rights, as

---

the state involved, and its agents'. The *Liberia Truth and Reconciliation Report*, 51, also did not attribute responsibility for human rights violations to ANSAs.

227 For one of the recent exceptions see UN Doc A/HRC/22/33.

228 The motives of states might vary from humanitarian reasons to self-interest, in order to divert attention from their own atrocities. It is probable that the human rights obligations of an ANSA would also ease, up to a point, the burden from the state.

229 UN Docs S/PV. 3705, 24 and S/PV. 3765, 12. See also Afghanistan in UN Doc S/PV. 3705, 4, referring to human rights violations by the Taliban as well as Indonesia, 17, calling ' ... upon the parties to respect the human rights of all civilians'.

230 UN Doc S/PV. 3921 (Resumption) 12. See also the Statement by H.E. Andrej Logar in the 9th Emergency Session of the UNHRC.

231 UN Doc S/PV.4046 (Resumption 2) (17 September 1999) 2. See also the Statement by H.E Mr. Mothusi B.R. Palai, Permanent Representative of Botswana to the UN Office in Geneva, at the 23rd Session of the HRC, condemning human rights violations by the Syrian opposition groups.

232 UN Doc S/PV.4046, 23.

233 UN Doc S/PV.4312 (Resumption 1) 26. See also the Statement in the 23rd Session of the HRC.

234 UN Doc S/PV.4414 (13 November 2001) 16 and 17.

235 UN Doc S/PV.5953, 14.

236 UN Doc S/PV.6063, 9. See also the Statement by Ambassador Christian Strohal in the 9th Emergency Session of the UNHRC.

237 UN Doc S/PV.6061 (6 January 2009) 15.

well as humanitarian law.[238] On the other hand, Argentina and Kenya,[239] when discussing the 'protection of civilians in armed conflict', avoided mentioning human rights law as a tool for the responsibility of ANSAs.[240] This does not necessarily suggest that human rights do not apply with regard to ANSAs, since the conflict situation gives a first, but not exclusive role, to humanitarian law. With regard to terrorism, some states, such as the USA and the UK,[241] deny that it is a human rights violation, considering it only a crime.[242] Other states appear to hold mixed views. Brazil 'underline[d] the need for … the forces [of Abkhazia], to respect human rights … '[243] and the need for 'all parties in conflict [to] strictly abide by their obligations established by international human rights and humanitarian law',[244] including Hamas, but it avoided similar references with regard to

---

238 See also the General Statement of Philippines in the 2nd Emergency Session of the UNHRC, with regard to Hezbollah. Calls to respect human rights law from both parties to the conflict (and therefore including Hamas) were made in the 9th Emergency Session of the UNHRC, see Statement by the Republic of Korea; (Statement by the) Delegation of Vietnam; Intervention de la Délégation Sénégalaise lors de la Session Extraordinaire du Conseil des Droits de l'Homme sur le Situation à Gaza; Statement by H.E. Giovanni Caracciolo Di Vietri Permanent Representative of Italy; the (Angola) Statement by H.E. Ambassador Arcanjo Nascimento before the Human Rights Council Special Session on the Situation in Gaza; the Statement by Nigeria; and the Statement by H.E. Ambassador Sihasak Phuangketkeow, Permanent Representative of Thailand to the United Nations Office in Geneva. Similar calls or expectations were projected or violations of human rights were condemned during the debate for Syria in the 23rd Session of the UNHRC, see (the Statement of) Estonia; the Statement by H.E. Ms Iruthisam Adam, Permanent Representative of the Republic of Maldives; the Statement by New Zealand; and the Intervention de la Belgique.

239 UN Doc S/PV.6216 (Resumption 1) (11 November 2009) 22–3 and 46 respectively. See also Gabon, UN Doc S/PV.6494 (10 March 2011) 11 and Lebanon, UN Doc S/PV.6690 (19 December 2011) 11.

240 This seems to come in sharp contrast to S/RES/1894 [1], while it is consistent with the reluctant approach of the Secretary General in UN Doc S/2009/277.

241 See also UN Doc E/CN.4/2003/63, 20: '[t]he United Kingdom believed that only States could violate HR law. But see S/PV. 3705, 16, where the UK, ' … call[ed] on all the factions to respect international human rights norms and to act in accordance with those international instruments which Afghanistan has signed and ratified, for example the [ICESCR] and the [ICCPR]'.

242 *Clapham* 2006, 39. See also Sweden's opinion in UNSG, 'Human Rights and Terrorism: Report' (26 October 1995) A/50/685, 5. Similar concerns were voiced in the *Annual Report 1990–1* of the Inter-American Commission on Human Rights, chapter V, since 'some [unnamed] member states of the Organization are not in favour of the idea of associating acts perpetrated by irregular groups with the concept of human rights'.

243 UN Doc S/PV. 3912 (30 July 1998) 11–12.

244 Statement by Brazilian Delegation, 9th Emergency Session of the UNHRC.

Hezbollah[245] and the Taleban.[246] Canada also did the same,[247] unlike its stance in the past.[248] Yet this ambiguity cannot be reconciled with their positive (or consensual) vote on many of the Council resolutions that have been mentioned above. Colombia appears to be a case of evolution, since it mentioned only humanitarian law in the past[249] and has moved towards a more inclusive approach.[250]

As regards ANSA practice, support of the applicability of human rights law to them can be found in their constitutional-type texts. Art 11 of the Constitution of the Republic of Abkhazia provides for the ' … guarantee [of] the rights and freedoms proclaimed in the Universal Declaration of Human Rights, the International covenants of economic, social, cultural, civil and political rights and other universally recognized international legal instruments'. Somaliland professes its respect (art 10.2 of its Constitution) to the UDHR as well, while the Fifteen-Point Programme of the SPLM contained (point 2.13) a pledge to 'support and respect […] international Conventions on human rights and similar international protocols on human rights' and to 'adhere to and respect internationally accepted norms and standards of human rights'.[251] The LTTE has created the North East Secretariat on Human Rights and released a Charter in October 2005. Finally the signatories of the Geneva Call's Deed of Commitment accept, in the preamble, that human rights law applies and obliges all parties to armed conflict.[252]

The positive intention of ANSAs (and states) can also be seen in specific (human rights) agreements concluded with the opposing state. The Agreement on Human Rights[253] in El Salvador is a relative proof, since the FMLN ' … assumes the commitment to respect the inherent attributes of the human person' (preamble). In that regard, it appears that, apart

245 Intervention by the Permanent Representative of Brazil in Geneva, Ambassador Clodoaldo Hugueney, 2nd Emergency Session of the UNHRC. See also the calls to the parties to the conflict to put an end to human rights violations in the Intervention of Brazil to the 23rd Session of the UNHRC.

246 UN Doc S/PV.6625, 16.

247 Statement by Ambassador Paul Meyer of Canada, 2nd Emergency Session of the UNHRC. In the Canadian Intervention to the 23rd session of the UNHRC, there was a call to the parties 'uphold their international legal obligations', without expressly referring to human rights law.

248 UN Doc S/PV.4046, 8. See also Norway's positive stance, UN Doc S/PV.4046 (Resumption 1) 12 and Statement by Mrs Astrid Helle Ajamay, Minister Counsellor, 2nd Emergency Session of the UNHRC, while avoiding mentioning human rights law in UN Doc S/PV.4312 (23 April 2001) 29; and Portugal's positivity in UN Docs S/PV. 3765 (Resumption) 13, S/PV. 3921 (Resumption) 4 and S/PV. 6494, 24, and ambiguity with regard to Hamas, Statement by Portugal, 9th Emergency Session of the UNHRC. Similarly with Russia, see UN Doc S/PV. 3705, 12 as well as UN Doc S/PV.6625 (29 September 2011) 11.

249 UN Doc S/PV.4312, 26.

250 UN Doc S/PV.6625, 16 and S/PV.6690, 12.

251 See also the Agreement on the Implementation of Principles Governing the Protection and Provision of Humanitarian Assistance to War Affected Civilian Populations, preamble and Part 3.

252 See also the *Statement by the Opposition Movements (JEM and SLM-Unity)* as well as other practice in *Sivakumaran* 2012, 124.

253 San José, 26 July 1990.

from evincing the ANSA's positive intention, it is the medium creating accountability. Yet its character was mostly symbolic with regard to the obligations and accountability of the ANSA,[254] although it might have contributed to a decrease in certain human rights violations, as evidenced by non-governmental sources.[255] The Comprehensive Agreement on Human Rights in Guatemala reveals also that it is the medium which creates human rights obligations[256] for the non-state party and this is evident in the preamble.[257] But the bulk of the burden is placed on the government and not the ANSA, since the general commitment regarding human rights, in art I, as well as the majority of stipulations refer to the governmental party only. In any case, it appears that, initially, the ANSA's activities were scrutinized through IHL[258] and that, as time passed by, the UN organs were more at ease with assessing the ANSA's conduct through human rights law and/or the agreement.[259] On the positive side, there was an amelioration of the ANSA's conduct.[260] The Philippines Comprehensive Agreement seems, on the other hand, to be an additional tool, since it 'reaffirm[s] their continuing commitment to the aforesaid principles [of human rights and humanitarian law]' in the preamble.[261] Moreover, it 'realiz[es] the necessity and significance

---

254 In UNSG, 'Note Transmitting the Report on the Situation of Human Rights in El Salvador Prepared by the Independent Expert of the Commission on Human Rights in Accordance with Paragraph 13 of Commission Resolution 1991/75 of 6 March 1991 and Economic and Social Council Decision 1991/257 of 31 May 1991' (11 October 1991) A/46/529 and UN Docs A/46/876, 28 ff. and A/47/596, 28 ff. the violations of rights by the ANSA are examined under IHL, rather than the agreement.

255 See UN Doc A/45/630, 25. Governmental sources also seem to corroborate this view, see UN Doc A/46/529, 17, 20 and 27–8, with the Special Rapporteur coming to the conclusion that violations of rights continued but on a 'slightly lesser scale'.

256 For *Schoiswohl* 2004, 232, the agreement operates on the assumption of an already existing commitment to human rights; nonetheless his conclusion seems to be relevant only for the government, since it only ' … reaffirms its adherence to the principles and norms designed to guarantee and protect the full observance of human rights' (art I.1).

257 'Considering further that the Unidad Revolucionaria Nacional Guatemalteca undertakes to respect the inherent attributes of the human being … '.

258 UN Docs A/49/856, 30 ff. and E/CN.4/1995/15, 48.

259 See 'Note Transmitting the Third Report of the Director of the United Nations Mission for the Verification of Human Rights and of Compliance with the Commitments of the Comprehensive Agreement on Human Rights in Guatemala' (12 October 1995) A/50/482, 38, referring to the war tax as a violation of human rights and 'Note Transmitting the Fourth Report of the Director of the United Nations Mission for the Verification of Human Rights and of Compliance with the Commitments of the Comprehensive Agreement on Human Rights in Guatemala' (24 February 1996) A/50/878, 13, on freedom of movement. See also UN Doc A/49/929, 13, 18 and 39.

260 UN Doc A/50/878, 26 and 32, especially since the assessment in UN Doc A/50/482, 38, was not particularly encouraging. See also Portugal in UN Doc S/PV.3730 (10 January 1997) 11.

261 See also art 2 of Part VI where 'the Parties recognize the applicability of the principles of human rights … and the continuing force of obligations arising from these principles'. Obviously if the agreement was the essential way of creating human rights responsibilities, the 'force of obligations' would not be continuing. See also the *Agreement on Civilian Protection Component of the International Monitoring Team*, art 1.

of assuming separate duties and responsibilities ... ' (preamble) and therefore, after proceeding to a rather impressive enumeration of applicable human rights (Part III, art 2), the government undertakes further obligations with regard to employment and property rights (Part III, arts 11–2), as well as the right to security (Part III, art 2.6).

Apart from these agreements, which are rare, human rights feature prominently in peace and ceasefire agreements. The implication is that the state party to such agreements assesses the ANSA as able and willing to respect human rights and, simultaneously, this body of law as relevant and applicable to the ANSA. In fact they are more important in ceasefire agreements, not only because they might create a basis for obligations but also because the ceasefire period might not be covered by humanitarian law. In the 'Agreement on Permanent Ceasefire and Security Arrangements Implementation Modalities between the Government of the Sudan (GOS) and the Sudan People's Liberation Movement/Sudan People's Liberation Army (SPLM/SPLA) During the Pre-interim and Interim Periods',[262] the parties agreed that violations of human rights and humanitarian law constitute a breach of the agreement. In the 1996 Peace Agreement between the Government of the Republic of Sierra Leone and the Revolutionary United Front of Sierra Leone, the parties agree to guarantee and promote human rights (art 19). The subsequent 1999 effort towards peace[263] refers to full protection and promotion of 'the basic civil and political liberties ... contained in the declarations and principles of Human Rights adopted by the UN and OAU, especially the Universal Declaration of Human Rights and the African Charter on Human and People's Rights'. The preamble to the Ceasefire Code of Conduct Agreed between the Government of Nepal and CPN (Maoist) reads as follows: 'Remaining committed towards the Universal Declaration of Human Rights – 1948, and fundamental principles and values of ... human rights'. Subsequently in the Nepali Peace Agreement (art 7.1.1) 'both sides reiterate[d] their commitment to the respect and protection of human rights ... '.[264]

It is not certain whether these agreements have a standard-setting character or whether they are just re-affirming pre-existing obligations. The language in some agreements and the use of verbs such as reiterate or re-affirm could hint at obligations that predated the agreements, but, generally speaking, the record appears mixed. References to the UDHR could be read as affirmation that customary law applies – but would it really make sense to 'commit' to customary law at all, if it already applies? This, also, implies pre-existing obligations. As a minimum these agreements should evince an intention of ANSAs to accept or affirm human rights obligations and, therefore, serve as attestations of the

262 Naivasha, Kenya, 31 December 2004, art 10.1.6.

263 Peace Agreement between the Government of Sierra Leone and the Revolutionary United Front of Sierra Leone, Lomé, Togo,7 July 1999, art XXIV (hereafter Sierra Leone Peace Agreement).

264 See also the *Uganda Peace Talks Agreement,* preamble and art 1f, the Lincoln Agreement on Peace, Security and Development on Bougainville, Christchurch, 23 January 1998, art 1, the General Framework of Agreement of Intent between the Government of the Republic of Philippines (GRP) and the Moro Islamic Liberation Front (MILF), Dawah Center, Crossing Simuay, Sultan Kudarat, Maguindanao, 27 August 1998, art II, the *Liberia Peace Agreement*, art XII.1a, the *Darfur Declaration of Principles*, preambular [5], the *Darfur Peace Agreement*, arts 1.7, 3.24 and the preamble, the *Eastern Sudan Peace Agreement*, art 6.13, the Acte D'Engagement in North Kivu, Goma, Democratic Republic of Congo, 23 January 2008, art III and the *(Central African Republic) Accord De Cessez-le-Feu*, art 1.

tendencies of states and international organs in this regard. There are good reasons not to consider such agreements as the only medium for compliance with human rights law: firstly they might come quite late with regard to the 'danger' that the ANSA presents for human rights. A commitment to respect human rights in the post-conflict period might not be very useful, since the usual fate of the ANSA, after the peace agreement, is to dissolve or to transform into a radically different collectivity. Secondly it is not certain that they survive their breakdown, especially ceasefire agreements. Thus the role of human rights law in such agreements remains minimal, with regard to the period that the ANSA is functional, although, certainly, it is not unimportant if the ANSA has not exhibited its relevant volition before.

Concluding Remarks

In conclusion, it seems that there is significant and growing support for the position that ANSAs have human rights obligations and we might be able to conclude that a proposition *de lege ferenda* is slowly becoming *lex lata* and that a customary rule is emerging, if it has not already been established. It is not only the fact that states, whether individually or through international organizations, seem to consent in this regard; it is also that categorical negations, from states or human rights organs, seem to disappear. Even this part of academia which denies applicability (and there are reasons to do so) is careful not to include ANSAs with a (non-exclusive) government-like function within a part of the national territory. ANSAs have shown a positive *opinio juris* (limited or not) towards the expansion of their obligations within human rights law, although their actual practice shows the same inconsistencies as state practice in human rights law and might not always comply with their unilateral or written commitments. The type of ANSAs that have shown this *opinio juris*, usually ranging from *de facto* entities to ANSAs in control of territory, would suggest the limited cover of the emerging customary rule. More proof of *opinio juris*, practice and, possibly, state consent is needed in order to substantiate that human rights law has become a standard of accountability for *all* ANSAs and that the customary rule is firmly established. Although the human rights applicability to ANSAs might be the majority view, contrary to the relevant comment in the CIHL Study,[265] it is not overwhelming so that it becomes a norm beyond doubt, as has happened with humanitarian law. This would become more evident in the following sub-chapter, which attempts to sketch an uncharted area: the types of ANSAs that incur obligations, the extent of their obligations and the problem of enforceability.

Mapping Accountability: Actors, Extent of Obligations and Implementation

As became evident, there is considerable support for the existence of human rights obligations for ANSAs, despite the lack of a generally supported base. But even so, basic questions have not yet been answered or they have been answered partially and *in passim*: the type of actors bound and the extent of their obligations. In comparison with humanitarian

265 Vol. 1, 299.

law, 'human rights provisions need much more practical translation and adjustment … '.[266] The present part will be an attempt to formulate a principled approach to these issues, which are necessary for the overall accountability of the ANSA.

Which Actors Are Bound?

ANSAs have been classified in three categories, representing different layers of international obligations and a varied degree of accountability, mainly in IHL and, more generally in public international law: *de facto* regimes could either be bound by inter-state customary IHL or only the rules that apply in non-international armed conflict, depending on factors such as recognition; ANSAs in control of territory might have obligations under Protocol II and all other ANSAs are bound by common article 3 and other international treaties or customary law that applies in comparable conflict situations.

The classification scheme is relevant with regard to the human rights obligations of ANSAs, since the different categories of representativeness, recognition, effectiveness and organization of ANSAs correspond to variable layers of obligations and to differentiated expectations by the international community.[267] To a certain extent, the above-mentioned practice of international organs, states and ANSAs reflects this reality.

De facto entities exercise effective and probably exclusive[268] control over a territory and have acquired the characteristics of a state, through the passage of time and outside the strict confines of armed violence. Consequently they are objectively in a better position than other ANSAs to assume human rights obligations and the need to do so, for the benefit of individuals, is more compelling, as the regime of IHL might not be applicable at all. Several UN Reports[269] commented emphatically on the obligation of non-state actors with government-like functions and control over a territory to respect human rights. Effectiveness is, of course, essentially coupled with a high degree of organization, although there might be other reasons which were critical for the creation and endurance of *de facto* entities in time (such as help from states with a special interest or the inability of the parent state to counter their actions). It should not, generally, matter whether control over territory was fought for and won or whether it was gained because the central state institutions are weak and/or collapsing. But if the first scenario applies, the effectiveness (and possibly the organization) of the ANSA would be easier to presume. *De facto*

266 *Sassòli* 2003, 4. Similarly *Knox*, 40, for transnational corporations.

267 This applies for states as well, as the extent of obligations would differ according to recognition (for example with regard to the recognizing state), effectiveness (for example a situation of armed conflict or partial state collapse might negate effective control on the part of a state and could mitigate the extent of its international responsibility) and organization (for example a newly born state or a state coming out of a situation of turbulence would not be expected to (re-) realize economic and social rights to the same extent as a developed country).

268 With regard to the parent state; otherwise the ties between certain neighbouring states and *de facto* entities might be of such magnitude that authority over people rests on a third state rather than the *de facto* entity, in which case it is a matter of state responsibility rather than ANSA accountability.

269 See *supra* sub-chapter *Devolution of Human Rights Obligations*, at 163.

entities are objectively able, at some point, to administer territories and 'succeed' to some responsibilities of the parent state. But this should not be automatically assumed for all ANSAs which control territory.

The latter type of ANSAs could trigger the applicability of Protocol II and they are also, as a matter of fact, in a position to incur human rights responsibilities. They are organized groups, probably with significant membership, and, at times, with a political wing in addition to an armed element. Furthermore they are effective in mounting an armed conflict of considerable proportions, while they also exercise control over territory and people. This latter element is considered as sufficient for their obligation to protect human rights.[270] The FMLN assumed human rights obligations because it had the capacity to do so, according to the preamble of the human rights agreement with the Salvadorian government, a capacity which relates also to its control over certain territory. Consequently, it is clear that *effectiveness* is the key element, regardless of the existence of armed violence and the actuality of governmental functions. Yet control over territory which is gained randomly might have an impact on the extent of the ANSA's obligations, because it might not match the actual capacity of the ANSA to incur human rights accountability.

It is important to note that control over territory does not necessarily entail exclusivity. In a UN Report,[271] the accountability of Hezbollah was mentioned, which functions as a political party, although it has also an armed wing and therefore falls under the heading of an ANSA. Nevertheless, Hezbollah does not function as a state within a state and therefore its control over territory (and population) is competing with that of the state of Lebanon; yet this has not barred the Rapporteurs (as well as states) from considering it as an entity that may incur human rights obligations. Possibly the environment of Lebanon, akin to a failed state, has contributed to this outcome.

Common article 3 ANSAs are organized and effective enough to mount an armed conflict (probably a low-intensity one), but they do not in principle displace governmental control or create exclusive territorial boundaries. Consequently they cannot, as a matter of fact, be bound to the same extent as other ANSAs. Actually, most of the several UN Reports are usually concerned with ANSAs of a different capacity.[272] Since these ANSAs do not control territory, they seem to be automatically excluded from the field of human rights as possible violators. Emphatically enough, the Special Rapporteur on Sri Lanka has refrained from holding an LTTE splinter group (Karuna) as liable for human rights violations.[273] However, the UN Reports on Syria, which are occasionally concerned with

270 UN Doc E/CN.4/Sub.2/2004/40, 24. See also other similar references in sub-chapter *Devolution of Human Rights Obligations*, at 163–4.

271 UN Doc A/HRC/2/7, 7.

272 Further examples of this reluctance in *Rodley*, 300 and *Ryngaert* 2008, 363.

273 UN Doc E/CN.4/2006/53/Add.5. See also UN Doc E/CN.4/Sub.2/2005/40, 7, where the Special Rapporteurs write that '[i]f we accept that organized criminal groups with transnational ramifications, or mercenaries used to prevent the realization of the right of peoples to self-determination are to be considered also as non-State actors in international relations, it is hard to imagine that such actors would freely undertake, for example, obligations to respect human rights'. The ensuing difficulty to make them uphold human rights standards is partly different from holding them accountable for certain human rights violations

common article 3 ANSAs, depending on the situation on the ground, as well as other disparate Reports, show an increasing change of direction. Furthermore, the practice of the Security Council[274] and the Institute of International Law[275] implies that even such types of ANSAs have certain human rights obligations.

From a policy and humanitarian perspective this position seems justified: these ANSAs *could* exercise *de facto* control over people and they are able to commit human rights violations[276] within their sphere of influence. This is exemplified by a situation where they apprehend people.[277] Consequently, the need to bind them might be as great as in the case of other ANSAs, especially if, for example, these ANSAs function in the lawless environment of a failed or weak state. The difficulty, though, of relying on the theory of functional succession or the analogous application of military occupation rules (which essentially denote control over territory) would mean that alternative justifications might come into place, and only certain armed groups would be bound by human rights law. Or else, it might be proper to resort to the *jus cogens* quality of certain human rights, to human rights as a tool of interpretation of humanitarian law or a combination thereof.

In addition to the foundation, the difference between common article 3 ANSAs and others should lie in the *extent* of obligations. After all, this is reflected in the different layers of obligations under humanitarian law and this is how accountability under human rights law should be drawn for each type of ANSA, in accordance with their respective capacity, organization and effectiveness.

The Extent of Human Rights Obligations

As a consequence of the different types of ANSAs, different layers of obligations (should) apply; otherwise violations will take place as a consequence of the lack of capacity to uphold the standards[278]. This is similarly evident in the distinction between the legal regimes applicable to ANSAs with and without control of territory in IHL, which, in treaty law, had a differentiation, although the advance of customary law has, supposedly, eroded this distinction. A certain flexibility should be retained in the applicability of human rights to the respective ANSA, if we do not want to create impossible and therefore untenable obligations, which certainly will not promote respect for human rights. It would also be absurd to expect *provisional* and *temporary* entities, some of which do not have a reasonable prospect of gaining the governmental position,[279] to have the exact same obligations with

---

274 Apart from the cases where the Council referred to *de facto* control or authority of the ANSA, it did not generally distinguish between parties to the conflict controlling territory or not.

275 *IDI 1999 Resolution.*

276 UN Doc A/HRC/11/31, 7, 'lack of control over territory should not … lead to ignoring the human rights paradigm'.

277 See a similar example in UN Doc S/2007/584, 89.

278 This has been mentioned by the *ILA Committee on Non-State Actors 2014*, 693 as an argument for the difficulty of recognizing ANSAs as ' … subjects of human rights law … '.

279 There are internal armed conflicts which are virtually forgotten by the international community, in spite of the fact that they take place for decades, such as the one in Senegal.

a permanent international entity with substantial resources.[280] The differentiation in several intra-state agreements of the obligations incurred by the government and the ANSA might be an acknowledgement of this reality.[281] And since human rights law was created with the state in mind, one should be cautious and flexible with regard to the human rights obligations of ANSAs.

The lack of clarity on the international plane with regard to the scope of obligations is evident. Actors in favour of human rights applicability do not usually refer to specific obligations. For example the Institut de Droit International has made a corresponding reference to 'fundamental human rights',[282] which could imply only 'a certain spectrum of human rights .... If, however, [this reference] is equated with non-derogable rights[283] under the relevant treaties, then almost all of them are protected explicitly by humanitarian law treaties, provided, of course, that an armed conflict exists'.[284] However, when the Commission of Inquiry on Libya[285] made a similar reference to ' ... respect fundamental human rights of persons ... ' by ANSAs, it went beyond non-derogable rights, as it examined freedom of expression issues (although not specifically for the ANSA). More significantly, Meron[286] noted that the language of treaties and other instruments does not show a differentiation between fundamental and ordinary human rights.

There is also the issue of whether ANSAs have an obligation to respect or ensure compliance. This is especially important because it would give ANSAs an additional and significant burden with regard to their substantive obligations. In addition, the extent of obligations for second-generation rights is also important.[287] Are the three different layers of obligations, to respect, protect and fulfil the relevant rights,[288] all relevant to ANSAs?

---

280 See also *Ronen*, 25. Similarly, '[c]orporations do not have a general role in relation to human rights as do States; they have a specialized one'; UNCHR, 'Interim Report of the Special Representative of the Secretary-General on the Issue of Human Rights and Transnational Corporations and Other Business Enterprises' (22 February 2006) E/CN.4/2006/97, 17.

281 See for example the *Philippines Comprehensive Agreement* and the *Comprehensive Agreement on Human Rights in Guatemala, supra* sub-chapter on *The Approach of States and Armed Non-State Actors*, at 180–81, as well as the *Darfur Peace Agreement*, art 21.180.

282 *IDI 1999 Resolution*, arts II, III and IV. See also the Déclaration de S.E. M. Blaise Godet Représentant Permanent de la Suisse auprès de l'Office des Nations Unies et autres Organisations Internationales à Genève in the 2nd Emergency Session of the UNHRC referring to 'droix fondementaux de la personne humaine'. Furthermore, see *Walker*, 153 and UNCHR, 'Report on the Situation of Human Rights in Afghanistan Prepared by the Special Rapporteur, Mr. Felix Ermacora, in Accordance with Commission on Human Rights Resolution 1988/67' (16 February 1989) E/CN.4/1989/24, 13, implying the non-derogable human rights.

283 The understanding, though, seemed to be different and wider in scope, *Clapham* 2006, 111. See also Theodor Meron, 'On a Hierarchy of International Human Rights' (1986) 80 AJIL 1, 9–10 and 18, disagreeing on confusing non-derogable with fundamental rights, while highlighting a use of 'fundamental human rights' by the Institute, as implying *jus cogens*.

284 *Mastorodimos* 2009, 139.

285 UN Doc A/HRC/17/44, 33.

286 *Meron* 1986, 5.

287 The body of humanitarian law is mostly concerned with civil rights only, with certain exceptions such as the right to education, the right to food and so on.

288 See Asbjørn Eide, 'Realisation of Social-Economic Rights and the Minimum Threshold Approach' (1989) 10 HRLJ 35, 37.

In order to formulate the obligations of ANSAs, at least in a nutshell, various comparable situations could offer some guidance. Humanitarian law could be the first point of reference, as the principal legal regime applicable to ANSAs in the event of an armed conflict.[289] If we consider that a conflict might also be a public emergency, IHL could provide a list of rights (or aspects thereof) that are non-derogable. The generally accepted *jus cogens* norms of human rights law[290] could equally constitute a starting point. Non-derogable rights in human rights treaties could also offer guidance,[291] especially since they are occasionally considered to approximate *jus cogens* in international human rights law.[292] Although this is not necessarily so,[293] '[p]erhaps it is sound to agree that those rights which are commonly described in the relevant conventions as non-derogable form part of *jus cogens*'.[294] Agreements between states and ANSAs could also give some measure of the volition of states and ANSAs regarding the latter's substantive obligations, especially with regard to similar ANSAs in terms of organization, capacity and effectiveness.[295] The various private initiatives, such as the Minimum Humanitarian Standards[296] and similar codes, although partially outdated, could also give a measure of what is considered as indispensable in human rights. UN documents could also hint at what is expected from ANSAs.[297] More generally, ANSA practice could also give a measure of what is (or is not) considered as 'necessary' for self-regulation of conduct towards people, as well as sufficient for their capabilities.

Firstly, the 'usual suspects' for the *jus cogens* quality of certain human rights norms are a) equality and non-discrimination, including racial discrimination[298], b) the prohibitions of cruel, inhuman or degrading treatment or punishment, c) slavery and d) torture. This

289 See this approach in UN Doc A/53/928, since prohibited acts in humanitarian law are explained partly with reference to human rights law.

290 See *supra* sub-chapter *Preliminaries*, at 146–7.

291 See also Dinah Shelton, 'Hierarchy of Norms and Human Rights: Of Trumps and Winners' (2002) 65 Sask. L.Rev. 301, 316.

292 'General Comment No 29', 4.

293 See *Meron* 1986, 16 (on art 11 of the ICCPR and 23 of the ACHR), *Moir*, 209 (on art 23 of the ACHR) and Eckart Klein, 'Establishing a Hierarchy of Human Rights: Ideal Solution or Fallacy?'(2008) 41 Israel L.Rev. 477, 481 (non-derogability does not contribute to a hierarchy of human rights norms).

294 *Klein*, 482.

295 Yet it is possible that insistence on specific rights might be the fruit either of the weight given by a specific party to the conflict or, as Christine Bell, *Peace Agreements and Human Rights* (OUP 2000) 313, notes, of past abuses. In addition, several of these agreements are destined for a post-conflict environment (where the role of the ANSA is different to the one during the armed conflict period) and consequently, they only constitute an *indication*.

296 Note that in UN Doc A/HRC/19/69, 23, the Commission recommended the adoption of rules on conduct, which should include this Declaration.

297 But at least Security Council resolutions are too abstract to help in this regard, let alone that they do not seem to differentiate on the quality of ANSAs.

298 But see *Shelton*, 311, claiming that only racial discrimination appears to enjoy a higher status in state practice.

part of human rights law is not only usually considered as non-derogable in the ICCPR,[299] but also in the European Convention,[300] ACHR[301] and the Arab Charter.[302] The African Charter is a special case, since there is no derogation clause and, therefore, all rights included are considered as non-derogable:[303] such rights include equality and non-discrimination (arts 2–3), the prohibitions of cruel, inhuman or degrading treatment or punishment, slavery and torture (art 5). Taking also into account that those rights are reflected partly in humanitarian/criminal treaties and customary law applicable in non-international armed conflicts, which have the character of absolute prohibition in a period of turbulence,[304] it is possible to claim that also in a period of negative peace (absence of armed conflict), these same standards should continue to apply for the benefit of human beings. They are also included in the soft law document on Minimum Humanitarian Standards.[305]

Apart from norms that are commonly cited as *jus cogens*, non-derogable rights could give a further indication of a framework of obligations, especially if they are repetitively considered as such in treaties beyond the universal level. Table 4.1 shows some possible candidates.

If anything, this table shows that, through repetition, some rights are better candidates with regard to their placement in a hierarchy. In fact the better case is for those rights that are protected both at the regional and the universal level. Among them the right to life is prevalent; the principle of legality as well as other basic guarantees in criminal trials; recognition of person before the law; and freedom of thought, conscience and religion. Humanitarian/criminal treaty and customary law applicable in non-international armed conflicts protects aspects of the right to life and of the freedom of religion as well as the basic guarantees in criminal trials.[306] They further encompass the forced labour prohibition, some rights of the family and the child, some essential judicial guarantees as well as the aspect of human dignity of persons deprived of their liberty.

---

299 See art 4.2, referring to freedom from torture and degrading treatment (art 7), prohibition of slavery and servitude (art 8.1 and 2). The UN Human Rights Committee, 'General Comment No 29', 4 has deemed discrimination for reasons relating to 'colour, sex, language, religion or social origin' as non-derogable.

300 In the European Convention (art 15.2), no derogations may be made with respect to arts 3 (prohibition of torture) and 4.1 (prohibition of slavery and servitude). The same pattern is followed by the CIS Convention, art 35.2.

301 ACHR's non-derogable rights (art 27.2) include arts 3 (right to juridical personality), 5 (right to humane treatment) and 6 (freedom from slavery, including forced labour).

302 The non-derogable rights (art 4.2) are humane treatment (art 8) and prohibition of medical or scientific experimentation (art 9) as well as freedom from slavery, servitude and forced labour (art 10).

303 *Commission Nationale des Droits de 1'Homme et des Libertés Case* [21].

304 The freedom from torture and inhumane treatment, the prohibition of slavery and non-discrimination (termed as adverse distinction).

305 The prohibition of slavery appears to be missing. The Paris Minimum Standards, see Richard Lillich, 'The Paris Minimum Standards of Human Rights Norms in a State of Emergency' (1985) 79 AJIL 1072–81, contain also the prohibition of slavery.

306 Rule 101 of the *CIHL Study*.

Table 4.1 Non-derogable rights in international conventions

	ICCPR (art 4.2)	European Convention (art 15.2)[1]	ACHR (art 27.2)	Arab Charter (art 4.2)	African Charter
Right to life	X (art 6)	X (art 2)	X (art 4)	X (art 5)	X (art 4)
Non-imprisonment for inability to fulfil contractual obligations	X (art 11)	-	-	X (art 18)	-
Basic guarantees in criminal trials	X (art 15)	X (art 7)[2]	X (art 9)	X (art 15)	X (art 7)
Ne bis in idem	-	X[3]	-	X (art 19)[4]	-
Recognition of person before the law	X (art 16)	-	X (art 3)	X (art 22)	X (art 5)
Freedom of thought, conscience and religion	X (art 18)	-	X (art 12)	X (art 30)	X (art 8)
Abolition of death penalty	X[5]	X[6]	-	-	-
Prohibition of war propaganda	X (art 20)	-	-	-	-
Forced labour prohibition	-	-	X (art 6)	X (art 10)	-
Rights of the family	-	-	X (art 17)	-	X (art 18)
Right to a name	-	-	X (art 18)	-	-
Rights of the child	-	-	X (art 19)	-	X (art 18)
Right to nationality	-	-	X (art 20)	X (art 29)	-
Right to participate in government	-	-	X (art 23)	-	X (art 13)
Judicial guarantees essential for the protection of non-derogable rights	-[7]	-	X	X	-
Fair trial	-	-	-	X (art 13)	X (art 7)
Habeas corpus	-[8]	-	-	X (art 14.6)	-
Human dignity of persons deprived of their liberty	-[9]	-	-	X (art 20)	-
Freedom of movement	-	-	-	X (art 27)	X (art 12)

1 The same pattern is followed by the CIS Convention, art 35.2.

2 But only with regard to the principle of legality.

3 Art 4 of Protocol No. 7 to the Convention for the Protection of Human Rights and Fundamental Freedoms as Amended by Protocol No. 11 (adopted 22 July 1984, entered into force 1 November 1998) CETS No.: 155.

4 Significantly, this article includes also a *habeas corpus* right as well as an entitlement to compensation if innocence is established.

5 Art 1 of the Second Optional Protocol to the International Covenant on Civil and Political Rights, Aiming at the Abolition of the Death Penalty (adopted 15 December 1989, entered into force 11 July 1991) 1642 UNTS 414.

6 Art 3 of Protocol No. 6 to the Convention for the Protection of Human Rights and Fundamental Freedoms Concerning the Abolition of the Death Penalty as Amended by Protocol No. 11 (adopted 28 April 1983, entered into force 1 November 1998) CETS No.: 155.

7 But see the 'General Comment No 29', 6–7.

8 Ibid.

9 Ibid., 5. Note also that for the Committee other rights should be acknowledged as non-derogable, such as effective remedy, human dignity of persons, some minority rights, elements of the right to liberty (prohibitions of hostage-taking, abductions and unacknowledged detention). For an analysis of this Comment see *Arai-Takahashi*, 468 ff.

Almost the entirety of non-derogable rights is also included in the soft law document on Minimum Humanitarian Standards.[307] Agreements between the state and ANSAs include these rights occasionally – usually those referred to as *jus cogens*. Regardless of whether they were duly implemented or not, they show the intent of the ANSAs (and the states) that signed them to respect certain human rights as well as the corresponding assessment by the parties regarding their relevant capacity. The Ceasefire Agreement in Lusaka protects the right to life and freedom from torture (art I.3c), while the Darfur Declaration of Principles (principle 3) outlaws non-discrimination.[308] The Gaborone Acte guarantees the right to life and physical integrity, as well as freedom from torture and forced labour.[309] The Darfur Peace Agreement protects the right to life (art 3.26), [non-]discrimination (art 3.27) and religious belief (art 3.36), while it prohibits torture and slavery.[310] The Philippines Comprehensive Agreement (art 2, Part III) recognizes the protection of the right to life, freedom from torture and slavery, non-discrimination, freedom of conscience, thought and religion, family, as well as children and minority rights. Similarly, the Agreement on Human Rights in El Salvador protects against torture and inhuman treatment (art 2f). The Liberia Peace Agreement (art XII.1b) and the Sierra Leone Peace Agreement (art XXIV.1) deem, also, the right to life, freedom from torture and freedom of conscience to be basic civil rights, while the Sri Lanka Ceasefire prohibits several acts relevant to the right to life (art 1.2a) and freedom from torture (art 2.1).[311] But we have to note that the majority of agreements do not concern common article 3 ANSAs, but mainly ANSAs in control of territory, so that the *jus cogens* quality of (certain) non-derogable rights is a better argument than the intent of similar ANSAs. Violations of these rights, mostly those considered as *jus cogens*, have also been mentioned by several UN Reports, showing the corresponding obligations by ANSAs.[312]

The escape clauses with regard to the obligations of ANSAs, as reflected in international humanitarian and criminal law treaties, should formulate the limitations on non-derogable

---

307 The exceptions are art 11 and the prohibitions of art 20 of the ICCPR as well as arts 17, 18, 20 and 23 of the ACHR and arts 18, 27 (partially) and 29 of the Arab Charter. The prohibition of forced labour also appears to be missing. The *Paris Minimum Standards* contain also arts 17, 18, 20 and 23 of the ACHR as well as arts 18 and 29 of the Arab Charter. Both *Minimum Humanitarian Standards* and the *Paris Minimum Standards* contain aspects of the right to liberty and fair trial as well as minority protection.

308 Similarly the *Acte D'Engagement in North Kivu*, art III.

309 The *Nuba Mountains Cease Fire Agreement* (art II.3d) protects the right to life and prohibits torture.

310 Arts 3.29 and 3.30 respectively. It also contains provisions on the right to vote (art 3.31) and minority rights (art 3.39).

311 See also the *Nepali Peace Agreement* prohibiting violations of the right to life (art 5.1.1 and 7.2.1), non-discrimination (arts 5.2.10 and 7.1.1) and freedom of thought (7.7.1) as well as torture (arts 5.1.1, 7.1.4. and 7.3.1).

312 See the condemnations of violations of the right to life and freedom from torture in UN Doc A/53/928, 29 ff. and torture in UN Doc A/56/36, 3. In UN Doc E/CN.4/1987/23, 5, the right to life is mentioned, while UN Docs A/HRC/21/50, 16 and A/HRC/24/46, 13 refer to torture and inhuman treatment. See also UN Doc E/CN.4/1989/24, 13.

human rights, provided of course that an armed conflict exists; otherwise humanitarian law would be replaced by human rights law. Freedom of religion would be impaired by the destruction of churches which are used by the adversary as military objects; yet a proper interpretation of human rights law through the lenses of humanitarian law could allow for such action.[313] Similarly it could be prohibited to hold ceremonies in certain religious buildings near or in the battlefield for military reasons; such a restriction could be considered as legitimate, if not required also for the protection the non-derogable right to life of anyone who manifests their religion.

In sum, it appears that, initially, the obligations of ANSAs should be formulated particularly from a) the several norms identified as *jus cogens*, b) some of the rights that are commonly described as non-derogable by the universal, and one or more regional, systems and c) those that are commonly described as non-derogable by more than one legal systems and are contained in IHL.

With regard to civil rights that are covered by humanitarian law (such as the right to fair trial and the right to property) there is a question mark. Is that inclusion sufficient to make them in their entirety part of the ANSA's obligations, especially those under common article 3? Much would depend on the legal basis that we pick and choose, as they lack a *jus cogens* quality, while a foundational customary law basis is still missing. Yet military necessity implies that the use of force or other supportive acts are permissible against the state and its (military) agents, not against the people residing in the territory.[314] Moreover, violations of such rights do not, in general, support the war aim of the ANSA, when judged properly according to the balance between military necessity and humanity. It makes sense not to exclude such rights as coming within the scope of obligations for common article 3 ANSAs. Although intra-state agreements are not particularly substantial in this regard,[315] it does not appear that agreements between ANSAs in control of territory and states are particularly different in scope.[316] Some of those rights, as the freedom of

---

313 See also the reasonable restrictions of the freedom of religion for detainees through military regulations for order and discipline, *CIHL Study* Vol. I, 451.

314 See Rule 1 of the *CIHL Study*.

315 Most agreements mention freedom of movement as a right to be respected by ANSAs, see the *Comprehensive Agreement on Human Rights in Guatemala*, art V, the *Ceasefire Agreement in Lusaka*, art III.6, the Accord De Cessez-Le-Feu et de Cessation des Hostilités Entre le Haut Commandement de la Force Publique et le Haut Commandement des Forces D'Autodéfense de la Résistance (FADR) en République Du Congo-Brazzaville, Brazzaville, 29 December 1999, art 5, the *Gaborone Acte*, art 4, the Humanitarian Cease Fire Agreement on the Conflict in Darfur, N'Djamena, Chad, 8 April 2004, art 2, the Agreement between the Government of Sudan, the Sudan Liberation Movement, and the Justice and Equality Movement, N'Djamena, 25 April 2004, art 4e, the *Darfur Peace Agreement*, art 3.34. Property is protected, *inter alia*, in the *Gaborone Acte*, art 6, the *Darfur Peace Agreement*, art 3.33 and the *Agreement on a Permanent Ceasefire*, art 5.2(c). The *Darfur Peace Agreement* mentions also fair trial (art 3.25).

316 In the *Agreement on Human Rights in El Salvador*, there is a provision on freedom of movement (arts 7–8). The *Philippines Comprehensive Agreement* protects the rights to free movement and property. The *Sierra Leone Peace Agreement*, art XII.1b and the *Liberia Peace Agreement*, art XXIV.2 pick out the right to a fair trial, the *Nuba Mountains Cease Fire Agreement*, art II.2, focuses on movement and the

movement, the right to marry and found a family, as well as judicial guarantees for the protection of certain (non-derogable) human rights are considered as non-derogable in certain corners worldwide, and therefore, local (human rights) traditions could entail a need for their respect. On the other hand, though, the minimum standards rationale from soft law documents does not generally make reference to all of them, with certain exceptions noted above, such as aspects of the right to fair trial as well as the right to marry and found a family (Paris Minimum Standards). Therefore it is less evident what the course should be, although the volition of states and ANSAs alike show, to a certain extent, that there is a good case in this regard. Several UN documents also make reference to some of these rights.[317]

As with the more basic human rights, the several escape clauses, coming directly (or indirectly) from humanitarian law, should also be taken into account; an example could include the limitations on the freedom of movement (subject to military reasons or the security of civilians).[318]

With regard to civil rights which are not covered *rationae materiae* by IHL (such as the freedoms of demonstration or assembly and, arguably, the right to liberty), the same rationale could apply: military necessity cannot easily be reconciled with a conduct that violates the human rights of people. Yet there is insufficient evidence on the obligation of common article 3 ANSAs to respect such rights, not only from signed agreements,[319] but also from the soft law documents on minimum standards, with the exception of the right to liberty. With regard to ANSAs in control of territory, several agreements make reference to them: The Liberian and Sierra Leonean peace agreements pick out the freedoms of expression and association, in addition to the right to liberty.[320] The

---

Sri Lanka Ceasefire (art 1.2a) protects civilian property. The *Liberia Ceasefire* protects free movement, the right to return and the right to property. See also the *Nepali Peace Agreement* on property (arts 5.1.1., 5.2.1, 5.2.8, 7.5.5 and 7.7.1) and movement (arts 5.2.8, 7.3.3 and 7.7.1).

317 For example, the High Commissioner for Human Rights, UN Doc A/56/36, 3, condemned violations of the rights to movement and fair trial in rebel-held areas. In E/CN.4/RES/2005/85 [5], the UNCHR urged parties to respect freedom of movement of civilians. Similarly, the SG in UN Doc S/2012/376, 10, claimed that 'the right to freedom of movement and to leave one's country and seek asylum must always be respected'.

318 See Rule 132 of the *CIHL Study* and UNCHR, 'Report of the Representative of the Secretary-General, Francis M. Deng, Submitted Pursuant to Commission Resolution 1997/39, Addendum: Guiding Principles on Internal Displacement' (11 February 1998) E/CN.4/1998/53/Add.2, Principle 6.3.

319 The *Comprehensive Agreement on Human Rights in Guatemala* refers specifically to freedom of association (art V), the *Gaborone Acte*, art 2, guarantees freedom of expression, the *Darfur Declaration of Principles*, Principle 3, protects freedom of expression and association and the *Darfur Peace Agreement* protects freedom of expression (art 3.37) and peaceful assembly and association (art 3.38a). The case for the right to liberty is a much better one, since it is protected in the *Accord de Cessez-le-Feu et de Cessation des Hostilités entre le Haut Commandement de la Force Publique et le Haut Commandement des Forces D'Autodéfense de la Resistance (FADR) en Republique du Congo Brazzaville*, art 5, the *Gaborone Acte*, art 7, the *Darfur Peace Agreement*, art 3.25 and the *Agreement on a Permanent Ceasefire*, art 5.2(c).

320 See also the *Liberia Ceasefire* [9c] and the *Nuba Mountains Cease Fire Agreement*, art II.3d on the right to liberty.

Philippines Comprehensive Agreement also depicts, assembly and information (art 2.12), while the respective Agreement on Human Rights in El Salvador provides for the protection of associations and expression (arts 5–6) in addition to the right to liberty and security (arts 2 and 4). The Nepali Peace Agreement provides for freedom of speech, expression, association and peaceful assembly (art 7.4.1) as well as information (art 7.4.3) and liberty (arts 5.1.1, 5.2.2, 5.2.7 and 7.3.2). The High Commissioner for Human Rights[321] condemned violations of free expression and association in rebel-held areas in addition to arbitrary detention. Therefore there is a better argument for the extension of their obligations in this regard.

This, of course, does not imply that such rights are absolute, since limitations, according to the exigencies of the situation, should be considered possible. For example a notification that demonstrations should not take place near military bases because an attack will take place is not only a precautionary measure under humanitarian law, but it should also be considered a permissible *limitation* of the freedom of demonstration. Another potential example could include the freedom to impart information with regard to the position of the rebel army; this could be restricted by the respective ANSA (for example by temprorary confiscation of the means of communication), as it concerns its security and it would be immaterial to expect an open flow of information on certain aspects that are critical for the war aims of the ANSA.

If the obligations of common article 3 ANSAs are limited according to the above, it makes sense to consider that obligations of due diligence should not in principle form part of the legal obligations for common article 3 ANSAs, except for people detained and mainly for absolute human rights. Several Security Council resolutions would suggest otherwise.[322] The Syrian Commission of Inquiry has also *recommended* ' … that opposition groups ensure respect for and act in accordance with international human rights law',[323] while the Human Rights Council[324] has urged ' … all parties to the conflict to prevent … human rights violations and abuses'. Based, however, on incremental practice, these documents should be viewed as exceptions to the rule, rather than its re-affirmation. To the extent that there is substantial ambiguity on such general requirement in humanitarian law, it would be over-ambitious to expect something more extensive in human rights law.

---

321 UN Doc A/56/36, 3. See also UN Docs A/HRC/8/17, 20, regarding incidents in Gaza that affected freedom of expression and opinion and the right of peaceful assembly, and A/HRC/22/33, 12, condemning violations of freedom of expression and of the right to information by the ANSAs in Mali. A UN Special Rapporteur, UN Doc E/CN.4/1987/23, 5, mentioned personal freedom.

322 See *supra* sub-chapter *The Approach of United Nations Primary Organs, with Emphasis on the Security Council*, at 169–70. See also UN Doc E/CN.4/RES/1995/74 [12], calling on 'all the Afghan parties to ensure respect for the human rights and fundamental freedoms of women in accordance with international human rights instruments'.

323 A/HRC/S-17/2/Add.1, 22. The recommendation in A/HRC/23/58, 25, towards ' … anti-Government armed groups' to ' … compel all groups to respect human rights … ', appears even more unrealistic.

324 A/HRC/RES/24/22 [7].

Even intra-state agreements that suggest due diligence obligations[325] are not numerous and imply a partial and not a generalized obligation. More realistically, it seems justified to claim that the ANSA 'must not undermine state efforts to comply with their human rights obligations',[326] at least not deliberately, as it would not conform with a proper reading of military necessity.[327]

As regards social-economic rights, they are not described as possessing the quality of *jus cogens*. Therefore another way should be found in order to assess the extent of obligations. For common article 3 ANSAs the answer should reside mainly in the existence of specific humanitarian law stipulations which protect certain aspects, for example the right to health[328] and food.[329] Otherwise, they do not usually seem to be part of their obligations in intra-state agreements,[330] unlike similar agreements with stronger ANSAs.[331] On an additional level, it is to be questioned whether further guidance can be provided by the 'minimum core obligations'.[332] By way of an example the UN Committee on Economic, Social and Cultural Rights mentioned essential foodstuffs, essential primary health care, basic shelter and housing as well as the most basic forms of education, which depict rights that are, in one way or another, directly or indirectly, protected by IHL. A second level of obligations could be formulated by rights that are considered to be of an immediate effect.[333] Furthermore, a proper reading of military necessity could, arguably, suggest that the basic obligations to respect should form part of the ANSA's conduct.[334] It seems more sustainable, though, to envisage a general duty not to destroy such resources which would help the government abide by its increased (to the ANSA) obligations (for example warehouses containing crops). For persons 'in the hands of' the ANSA a standard of diligence should apply, equivalent to the obligation to protect. Similarly the limitations

325 See the example of the *Gaborone Acte*, referring to assurance of protection of the civil population from torture, rape, arbitrary arrest and so on. Therefore it's a partial due diligence clause for specific acts and rights.

326 *Ssenyonjo*, 128.

327 Otherwise the conduct of the ANSA is a constant incidental undermining of the human rights efforts of the state.

328 Rules 110–11 of the *CIHL Study*.

329 Rules 53–4 and 118 of the *CIHL Study*.

330 See the exception of the *Darfur Peace Agreement*, arts 3.35 and 17.97, referring to, among others, the rights to work, food, sustainable livelihood, water, education and health.

331 The *Agreement on Human Rights in El Salvador* includes labour rights in its protective scope, the *Sri Lanka Ceasefire* and the *Philippines Comprehensive Agreement* protect education and the *Nepali Peace Agreement* contains provisions on the individual's right to livelihood through employment of their choice or acceptance (art 7.5.1), right to food (art 7.5.2), right to health (art 7.5.3) and the right to education (art 7.5.4).

332 UN Committee on Economic, Social and Cultural Rights, 'General Comment No 3: The Nature of States Parties' Obligations (Art. 2, Para. 1, of the Covenant)' (14 December 1990) E/1991/23, 3 and *Ssenyonjo*, 65 ff.

333 'General Comment No 3', 2, referring to arts 3, 7(a)(i), 8, 10(3), 13(2)(a), (3) and (4) and 15(3) of the ICESCR. See also, similarly, *Vité*, 633 (non-discrimination and art 10.3) and *Arai-Takahashi*, 372 (on art 8).

334 For possible measures in this regard see *Vité*, 639.

(practicability or military reasons) should also be retained for interpretational reasons of human rights law, and, as with civil rights, the invocation of military necessity could only justify certain limitations (for example the right to adequate housing in cases of a private home's use for temporary shelter).

For ANSAs in control of territory (including *de facto* entities) the degree of obligations should be different. Almost invariably their control over territory is coupled with control over people and the need to uphold higher standards for the benefit of the latter is more pressing. Subject to the degree of control and in accordance with their resources, capabilities and the existence (or possibly even the prospect) of competing control by the state or other entities, there might also be different standards among these entities, apart from derogable human rights, whether covered by IHL or not. A Protocol II type of control is not necessarily government-like control, and this is reflected partly in the language of this treaty. Consequently, the possibility that control might change overnight is a variable that could have consequences on the extent of obligations, but does not limit them so much as to equate them with the basic (mainly prohibitive) obligations of common article 3 ANSAs. In fact their agreements with states show, exactly, an increased level of accountability. The same applies with regard to due diligence, which forms part of several Protocol II provisions. Consequently, and subject to the capabilities of the ANSA, the latter should be responsible for acting with due diligence,[335] at least with regard to *jus cogens* or other certain non-derogable rights. Walter Kälin appealed to the *de facto* authorities in Abkhazia and the Tskhinvali Regional/South Ossetia to 'prevent … acts of violence against returnees and other violations of their human rights'.[336] Once again, if the capabilities of the ANSA do not permit compliance (for example the area where the control of the government is displaced is too large for the ANSA to handle), it would not be possible to require an obligation of result, but only one of conduct.

With regard to social-economic rights, the Protocol II ANSA should be held responsible for the basic layer only, that is, the obligation to respect;[337] all other layers of responsibility are essentially linked with (more or less) exclusive and firm control (obligation to protect) and sovereignty (obligation to fulfil).[338] The exception should be people interned or detained by the ANSA (that is, persons who are in the exclusive jurisdiction of the ANSA), in which case respect for social-economic rights should include the obligation to protect.[339]

335 For *Ronen* 2013, 26 'effective territorial control is necessary in order to protect rights as opposed to merely respecting them'.

336 UN Doc E/CN.4/2006/71/Add.7, 17. See also UN Docs E/CN.4/1999/79/Add.2, 9, A/56/336, 14 and S/2007/584, 89.

337 As indirect support, see A/HRC/22/33, 12 ff., where violations of the rights to education, health and culture by Malian ANSAs are condemned but there is no expectation (or recommendation) that they act in this regard.

338 This is obvious in the *Sierra Leone Peace Agreement*, art XXXI, as only the government is under the obligation to provide for the rights of education and health.

339 Although for these situations it seems that humanitarian law provides for almost all aspects of human rights protection. Consequently human rights law serves mostly as strengthening the protection already offered.

In a situation of state failure (Somalia type situation), the actual need for an entity to step up and administer the territory is more compelling; yet to transplant the potential effective control test of military occupation, which 'stresses the capability of belligerent forces to exercise effective powers of government (while the sovereign cannot), even if they actually do not',[340] is not convincing for two reasons. Firstly it is not firmly established in international law[341] and secondly it implies that relevant ANSAs have the same level of capabilities as a state, something that is hardly the case. In essence one might have to turn to non-legal reasons in order to widen the scope of obligations: for example it is expectable that an ANSA with distinct ties to a certain group would claim and attempt 'liberation' of the territory where this group resides and therefore it would have a measure of self-interest in applying more than its objective capabilities allow or demand. Representativeness could become the vehicle of a more extensive scope of obligations for the ANSA. It is presupposed, of course, that the ANSA has not assumed the governmental position within a failed state, because in this case we should look on the context of state responsibility exclusively.

Finally, *de facto* entities are not only in a position where they can protect rights, but the necessity to hold them accountable on higher standards is significant, in light of the continuing incapability of the parent state to use its law-enforcement machinery to promote respect for human rights and the insecurity on whether humanitarian law applies at all. However, the extent of obligations should not in principle be different from those of the Protocol II ANSAs, which do not confront any impediment to their jurisdiction. The substantial differentiation could lie in the fact that *de facto* entities are in a much better position to enforce rights through regulations, laws, police and judicial enforcement. Consequently, accountability for civil rights through positive measures should, in principle, exist,[342] including the obligation to protect in the field of social-economic rights. The provisions on military occupation could provide a measure of how the *de facto* entity could realize those second-generation rights.[343] With regard to the obligation to fulfil, which requires taking measures progressively that would ensure certain and permanent results in human rights achievement, the answer should depend on certain variables: since the future of the *de facto* entity is not necessarily secure, it might be premature to expect increased legal standards immediately after *de facto* independence. Again the passage of time[344] (and the attitudes of the parent state) as well as the overall situation of human rights might be crucial: for Somaliland, the need for progressive realization intensifies as the ANSA stands more firmly on its own feet. The 60 years that Taiwan has functioned as a state should be an adequate indication that social-economic rights should not be fulfilled only to a minimum degree. Likewise in the TRNC entity, 45 years of peace, the commitment of Cyprus to a

340 Konstantinos Mastorodimos, 'The Current Legal Status of Gaza Strip: Has the Occupation Ended?' in David A. Frenkel and Carsten Gerner-Beuerle (eds), *Challenges of the Law in a Permeable World* (ATINER 2009) 227.

341 If not for Gaza, it is debatable if it would be discussed at all.

342 For a rare example that the Security Council expects ANSAs to exercise its positive human rights obligations based on the fact that it constitutes the *de facto* authority see S/RES/1417 [4–5].

343 See the provisions of arts 55–6 of the Fourth Geneva Convention.

344 Similarly for prolonged military occupations, see *Arai-Takahashi*, 370.

peaceful settlement to the conflict or, generally, the faint perspective that it will ever use force should be elements that affirm the degree of control and the durability required to achieve a higher standard for these rights.[345] Nonetheless, *de facto* entities should take into account their non-conclusive character (whether temporary or not) and should not generate permanent results on the way that they form the standards,[346] with the possible exception of human rights responsibilities of the parent state which have not been duly implemented. In a similar vein, for the category of national liberation movements that have achieved a similar degree of control a different level of obligations could be envisaged. Knowing that they will eventually become a state, the obligation to fulfil social-economic rights is coupled with (future) sovereignty over the same territory and people.

In conclusion, it appears that the obligations of ANSAs will be commensurate mainly with their effectiveness and objective capabilities; representativeness, legitimacy and recognition could play a certain residual role in the extent of obligations in the sense that there would be expectations to uphold them automatically (in the cases of liberation movements) or, at least, unilaterally (in cases of ANSAs with control over territory and/ or *de facto* regimes). International humanitarian law, past intra-state agreements, UN documents and soft law instruments also constitute useful tools of guidance in order to formulate the extent of obligations and the accountability of each ANSA. This principled approach, however, leaves a measure of discretion and uncertainty as to the extent of ANSAs' obligations and there might be a need to adopt a minimum code of conduct, similar to the Minimum Humanitarian Standards, as a basis for obligations. Furthermore, it would appear that, regardless of the extent of obligations, their enforceability is debatable, in light of their lack of an international legal standing in the current phase of international law's development.

Putting the Accountability of Armed Non-State Actors into Operation

The redress of victims of human rights violations by the state has evolved during the years. The national institutions are, certainly, the first point of reference, but thereafter, victims have a variety of international bodies to turn to, to exercise their effective remedy and to ask for redress. In that regard human rights law is much more advanced than international humanitarian law, despite the older origins of the latter. This is, in fact, one additional argument in favour of the applicability of human rights law during armed conflicts, generally, and to ANSAs, specifically. And although Tomuschat[347] notes that it is difficult

---

345 On the other hand, the situation in the *de facto* entities of Caucasus seems more unstable.

346 Similarly for military occupiers, see *Vité*, 641.

347 2008, 371 and 374. See also the position of Chile in UNSG, 'Views and Comments Received from States on the Note and Revised Draft Basic Principles and Guidelines on the Right to Reparation for Victims of Gross Violations of Human Rights and International Humanitarian Law: Report of the Secretary-General' (22 December 1997) E/CN.4/1998/34, 3, on their ' … agreement with the principle that the victims of all violations *should* have the right to reparation … ' (emphasis added) and the reluctance of *Van Boven* 2009, 27.

to extract from human rights treaties, let alone customary law,[348] a secondary reparation right when the primary right has been infringed, this is not the majority opinion.[349]

One can understand that the accountability of ANSAs for human rights law violations is more problematic, to the extent that treaty law did not generally envisage a role for them. Nonetheless, the prospect of ANSAs' reparations in IHL seems to have posed the possibility of reparations for violations of human rights law. The ILA Reparations Committee 2010[350] does not differentiate between violations of human rights and humanitarian law, while the accountability of ANSAs is acknowledged. The Basic Principles could also suggest the accountability of ANSAs, although confined only to gross violations.[351] In Guatemala, both parties 'recognize[d] that it is a humanitarian duty to compensate and/or assist victims of human rights violations',[352] while in the Philippines Comprehensive Agreement (Part III, art 2.3), there is a further acknowledgment of this reality.[353] Similarly in the Nepali Peace Agreement, the signatories also 'agree to take ... collective responsibility for ... making correction gradually in the future' (art 8.1). The Commission of Inquiry on the Syrian Arab Republic[354] similarly expects anti-Government armed groups to ' ... provide effective redress for victims based on international standards ... '.

If, however, there is a reparation right against ANSAs, it will be difficult for the victims of violations, be they individuals, groups, states or international organizations, to find a forum to turn to. Even the proposition to create a World Court of Human Rights[355] included non-state actors[356] but avoided mentioning ANSAs expressly. In many respects an inclusion of human rights claims against ANSAs could prove beneficial to state actors, because less strain would be exerted towards them in instances of human rights violations. On the one hand, their exclusion is understandable, based on their transitory and provisional character as well as their illegality under national law. To give even a limited (international) legal

348 Also *Zwanenburg*, 654. But see the *Darfur Inquiry*, 151–2.

349 *Velasquez Rodriguez Case* [166] and [174], UN Human Rights Committee, 'General Comment No 31', 6, UNCHR, 'Report of the Independent Expert to Update the Set of Principles to Combat Impunity, Diane Orentlicher: Addendum' (8 February 2005) E/CN.4/2005/102/Add.1, Principle 31 and *Schwager*, 421. The European Court in *Aksoy v Turkey* (App no 21987/93) Reports 1996-VI [98] linked the right to an effective remedy with 'the payment of compensation where appropriate'.

350 At 308. See also UN Doc S/2009/277, 15.

351 See also the *Darfur Inquiry*, 150 ff.

352 Part VIII, *Comprehensive Agreement on Human Rights in Guatemala*. However, an expectation of fulfilment fell into the hands of the government, see UN Doc A/49/929, 41.

353 Significantly this same agreement does not envisage a similar right for violations of humanitarian law!

354 UN Doc A/HRC/22/59, 25.

355 Manfred Nowak, 'The Need for a World Court of Human Rights' (2007) 7 H.R.L.Rev. 251, 255. The idea is barely new, see Jochen von Bernstorff, 'The Changing Fortunes of the Universal Declaration of Human Rights: Genesis and Symbolic Dimensions of the Turn to Rights in International Law' (2008) 19 EJIL 903, 906.

356 *Nowak* 2007, 256–7 and *Ssenyonjo*, 146, further pinching the idea of a global ombudsman.

standing to ANSAs, even for purposes of human rights protection,[357] would constitute the same anathema for states as the limited legal personality for humanitarian law purposes, while it could reduce the government's authority over ANSAs. A similar concern was raised by the Inter-American Commission on Human Rights[358] on 'the repercussions that the activities of an intergovernmental organ can have on the international standing of a group that is a party to an internal armed conflict', without, however, commenting any further on this point. On the other hand, though, it is the lack of an effective domestic system of enforcement that creates the need for the direct international accountability of ANSAs for human rights violations.

Nonetheless, the lack of an international standing of ANSAs does not mean that their accountability is not an option. It is not only that a victim's reparation right includes a corresponding remedy. Additionally, on the procedural aspect, the ICCPR (art 2.3) and other human rights treaties, such as the European Convention (art 13) and ACHR (art 25), provide for an effective remedy in case of human rights violations.[359] Depending on the legal basis for obligations, an individual's right to an effective remedy would, therefore, constitute an ANSA's duty. Such obligation could call for the development of justice structures in order to provide for reparations.[360] The possibility of criminal court mechanisms in combination with a victim's participation has already been mentioned in Chapter 3, sub-chapter on *Remedies/Reparation Mechanisms*. The right to an effective remedy is considered as including the necessity of individual criminal accountability in certain circumstances.[361] Several Security Council resolutions envisage also the need to bring to justice those responsible for human rights violations.[362] Although it is probable that they refer to existing forms of judicial systems (international or national), one could include ANSA justice mechanisms. After all, the reference to Somalia, where the national justice system is of dubious capacity (if not existence) could indicate that ANSA justice systems could provide an alternative. In essence this is a channel for the right to remedy as well as a form of reparation (satisfaction)

---

357 Similarly see *Knox*, 19, claiming that international law 'lacks the *practical* and *political* capacity to *enforce* those duties'.

358 *Annual Report 1990–1*, chapter V.

359 For Pierre D'Argent, 'Le Droit de la Responsabilité Internationale Complété? Examen des Principes Fondamentaux et Directives Concernant le Droit à un Recours et à Réparation des Victimes de Violations Flagrantes du Droit International des Droits de l'Homme et de Violations Graves du Droit International Humanitaire' (2005) 51 AFDI 27, 41, the regional treaties are more convincing on the existence of a right to an effective remedy. But see UN Doc E/CN.4/2005/102/Add.1, Principle 32. Note that this right is considered as non-derogable for the UN Human Rights Committee, 'General Comment No 29' and the Inter-American Court of Human Rights in *Judicial Guarantees in States of Emergency (Arts. 27(2), 25 and 8 American Convention on Human Rights)*, Advisory Opinion OC-9/87, Inter-American Court of Human Rights Series A No 9 (6 October 1987) [23 ff.].

360 See also the disciplinary measures for human rights violations envisaged in the *Uganda Peace Talks Agreement*, art 1f.

361 See *Nowak* 2005, 66–7, concerning gross violations of human rights.

362 S/RES/1509 [10] on Liberia and S/RES/1814 [16] on Somalia. But see UNSC Res 2088 (24 January 2013) [16] referring to the government specifically, as well as Res 2144 (13 March 2014) [4].

that could be expected from ANSAs.[363] Similarly a Panel on Sudan[364] has posited on the responsibility of ANSAs 'to investigate and address violations of human rights … ' as well as 'to enforce accountability among members of the group',[365] while the Philippines Comprehensive Agreement (Part III, art 4) provides that 'persons liable for violations and abuses of human rights shall be subject to investigation and, if evidence warrants, to prosecution and trial … '.[366] But the capability of ANSAs to have such functional institutions is dubious while relevant practice with regard to criminal prosecutions has neither been widespread nor hailed as compatible with human rights standards.[367]

Apart from this possibility, it is expected, if not required under the right to an effective remedy, that *de facto* entities and other ANSAs who are in semi-permanent control of territory will create some basic institutions which would include civil/administrative courts. Within the latter, the possibility of reparations for human rights violations is increased. It is worth mentioning that for a large number of years Turkey was objecting to complaints by Cypriots in front of the European Court of Human Rights, for non-exhaustion of local remedies (referring to the institutions of the local North-Cypriot administration). Recently the Court upheld that, for violations of the right to property, Greek Cypriots should resort to such institutions, thus recognizing their importance as a tool to protect human rights standards and to provide reparations.[368] It is another matter whether such institutions and procedures are adequate, but it is, nevertheless, a remedy and certainly a way to operationalize ANSA accountability.

It is also possible that non-judicial mechanisms on the part of ANSAs could offer an alternative path for the rectification of rights violations. *De facto* entities and some ANSAs with firm control over territory have administrative institutions to which an individual victim can turn. It might be advisable for organizations that are working in the field (and with ANSAs) to help them set up such procedures, wherever they do not exist, or reform them with the ultimate goal of gaining the capacity to provide reparations. Of course

363 Administrative – internal investigations were also expected from the CPN (Maoist) by the *United Nations Office of the High Commissioner for Human Rights in Nepal*, 2–3 and 8.

364 UN Doc S/2007/584, 89.

365 Also UN Doc A/HRC/22/59, 25.

366 For P. Alston, UN Doc A/HRC/8/3/Add.2, 14, it is controversial whether this supplies a legal basis (with regard to ANSAs).

367 See the European Court of Human Rights' assessment of the 'Supreme Court of the MRT', in *Ilascu* [436], which could imply that all non-state judicial institutions are illegal *per se* and, possibly, incompatible with the Convention. However, in [460], it asserts that 'in certain circumstances a court belonging to the judicial system of an entity not recognised under international law may be regarded as a tribunal "established by law" provided that it forms part of a judicial system operating on a "constitutional and legal basis" reflecting a judicial tradition compatible to the Convention, in order to enable individuals to enjoy the Convention guarantees'. See also *United Nations Office of the High Commissioner for Human Rights in Nepal*, 4.

368 *Demopoulos* [96 ff.]. See also *Cyprus v Turkey* [98], [236] as well as operative [III.5] and *Xenides-Arestis* [40] and operative [5] which exemplified the need to have organs which would provide remedies for violations of human rights law. The Court focuses on issues of substantive justice rather than the formalities which derive from the illegality of the entity and its non-recognition.

this aspiration would be relevant only for those ANSAs that take human rights seriously and want to increase their internal or external legitimacy. Also, in accordance with the principle of effectiveness, the outcome of such procedures, whether judicial or not, should be validated, even after pacification and dissolution of the ANSA, especially if they contribute to respect for human rights.

But such remedies will not in principle exist for the majority of ANSAs, while their actual capacity to provide reparations will be even more dubious. Szablewska[369] is even more pessimistic, since

> some of the duties put on states are very specific, including restitution, compensation and rehabilitation, as well as satisfaction and guarantees of non-repetition … . It is not easy to comprehend how a non-state actor (unless it achieves state power) would be able to fulfil most of these obligations, especially since even states, torn apart and destroyed by years of violence and conflict, frequently [are] unable to fully comply.

This difficulty, however, should not draw us to the conclusion that all forms of reparations are inexistent, even during an armed conflict. Restitution, satisfaction and guarantees of non-repetition should be considered as an open possibility for ANSAs as well[370] and there are some weak signs towards their provision. The Security Council[371] has called for ' … the immediate release of all individuals arbitrarily arrested or detained in Libya, including foreign nationals … ' (a measure of restitution). The JEM has instituted a Committee for Human Rights[372] with the task to monitor, supervise and spread the word of human rights (a guarantee of non-repetition). Moreover, even when the resources, material or other, are missing, external help should not be excluded as an element of the accountability of ANSAs. The Chin National Front[373] has requested external assistance on the ' … physical and psychological well-being and social reintegration of demobilized or released children … '.

Furthermore, the possibility that certain ANSAs (or at least their leaders) have become rich during the conflict should not be dismissed, in which case even compensation might be an option. A combination with the proposition of the UN Secretary General[374] could provide some material means of compensation, although there might be associated problems with regard to the ANSA's capability to sustain its war effort and the effect that its financial strangulation could have on the local population.

---

369 Natalia Szablewska, 'Non-State Actors and Human Rights in Non-International Armed Conflicts' (2007) 32 SAYIL 345, 356.

370 For such measures see Chapter 3 sub-chapter on *Reparations*, at 127–8, as well as *United Nations Office of the High Commissioner for Human Rights in Nepal*, 2.

371 S/RES/2144 [4]. See also HRC/RES/27/16 [12] on the ' … immediate and unconditional release' of human rights defenders and [15] on the ' … release [of] all civilians detained'.

372 Decree, No 71 (2010): Establishment of a JEM Committee for Human Rights (JCHRs).

373 *Chin National Front's Perspective on Child Protection in Armed Conflict.*

374 UN Docs A/52/871, 11 and S/1999/957, 9. Significantly, the Security Council appears to have adopted this approach, to the extent that frozen assets would be ' … made available to and for the benefit of the people of [Libya]', Res 1970 (26 February 2011) [18].

Accountability in the post-conflict environment could also come about through certain intra-state agreements, tending to provide remedies and make reparations for previous violations of individuals into account or, at least, leave a window of opportunity for the future. For example the General Framework Agreement for Peace in Bosnia and Herzegovina[375] created the Commission for Real Property Claims of Displaced Persons and Refugees. Art XXIX of the Sierra Leone Peace Agreement envisaged the creation of a Special Fund for War Victims.[376] The Darfur Peace Agreement (art 21.200) foresaw the institution of Compensation Commissions for war-affected individuals as well as the right to restitution (or compensation) of property for internally displaced persons (art 21.194).[377]

The above-mentioned agreements indicate also that, at times, ANSA accountability (towards individuals) would be absorbed by the state,[378] with or without some form of help from the international community. This makes sense from a political point of view, because the ANSA's concession in abandoning its dominant position in one part of the state might be the transposition, partly, of its duty to make reparations. It does not make sense, though, from a justice perspective and in terms of the deterrent effect that accountability could have. If the conflict finishes up with the defeat of the ANSA, it is impossible to expect accountability outside individual criminal and/or civil responsibility[379] – it would be different in the case where the ANSA becomes the government, in which case the state would be liable for both the ANSA's and the adversary's illegal conduct.[380] The transitional government paradigm is, allegedly, not covered by 10.1 of the State Responsibility articles, nor would it be likely to cover the situation that after a period of ruling by the transitional government and elections where the former ANSA (and now political party) triumphed.[381] In these cases, again, the state cannot be held liable and it is doubtful whether ANSA accountability could be actively pursued.

The Basic Principles[382] have foreseen the role of the states as substitutes for the inability or unwillingness of ANSAs to provide reparations.[383] We have to note though that this instrument, along with the Chicago Principles, is concerned with ANSA accountability

375 Chapter II of Annex 7.

376 See also the *Sierra Leone Truth and Reconciliation Report*, 227 ff.

377 See also the *Darfur Declaration of Principles*, Principle 10.

378 This is acknowledged explicitly in the *Comprehensive Agreement on Human Rights in Guatemala*, Part VIII, while the special fund for war victims in the *Sierra Leone Peace Agreement* would be designed and implemented by the government.

379 See Annex to A/RES/60/147 [17].

380 UN Doc E/CN.4/2000/62, 10: 'In cases where the State or Government under whose authority the violation occurred is no longer in existence, the State or Government successor in title should provide reparation to the victims'.

381 In agreement, *D'Aspremont* 2009, 437.

382 Annex to A/RES/60/147 [16]. See also the *Chicago Principles*, 30.

383 Such possibility was already envisaged in UNGA Res 40/34 (29 November 1985) [12–13] and art 2 of the European Convention on the Compensation of Victims of Violent Crimes (adopted 24 November 1983, entered into force 1 February 1988) CETS No.: 116. Even the Trust Fund of the Rome Statute draws its resources from voluntary contributions; the fines and forfeitures that would be imposed were deemed as inadequate in themselves for the purpose of compensation.

towards individuals and implies a soft law obligation. Moreover resort to the state is not a panacea; practical considerations would probably preclude reparations through the court system, as well as full reparations, and therefore alternatives would have to be found.[384] In fact there might be a need to prioritize reparation for certain rights violations (or violations suffered by certain classes of people[385]), if not with regard to gravity at least with the aim of post-conflict reconstruction of the national society and certainly not at the expense of the needs of the local population.[386]

The conclusion that we can come to is that ANSA accountability for human rights violations is in an embryonic stage and this could explain why the applicability of human rights, while debated for some time now, has not been pursued further. It is difficult to envisage how it will be possible to give specific teeth to accountability and reparations, unless the ANSA itself takes action and/or the international community seriously addresses the issue through a concerted effort. After the end of the conflict, the available options are criminal law mechanisms (which, of course, are limited to certain human rights violations), symbolic reparations (if this is possible) or the stepping-up by the state, within the inherent limitations of its post-conflict capabilities, and possibly the involvement of the international community, in the form of funding and support for reparation purposes.

Concluding Remarks

The topic of ANSAs' obligations in human rights law and the corresponding accountability for violations constitutes a new and still-evolving field in international law. Relevant condemnations have occasionally featured in resolutions or other texts of international bodies while states as well as ANSAs have concurred. Doctrine, however, has only very recently received attention, overwhelmed, probably, by the rise of international criminal law. In terms of evolution, the present situation can be compared with the conditions that existed on the applicability of humanitarian law to ANSAs in the 1960s to 1970s: it was not obvious where the law would be directed and doubts existed as to the accountability of ANSAs.

ANSAs should have human rights obligations for a number of reasons. First and foremost, state responsibility might not be adequate and international humanitarian law leaves certain

384 See the references in the Chapter 3, sub-chapter *Reparations and Remedies: Further Prospects*, at 133–5. Similarly, see the doubts of Germany in UN Doc E/CN.4/1998/34, 9, on '… whether full restitution, compensation or rehabilitation of persons affected by violations of human rights can constitute a realistic goal'.

385 See also the *Lubanga* Decision 2012 [189]. Such priority is not considered as a violation of equal treatment in the implementation of the reparation right, see *ILA Reparations Committee 2014*, 792.

386 As *Schwager*, 436, notes: 'the economic and political situation cannot lead to denying the existence of internationally and nationally guaranteed rights and judicial procedures under domestic law. A differentiation must be made between the legal conditions for a claim and the economical resources which might have an impact on the performance of the claim. Whilst the claim has to be recognized, its potential amount might be limited due to the lack of resources of the respondent debtor, the impossibility of the debtor to fulfil all claims or other special circumstances.'

gaps with regard to specific situations (that is, internal disturbances) or particular rights. Most importantly though, individual responsibility, whether criminal or civil, might not be able to capture the role that the group plays and how the violating conduct would not have existed without the collective apparatus. To a certain extent ANSAs do have human rights obligations, although the legal foundations are not necessarily adequate or satisfactory. Due to a growing trend to acknowledge the applicability of human rights to ANSAs (and their responding accountability), it might be possible to refer to the emergence of a corresponding customary rule at least with regard to *de facto* entities and other ANSAs with a firm control over territory. Nonetheless, this is hardly adequate, because, until such rule is firmly established, the legal basis for their accountability will be differentiated in accordance with the type of ANSA in question. In this regard it seems appropriate to approach the extent of ANSAs' obligations qualitatively, based on their characteristics: from the minimum *jus cogens* human rights, applicable to all types of ANSAs to obligations to fulfil social and economic rights, being applicable only to *de facto* entities, under certain circumstances.

The subject matter of humanitarian law, intra-state agreements, soft law instruments and UN documents appear to espouse this approach, at least indirectly. Such an approach would constitute a response to the less than comprehensive character of humanitarian law with regard to the substantive obligations of certain ANSAs, mainly *de facto* entities and ANSAs in control of territory. It is the subject of remedies, mainly, and reparations that follows the under-development of IHL and it cannot offer any viable alternative to it,[387] unless ANSAs become the subject of scrutiny in front of international judicial or semi-judicial organs. The prospect of remedies within the structures of the ANSA seems, again, the most promising option during the period of its existence, unless the international community enforces sanctions against ANSAs (for example frozen assets) that would in sequence be directed towards reparation schemes. After the effective end of violence the available reparations would depend not only on the fate of the ANSA but also on the post-conflict situation of the state and the substantial involvement of the international community, in order to achieve tangible results. Yet even with such a dim future prospect, the need to create a culture of human rights compliance by ANSAs is almost self-evident. Attributing the human rights violation to the state or resorting to due diligence obligations might not be effective in itself: the aim should equally be to prevent the potential violation from occurring in the first place; and without the 'participation' of non-state actors and especially ANSAs this might prove to be impossible.[388] Individual criminal responsibility is also inadequate in order to cover all violations of human rights. In essence, the accountability of ANSAs for violations of human rights law is a further step from their acknowledged accountability in IHL and, maybe, the step before their international accountability for violations of other treaties or agreements, customary rules beyond IHL and human rights law or acts of international organs with a binding effect on them.

---

387 However, this under-development can be explained partly by the fact that the extent of the primary obligations still remains nuanced in international practice.

388 As an alternative, a human rights treaty to be applied specifically to ANSAs might be a potential answer, since, '[i]nternational law imposes no conceptual obstacle to an agreement among states to impose obligations directly on private parties', *Vasquez*, 930.

Chapter 5
The Obligations and Accountability of Armed Non-State Actors: Concluding Remarks

The accountability of ANSAs has been a rather neglected field of international law, despite the fact that these entities challenge, in some aspects, its state-centred approach. Even though the effect of ANSAs in armedconflict situations has been long acknowledged, their accountability has not been considered in depth until recently. The proliferation of power sources outside the state has sparked the debate on the place of non-state actors in international law and this book constitutes part of it. For methodological and ontological reasons ANSAs have been divided into three different categories. *De facto* entities, ANSAs in control of territory and armed actors without territorial control (common article 3 ANSAs) should correspond to a differentiated extent of obligations and accountability both in IHL and human rights law. Although the tendency in IHL is to equate the different categories of actors with regard to substantive obligations, this is an incorrect approach since it does not take into account the responding capacity of ANSAs. A similar tendency is shown with regard to regulation of their activities under human rights law. The author has argued that the obligations of ANSAs under human rights law should follow a principled approach based on a hierarchy of international sources and the quality of the respective ANSA. In fact even humanitarian law obligations should have followed a different approach. Additionally, the limits of an all-inclusive approach become obvious in the available reparations and remedies. The powerful ANSA is able grant them, sometimes willingly, while the less powerful ANSA cannot, even if it is willing to.

The examination of ANSAs' obligations and accountability reveals a need to move away from the traditional state-centred approach and to adapt international law to the particularities of armed non-state actors. After all, ANSAs increasingly have *direct* international legal obligations and have shown a capacity to enter into relations with subjects of international law, while they might, occasionally, exhibit evidence of state features (government, effective control of territory and even a population). The lack of accountability mechanisms specifically addressed to ANSAs is a symptom of a state-centred approach and it is likely to reach a dead end if we stick to the existing avenues. At the same time, the lack of accountability pushes the limits of state responsibility beyond its objective capabilities. To the extent that the state undertakes to provide reparations to victims of international law violations after the armed conflict period, the strain is enormous. Furthermore, there is a possibility that individual criminal accountability would be expanded to such a degree that the principle of personal culpability might be endangered. A regime of accountability has the potential to enhance compliance by armed non-state actors especially if it is coupled with scrutiny from international organs. Consequently, it could lead to a decrease in primary rules violations, thus serving a preventive role, while it would also contribute to the values of justice.

The challenge that the variety of non-state actors (including ANSAs) pose to the state paradigm currently is significant, but it does not appear to de-construct it. The several processes that gave a limited legal standing to non-state actors, particularly individuals, has barely changed the state primacy in international affairs. In fact these approaches have been realized with the consent of states and have led towards more participatory and inclusive forms in international law. In light of the role played by armed non-state actors there is a need to move towards a functional, rather than a formal, theory of status.[1] The politics of exclusion have not generated the positive results that states wanted or expected. On the contrary, ANSAs' participation has on many occasions proved to be a step forward in regards to the interests both of the individual and the international community.[2] Although not all unilateral declarations or intra-state agreements have led to an amelioration of conduct, there are, occasionally, positive signs. The assumption that ANSAs are generally non-abiding by legal standards tends to collapse if one searches a bit beyond state condemnations. Furthermore, there are ANSAs that 'deserve' to be treated more seriously than certain governments and constitute a part of the solution rather than a part of the problem that has generated the armed conflict (or the dispute behind the conflict).

The move of the international community towards inclusion of ANSAs could take several forms. Direct law-making through treaties is certainly unimaginable and, at best, an unsubstantiated proposal. It would be more logical to envisage a role for ANSAs within customary IHL and human rights law, at least with regard to their own obligations. Another approach is to create or amend treaties[3] which would explicitly be addressed to ANSAs either exclusively or within the inter-state relations paradigm. Yet this approach might also be inadequate if it does not take into account the capabilities and/or practice of ANSAs, while it could generate negative responses from ANSAs and become ineffective. The approach of the Kampala Convention, which has passed over armed groups and is addressed to individuals, shows, once more, the statist approach to international law, where collective entities that could challenge the state are not accommodated. Although it is mainly a matter of architecture, it still fails to capture the significant role of ANSAs within its subject matter.

A certain prospect could be offered by unilateral declarations and agreements with ANSAs and, so far, it appears to be the most fruitful way to accommodate their inclusion,

1 See also *ILA Committee on Non-State Actors 2010*, 659: 'The challenge now appears to be to clarify and develop attributes relating to their legal position, so that they can become genuine *subjects* of international law (implying consent on the part of NSAs to be bound), and *de jure* participants in international law processes. This will require States to recognise that formalising the status of at least particular NSAs is in the best interest of the broader international community of which States form the principal part.'

2 See alsoibid, 692: '[i]nvolvement of NSAs is all the more desirable if the effectiveness of regulation hinges in large part on the implementation efforts of NSAs rather than States (e.g., regulation of the shipping industry, regulation of the conduct of armed opposition groups)'.

3 See the relevant comments of *Bassiouni*, 809, with regard to international crimes.

although there might be some doubts with regard to whether they function at the level of secondary rules regarding accountability. Model agreements or unilateral declarations could be devised in this regard, depending on the quality of the ANSA. Such acts would not only re-affirm (and/or clarify) obligations under IHL and human rights law; they could also expand obligations or, mainly, envisage available remedies for victims of violations of the general legal regimes applicable and/or the specific one (agreement, unilateral declaration).

Certainly, none of the above suggests that ANSAs deserve an equal role to that played by states. Apart from the fact that some of them are notorious for their disregard of any rules, the representativeness and legitimacy of most governments could not (and should not) equate the latter with ANSAs. Nonetheless, there is a great gap between being given an equal role to acquiring no role whatsoever. Obviously, 'a regime of responsibility for non-State actors [is] not [to] be interpreted as an acknowledgement of their legitimacy or lawfulness'.[4] But it is an acknowledgement that ANSAs should carry the burden of the effects of their own activities and it should constitute an alternative and/or complementary regime to the individual and state responsibility schemes, in light of a particular act and its source. The interests of the international community do not coincide with those of states and the international accountability of ANSAs could serve communal values as regards to justice. The time has come to grapple with this problem more seriously and the international community needs to be thoroughly engaged with armed non-state actors or at least certain types of them. Humanitarian and human rights rules need to be adjusted to the capabilities and strengths of armed non-state actors, while rules of attribution, remedies and reparations need to be devised in a more comprehensive manner. This is certainly a long and difficult task, but it is definitely worthwhile.

4 *ILA Reparations Committee 2010*, 309. See, also, *Cahin*, 338.

Bibliography

1. Books

Arai-Takahashi Y, *The Law of Occupation: Continuity and Change of International Humanitarian Law, and its Interaction with International Human Rights Law* (Nijhoff 2009)

Aust A, *Modern Treaty Law and Practice* (CUP, Cambridge 2007)

——— *Handbook of International Law* (2nd edn, CUP 2010)

Babiker MA, *Application of International Humanitarian and Human Rights Law to the Armed Conflicts of the Sudan: Complementary or Mutually Exclusive Regimes?* (Intersentia 2007)

Bedjaoui M, *Law and the Algerian Revolution* (International Association of Democratic Lawyers 1961)

Bell C, *Peace Agreements and Human Rights* (OUP 2000)

——— *On the Law of Peace: Peace Agreements and the Lex Pacificatoria* (OUP 2008)

Bond J, *The Rules of Riot: Internal Conflict and the Law of War* (Princeton University Press 1974)

Boothby WH, *Weapons and the Law of Armed Conflict* (OUP 2009)

Brownlie I, *Principles of Public International Law* (7th edn, OUP 2008)

Brownlie I and Goodwin-Will G, *Basic Documents on Human Rights* (4th edn, OUP 2002)

Castren E, *Civil War* (Suomalainen Tiedeakatemia 1966)

Chadwick E, *Self-Determination, Terrorism and the International Humanitarian Law of Armed Conflict* (Martinus Nijhoff 1996)

Chen TC, *The International Law of Recognition* (Preager 1951)

Clapham A, *Human Rights Obligations of Non-State Actors* (OUP 2006)

——— *Human Rights in the Private Sphere* (Clarendon Press 1993)

Crawford E, *The Treatment of Combatants and Insurgents under the Law of Armed Conflict* (OUP 2010)

Crawford J, *The Creation of States in International Law* (2nd edn, Clarendon Press 2006)

Cullen A, *The Concept of Non-International Armed Conflict in International Humanitarian Law* (CUP 2010)

Daes E-I A, *Freedom of the Individual under Law: An Analysis of Article 29 of the Universal Declaration of Human Rights* (United Nations 1990)

de Schutter O, *International Human Rights Law: Cases, Materials, Commentary* (CUP 2010)

Detter I, *The Law of War* (2nd edn, CUP 2000)

Dinstein Y, War, *Aggression and Self-Defence* (4th edn, CUP 2005)

——— *The International Law of Belligerent Occupation* (CUP 2009)

Draper GIAD, *The Red Cross Conventions* (Stevens 1958)

Duffy H, *The 'War on Terror' and the Framework of International Law* (CUP 2005)

Green LC, *The Contemporary Law of Armed Conflict* (2nd edn, Manchester University Press 2000)

Hall WE, *A Treatise on International Law* (8th edn, Clarendon Press 1924)

Harris DJ, O'Boyle M and Warbrick C, *Law of the European Convention on Human Rights* (2nd edn, OUP 2009)

Henckaerts JM and Doswald-Beck L, *Customary International Humanitarian Law* Vols. 1–2 (CUP 2005)

Higgins N, *Regulating the Use of Force in Wars of National Liberation, the Need for a New Regime: A Study of the South Moluccas and Aceh* (Nijhoff 2010)

Hodgson D, *Individual Duty within a Human Rights Discourse* (Ashgate 2003)

Jennings R and Watts A (eds), *Oppenheim's International Law* Vol. 1 (9th edn, Longman 1992)

Kirk-Greene AHM (comp.*), Crisis and Conflict in Nigeria: A Documentary Sourcebook 1966–1970* Vol. II, June 1967–January 1970 (OUP 1971)

Kolb R and Hyde R, *An Introduction to the International Law of Armed Conflicts* (Hart Publishing 2008)

Lauterpacht H, *Recognition in International Law* (CUP 1947)

Lubell N, *Extraterritorial Use of Force against Non-State Actors* (OUP 2010)

McCoubrey H, *International Humanitarian Law: Modern Developments in the Limitation of Warfare* (2nd edn, Ashgate 1998)

Meron T, *Human Rights and Humanitarian Norms as Customary Law* (Clarendon Press 1989)

Milano E, *Unlawful Territorial Situations in International Law: Reconciling Effectiveness, Legality and Legitimacy* (Martinus Nijhoff 2004)

Moir L, *The Law of Internal Armed Conflict* (CUP 2002)

Nowak M, U.N. *Covenant on Civil and Political Rights: CCPR Commentary* (2nd edn, N.P. Engel 2005)

O'Connell DP, *International Law* (2nd edn, Stevens 1970)

Okeke CN, *Controversial Subjects of Contemporary International Law* (Rotterdam University Press 1974)

Pictet J (ed.), *Commentary to the Geneva Convention IV Relative to the Protection of Civilian Persons in Time of War* (International Committee of the Red Cross 1958)

Provost R, *International Human Rights and Humanitarian Law* (CUP 2002)

Rogers APV, *Law on the Battlefield* (2nd edn, Manchester University Press 2004)

Roth B, *Governmental Illegitimacy in International Law* (OUP 2000)

Samuels K, *Political Violence and the International Community: Developments in International Law and Policy* (Nijhoff 2007)

Sassòli M and Bouvier A, *How Does Law Protect in War* (2nd edn, International Committee of the Red Cross 2006)

Schoiswohl M, *Status and (Human Rights) Obligations of Non-Recognized De Facto Regimes in International Law: the Case of 'Somaliland': the Resurrection of Somaliland against all International 'Odds': State Collapse, Secession, Non-Recognition and Human Rights* (Nijhoff 2004)

Shaw MN, *International Law* (5th edn, CUP 2003)

Siotis J, *Le Droit de la Guerre et les Conflits Armés d'un Caractère Non-International* (Librairie Générale de Droit et de Jurisprudence 1958)

Sivakumaran S, *The Law of Non-International Armed Conflict* (OUP 2012)

Solis GD, *The Law of Armed Conflict* (CUP 2010)
Ssenyonjo M, *Economic, Social and Cultural Rights in International Law* (Hart 2009)
Talmon S, *Recognition of Governments in International Law: With Particular Reference to Governments in Exile* (Clarendon Press 1998)
Tomuschat C, *Human Rights: Between Idealism and Realism* (2nd edn, OUP 2008)
Villiger ME, *Commentary on the 1969 Vienna Convention on the Law of Treaties* (Nijhoff 2009)
Von Glahn G, *Law among Nations: An Introduction to Public International Law* (5th edn, Collier Macmillan 1986)
Whiteman M, *Digest of International Law* Vol. 12 (Department of State Publications 1963)
Wilson H, *International Law and the Use of Force by National Liberation Movements* (Clarendon Press 1988)
Zegveld L, *Accountability of Armed Opposition Groups in International Law* (CUP 2002)

2. Articles

A. In Journals

Abresch W, 'A Human Rights Law of Internal Armed Conflict: The European Court of Human Rights in Chechnya' (2005) 16 The European Journal of International Law 741
Akehurst M, 'State Responsibility for the Wrongful Acts of Rebels – an Aspect of the South Rhodesian Problem' (1968–9) 43 British Yearbook of International Law 49
Alder JL, 'The Unrecognized Government in the Courts of the United States' (1964–5) 5 Virginia Journal of International Law 36
Aldrich GH, 'Customary International Humanitarian Law – An Interpretation on behalf of the International Committee of the Red Cross' (2006) 76 British Yearbook of International Law 503
Andreopoulos GJ, 'The International Legal Framework and Armed Groups' (2010) 11 Human Rights Review 223
Anonymous, 'The Geneva Convention and the Treatment of Prisoners of War in Vietnam' (1966–7) 80 Harvard Law Review 851
Ary VA, 'Concluding Hostilities: Humanitarian Provisions in Cease-Fire Agreements' (1995) 148 Military Law Review 186
Backer LC, 'On the Evolution of the United Nations' "Protect–Respect–Remedy" Project: The State, the Corporation and Human Rights in a Global Governance Context' (2011) 9 Santa Clara Journal of International Law 37
Bailey S, 'Cease-fires, Truces, and Armistices in the Practice of the UN Security Council' (1977) 71 The American Journal of International Law 461
Baloro J, 'International Humanitarian Law and Situations of Internal Armed Conflicts in Africa' (1992) 4 African Journal of International and Comparative Law 449
Barbour SA and Salzman ZA, 'The "Tangled Web": The Right of Self-Defense Against Non-State Actors in the Armed Activities Case' (2008) 40 New York University Journal of International Law and Politics 53

Bassiouni CM, 'The New Wars and the Crisis of Compliance with the Law of Armed Conflict by Non-State Actors' (2007–8) 98 Journal of Criminal Law & Criminology 711

Bellal A, Giacca G and Casey-Maslen S, 'International Law and Armed Non-State Actors in Afghanistan' (2011) 93 International Review of the Red Cross 1

Blank LR, 'Defining the Battlefield in Contemporary Conflict and Counterterrorism: Understanding the Parameters of the Zone of Combat' (2010) 39 Georgia Journal of International and Comparative Law 1

Boister N, 'The Legal Regulation of the South African "Armed Conflict" by Common Article 3 of the 1949 Geneva Conventions' (1988–9) 14 South African Yearbook of International Law 129

Bond JE, 'Internal Conflict and Article Three of the Geneva Conventions' (1971–2) 48 Denver Law Journal 263

Bondzie SE, 'A Critique of the African Charter on Human and People's Rights' (1988) 31 Howard Law Journal 643

Boothby WH, 'Direct Participation in Hostilities – A Discussion of the ICRC Interpretive Guidance' (2010) 1 International Humanitarian Legal Studies 143

Bothe M, 'Article 3 and Protocol II: Case studies of Nigeria and El Salvador' (1981–2) 31 American University Law Review 899

——— 'Customary International Humanitarian Law: Some Reflections on the ICRC Study' (2005) 8 Yearbook of International Humanitarian Law 143

Breau S, 'The International Law Implications of the Turkish/Kurdish Conflict' (2008) 41 Revue Belge de Droit International 426

Brinktrine R, 'The Horizontal Effect of Human Rights in German Constitutional Law: the British Debate on Horizontality and the Possible Role Model of the German Doctrine of "Mittelbare Drittwirkung der Grundrechte"' (2001) 4 European Human Rights Law Review 421

Brunnée J, 'International Legal Accountability through the Lens of the Law of State Responsibility' (2005) 36 Netherlands Yearbook of International Law 21

Bugnion F, '*Jus ad Bellum, Jus in Bello* and Non-International Armed Conflicts' (2003) 6 Yearbook of International Humanitarian Law 167

Cameron L, 'Private Military Companies: Their Status under International Humanitarian Law and its Impact on their Regulation' (2006) 88 International Review of the Red Cross 573

Carrillo-Suarez A, 'Hors de Logique: Contemporary Issues in International Humanitarian Law as Applied to Internal Armed Conflict' (1999) 15 American University International Law Review 1

Cassese A, 'The Status of Rebels under the 1977 Geneva Protocol on Non-International Armed Conflict' (1981) 30 International & Comparative Law Quarterly 416

——— 'The Geneva Protocols of 1977 on the Humanitarian Law of Armed Conflict and Customary International Law' (1984) 3 UCLA Pacific Basin Law Journal 55

——— 'The Martens Clause: Half a Loaf or Simply Pie in the Sky?' (2000) 11 The European Journal of International Law 187

Cayci S, 'Countering Terrorism and the Law of Armed Conflict: the Turkish Experience' (2002) 8 International Peacekeeping 333

Cerna CM, 'Reflections on the Normative Status of the American Declaration of the Rights and Duties of Man' (2008–9) 30 University of Pennsylvania Journal of International Law 1211

Cerone J, 'Human Dignity in the Line of Fire: The Application of International Human Rights Law during Armed Conflict, Occupation, and Peace Operations' (2006) 39 Vanderbilt Journal of Transnational Law 1447

Chan PCW, 'The Legal Status of Taiwan and the Legality of the Use of Force in a Cross-Taiwan Strait Conflict' (2009) 8 Chinese Journal of International Law 455

Charney J and Prescott JRV, 'Resolving Cross-Strait Relations between China and Taiwan' (2000) 94 The American Journal of International Law 453

Charnovitz S, 'Nongovernmental Organizations and International Law' (2006) 100 The American Journal of International Law 348

Clapham A, 'Human Rights Obligations of Non-State Actors in Conflict Situations' (2006) 88 International Review of the Red Cross 491

Constantinides A, 'Human Rights Obligations and Accountability of Armed Opposition Groups: The Practice of the UN Security Council' (2010) 4 Human Rights & International Legal Discourse 89

Cryer R, 'The Interplay of Human Rights and Humanitarian Law: The Approach of the ICTY' (2010) 14 Journal of Conflict & Security Law 511

Cullen A and Wheatley S, 'The Human Rights of Individuals in *De Facto* Regimes under the European Convention on Human Rights' (2013) 13 Human Rights Law Review 691

Daboné Z, 'International Law: Armed Groups in a State-Centric System' (2011) 93 International Review of the Red Cross 395

D'Argent P, 'Le Droit de la Responsabilité Internationale Complété? Examen des Principes Fondamentaux et Directives Concernant le Droit à un Recours et à Réparation des Victimes de Violations Flagrantes du Droit International des Droits de l'Homme et de Violations Graves du Droit International Humanitaire' (2005) 51 Annuaire Français de Droit International 27

D'Aspremont J, 'Rebellion and State Responsibility: Wrongdoing by Democratically Elected Insurgents' (2009) 42 International & Comparative Law Quarterly 427

de Beco G, 'Compliance with International Humanitarian Law by Non-State Actors' (2005) 18 Humanitäres Völkerrecht 190

Decaux E, 'The Definition of Traditional Sanctions: Their Scope and Characteristics' (2008) 90 International Review of the Red Cross 249

Deeks AS, 'Administrative Detention in Armed Conflict' (2009) 40 Case Western Reserve Journal of International Law 403

De Hoogh AJJ, 'Articles 4 and 8 of the 2001 ILC Articles on State Responsibility, the *Tadic Case* and Attribution of Acts of Bosnian Serb Authorities to the Federal Republic of Yugoslavia' (2002) 72 British Yearbook of International Law 255

Dennis MJ, 'Application of Human Rights Treaties Extraterritorially to Detention of Combatants and Security Internees: Fuzzy Thinking all Around?' (2006) 12 ILSA Journal of International and Comparative Law 459

——— 'Application of Human Rights Treaties Extraterritorially in Times of Armed Conflict and Military Occupation' (2005) 99 The American Journal of International Law 119

Devereux A, 'Should Duties Play a Larger Role in Human Rights – A Critique of Western Liberal and African Human Rights Jurisprudence' (1995) 18 University of New South Wales Law Journal 464

Dinstein Y, 'The International Law of Civil Wars and Human Rights' (1976) 6 Israel Yearbook on Human Rights 62

Domingo R, 'The Crisis of International Law' (2009) 42 Vanderbilt Journal of Transnational Law 1543

Doswald-Beck L, 'The Legal Validity of Military Intervention by Invitation of the Government' (1985) 56 British Yearbook of International Law 189

——— 'The Civilian in the Crossfire' (1987) 24 Journal of Peace Research 251

Draper GIAD, 'The Relationship between the Human Rights Regime and the Law of Armed Conflict' (1971) 1 Israel Yearbook on Human Rights 191

——— 'Human Rights and the Law of War' (1972) 12 Virginia Journal of International Law 326

——— 'Humanitarian Law and Internal Armed Conflicts' (1983) 13 Georgia Journal of International and Comparative Law 253

Drumbl MA, 'Collective Violence and Individual Punishment: The Criminality of Mass Atrocity' (2004–5) 99 Northwestern University Law Review 539

——— 'Accountability for System Criminality' (2010) 8 Santa Clara Journal of International Law 373

Drzemczewski A, 'The European Human Rights Convention and Relations Between Private Parties' (1979) 26 Netherlands International Law Review 163

Dumberry P, 'New State Responsibility for Internationally Wrongful Acts by an Insurrectional Movement' (2006) 17 The European Journal of International Law 605

——— 'Is a New State Responsible for Obligations Arising from Internationally Wrongful Acts Committed before its Independence in the Context of Secession?' (2005) 43 The Canadian Yearbook of International Law 419

Dudai R, 'Closing the Gap: Symbolic Reparations and Armed Groups' (2011) 93 International Review of the Red Cross 783

Eide A, 'Realisation of Social-Economic Rights and the Minimum Threshold Approach' (1989) 10 Human Rights Law Journal 35

Eissen MA, 'The European Convention on Human Rights and the Duties of the Individual' (1962) 32 Nordisk Tidsskrift for International Ret 230

Elder D, 'The Historical Background of Common Article 3 of the Geneva Convention of 1949' (1979) 11 Case Western Reserve Journal of International Law 37

Elias TO, 'The Nigerian Crisis in International Law' (1971) 5 The Nigerian Law Journal 1

Emanuelli CC, 'Comments on the ICRC Study on Customary International Humanitarian Law' (2006) 44 Canadian Yearbook of International Law 437

Engle E, 'Third Party Effect of Fundamental Rights (Drittwirkung)' (2009) 5 Hanse Law Review 165

Ewumbue-Monono C, 'Respect for International Humanitarian Law by Armed Non-State Actors in Africa' (2006) 88 International Review of the Red Cross 905

Fleck D, 'The Protocols Additional to the Geneva Conventions and Customary International Law' (1990) 29 Military Law & Law of War Review 497

——— 'International Accountability for Violations of the *Ius In Bello*: The Impact of the ICRC Study on Customary International Humanitarian Law' (2006) 11 Journal of Conflict & Security Law 179

Flory M, 'Algérie et Droit International' (1959) 5 Annuaire Français de Droit International 817

Forsythe DP, 'Legal Management of Internal War: The 1977 Protocol on Non-International Armed Conflicts' (1978) 72 The American Journal of International Law 272

Franck TM and Rodley NS, 'Legitimacy and Legal Rights of Revolutionary Movements with Special Reference to the Peoples Revolutionary Government of South Vietnam' (1970) 45 New York University Law Review 679

——— 'Legitimacy in the International System' (1988) 82 The American Journal of International Law 705

Frey B, 'The Legal and Ethical Responsibilities of Transnational Corporations in the Protection of International Human Rights' (1997) 6 Minnesota Journal of Global Trade 153

Gayim E, 'Reflections on the Draft Articles of the International Law Commission on State Responsibility: Articles 14;15;&19 in the Context of the Contemporary International Law of Self-Determination' (1985) 54 Nordisk Tidsskrift for International Ret 85

Geiss R, 'Armed Violence in Fragile States: Low-Intensity Conflicts, Spillover Conflicts, and Sporadic Law Enforcement Operations by Third Parties' (2009) 91 International Review of the Red Cross 127

Gillard E-C, 'Reparation for Violations of International Humanitarian Law' (2003) 85 International Review of the Red Cross 529

Gittleman R, 'The African Charter on Human and Peoples' Rights: A Legal Analysis' (1981–2) 22 Virginia Journal of International Law 667

Goldman RK, 'International Humanitarian Law and the Armed Conflicts in El Salvador and Nicaragua' (1987) 2 American University Journal of International Law and Policy 539

Green F, 'Fragmentation in Two Dimensions: The ICJ's Flawed Approach to Non-State Actors and International Legal Personality' (2008) 9 Melbourne Journal of International Law 47

Greenberg EVC, 'Law and the Conduct of the Algerian Revolution' (1970) 11 Harvard International Law Journal 37

Greenwood C, 'International Humanitarian Law and the Tadic Case' (1996) 7 The European Journal of International Law 265

Hadden T and Harvey C, 'The Law of Internal Crisis and Conflict: An Outline Prospectus for the Merger of International Human Rights Law, the Law of Armed Conflict, Refugee Law, and the Law on Humanitarian Intervention' (1999) 81 International Review of the Red Cross 119

Halabi SF, 'Traditions of Belligerent Recognition: The Libyan Intervention in Historical and Theoretical Context' (2012) 27 American University International Law Review 321

Hannum H, 'The Right of Self-Determination in the Twenty-First Century' (1998) 55 Washington & Lee Law Review 773

Hansen MMA, 'Preventing the Emasculation of Warfare: Halting the Expansion of Human Rights Law into Armed Conflict' (2007) 194 Military Law Review 1

Heintze HJ, 'Are De Facto Regimes Bound by Human Rights?' (2009) 15 OSCE Yearbook 267

Helle D, 'Optional Protocol on the Involvement of Children in Armed Conflict to the Convention on the Rights of the Child' (2000) 82 International Review of the Red Cross 797

Henckaerts JM, 'Binding Armed Opposition Groups through Humanitarian Treaty Law and Customary Law' (2003) 27 Collegium 123

——— 'Customary International Humanitarian Law – A Rejoinder to Judge Aldrich' (2006) 76 British Yearbook of International Law 525

Henderson C and Green JA, 'The *Jus ad Bellum* and Entities Short of Statehood in the Report on the Conflict in Georgia' (2010) 59 International & Comparative Law Quarterly 129

Henkin L, 'The Universal Declaration at 50 and the Challenge of Global Markets' (1999) 25 Brooklyn Journal of International Law 17

Hessbruege JA, 'Human Rights Violations Arising from Conduct of Non State Actors' (2005) 11 Buffalo Human Rights Law Review 21

Hoffman MH, 'The Application of International Humanitarian Law in Sri Lanka: A Compliance Based Case Study on the Rules of War' (2001) 30 Israel Yearbook of Human Rights 209

Horowitz J, 'Human Rights, Positive Obligations, and Armed Conflict: Implementing the Right to Education in Occupied Territories' (2010) 1 International Humanitarian Legal Studies 304

Hsiao AHA, 'Is China's Policy to Use Force against Taiwan a Violation of the Principle of Non-Use of Force under International Law?' (1998) 32 New England Law Review 715

Jaramillo DGP, 'Humanitarian Protection in Non-International Conflicts: A Case Study of Colombia' (2001) 30 Israel Yearbook of Human Rights 179

Junod S, 'Additional Protocol II: History and Scope' (1983) 33 American University Law Review 29

Kaladharan Nayar MG, 'Self Determination beyond the Colonial Context: Biafra in Retrospect' (1975) 10 Texas International Law Journal 321

Kalshoven F, 'State Responsibility for Warlike Acts of the Armed Forces: From Article 3 of the Hague Convention IV of 1907 to Article 91 of Additional Protocol I of 1977 and Beyond' (1991) 40 International & Comparative Law Quarterly 827

Kamminga MT, 'State Succession in Respect of Human Rights Treaties' (1996) 7 The European Journal of International Law 469

Kelly JB, 'Legal Aspects of Military Operations in Counterinsurgency' (1963) 21 Military Law Review 95

Kinley D and Tadaki J, 'From Talk to Walk: The Emergence of Human Rights Responsibilities for Corporations at International Law' (2004) 44 Virginia Journal of International Law 931

Klabbers J, 'Rebel with a Cause? Terrorists and Humanitarian Law' (2003) 14 The European Journal of International Law 299

Kleffner JK and Zegveld L, 'Establishing an Individual Complaints Procedure for Violations of International Humanitarian Law' (2000) 3 Yearbook of International Humanitarian Law 384

——— 'The Applicability of International Humanitarian law to Organized Armed Groups' (2011) 93 International Review of the Red Cross 443

Klein E, 'Establishing a Hierarchy of Human Rights: Ideal Solution or Fallacy?'(2008) 41 Israel Law Review 477

Knox JH, 'Horizontal Human Rights Law' (2008) 102 The American Journal of International Law 1

Kretzmer D, 'Rethinking the Application of IHL in Non-International Armed Conflicts' (2009) 42 Israel Law Review 8

Kwakwa E, 'The Current Status of Mercenaries in the Law of Armed Conflict' (1990) 14 Hastings International and Comparative Law Review 67

La Rosa AM and Wuerzner C, 'Armed Groups, Sanctions and the Implementation of International Humanitarian Law' (2008) 90 International Review of the Red Cross 327

——— 'Sanctions as a Means of Obtaining Greater Respect for Humanitarian Law: A Review of Their Effectiveness' (2008) 90 International Review of the Red Cross 221

Lazarus C, 'Le Statut des Mouvements de Libération Nationale à l'Organisation des Nations Unies' 20 (1974) Annuaire Français de Droit International 173

Levie HS, 'The Nature and Scope of the Armistice Agreement' (1956) 50 The American Journal of International Law 880

Lillich R, 'The Paris Minimum Standards of Human Rights Norms in a State of Emergency' (1985) 79 The American Journal of International Law 1072

Lootsteen YM, 'The Concept of Belligerency in International Law' (2000) 166 Military Law Review 109

Lysaght C, 'The Scope of Protocol II and its Relation to Common Article 3 of the Geneva Conventions of 1949 and Other Human Rights Instruments' (1983) 33 American University Law Review 9

Maslen S and Herby P, 'An International Ban on Anti-Personnel Mines: History and Negotiation of the "Ottawa Treaty"' (1998) 38 International Review of the Red Cross 693

Mastorodimos K, 'The Utility and Limits of International Human Rights Law and International Humanitarian Law's Parallel Applicability' (2009) 5 Review of International Law and Politics 129

——— 'The Character of the Conflict in Gaza: Another Argument towards Abolishing the Distinction between International and Non-international Armed Conflicts' (2010) 12 International Community Law Review 437

——— 'Belligerency Recognition: Past, Present and Future' (2014) 29 Connecticut Journal of International Law 301

Matas D, 'Armed Opposition Groups' (1996–7) 24 Manitoba Law Journal 621

MacBride S, 'Human Rights in Armed Conflicts: The Inter-Relationship between the Humanitarian Laws and the Law of Human Rights' (1970) 9 Military Law & Law of War Review 373

McCorquodale R, 'Self-Determination: A Human Rights Approach' (1994) 43 International & Comparative Law Quarterly 857

——— 'An Inclusive International Legal System' (2004) 17 Leiden Journal of International Law 477

Meron T, 'Applicability of Multilateral Conventions to Occupied Territories' (1978) 32 The American Journal of International Law 542

——— 'On a Hierarchy of International Human Rights' (1986) 80 The American Journal of International Law 1

——— 'Classification of Armed Conflict in the Former Yugoslavia: Nicaragua's Fallout' (1998) 92 The American Journal of International Law 236

——— 'The Humanization of Humanitarian Law' (2000) 94 The American Journal of International Law 239

Meron T and Rosas A, 'Declaration on Minimum Humanitarian Standards' (1991) 85 The American Journal of International Law 375

Meyrowitz H, 'Le Droit de la Guerre dans le Conflit Vietnamien' (1967) 13 Annuaire Français de Droit International 153

Milanovic M, 'State Responsibility for Acts of Non-state Actors: A Comment on Griebel and Plücken' (2009) 22 Leiden Journal of International Law 307

——— 'From Compromise to Principle: Clarifying the Concept of State Jurisdiction in Human Rights Treaties' (2008) 8 Human Rights Law Review 411

Miyazaki S, 'The Application of the New Humanitarian Law' (1980) 20 International Review of the Red Cross 184

Mulaj K, 'Resisting an Oppressive Regime: The Case of Kosovo Liberation Army' (2008) 31 Studies in Conflict & Terrorism 1103

Murphy SD, 'Democratic Legitimacy and the Recognition of States and Governments' (1999) 48 International & Comparative Law Quarterly 545

Nair R, 'Confronting the Violence Committed by Armed Opposition Groups' (1998) 1 Yale Human Rights & Development Law Journal 1

Nedjati ZM, 'Acts of Unrecognized Governments' (1981) 30 International & Comparative Law Quarterly 388

Nollkaemper A, 'Concurrence between Individual Responsibility and State Responsibility in International Law' (2003) 52 International & Comparative Law Quarterly 615

——— 'Systemic Effects of International Responsibility for International Crimes' (2010) 8 Santa Clara Journal of International Law 313

Nowak M, 'The Need for a World Court of Human Rights' (2007) 7 Human Rights Law Review 251

O'Donnell D, 'Trends in the Application of International Humanitarian Law by United Nations Human Rights Mechanisms' (1998) 38 International Review of the Red Cross 481

Paust J, 'The Other Side of Right: Private Duties under Human Rights Law' (1992) 5 Harvard Human Rights Journal 51

——— 'Human Rights Responsibilities of Private Corporations' (2002) 35 Vanderbilt Journal of Transnational Law 801

Pejic J, 'Procedural Principles and Safeguards for Internment/administrative Detention in Armed Conflict and Other Situations of Violence' (2005) 87 International Review of the Red Cross 375

Plattner D, 'La Portée Juridique des Déclarations de Respect du Droit International Humanitaire qui Emanent de Mouvements en Lutte dans un Conflit Armé' (1984–5) 18 Revue Belge de Droit International 298

——— 'The 1980 Convention on Conventional Weapons and the Applicability of Rules Governing Means of Combat in a Non-International Armed Conflict' (1990) 30 International Review of the Red Cross 551

Powers Jr RD, 'Insurgency and the Law of Nations' (1962) 16 JAG Journal 55

Quigley J, 'The Relation between Human Rights Law and the Law of Belligerent Occupation: Does an Occupied Population have a Right to Freedom of Assembly and Expression?' (1989) 12 Boston College International & Comparative Law Review 1

——— 'The Israel–PLO Interim Agreements: Are They Treaties?' (1997) 30 Cornell International Law Journal 717

Ramcharan BG, 'The Legal Status of the International Bill of Human Rights' (1986) 55 Nordic Journal of International Law 366

Rasulov A, 'Revisiting State Succession to Humanitarian Treaties: Is There a Case for Automaticity?' (2003) 14 The European Journal of International Law 141

Ratner SR, 'Revising the Geneva Conventions to Regulate Force by and against Terrorists: Four Fallacies' (2003) 1 Israel Defence Forces Law Review 7

——— 'Foreign Occupation and International Territorial Administration: The Challenges of Convergence' (2005) 16 The European Journal of International Law 695

Roberts A, 'Righting Wrongs or Wronging Rights? The United States and Human Rights Post-September 11' (2004) 15 The European Journal of International Law 721

——— and Sivakumaran S, 'Lawmaking by Nonstate Actors: Engaging Armed Groups in the Creation of International Humanitarian Law' (2012) 37 The Yale Journal of International Law 107

Rogers APV, 'Armed Forces and the Development of the Law of War' (1982) 21 Military Law & Law of War Review 201

——— 'Direct Participation in Hostilities: Some Personal Reflections' (2009) 48 Military Law & Law of War Review 143

Rona G, 'Interesting Times for International Humanitarian Law: Challenges from the "War on Terror"' (2003) 27 Fletcher Forum of World Affairs 55

Rondeau S, 'Participation of Armed Groups in the Development of the Law Applicable to Armed Conflicts' (2010) 93 International Review of the Red Cross 649

Ronen Y, 'Human Rights Obligations of Territorial Non-State Actors' (2013) 46 Cornell International Law Journal 21

Ronzitti N, 'Compensation for Violations of the Law of War and Individual Claims' (2002) 12 Italian Yearbook of International Law 39

Rose C, 'An Emerging Norm: The Duty of States to Provide Reparations for Human Rights Violations by Non-State Actors' (2010) 33 Hastings International & Comparative Law Review 307

Rosenne S, 'State Responsibility and International Crimes: Further Reflections on Article 19 of the Draft Articles on State Responsibility' (1997) 30 New York University Journal of International Law and Politics 145

Rubin AP, 'The Status of Rebels under the Geneva Conventions of 1949' (1972) 21 International & Comparative Law Quarterly 472

Rudolf B, 'Non-State Actors in Areas of Limited Statehood as Addressees of Public International Law Norms on Governance' (2010) 4 Human Rights & International Legal Discourse 127

Ryngaert C, 'Human Rights Obligations of Armed Groups' (2008) 41 Revue Belge de Droit International 355

Sassòli M, 'State Responsibility for Violations of International Humanitarian Law' (2002) 84 International Review of the Red Cross 401

——— 'The Implementation of International Humanitarian Law: Current and Inherent Challenges' (2007) 10 Yearbook of International Humanitarian Law 45

——— 'Taking Armed Groups Seriously: Ways to Improve their Compliance with International Humanitarian Law' (2010) 1 Journal of International Humanitarian Legal Studies 5

Saul B, 'In the Shadow of Human Rights: Human Duties, Obligations, and Responsibilities' (2001) 32 Columbia Human Rights Law Review 565

Savarese E, 'Issues of Attribution to States of Private Acts: Between the Concept of *De Facto* Organs and Complicity' (2005) 15 Italian Yearbook of International Law 111

Schlögel A, 'Civil War' (1970) 10 International Review of the Red Cross 123

Schoiswohl M, '*De facto* Regimes and Human Rights Obligations – the Twilight Zone of Public International Law?' (2001) 6 Austrian Review of International & European Law 45

Schwager E, 'The Right to Compensation for Victims of an Armed Conflict' (2005) 4 Chinese Journal of International Law 417

Selassie BH, 'Self-determination in Principle and Practice: The Ethiopian-Eritrean Experience' (1997) 29 Columbia Human Rights Law Review 91

Shah S, 'Seeking Remedies for Violations of International Humanitarian Law: *Markovic v Italy*' (2007) 7 Human Rights Law Review 412

Shelton D, 'Hierarchy of Norms and Human Rights: Of Trumps and Winners' (2002) 65 Saskatchewan Law Review 301

Siordet F, 'Les Conventions de Genève et la Guerre Civile' (1950) 32 Revue Internationale de la Croix Rouge 104

Siotis J, 'La Protection de la Personne Humaine dans les Conflits Armés ne Présentant pas in Caractère International' (1973) 12 Military Law & Law of War Review 281

Sivakumaran S, 'Binding Armed Opposition Groups' (2006) 55 International & Comparative Law Quarterly 369

——— 'Courts of Armed Opposition Groups: Fair Trials or Summary Justice?' (2009) 7 Journal of International Criminal Justice 489

Smith C, 'Special Agreements to Apply the Geneva Conventions in Internal Armed Conflicts: The Lessons of Darfur' (2007) 2 The Irish Yearbook of International Law 91

Somer J, 'Jungle Justice: Passing Sentence on the Equality of Belligerents in Non-International Armed Conflict' (2007) 89 International Review of the Red Cross 655

Szablewska N, 'Non-State Actors and Human Rights in Non-International Armed Conflicts' (2007) 32 South African Yearbook of International Law 345

Talmon S, 'The Responsibility of Outside Powers for Acts of Secessionist Entities' (2009) 58 International & Comparative Law Quarterly 493

——— 'Recognition of Opposition Groups as the Legitimate Representative of a People' (2013) 12 Chinese Journal of International Law 219

Tenefrancia RC, 'A Breed of its Own: Characterizing the CARHRIHL as a Legal Document' (2009) 59 Ateneo Law Journal 149

Tomuschat C, 'The Arabellion: Legal Features' (2012) 72 Zeitschrift für ausländisches öffentliches Recht und Völkerrecht 447

Turns D, 'Weapons in the ICRC Study on Customary International Humanitarian Law' (2006) 11 Journal of Conflict & Security Law 201

Umozurike UO, 'The Application of International Humanitarian Law to Civil Conflicts' (1992) 4 African Journal of International & Comparative Law 493

Valencia EM, 'Theories of Compliance in International Conflict: The Place of the Third Geneva Convention in the Colombian Armed Conflict' (2007) 21 Temple International and Comparative Law Journal 445

Van Essen J, 'De Facto Regimes in International Law' (2012) 28 Merkourios 31

Van den Herik L and Cernic JL, 'Regulating Corporations under International Law, From Human Rights to International Criminal Law and Back Again' (2010) 8 Journal of International Criminal Justice 725

Van der Oije PJCS, 'International Humanitarian Law from a Field Perspective: Nepal' (2006) 9 Yearbook of International Humanitarian Law 394

Vasak K, 'The European Convention on Human Rights: A Useful Complement to the Geneva Convention' (1965) 5 International Review of the Red Cross 399

Vasquez CM, 'Direct vs. Indirect Obligations of Corporations Under International Law' (2004–5) 43 Columbia Journal of Transnational Law 927

Verplaetse JG, 'The *Ius in Bello* and Military Operations in Korea 1950–1953' (1963) 23 Zeitschrift für Ausländisches Offentliches Recht und Völkerrecht 679

Veuthey M, 'Implementation and Enforcement of Humanitarian Law and Human Rights Law in Non-International Armed Conflicts: The Role of the International Committee of the Red Cross' (1983) 33 American University Law Review 83

Vité S, 'The Interrelation of the Law of Occupation and Economic, Social and Cultural Rights: The Examples of Food, Health and Property' (2008) 90 International Review of the Red Cross 629

Von Bernstorff J, 'The Changing Fortunes of the Universal Declaration of Human Rights: Genesis and Symbolic Dimensions of the Turn to Rights in International Law' (2008) 19 The European Journal of International Law 903

Von der Groeben C, 'The Conflict in Colombia and the Relationship between Humanitarian Law and Human Rights Law in Practice: Analysis of the New Operational Law of the Colombian Armed Forces' (2011) 6 Journal of Conflict & Security Law 141

Von Glahn G, 'The Protection of Human Rights in Time of Armed Conflicts' (1971) 1 Israel Yearbook of Human Rights 208

Walker W, 'The International Law Applicable to Guerrilla Movements in Internal Armed Conflicts: A Case Study of Contra Attacks on Nicaraguan Farming Cooperatives' (1988–9) 21 New York University Journal of International Law & Politics 147

Watkin K, 'Controlling the Use of Force: A Role for Human Rights Norms in Contemporary Armed Conflict' (2004) 98 The American Journal of International Law 1

Wellens K, 'The Practice of the (UN) Security Council with regard to Treaties and (Other) Agreements Governed by International Law' (2003) 2 Revista Colombiana de Derecho Internacional 11

Wilde R, 'The Applicability of International Human Rights Law to the Coalition Provisional Authority (CPA) and Foreign Military Presence in Iraq' (2005) 11 ILSA Journal of International & Comparative Law 485

Williamson JA, 'Challenges of Twenty-First Century Conflicts: A Look at Direct Participation in Hostilities' (2010) 20 Duke Journal of Comparative & International Law 457

Wolfrum R and Philipp CE, 'The Status of the Taliban: Their Obligations and Rights under International Law' (2002) 6 Max Planck Yearbook of United Nations Law 559

Wright Q, 'Legal Aspects of the Viet-Nam Situation' (1966) 60 The American Journal of International Law 750

Yihdego Z, 'Darfur and Humanitarian Law: The Protection of Civilians and Civilian Objects' (2009) 14 Journal of Conflict & Security Law 37

Yingling RT, and Ginnane RW, 'The Geneva Conventions of 1949' (1952) 46 The American Journal of International Law 393

Zorzi Giustiniani F, 'New Hopes and Challenges for the Protection of IDPs in Africa: the Kampala Convention for the Protection and Assistance of Internally Displaced Persons in Africa' (2010–2011) 39 Denver Journal of International Law and Policy 347

Zwanenburg M, 'The Van Boven/Bassiouni Principles: An Appraisal' (2006) 24 Netherlands Quarterly of Human Rights 641

B. Contributions to Edited Books

Abi-Saab R, 'Human Rights and Humanitarian Law in Internal Conflicts' in Warner D (ed.), *Human Rights and Humanitarian Law: The Quest for Universality* (Martinus Nijhoff 1997) 107

Alkema EA, 'The Third-Party Applicability of "Drittwirkung" of the European Convention on Human Rights' in Matscher F and Petzold H (eds), *Protecting Human Rights: The European Dimension* (2nd edn, Karl Heymanns 1990) 33

Alston P, 'The "Not-a-Cat" Syndrome: Can the International Human Rights Regime Accommodate Non-State Actors?' in Alston P (ed.), *Non-State Actors and Human Rights* (OUP 2005) 3

Atlam H, 'National Liberation Movements and International Responsibility' in Spinedi M and Simma B (eds), *United Nations Codification of State Responsibility* (Oceana Publications 1987) 35

Barbier S, 'Assurances and Guarantees of Non-Repetition' in Crawford J, Pellet A and Olleson S (eds), *The Law of International Responsibility* (CUP 2010) 551

Baxter R, 'Jus in Bello Interno: The Present and Future Law' in Moore JN (ed.), *Law and Civil War in the Modern World* (Johns Hopkins University Press 1974) 518

Boals K, 'The Relevance of International Law to the Internal War in Yemen' in Falk RE (ed.), *The International Law of Civil War* (Johns Hopkins University Press 1971) 303

Bothe M, 'International Legal Aspects of the Darfur Conflict' in Reinisch A and Kriebaum U (eds), *The Law of International Relations: Liber Amicorum Hanspeter Neuhold* (Eleven International Publishing 2007) 1

Buergenthal T, 'To Respect and to Ensure: State Obligations and Permissible Derogations' in Henkin L (ed.), *The International Bill of Rights: The Covenant on Civil and Political Rights* (Columbia University Press 1981) 72

Cahin G, 'The Responsibility of other Entities: Armed Bands and Criminal Groups' in Crawford J, Pellet A and Olleson S (eds), *The Law of International Responsibility* (CUP 2010) 331

——— 'Attribution of Conduct to the State: Insurrectional Movements' in Crawford J, Pellet A and Olleson S (eds), *The Law of International Responsibility* (CUP 2010) 247

Calogeropoulos-Stratis A, 'Droit Humanitaire – Droits de l'Homme et Victimes des Conflits Armés' in Pictet JS and Swinarski C (eds), *Études et Essais sur le Droit International Humanitaire et sur les Principes de la Croix-Rouge en l'Honneur de Jean Pictet* (Comité International de la Croix-Rouge 1984) 654

Castagnetti L, 'The Claims on Behalf of Individuals before the Eritrea-Ethiopia Claims Commission' in de Guttry A, Venturini G and Post HHG (eds), *The 1998–2000 War between Eritrea and Ethiopia: An International Legal Perspective* (TMC Asser Press 2009) 409

Cheng B, 'Introduction to Subjects of International Law' in Bedjaoui M (ed.), *International Law: Achievements and Prospects* (UNESCO 1991) 23

Christakis T, 'The State as a "Primary Fact": Some Thoughts on the Principle of Effectiveness' in Cohen M (ed.), *Secession-International Law Perspectives* (CUP 2006) 138

Condorelli L and Kress C, 'The Rules of Attribution: General Considerations' in Crawford J, Pellet A and Olleson S (eds), *The Law of International Responsibility* (CUP 2010) 221

Corten O, 'Are there Gaps in the International Law of Secession?' in Kohen MG (ed.), *Secession: International Law Perspectives* (CUP 2006) 231

David E, 'Article 34 (1969)' in Corten O and Klein P (eds), *The Vienna Conventions on the Law of Treaties: A Commentary* (OUP 2011) 887

de Frouville O, 'Attribution of Conduct to the State: Private Individuals' in Crawford J, Pellet A and Olleson S (eds), *The Law of International Responsibility* (CUP 2010) 257

de Preux J, 'Article 91, Protocol I' in Sandoz Y, Swinarski C and Zimmermann B (eds), *Commentary on the Additional Protocols of 8 June 1977 to the Geneva Conventions of 12 August 1949* (International Committee of the Red Cross 1987) 1053

Del Ponte C, 'The case of Syria' in Veuthey M and Beruto GL (eds), *Respecting International Humanitarian Law: Challenges and Responses* (Franco Angeli 2014) 51

Dickson B, 'The Horizontal Application of Human Rights Law' in Hegarty A and Leonard S (eds), *Human Rights. An Agenda for the 21st Century* (Cavendish Publishing Ltd 1999) 59

Dinstein Y, 'The ICRC Customary International Humanitarian Law Study' in Helm AM (ed.), *The Law of War in the 21st Century: Weaponry and the Use of Force* (International Law Studies Vol. 82, Naval War College 2006) 99

Dugard J and Raič D, 'The Role of Recognition in the Law and Practice of Secession' in Kohen MG (ed.), *Secession: International Law Perspectives* (CUP 2006) 94

Eide A, 'Internal Disturbances and Tensions' in *International Dimensions of Humanitarian Law* (Henry Dunant Institute 1988) 241

Fleck D, 'Non-International Armed Conflicts' in Fleck D (ed.), *Handbook of International Humanitarian Law* (2nd edn, OUP 2008) 605

Franco A, 'Armed Nonstate Actors' in Malone DM (ed.), *The UN Security Council: From the Cold War to the 21st Century* (Rienner 2004) 117

Frowein JA, 'De Facto Regimes' in Bernhardt R (ed.), *Encyclopaedia of Public International Law* Instalment 10 (North-Holland 1987) 73

Frowein J and Kirsch P, 'Introduction to Chapter VII' in Simma (ed.), *The Charter of the United Nations: A Commentary* (2nd edn, OUP 2002) 701

Gal-Or N, 'Observations on the Desirability of an Enhanced International Legal Status of the Non-State Actor' in Noortmann M and Ryngaert C (eds), *Non-State Actor Dynamics in International Law: From Law-Takers to Law-Makers* (Ashgate 2010) 125

Goodman R, 'Rationales for Detention: Security Threats and Intelligence Value' in Schmitt MN (ed.), *The War in Afghanistan: A Legal Analysis* (International Law Studies Vol. 85, Naval War College 2009) 371

Gray C, 'The Different Forms of Reparation: Restitution' in Crawford J, Pellet A and Olleson S (eds), *The Law of International Responsibility* (CUP 2010) 589

Greenwood C, 'A Critique of the Additional Protocols to the Geneva Conventions of 1949' in Greenwood C, *Essays on War in International Law* (Cameron May 2006) 201

Grewe WG, 'Peace Treaties' in Bernhardt R (ed.), *Encyclopaedia of Public International Law* Instalment 4 (North-Holland 1982) 102

Haines S, 'Weapons, Means and Methods of Warfare' in Wilmshurst E and Breau S (eds), *Perspectives on the ICRC Study on Customary International Humanitarian Law* (CUP 2007) 258

Hampson F, 'Human Rights and Humanitarian Law in Internal Conflicts' in Meyer MA (ed.), *Armed Conflict and the New Law* (British Institute of International and Comparative Law 1989) 53

——— 'Fundamental Guarantees' in Wilmshurst E and Breau S (eds), *Perspectives on the ICRC Study on Customary International Humanitarian Law* (CUP 2007) 282

Heintze HJ, 'Do Non-State Actors Challenge International Humanitarian Law?' in von Heinegg WH and Epping V (eds), *International Humanitarian Law Facing New Challenges: Symposium in Honour of Knut Ipsen* (Springer 2007) 163

Higgins R, 'Internal War and International Law' in Falk RA and Black CE (eds), *The Future of the International Legal Order* Vol. III (Princeton University Press 1971) 81

Jimenez de Arechaga E, 'International Responsibility' in Sorensen M (ed.), *Manual of Public International Law* (MacMillan 1968) 533

Junod SS, 'Article 1, Protocol II' in Sandoz Y, Swinarski C and Zimmermann B (eds), *Commentary on the Additional Protocols of 8 June 1977 to the Geneva Conventions of 12 August 1949* (International Committee of the Red Cross 1987) 1347

——— 'Article 6, Protocol II' in Sandoz Y, Swinarski C and Zimmermann B (eds), *Commentary on the Additional Protocols of 8 June 1977 to the Geneva Conventions of 12 August 1949* (International Committee of the Red Cross 1987) 1395

Kalshoven F, 'Applicability of Customary International Law in Non-International Armed Conflicts' in Cassese A (ed.), *Current Problems of International Law: Essays on U.N. Law and on the Law of Armed Conflict* (Dott. A. Giuffrè 1975) 267

Kamenov T, 'The Origin of State and Entity Responsibility for Violations of International Humanitarian Law in Armed Conflicts' in Kalshoven F and Sandoz Y (eds), *Implementation of International Humanitarian Law* (Martinus Nijhoff 1989) 169

Kerbrat J, 'Interaction Between the Forms of Reparation' in Crawford J, Pellet A and Olleson S (eds), *The Law of International Responsibility* (CUP 2010) 573

Kleffner JK, 'The Collective Accountability of Organized Armed Groups for System Crimes' in van der Wilt H and Nollkaemper A (eds), *System Criminality in International Law* (CUP 2009) 238

Kooijmans PH, 'In the Shadowland between Civil War and Civil Strife: Some Reflections on the Standard-Setting Process' in Delissen AJM and Tanja GJ (eds), *Humanitarian Law of Armed Conflict Challenges ahead: Essays in Honour of Frits Kalshoven* (Nijhoff Publishers 1991) 225

Koskienniemi M, 'Preamble' in Alfredsson G and Eide A (eds), *The Universal Declaration of Human Rights: A Common Standard of Achievement* (Nijhoff 1999) 27

Laly-Chevalier C, 'Article 35 (1969)' in Corten O and Klein P, *The Vienna Conventions on the Law of Treaties: A Commentary* (OUP 2011) 902

Magliveras KD, 'Devising New Rules for Regulating International Terrorism Warfare and Engaging Non-State Actors in the Negotiations' in Quenivet N and Shah-Davis S (eds), *International Law and Armed Conflict* (TMC Asser Press 2010) 338

Mastorodimos K, 'The Current Legal Status of Gaza Strip: Has the Occupation Ended?' in Frenkel DA and Gerner-Beuerle C (eds), *Challenges of the Law in a Permeable World* (ATINER 2009) 223

McNemar DW, 'The Post Independence War in Congo' in Falk RE (ed.), *The International Law of Civil War* (Johns Hopkins University Press 1971) 244

Miyazaki S, 'The Martens Clause and International Humanitarian Law', in Pictet JS and Swinarski C (eds*), Études et Essais sur le Droit International Humanitaire et sur les Principes de la Croix-Rouge en l'Honneur de Jean Pictet* (Comité International de la Croix-Rouge 1984) 433

Muchlinski P, 'Multinational Enterprises as Actors in International Law: Creating "Soft Law" Obligations and "Hard Law" Rights' in Noortmann M and Ryngaert C (eds), *Non-State Actor Dynamics in International Law: From Law-Takers to Law-Makers* (Ashgate 2010) 9

Neuhold H, 'Legitimacy: A Problem in International Law and for International Lawyers?' in Wolfrum R and Rφben V (eds) *Legitimacy in International Law* (Springer 2008) 335

Opsahl T, 'Articles 29 and 30: The Other Side of the Coin' in Eide A and Swinehart T (eds), *The Universal Declaration of Human Rights: A Commentary* (Scandinavian University Press 1992) 449

Opsahl T and Dimitrijevic V, 'Articles 29–30' in Alfredsson G and Eide A (eds), *The Universal Declaration of Human Rights: A Common Standard of Achievement* (Nijhoff 1999) 633

Ouguergouz F, 'La Palestine et les Conventions de Genève du 12 Août 1949 ou l'Histoire d'une Adhésion Avortée' in Boisson de Chazournes L and Gowlland-Debbas V (eds), *The International Legal System in Quest of Equity and Universality: Liber Amicorum Georges Abi-Saab* (Nijhoff 2001) 507

Partsch KJ, 'Preamble, Protocol II' in Bothe M, Partsch KJ and Solf WA (eds), *New Rules for Victims of Armed Conflicts: Commentary on the Two 1977 Protocols Additional to the Geneva Conventions of 1949* (Martinus Nijhoff Publishers 1982) 618

——— 'Article 1, Protocol II' in Bothe M, Partsch KJ and Solf WA (eds), *New Rules for Victims of Armed Conflicts: Commentary on the Two 1977 Protocols Additional to the Geneva Conventions of 1949* (Martinus Nijhoff Publishers 1982) 622

——— 'Article 6, Protocol II' in Bothe M, Partsch KJ and Solf WA (eds), *New Rules for Victims of Armed Conflicts: Commentary on the Two 1977 Protocols Additional to the Geneva Conventions of 1949* (Martinus Nijhoff Publishers 1982) 648

Pazartzis P, 'Secession and International Law: The European Dimension' in Kohen MG (ed.), *Secession: International Law Perspectives* (CUP 2006) 355

Pejic J, 'Status of Armed Conflicts' in Wilmshurst E and Breau S (eds), *Perspectives on the ICRC Study on Customary International Humanitarian Law* (CUP 2007) 77

Pocar F, 'Some Remarks on the Continuity of Human Rights and International Humanitarian Law Treaties' in Cannizzaro E (ed.), *The Law of Treaties Beyond the Vienna Convention* (OUP 2011) 279

Popovski V, 'Protection of Children in International Humanitarian Law and Human Rights Law' in Arnold R and Quénivet NNR (eds), *International Humanitarian Law and Human Rights Law: Towards a New Merger in International Law* (Nijhoff 2008) 383

Randelzhofer A, 'Article 2(4)' in Simma B (ed.), *The Charter of the United Nations: A Commentary* (2nd edn, OUP 2002) 112

Reinisch A, 'The Changing International Legal Framework for Dealing with Non-State Actors' in Alston P (ed.), *Non-State Actors and Human Rights* (OUP 2005) 37

Rodley N, 'Can Armed Opposition Groups Violate Human Rights?' in Mahoney KE and Mahoney P (eds), *Human Rights in the Twenty-First Century: A Global Challenge* (Nijhoff 1993) 297

Ronzitti N, 'Resort to Force in Wars of National Liberation' in Cassese A (ed.), *Current Problems of International Law: Essays on UN Law and on the Law of Armed Conflict* (Dott. A. Giuffrè 1975) 319

Ruda JM, 'Recognition of States and Governments' in Bedjaoui M (ed.), *International Law: Achievements and Prospects* (UNESCO 1991) 449

Ryngaert C, 'Imposing International Duties on Non-State Actors and the Legitimacy of International Law' in Noortmann M and Ryngaert C (eds), *Non-State Actor Dynamics in International Law: From Law-Takers to Law-Makers* (Ashgate 2010) 69

Sassòli M, 'The Legal Qualification of the Conflicts in the Former Yugoslavia: Double Standards or New Horizons for International Humanitarian Law?' in Yee S and Tieya W (eds), *International Law in the Post-Cold War World: Essays in Memory of Li Haopei* (Routledge 2001) 307

Schmitt MN, 'The Law of Targeting' in Wilmshurst E and Breau S (eds), *Perspectives on the ICRC Study on Customary International Humanitarian Law* (CUP 2007) 131

Scobbie I, 'The Approach to Customary International Law in the Study' in Wilmshurst E and Breau S (eds), *Perspectives on the ICRC Study on Customary International Humanitarian Law* (CUP 2007) 15

Simma B and Tams CJ, 'Article 60 (1969)' in Corten O and Klein P, *The Vienna Conventions on the Law of Treaties: A Commentary* (OUP 2011)

Siordet F, 'Common Article 3' in Pictet J (ed.), *Commentary to the Geneva Convention for the Amelioration of the Condition of the Wounded and Sick in Armed Forces in the Field* (International Committee of the Red Cross 1952) 37

Solf WA, 'Article 43, Protocol I' in Bothe M, Partsch KJ and Solf WA (eds), *New Rules for Victims of Armed Conflicts: Commentary on the Two 1977 Protocols Additional to the Geneva Conventions of 1949* (Martinus Nijhoff Publishers 1982) 232

Sommario E, 'State Responsibility for Violations of International Humanitarian Law in the Work of the Eritrea-Ethiopia Claims Commission' in de Guttry A, Venturini G and Post HHG (eds), *The 1998–2000 War between Eritrea and Ethiopia: An International Legal Perspective* (TMC Asser Press 2009) 393

Tomuschat C, 'The Applicability of Human Rights Law to Insurgent Movements' in Fischer H, Froissart U, von Heinegg WH and Raap C (eds), *Krisensicherung und Humanitärer Schutz – Crisis Management and Humanitarian Protection: Festschrift für Dieter Fleck* (Berliner Wissenschafts-Verlag 2004) 573

——— 'Reparation in Favour of Individual Victims of Gross Violations of Human Rights and International Humanitarian Law' in Kohen MG (ed.), *Promoting Justice, Human Rights and Conflict Resolution through International Law: Liber Amicorum Lucius Caflisch* (Brill 2007) 569

Turns D, 'Implementation and Compliance' in Wilmshurst E and Breau S (eds), *Perspectives on the ICRC Study on Customary International Humanitarian Law* (CUP 2007) 354

Van Boven TC, 'Reliance on Norms of Humanitarian Law by United Nations' Organs' in Delissen AJM and Tanja GJ (eds), *Humanitarian Law of Armed Conflict Challenges ahead: Essays in Honour of Frits Kalshoven* (Nijhoff Publishers 1991) 495

——— 'Victims' Rights to a Remedy and Reparation: The New United Nations Principles and Guidelines' in Ferstman C, Goetz M and Stephens A (eds), *Reparations for Victims of Genocide, War Crimes and Crimes Against Humanity* (Brill 2009) 19

Veuthey M, '*Les Conflits Armés de Character Non-Internationals*' in Cassese A (ed.), *Current Problems of International Law: Essays on UN Law and on the Law of Armed Conflict* (Dott. A. Giuffrè 1975) 179

Vierucci L, 'Private Military and Security Companies in Non-International Armed Conflicts: "Ius ad Bellum" and "Ius in Bello" Issues' in Francioni F and Ronzitti N (eds) *War by Contract: Human Rights, Humanitarian Law and Private Contractors* (OUP 2011) 235

von Hebel H and Robinson D, 'Crimes within the Jurisdiction of the Court' in Lee RS (ed.), *The International Criminal Court: The Making of the Rome Statute – Issues, Negotiations, Results* (Kluwer Law International 1999) 79

Weissbrodt D., 'Human Rights and Responsibilities of Individuals and Non-State Entities' in Alfredsson G and Stavropoulou M (eds), *Justice Pending: Indigenous People and Other Good Causes: Essays in Honour of Erica-Irene A. Daes* (Martinus Nijhoff 2002) 239

——— and Kruger M, 'Human Rights Responsibilities of Businesses as Non-State Actors' in Alston P (ed.), *Non-State Actors and Human Rights* (OUP 2005) 315

Willets P, 'Transnational Actors and International Organizations in Global Politics' in Baylis J and Smith S (eds), *The Globalization of World Politics. An Introduction to International Relations* (OUP 2001) 356

Wolfrum R, 'Legitimacy in International Law from a Legal Perspective: Some Introductory Considerations' in Wolfrum R and Røben V (eds), *Legitimacy in International Law* (Springer 2008) 1

Yutaka-Arai, 'Prohibition of Abuse of the Rights and Freedoms Set Forth in the Convention and of their Limitation to a Greater Extent than is Provided for in the Convention' in Van Dijk P (ed.), *Theory and Practice of the European Convention on Human Rights* (4th edn, Intersentia 2006) 1083

Zemanek K, 'Does the Prospect of Incurring Responsibility Improve the Observance of International Law?' in Ragazzi M (ed.) *International Responsibility Today: Essays in Memory of Oscar Schachter* (Martinus Nijhoff 2005) 125

Zimmermann A, 'Commentary on Para. 2(c) – (f) and Para. 3: War Crimes in an Armed Conflict Not of an International Character' in Triffterer O (ed.), *Commentary on the Rome Statute of the International Criminal Court: Observers' Notes, Article by Article* (Nomos 1999) 263

——— 'Secession and the Law of State Succession' in Kohen MG (ed.), *Secession: International Law Perspectives* (CUP 2006) 208

C. Web

D'Aspremont J, 'La Légitimité des Rebelles en Droit International' (2008) <http://www.ssrn.com/abstract=1266047>

Heffes E and Kotlik MD, 'Special Agreements Concluded by Armed Opposition Groups: Where is the Law?' (2014) <http://www.ejiltalk.org/special-agreements-concluded-by-armed-opposition-groups-where-is-the-law/>

Higgins N, 'The Application of International Humanitarian Law to Wars of National Liberation' (2004) Journal of Humanitarian Assistance <http://sites.tufts.edu/jha/files/2011/04/a132.pdf>

Hoffmann T, 'The Gentle Humanizer of Humanitarian Law – Antonio Cassese and the Creation of the Customary Law of Non-International Armed Conflicts' (2009) <http://ssrn.com/abstract=1531703>

Mack ML, 'Compliance with International Humanitarian Law by Non-State Actors in Non-International Armed Conflicts' (2003) <http://reliefweb.int/sites/reliefweb.int/files/resources/AC6DF550A5938F42C12571D4004A6AF1-Harvard-Nov2003.pdf>

Nieto-Navia R, 'International Peremptory Norms (*Jus Cogens*) and International Humanitarian Law' (2001) <http://www.iccnow.org/documents/WritingColombiaEng.pdf>

Peters A, 'Statehood after 1989: "*Effectivités*" between Legality and Virtuality' (2010) <http://papers.ssrn.com/sol3/papers.cfm?abstract_id=1720904>

Santos Jr S, 'The Recent MILF Agreements, Belligerency Status, International Law and the Philippine Constitution' <http://kalilintad.tripod.com/soliman_santos.htm>

D. Miscellaneous

Abi-Saab G, 'Wars of National Liberation in the Geneva Conventions and Protocols' (1979) 165 Recueil des Cours de l'Académie de Droit International 353

Barberis JA, 'Nouvelles Questions Concernant la Personnalité Juridique Internationale' (1983) 179 Recueil des Cours de l'Académie de Droit International 157

Cogen M, 'Correspondents' Report: Belgium' (1998) 1 Yearbook of International Humanitarian Law 412

Doswald-Beck L, 'Human Rights and Humanitarian Law: Are There Some Individuals Bereft of All Legal Protection?' (2004) 98 American Society of International Law Proceedings 353

Draper GIAD, 'The Geneva Conventions of 1949' (1965-I) 114 Recueil des Cours de l'Académie de Droit International 59

Forsythe DP, 'Comment' (1981–1982) 31 American University Law Review 833

Gasser HP, 'Determining Customary International Law Relative to the Conduct of Hostilities in Non-International Armed Conflicts: Remarks' (1987) 2 American University Journal of International Law & Policy 477

Kasutani H, 'Correspondent's Report: Japan' (1999) 2 Yearbook of International Humanitarian Law 388

Kovács P, 'Correspondent's Report: Hungary' (1998) 1 Yearbook of International Humanitarian Law 451

Matheson MJ, 'Session One: The United States Position on the Relation of Customary International Law to the 1977 Protocols Additional to the 1949 Geneva Conventions: Remarks' (1987) 2 American University Journal of International Law & Policy 419

Mohammed A, 'Correspondent's Report: Fiji' (2007) 10 Yearbook of International Humanitarian Law 326

Momtaz D, 'Le Droit International Humanitaire Applicable aux Conflits Armés Non Internationaux' (2001) 292 Recueil des Cours de l'Académie de Droit International 9

Pinto R, 'Les Règles du Droit International Concernant la Guerre Civile' (1965) 114 Recueil des Cours de l'Académie de Droit International 451

Provost R and Rikhof J, 'Correspondent's Report: Canada' (2000) 3 Yearbook of International Humanitarian Law 440

Rosenne S, 'The Perplexities of Modern International Law: General Course on Public International Law' (2001) 291 Recueil des Cours de l'Académie de Droit International 9

Santos Jr SM, 'Correspondent's Report: The Philippines' (2003) 6 Yearbook of International Humanitarian Law 561

Sassòli M, 'Possible Legal Mechanisms to Improve Compliance by Armed Groups with International Humanitarian and International Human Rights Law' (2003) (on file with the author)

Schindler D, 'The Different Types of Armed Conflicts According to the Geneva Conventions and Protocols' (1979-II) 163 Recueil des Cours de l'Académie de Droit International 117

Solf WA, 'Comment' (1981–2) 31 American University Law Review 927

Suy E, 'The Status of Observers in International Organizations' (1978) 160 Recueil des Cours de l'Académie de Droit International 75

3. Websites

<https://childrenandarmedconflict.un.org/our-work/action-plans/>

<http://www.genevacall.org/>

<http://theirwords.org/pages/home>

<http://www.un.org/sc/committees/>

Venezuelan Legislature Supports Belligerent Status for Colombian Rebels, 19 Jan 19 2008, by Kiraz Janicke, <http://venezuelanalysis.com/print/3080>

Index

For Product Safety Concerns and Information please contact our
EU representative GPSR@taylorandfrancis.com Taylor & Francis
Verlag GmbH, Kaufingerstraße 24, 80331 München, Germany